# The Classical Mind

Contents of *A History of Western Philosophy,* SECOND EDITION

# W. T. JONES

*California Institute of Technology*

# The
# Classical Mind

## A History of Western Philosophy

### SECOND EDITION

*Harcourt Brace Jovanovich, Inc.*

NEW YORK   CHICAGO   SAN FRANCISCO   ATLANTA

---

LIST OF COPYRIGHTS AND ACKNOWLEDGMENTS

The author records his thanks for the use of the selections reprinted in this book by permission of the following publishers and copyright holders:

GEORGE ALLEN & UNWIN LTD. for excerpts from Euripides' *Medea*, translated by G. Murray, from *Ten Greek Plays*; and from Euripides' *The Trojan Women*, translated by G. Murray.

GEORGE BELL & SONS, LTD., for excerpts from Euripides' *Medea*, translated by E. P. Coleridge, from *The Complete Greek Drama*, edited by W. J. Oates and E. O'Neill, Jr.

A. AND C. BLACK LTD. for excerpts from *Early Greek Philosophy*, translated by J. Burnet.

THE CLARENDON PRESS, OXFORD for excerpts from Aristotle's *De Anima*, translated by J. A. Smith; *Nichomachean Ethics*, translated by W. D. Ross; *Posterior Analytics*, translated by G. R. G. Mure; and *Physics*, translated by R. P. Hardie and R. K. Gaye; all from *The Works of Aristotle*, edited by J. A. Smith and W. D. Ross; for excerpts from *Epicurus: The Extant Remains*, translated by C. Bailey; from Lucretius' *On the Nature of Things*, translated by C. Bailey; from Simonides' "Human Imperfection," translated by G. Highet, from *The Oxford Book of Greek Verse*; from Sophocles' *Antigone*, translated by R. Whitelaw, from *Fifteen Greek Plays*, copyright 1943; for excerpts from *The Dialogues of Plato*, Fourth Edition, translated by Benjamin Jowett, copyright 1953; and for excerpts from Plato's *Republic*, translated by F. M. Cornford. All reprinted by permission of the Clarendon Press.

HARVARD UNIVERSITY PRESS for the following excerpts reprinted by permission of the publishers from the Loeb Classical Library: Cicero's *De Finibus* and *De Legibus*, translated by H. Rackham, copyright 1914; Hesiod's *Works and Days*, translated by H. G. Evelyn-White, copyright 1926; Marcus Aurelius Antonius' *Meditations*, translated by C. R. Haines, copyright 1924; Plato's *Apologia*, *Crito*, and *Phaedo*, translated by H. N. Fowler, copyright 1914, and Plato's *Symposium*, translated by W. R. M. Lamb, copyright 1925; Sextus Empiricus' *Outlines of Pyrrhonism*, translated by R. G. Bury, copyright 1933, and Empiricus' *Against the Logicians*, translated by Bury, copyright 1935.

HOUGHTON MIFFLIN COMPANY for excerpts from *Masters of Political Thought: Machiavelli to Bentham* by W. T. Jones.

HUMANITIES PRESS, INC., NEW YORK, for excerpts from *Plato and Parmenides*, *Plato's Cosmology: The Timaeus*, and *Plato's Theory of Knowledge: The Theaetetus*, all translated by F. M. Cornford.

DAVID MCKAY COMPANY, INC., NEW YORK, for an excerpt from Euripides' *The Bacchae*, translated by G. Murray, from *The Complete Greek Drama*, edited by W. J. Oates and E. O'Neill, Jr. Reprinted by permission of David McKay Company, Inc.

# Preface

The changes incorporated into this revision of A *History of Western Philosophy* reflect what I have learned, in the seventeen years since the book was first published, about the history of philosophy, the nature of the philosophical enterprise itself, and the role that philosophy plays in the general culture. They also reflect a good deal of thought about what characteristics make a textbook useful.

The most noticeable innovation is the division of the book into four separate volumes: *I. The Classical Mind; II. The Medieval Mind; III. Hobbes to Hume;* and *IV. Kant to Wittgenstein and Sartre.* This division has provided space for expansion of the text, especially in the fourth volume. It also conforms to the way in which courses in the history of philosophy are now organized and enables the reader to choose the periods on which he wishes to concentrate.

In my revision I have been able to condense and at the same time clarify the exposition materially. In addition, I have greatly simplified the elaborate system of subheadings used in the first edition, for I believe that today's generation of students no longer needs such a complex set of guideposts. The condensation of material and the elimination of superfluous heads have allowed me to expand the discussions of a number of thinkers and to add discussions of many others who were omitted from the earlier edition. For instance, in Volume I, I have added a short section on axiomatic geometry and a longer section on Greek Scepticism, with extracts from the writings of Sextus Empiricus. In Volume II, I have added a discussion of Gnosticism and have balanced this with a section on physical theory in the late Middle Ages, illustrated by quotations from John Buridan. It is Volume IV, however, that contains the most extensive additions. The sections on Hegel, Marx, and Nietzsche have been completely rewritten and greatly expanded; there are entirely new chapters on Kierkegaard, Wittgenstein, Husserl, and Sartre.

There are also a great many changes—some of them major—in my interpretation and evaluation of individual thinkers and their theories. For instance, I have softened my criticisms of Greek Atomism and of Augustine, and in the sections on St. Paul and on the author of the Fourth Gospel I have taken account of recent scholarship. There is, indeed, hardly a page that has not undergone extensive revision. This edition is a thoroughgoing and rigorous updating of the first version.

Despite all these alterations, my point of view remains basically the same. In revising, as in originally writing, this history, I have been guided by four principles—concentration, selectivity, contextualism, and the use of original sources.

An historian of philosophy can either say something, however brief, about everyone who philosophized, or he can limit himself to giving a reasonably consecutive account of a number of representative thinkers, omitting discussion of many second- and third-flight philosophers. I have chosen the latter approach, for two reasons. First, many works based on the first approach are already available, and I see no good reason for adding to their number. Second, such works are likely to be unintelligible to the beginning student. I still recall my own bewilderment as an undergraduate in seeking to understand a complicated theory that some expositor had "boiled down" to a summary. The principle of concentration rests on the thesis that it is better to understand a few theories than to be superficially acquainted with a great many.

But concentration implies selectivity, and I can hardly hope that even those who accept the principle of concentration will approve all my selections. There will probably be no difference of opinion about the great figures of the remote past. Everyone will surely agree that Plato and Aristotle are the masters of their age. And perhaps there will be general agreement that Augustine and Thomas occupy similar positions in the Middle Ages—that Augustine demands more attention than, say, Boethius, and Thomas more attention than Duns Scotus. But how is one to choose among philosophers of more recent times? Here one must try to anticipate the judgment of time. To some extent, I have simply avoided the issue by dealing with more philosophers in the modern period. The result is that, whereas the first two volumes cover more than two millenia, the last two focus on hardly more than four hundred years.

Even so, I have been forced to be selective by my determination that here, as in the earlier periods, I would not mention a philosopher unless I could deal with his views in some detail. Thus I have repressed a natural desire at least to mention Fichte and Schelling, in order to provide extended analyses of Hegel and Schopenhauer. All these thinkers represent reactions to Kantianism, and although they differ among themselves in many ways, it is better, I believe, to select and concentrate on a few than to attempt to give a complete enumeration.

Also underlying the writing of this history is the generally recognized but seldom adopted principle that philosophers are men, not disembodied spirits. Some histories of philosophy treat theories as if they were isolated from everything except other philosophical theories. But all the great philosophers have actually been concerned with what may be called "local" problems. To be understood, their theories must be seen as expressions—doubtless at a highly conceptualized level—of the same currents of thought and feeling that were moving the poets and the statesmen, the theologians and the playwrights, and the ordinary men, of the age. Otherwise, how could their philosophies ever have been accepted? These philosophers furnished satisfactory answers only because they were alert to the problems that were exercising their contemporaries and because they were harassed by the same doubts. The cultural milieu in which a given philosophy emerges can be ignored only at the risk of making the philosophy seem a detached (and so meaningless and inconsequential) affair.

In carrying out this principle I have begun my account of Greek philosophy by describing the state of affairs in Athens at the end of the Peloponnesian War, and I have drawn on the plays of Euripides and Aristophanes to illustrate the mood of the times. This, I believe, is a necessary setting for Plato, because his central thesis—the theory of forms—was an attempt to answer the scepticism and cynicism of his age. Plato's insistence on the existence of "absolute" standards for conduct and for knowledge is understandable only as a reflection of the social, economic, and political chaos and the moral and religious collapse that occurred at the end of the fifth century.

Similarly, my discussion of medieval philosophy is prefaced with an account of the dissolving Roman Empire, and I have tried to indicate the rich and diversified cultural background within which Christian philosophy developed. In discussing the theories of Augustine and Thomas I have kept in mind that, whereas Augustine expressed the eschatological fervor of a new sect fighting for its life, Thomas embodied the serenity of an imperial and universal religion whose piety had been softened by a new sense of responsibility for "that which is Caesar's."

Finally, in discussing the development of early modern philosophy I have tried to show the many factors—exploration and discovery, the rise of money

power, Humanism, the Reformation, and above all the new scientific method—
that combined to overthrow the medieval synthesis and to create new problems
that philosophy even today is struggling to resolve. In a word, I have conceived
the history of philosophy to be a part of the general history of culture and hence
to be intelligible only in its cultural context.

The fourth principle is my conviction that in philosophy—or in any discipline, for that matter—nothing takes the place of a direct, patient, and pains-
taking study of a great and subtle mind. For this reason there is much to be
said for the use of a source book. But a source book alone has serious limitations, because its selections are apt to be discontinuous and difficult to follow.
The advantage of a text is that it can explicate obscure passages and draw
comparisons. Even so, explication and interpretation are not substitutes for the
documents themselves. Therefore, each of the volumes in this series stands
halfway between textbook and source book and tries to combine the advantages
of both: I have set out a philosopher's thought in his own words by a careful
selection of key passages and have bound these together with my own comment and criticism. The quoted passages constitute about one third of the contents.

To undertake to give an account of the history of philosophy in its cultural
context is a formidable and perhaps presumptuous task for a single expositor.
In this undertaking I have received help from a wide variety of sources. In
addition to those who have read and commented on the first edition, whose names
I shall not repeat here, I wish to thank many friends and colleagues who have
called my attention to points that needed correction: Stanley M. Daugert,
Stewart C. Easton, Robert L. Ferm, John H. Gleason, Douglas Greenlee, Ray-
mond Lindquist, Edwin L. Marvin, James A. McGilvray, Philip Merlan, John E.
Smith, Robert T. Voelkel, Culver G. Warner, Rev. S. Y. Watson, S.J., and R. M.
Yost, Jr. I am much indebted to Robert J. Fogelin, from whom I learned a great
deal during the years we taught a joint course on nineteenth-century philosophy,
and to Clark Glymour, who has sent me extensive notes, especially on the history
of science. My greatest appreciation is due to Cynthia A. Schuster, who read the
revised version of Volumes I, II, and III and commented in immense—and
immensely helpful—detail, and to Stephen A. Erickson, on whom I have constantly leaned for advice about matters small as well as great and whose detailed
comments both on the first edition and on successive drafts of the revision have
been invaluable. These readers have saved me from many errors of fact and interpretation; for errors that remain I must be responsible, and I shall be grateful if
any that come to notice are pointed out to me.

I am obliged to the many publishers and copyright holders (listed on pages
iv–v) through whose cooperation the quotations used in these volumes appear.
Since I have followed the style of the various writers and translators I have
quoted, there is some variation in spelling, capitalization, and punctuation in
the reprinted passages. Full bibliographical notes, keyed to the text by letters
rather than numbers, appear at the end of each volume.

For the secretarial work on the manuscript I am chiefly indebted to Helen Armstrong, Dorothy Overaker, Catherine Tramz, and Judith Strombotne, who divided the typing. I am also grateful to Paul Cabbell, who checked all references in the first three volumes and made many helpful suggestions, to Joan McGilvray, who performed a similar function for the last volume, and to my good friend Margaret L. Mulhauser, who generously allowed me to impose on her the onerous task of proofreading.

W. T. Jones

# Contents

# 5

# 6

# 7

# 8

# Introduction

Greek philosophy was born out of the struggle to understand nature, for understanding nature proved to be less simple and straightforward than the earliest
Greek scientist had confidently assumed. Scientific inquiry became philosophical
when men discovered that it was necessary to ask questions about this inquiry
itself and about its method. The first scientists had taken for granted that underlying the visible changes in nature there is a material stuff in process. The
problem, they conceived, was simply to ascertain the nature of this material
(Is it water or air or fire?) and the changes it undergoes (evaporation, silting-up,
and so on). It gradually became clear, however, that the assumptions on which
this procedure rested were ambiguous. What does it mean to say that something
endures through change? What is the relation between the one real stuff and its
many appearances? Since the various answers suggested by the earliest philosophers contradicted one another, there came to be a widespread scepticism about

the power of reason as an instrument for obtaining knowledge. And if one could not trust reason, what *could* one trust? (Chapter 1.)

Meanwhile a parallel development was occurring in Greek thought about conduct. A new type of man had emerged from the changed economic and social conditions that had overthrown the old feudal nobility. The new-rich repudiated the old chivalric ideal of honor and loyalty, and "passion" became a justification for every excess. Natural science had its repercussions on this situation. In a world conceived to be a purely natural process, what place was there for man as a moral being? (Chapter 2.)

All these currents of thought and feeling came to a focus during the prolonged world war that took place in the last quarter of the fifth century B.C., and as a result of the political and economic dislocations that this exhausting struggle brought in its train. Zeus had been dethroned and whirlwind was king.

The central philosophical question, accordingly, was how to rehabilitate the old belief in the existence of an objective moral order and of a public truth cognizable by reason. To do this it was necessary to resolve those paradoxes about change, about the one and the many, and about appearance and reality that had led to the Sophists' scepticism. Two major solutions were worked out, each of which was to be a recurring influence on subsequent thought. One of these solutions was Atomism, according to which the universe is a purposeless congeries of small material particles differing only quantitatively. (Chapter 3.) The other was the theory of forms. As Plato conceived them, forms are super-sensible entities whose relation to the particulars of sense experience is incapable of clear formulation. (Chapters 4 and 5.) Aristotle sought to avoid this difficulty by introducing the concept of individual substance, which he held to be an amalgam of form and matter, of achievement and possibility. (Chapter 6.) Despite great differences in emphasis, both versions of the theory held the universe to be a purposive system, not a merely mechanical process. (Chapter 7.)

All these philosophers also sought to find a more rational basis for conduct than the religious myths that had once, but now no longer, provided a sanction for socially oriented behavior. And despite differences of detail, they agreed that this rationale is long-range happiness, which is attainable, they held, in an active life of personal culture and of public achievement, but which is limited to a relatively small elite who have the capacity for such activities and the leisure to pursue them. Unfortunately, in the time of troubles following the dissolution of Alexander's abortive empire, men began to abandon hope and to fall back on negative ideals of apathy and passivity. (Chapter 8.) Though the emergence of the Roman imperium for a time halted the collapse of classical culture and enabled the Stoics to develop a social theory that wove together strands from both the old and the new points of view, it too met with disaster. As the barbarians disrupted the ordered life of the West, the old classical poise and self-assurance vanished and men came more and more to lean on a greater-than-man.

But though the Greek belief in self-sufficiency thus disappeared for centuries, it proved astonishingly resilient. It was revived about five centuries ago, and even in the complex, interdependent societies of the twentieth century it remains an ideal. And, though our modern emphasis is less on contemplation as an end in itself than on knowledge as an instrument for changing the world, our notion of the universe is essentially secular and natural like that of the Greeks.

When people mention our heritage from Greece and Rome they may mean anything from the Apollo Belvedere and the Corinthian capital to natural law. But at the core of this rich and complex heritage are the ideas of nature as a process capable of being understood by man and of man as an autonomous and self-sufficient part of this natural order.

A good Greek land hath been
Thy lasting home, not barbary. Thou hast seen
Our ordered life, and justice, and the long
Still grasp of law not changing with the strong
Man's pleasure. . . .

EURIPIDES

The ruler of the world is Whirlwind, that hath unseated Zeus.

ARISTOPHANES

# CHAPTER 1

# Pre-Socratic Philosophy

Presumably a history of Western philosophy should begin with the beginning of Western philosophy. When, then, did Western philosophy begin? The standard answer is that it began in the sixth century B.C. with Thales, the father of Greek philosophy and thus the father of philosophy in the Western world. But this seemingly innocent question contains a booby trap that explodes any such simple answer. "Begin" is, in fact, a rather tricky word. A history of philosophy, in distinction from *the* history of philosophy, does indeed have a definitive beginning—for instance, this one has just opened with the sentence, "Presumably a history of Western philosophy should begin with the beginning of Western philosophy." But the history of philosophy itself does not have a definitive starting point. This is not merely due to the fact that most of the records have been lost. For even if the records were complete, it would be impossible to locate a particular moment in time and say, "Before this moment there wasn't philosophy; after this moment there was philosophy." Rather, there was a gradual change from a kind of thinking that no one would call philosophical (for example, mythic) to a kind of thinking that everyone would call philosophical. We are dealing with a continuum, not with abrupt transitions. The earlier type of thought was far more than sheer fantasy; it was animated by a desire to find explanations, even though its criteria for what constituted adequate explanations were very crude. And there is much in the later type of thought that remained anthropomorphic and mythic. Although it is not possible to trace this process in detail, an example or two of the earlier kind of thinking can be used to point up both the similarities and the differences between it and philosophy of the later type. The *Iliad* of Homer is one example.

## God and Nature in Homer

This epic poem is concerned with a single short episode during the ten-year struggle between the Greeks and the Trojans. Homer recounts how during the siege of Troy a dispute between Agamemnon and Achilles, two of the Greek chiefs, leads to "woes innumerable." The trouble begins with a quarrel over a woman, and pride and high-handedness bring matters to an impasse. Achilles loses the girl and refuses to take any further part in the war. Since Achilles is the greatest of all the Greek warriors, his compatriots are worsted in the ensuing fighting. In desperation they offer him all sorts of inducements to return to the battle. Odysseus, the most eloquent of the Greek leaders, tells Achilles that a man needs not only strength but moderation. And Achilles' old tutor Phoenix reminds Achilles that

> . . . your aged father sent me out to teach you . . . how to be a fine speaker and a man of action too. . . .
>
> Come, Achilles, tame that awful temper! You must not let your heart be hard. Even the gods can be moved, and they are greater than you in excellence and honour and might. They can be turned by the supplications of mankind, with burnt offerings and tender prayers, and the savour of sacrifice, when there has been transgression and error. Prayers are the daughters of Zeus Almighty. . . . If any man does reverence to Prayers when they come near, they bless him and hear his supplication; but if any one rebuffs them and stubbornly denies them, they go to Zeus Cronion and beseech him that . . . he may fall and be punished.
>
> And now you, Achilles, must see to it that reverence attend these daughters of Zeus, the reverence which bends the minds of other good men.[a]

But Achilles is too proud to heed this good advice. It is true that he has been wronged, but Homer believes his anger is excessive. Because he refuses to listen to the sweet voice of reason and moderation, the tragic sequel unfolds. First his best friend, Patroclus, is killed trying to help the Greeks; then, in revenge for Patroclus, Achilles seeks out and kills Hector, Patroclus' slayer, even though he knows that he is "fated" to die shortly after Hector. The poem ends with the passing of Achilles' anger as he awaits his death.

This, in outline, is the "argument" of the poem. Consider now the passage in which Homer describes how Achilles' goddess mother, Thetis, gets Zeus's help for her warrior son:

> Early in the morning she climbed to Olympos in the highest heavens. . . . There she knelt before [Zeus], and grasped his knees with her left hand, catching his chin with the right hand as she made her prayer:
> "O Father Zeus! If ever I have served you by word or deed, grant me this boon: . . . Satisfy my son, Zeus Olympian most wise! Let the Trojans prevail, until the Achaian nation shall satisfy my son and magnify him with honour!"
> . . . . . . . . . . . . . . . . . . . . . . . . . . . . . . . . . . . . . . . . . . . . . . . . . . .
> Zeus answered in great vexation:
> "Here's a bad business! You'll set me curry-worrying with Hera [his wife] and make her scold me again! She is always at me as it is before them all, and says I help the Trojans to win. You just go away again now, and don't let Hera see: I will manage to do what you want. . . ."
> But Hera had seen; she . . . lost no time in scolding at Zeus Cronion.
> "Who is it this time?" she began, "who has been confabulating with you now, you deceiver? You always like to go behind my back and make secret plans, and lay down the law! You never would tell me a word of your notions if you could help it!"
> The Father of men and gods made answer:
> "My dear Hera, do not expect to know everything I say. You must not expect as much as that, although you are my wife. Whatever is proper for you to hear, you shall be the first to hear before any in heaven or earth; but when I choose to consider things by myself, do not be inquisitive and ask questions about everything."
> Queen Hera said at once, opening her fine eyes:
> "O you dreadful creature, what a thing to say! I inquisitive? I ask you questions? I never did such a thing in my life! I just leave you alone, and you decide whatever you choose. But . . . I can't put it out of my mind that you may be cajoled by Silverfoot Thetis. . . ."[b]

Next look at the passage in which, after Patroclus is slain, Achilles goes out to find the slayer and destroy him. As Achilles pursues Hector, the gods look down from Olympus like men watching a chariot race. Zeus, who is pulled in as many diverse directions by his own impulsive nature as by his importuning relatives, has a sudden change of heart:

> "Confound it, I love that man whom I see hunted round those walls! I am deeply grieved for Hector, who has sacrificed many an ox on the heights of Ida or the citadel of Troy! and now there is prince Achilles, chasing him round the city of Priam. What do you think, gods? Just consider, shall we

save him from death, or shall we let Achilles beat him now? He is a brave man."

Athena Brighteyes replied:

"O Father Flashingbolt, O Thundercloud, you must never say that! A mortal man, long doomed by fate, and you will save him from death? Do as you please, but the rest of us cannot approve."

Zeus Cloudgatherer answered:

"Never mind, Tritogeneia, my love. I did not really mean it. . . ."

Achilles was now following at full speed and gave Hector no chance. . . . See now, the Father laid out his golden scales and placed in them two fates of death, one for Achilles and one for Hector. He grasped the balance and lifted it: Hector's doom sank down, sank down to Hades, and Apollo [who had been supporting Hector] left him.[c]

Thus, according to Homer, Zeus is far from being the omnipotent deity that the Christians, for instance, conceive their God to be. He is thwarted and harassed by his wife, by his numerous progeny, and by his still more numerous relatives, in much the same way that a human father is often dominated by the members of his household.

But a better analogy is the actual organization of a Greek community in Homer's day, for the Homeric heaven was a reflection of the Homeric state. The Greek state, as Homer described it, was monarchial in principle, but the king was by no means an absolute monarch. Public opinion, as represented by the warriors and nobles—not the "people," of course—clearly played a part in limiting the royal prerogative. On the other hand, Homer's state was not a limited monarchy in the modern sense, in which the powers of both ruler and ruled are clearly defined in a written document or at least in constitutional practice. When, as he often does, Agamemnon overrides the wishes of his council or rejects what is obviously the majority opinion, nobody protests. His actions have authority, even when they run counter to established precedents. Homer's was a society in which there was not yet any conception of law as a body of rules to which even the sovereign must bow.

Nor did Homer have any conception of nature as a system of regularly recurring sequences of events. Of course, he was aware—who was not?—that day follows night and summer follows winter. But he was also aware of the unpredictable irregularities of nature—the sudden thunderstorm, the unusually severe winter, the series of accidents that leads to an unexpected victory. For such irregularities, as well as for the order broken by them, he held the gods responsible. In Homer's works, the natural order of events is regulated by various gods who have a kind of viceregal suzerainty (under Zeus's final authority) for sea, earth, and sky; and the customs that men follow in their relations with one another are also handed down by Father Zeus. But the gods can never be counted on not to interrupt this order; in the depths of the blue sky there always lurks the thunderbolt of an impulsive Zeus. It is clear that Homer was, on the whole, much more impressed by the chaotic and the irregular than by the systematic and the predictable.

Though the gods' interference in human affairs is often capricious, some of it has a kind of rationale. They interfere, for instance, to punish men for lack of moderation[1]—in Achilles' case, as we have seen, for immoderate wrath. But even more fundamental for Homer than lack of moderation was *hübris*, or, as we might say, insubordination. The two concepts are closely connected. The moderate man "knows his place"; the immoderate man, who lets his pride or his anger or anything else get out of hand, is likely to become arrogant. This kind of forgetfulness the gods never fail to punish. Thus, though the assembly does not protest when Agamemnon ignores its wishes, retribution comes from on high.

Agamemnon is not punished because his act causes misery and suffering; he is punished because he has annoyed the gods by violating one of their regulations. Homer does not suggest that the divine rules were established for man's good nor that the gods are moral ideals for men to emulate. They are impetuous, childishly egotistical, lustful, selfish, vain, unscrupulous, and downright dishonest. In every respect a Homeric hero—an Achilles or a Hector—is the moral superior of Zeus. Homer's men do not worship the gods because they are *good* but because they are powerful (not all-powerful, but a great deal more powerful than men) and because it is therefore useful to have them on one's side and dangerous to have them against one. Worship is a business transaction and clearly understood as such on both sides: If a god is not promptly forthcoming with a suitable return after a handsome sacrifice in his honor, man feels cheated and is frank to say so. In fact, the gods as conceived by Homer are rather like children who happen, through some paradox of nature, to be endowed with great power. They must therefore be petted, coaxed, and flattered lest they disrupt the more serious pursuits of adult men. On the whole this system works fairly well, but there is no telling when sheer capriciousness on the part of the gods may cause the best laid plans of men to go astray. Thus the operation of divine causality as it affects man is anything but moral in the modern sense.

So far it has been noted that Homer's gods are causal agents—that they are responsible for both the regular order of events and the interruptions of that order. But above the gods is fate, a blind, inscrutable "will" to which even Zeus must yield. Homer was far from consistent in his account of fate and its relation to the powers of the gods.[2] The most that can be said is that he was feeling his

---

1 For an interpretation of Homer that puts less emphasis on moderation and the other "quieter" virtues, see Arthur W. H. Adkins, *Merit and Responsibility: A Study in Greek Values* (Oxford University Press, 1960), pp. 32–38 and 61–62.

2 In several places in the *Iliad* Zeus resorts to his scales to discover what is going to happen. It follows that fate is above the gods, just as the gods are above men. However, in other passages Homer writes as if what was fated to occur might well not have occurred but for the intervention of some deity or other. This certainly suggests that fate, far from being above the gods, is dependent on their will.

way toward the notion of a causal order that is nonpurposive in character—indifferent to all volition, whether human or divine. But before thought could attain this conception it had to pass through the stage of conceiving the single, pervasive order as a moral law binding on gods and men alike.

## God and Nature in Hesiod

Hesiod took an important step in this direction. Just as Homer's theology expressed the social structure of Greece in his period, Hesiod's was a product of a later period—probably the eighth century B.C.—and reflects the changed circumstances of the "time of troubles" that developed when economic pressures forced the small farmer to choose between serfdom and emigration.

Hesiod may have been such a small farmer. At least he wrote bitterly against grasping nobles who oppressed the poor. *Works and Days* describes how his brother Perses, by bribing one of these unjust lords, was able to steal Hesiod's inheritance from their father. As he raised his voice in protest, Hesiod envisaged an order that would correct such abuses. For him Zeus was not a hotheaded, magnified edition of Agamemnon or the other Homeric kings; he was the fashioner of a rule of justice that sooner or later would right wrongs, correct abuses, lift up the downtrodden, and punish the wicked and unjust.

This was a new conception. In Homer divine punishment had been directed less against human wrongdoing than against human insolence, against the man who set himself up as equal or superior to the gods. Here, of course, Homer had merely given expression to the warrior code of those among whom he lived. In a military system insubordination is the vilest of crimes, for the very existence of the system depends on every member's recognition and acceptance of his place. With Hesiod the moral life was differently conceived. Expressing the sentiments of the lower classes, who were not warriors but farmers, he considered the supreme offense to be oppression of the weak by the strong.

At the same time that Hesiod deepened the conception of wrongdoing, he radically changed the way in which the sanctions against immoral conduct operated. For Homer these sanctions had operated, on the whole, capriciously: Zeus was virtually at the mercy of whichever relative happened to catch his ear. For Hesiod, on the contrary, Zeus had the moral integrity to choose, and the power to enforce the rule of law. The law that he promulgated for man operated with complete certainty and regularity to reward the good for their goodness and to punish the wicked for their wickedness. It may be said, indeed, that Hesiod took over the old notion of fate and that, while retaining the notion of absolute necessity, he refined it by rejecting its indifference to humanity. In his hands fate became the concept of a pervasive moral law.

*Works and Days,* for instance, begins with this praise for Father Zeus:

> Through him mortal men are famed or unfamed, sung or unsung alike, as great Zeus wills. For easily he makes strong, and easily he brings the strong man low; easily he humbles the proud and raises the obscure, and easily he straightens the crooked and blasts the proud. . . . So is there no way to escape the will of Zeus. . . .
>
> Listen to right and do not foster violence. . . . The better path is to go by on the other side towards justice; for Justice beats Outrage when she comes at length to the end of the race. . . .
>
> For those who practise violence and cruel deeds far-seeing Zeus, the son of Cronos, ordains a punishment. Often even a whole city suffers for a bad man who sins and devises presumptuous deeds, and the son of Cronos lays great trouble upon the people, famine and plague together, so that the men perish away, and their women do not bear children, and their houses become few, through the contriving of Olympian Zeus. And again, at another time, the son of Cronos either destroys their wide army, or their walls, or else makes an end of their ships on the sea.
>
> You princes, mark well this punishment you also; for the deathless gods are near among men and mark all those who oppress their fellows with crooked judgments, and reck not the anger of the gods. For upon the bounteous earth Zeus has thrice ten thousand spirits, watchers of mortal men, and these keep watch on judgments and deeds of wrong as they roam, clothed in mist, all over the earth. . . . Keep watch against this, you princes, and make straight your judgments, you who devour bribes; put crooked judgments altogether from your thoughts. . . .
>
> Lay up these things within your heart and listen now to right, ceasing altogether to think of violence. For the son of Cronos has ordained this law for men, that fishes and beasts and winged fowls should devour one another, for right is not in them; but to mankind he gives right which proves far the best. For whoever knows the right and is ready to speak it, far-seeing Zeus gives him prosperity; but whoever deliberately lies in his witness and forswears himself, and so hurts Justice and sins beyond repair, that man's generation is left obscure thereafter.[d]

The last sentences express a typically Greek view: Man is different from the rest of nature; he has an obligation to live in a characteristically human way, to do certain acts and to abstain from doing others. The Greeks coupled the pride they felt in being human (a pride that the Hebrews, for instance, did not share) with a sense of *noblesse oblige:* Man must live up to his responsibilities as man. This is quite different from feeling that man must obey a divine overlord's commands.

These notions connect with another key concept, moderation.[3] Moderation, as the Greeks thought of it, is a peculiarly human trait. No one expects animals

3 See pp. 5 and 62.

to temper their violent impulses; the law for them is such that they must devour one another in order to survive. But men are capable of an inner discipline, a self-restraint in their dealings with one another. They ought to live by this uniquely human law; when they do not, they sooner or later pay for their violations, as Achilles did.

Further, the operation of this moral law is no longer conceived of as being in the hands of an arbitrary and temperamental divinity. In Homer there had usually been a "way to escape the will of Zeus," either by bribery or cajolery. Moreover, Zeus himself seemed not to know the extent of his will or whether it would be efficacious. Though Hesiod still speaks of the will of Zeus, it has now become a force operating uniformly, regularly, and pervasively throughout nature.

Despite these innovations, the *Theogony* shows that Hesiod retained much of the way of thinking of his predecessors. Hesiod's cosmogony—his account of the process by which the world came into existence—is still anthropomorphic:

> Tell how the first gods and earth came to be, and rivers, and the boundless sea with its raging swell, and the gleaming stars, and the wide heaven above, and the gods who were born of them, givers of good things. . . . These things declare to us from the beginning, ye Muses who dwell in the house of Olympus, and tell me which of them first came to be.
>
> Verily at first Chaos came to be, but next wide-bosomed Earth . . . and Eros [Love], fairest among the deathless gods. . . . From Chaos came forth Erebus and black Night: of Night were born Aether [the upper air] and Day. . . . Earth first bare the starry Heaven, equal to herself, to cover her on every side. . . . And she brought forth long Hills, forceful haunts of the goddess-Nymphs. . . . She bare also the fruitless deep with his raging swell. . . .[e]

Indeed, Hesiod's *Theogony* is a kind of divine *Burke's Peerage* that describes at once the genealogies of the gods and the process by which the world as we know it came to be. It is an indication of the mythic level of Hesiod's thought that for him these undertakings were identical.

## Thales

Thales lived in Miletus, a Greek colony in Ionia on the coast of Asia. He is said to have predicted an eclipse that modern astronomers have calculated to have occurred in 585 B.C. According to Aristotle, who lived almost two hundred and fifty years later, Thales believed that water is the cause of all things and that all things are filled with gods. This is virtually all that is known about Thales, but it clearly shows that he conceived of the world process in natural terms. With Thales, cosmogony had not yet become science, but it was no longer a genealogy of the gods. It had become something that could (and eventually did) develop into science.

Thales must have been impressed by the numerous physical transformations water is capable of—from ice through a liquid to a gaseous state—and by such phenomena as evaporation, rainfall, the silting-up of rivers at their mouths, and springs gushing forth from the earth. It must have seemed to him that in evaporation water "becomes" air, and in rain air becomes water. Similarly, in the formation of a delta, water becomes earth, and a spring represents the reverse process in which earth becomes water. Given a disposition to observe natural processes and a strong presupposition that the world is somehow one, Thales' assertion that the cause of everything is water is understandable.

To reach this conclusion he had to have, first, the notion of a single unifying principle (it is not too far-fetched to say this was Thales' inheritance from the religious past) and, second, a secular point of view that led him to seek this principle not in divine doings but in natural events and processes.

It is almost impossible to exaggerate the long-range importance of this shift in point of view. In the *Theogony* Hesiod purported to tell about the causes of natural occurrences; what he actually revealed was the inner life of his own spirit. Successive generations of poets might fashion more esthetically satisfying or more morally refined myths. If so, their verses would reflect an internal development of the poetic personality—a deeper moral sense, a more acute esthetic competence—not increased knowledge of nature. As a matter of fact, the myths not only failed to inform; they actually inhibited scientific advance. As long as the causes of events were attributed to the will of the gods, a science of meteorology, for instance, was impossible. For men appealing to untestable supernatural explanations (for example, a god's motives), any investigation of the conditions that actually determine changes in the weather was excluded from the outset. Instead of a science of weather forecasting, they offered a pseudo-science of divination, which purported to reveal Zeus's state of mind and tell how we might effect changes in it.

With Thales we reach an altogether different level of explanation, one from which an advance in natural knowledge is possible. From now on, there are indeed *theories*—public assertions, not private fantasies. That is, there are statements about the world that are open to criticism, revision, or rejection on the basis of their internal consistency and the empirical evidence. Of course, the criteria for evaluating theories did not emerge all at once; the formation of adequate criteria is itself a process involving the criticism and revision of earlier criteria. But this dual and reciprocal process, which is still going on, had to begin somewhere and sometime. As far as we know, it began in the Greek colonies in Ionia, and it is associated with Thales.

Thales' name is remembered, then, because he was the first person whom we know to have answered in natural terms the question, "Why do things happen as they do?" But there is a more significant reason for calling him the father of philosophy. His question implies a number of unconscious assumptions about the kind of answer called for—exactly as the question, "When did philosophy begin?" implies assumptions that are likely to affect the answer we give. Thales' assumptions determined the whole course of philosophy for a long time to come.

Indeed, the work of his successors, especially his immediate successors, can best be understood as, first, the gradual uncovering of his assumptions by the discovery of various paradoxes to which they led and, second, the revision of the assumptions in an attempt to avoid the paradoxes.

Though Thales' assumptions came to light slowly, it will be useful to set them out at once. To begin with, as we have already seen, Thales assumed that there is some *one* thing that was the cause of everything else. This means that Thales and his successors were all monists, that they were not content until they had reduced the diversity of the world to unity.

Second, Thales assumed that the answer to his question is a "thing." Here again all his successors followed him, for later on, when people abandoned monism, they still assumed that the answer must be in terms of "stuff," although they held that there are two or more basic, or ultimate, things. Even when, much later, the notion of a material stuff was abandoned as too crude, philosophers continued to think of the ultimate entities in the world as somehow being things. This concept has, in fact, survived extraordinary philosophical vicissitudes and in one form or another is still with us. Much of the history of philosophy is concerned with the gradual recognition by philosophers of the implications of the notion of "thing" and their constant attempts to rid it of the contradictions in which it seems involved.

This will become clearer as we proceed. For the moment it is enough to note that when Thales said that water is the cause of all, he was not thinking of it as something external to the effect (as when one billiard ball hits another) but rather as something that itself undergoes change and is transformed into the various objects we see about us. This may be put down as Thales' third assumption, namely, that the ultimate stuff is active and contains within itself a principle of change. This is probably what Thales meant when he said all things are "full of gods." In Greek theology the gods were conceived of as active agents. In fact, as we have seen, Homer thought of them primarily as agents rather than as objects of religious awe and veneration in our sense.[4] It seems likely, therefore, that in saying things are full of gods, Thales was not making a theological statement. Paradoxical as it may sound, he was tacitly denying divine causality. He meant that things, in order to be moved and to change, do not require force applied to them from outside by the gods but move of themselves, by a natural force within them. Here we doubtless have a first rudimentary concept of "process."

In contrasting Thales' views with those of Homer and Hesiod, it has been said that his position provided an opportunity for advance and improvement. The next generation of Greek thinkers illustrates the truth of this assertion. Instead of elaborating a myth, each new thinker submitted his predecessor's theory to an acute criticism from which, by the elimination of logical inconsistencies, an improved hypothesis emerged. Let us now examine the main steps in this process of criticism.

4 See p. 5.

# Anaximander

Anaximander, another citizen of Miletus in Ionia, is generally considered to have been a younger contemporary of Thales.[5] Unlike Thales, he appears to have written a book, one sentence of which has survived: "From what source things arise, to that they return of necessity when they are destroyed; for they suffer punishment and make reparation to one another for their injustice according to the order of time."[6]

This may, at first, sound a little obscure; as the Greek writer who quoted it said, these are "somewhat poetical terms." It is clear, however, that Anaximander was following Thales' basic position and at the same time correcting it in detail. He said (1) there is some "thing"—a one "stuff," and (2) there is a process by which this one becomes the many things of everyday experience. So far, he had made the same basic assumptions as Thales. He also held that (3) this process is "necessary." The language about "reparation for injustice" shows, incidentally, how the earliest thinking about natural law that can be called "scientific" was influenced by the speculation of such writers as Hesiod about moral law.

Though Anaximander agreed with Thales that there is one real, basic stuff that is in process, he differed with Thales both about what this stuff is and about the nature of the process by which it becomes many. According to later writers, he said that the basic stuff is "neither water nor any other of the so-called elements" but "a substance different from them, which is boundless." Possibly Anaximander argued that water could not be the one stuff of the world because it is too specific. We can see, he may have said, water becoming different things like air or ice or even earth. But how could it become *all* the multitudinous things of the world? In particular, how could it become the hot or the dry—things, in a word, the opposite of itself? This, it must be allowed, is a reasonable question. But whereas a modern scientist would probably set about designing experiments to see whether or not water does become any of these things and if so under what conditions, Anaximander raised a logical problem concerning the consistency, as we would say, of Thales' hypothesis. He thought there is a logical contradiction in the theory that things that are not water (rocks, fire, air, and so on) are "really" water. Accordingly, Anaximander modified the hypothesis in a way that was designed to meet this logical difficulty. Since the trouble with Thales' position was not simply that he said "water" (for obviously any other particular stuff—air or fire or earth—would involve the same problem), Anaximander argued that the one stuff must be without particular limiting characteristics, that is, infinite or "boundless."

5  Anaximander's birth date is usually put at 610 B.C. In any event he was younger, though probably not much younger, than Thales.
6  J. Burnet, in *Early Greek Philosophy* (Black, London, 1920), p. 52, points out that it is uncertain how much of this sentence is a direct quotation.

About the world process, Anaximander was much more specific than Thales, who may not even have felt it necessary to explain how the one real stuff becomes the many objects of this world. According to Anaximander, water, earth, air, fire, and the rest—the particular "stuffs"—issue from and return to the boundless. Anaximander conceived of the boundless, probably, as a kind of reservoir or bank.

He saw that the particular stuffs of the world fall into pairs of opposites: hot-cold, wet-dry, day-night, and so on. This observation, which is certainly not profound, was especially easy for a Greek to make, since the Mediterranean climate is one of such extremes—winter is cold and wet; summer, hot and dry. It is also true, of course, that what is hot is not at the same time cold. But hotness (summer) gives way eventually to cold, and cold in turn gives way to hotness. Hot and cold thus give way to each other in turn, each issuing from, and returning to, the reservoir of boundless, indeterminate stuff. This exchange happens with a regularity that seemed to Anaximander to imply some sort of compulsion. It is clear that, for Anaximander, the world was still basically disorderly, and that what required explanation was its orderliness.

So far we have an account of such stuffs as hot-cold, wet-dry. But we are a long way, of course, from an account of the particular objects—ships, sealing wax, cabbages, kings—that we see about us. Hence Anaximander proceeded to a more detailed statement of the world process. This proved to be a remarkable anticipation of modern evolutionary theories.

Anaximander argued that the world as we know it was separated out of the boundless by a kind of circular motion like an eddy. Our world is only one of many such separated-out worlds, which are coming into being and passing out of existence as eddies form and dissolve in the boundless. Hot and cold were first to separate out in this process of world formation, hot being an area of fire encircling cold "as the bark surrounds a tree." The sun, the moon, and the stars are "wheels of fire" that separated from this region of fire. As the heat from the outer fire dried up parts of the moist inner areas, differentiation between sea and land areas occurred. It was in the moist areas on the earth that life first arose. Man, therefore, "was like another animal, namely a fish, in the beginning." Moreover, man must have been born from animals of another species, since man requires a lengthy period of suckling, whereas other animals quickly find food for themselves. It follows, Anaximander reasoned, that in the early days of life man as he is now could never have survived.

## Anaximenes

This brings us to Anaximenes, the third of the Milesian philosophers. He subjected Anaximander's view to the same sort of criticism that Anaximander himself had leveled at Thales' view.

Anaximenes seems to have been a younger contemporary of Anaximander. He, too, was the author of a book, a number of references to which have survived in the writings of later philosophers. Like his two predecessors he thought that all the diversity of the world reduces to one ultimate stuff, and this, he said, is air. Thus he returned to Thales' conception of the world stuff as particular.

For this reason some historians have regarded Anaximenes' thought as a backward step from the position reached by Anaximander. But Anaximenes actually had good grounds for rejecting Anaximander's "boundless." The boundless is indefinite—it has no particular limiting characteristics. But though it is easy enough to *talk* about a boundless, what would such a thing actually be? Every thing we encounter has characteristics that make it a particular thing distinct from all other things. Indeed, since to be a thing is to have particular characteristics, the boundless cannot be a stuff, or thing. Two of Anaximander's basic assumptions—that there is one material stuff out of which everything else arises and that this one thing is boundless—are in conflict.

We understand why Anaximander was led to say that the boundless is nothing in particular; if it is any particular thing it is impossible to explain how it becomes its opposite. But talk about a "boundless" stuff does not solve the problem; it merely hides the fact that a problem exists—the problem, that is, of understanding how one can become many. Either the boundless is simply a kind of grab-bag collection of the specific stuffs (in which case it is not really one at all, and monism is abandoned), or it is an indefinite something, which, being nothing in particular, is not anything at all.

Thus, when Anaximenes declared that air is the basic stuff, he made a distinct advance over Anaximander. Further, his theory made an important contribution toward the understanding of change. He held that qualitative changes (for example, from a liquid to a gaseous state) can be explained as changes in density of the one stuff. Thus when air "is dilated into a rarer form it becomes fire, while on the other hand air that is condensed forms winds . . . if this process goes further, it gives water, still further earth, and the greatest condensation of all is found in stones."

Presumably Anaximenes was generalizing from familiar instances of qualitative changes that are linked to quantitative changes, such as the qualitative change from being sober to being drunk that results from a large quantity of wine being consumed. Here then is a change from one quality to its opposite. Why can we not find similar quantitative changes underlying the basic world changes (day-night, hot-cold, moist-dry)? Moreover, if all these qualitative changes are reducible to quantitative changes of *one* stuff, monism is "saved"; the experienced diversity is reconciled with the postulated unity. What is needed, then, is a stuff capable of quantitative variation. Such a stuff is air, which of course can vary in density, that is, quantitatively. Let us assume, therefore, that air is the basic world stuff.

If this, indeed, is how Anaximenes reasoned, a modern scientist would call the conclusion a provisional working hypothesis and would proceed to devise techniques for testing it; for example, he might subject air to varying degrees of pressure and see what happens. Not so Anaximenes: Like Thales and Anaximander he had no notion of experimentation or of evidence and so moved directly from brilliant guess to confident assertion.

Had Anaximenes tried to verify his hypothesis he would have found, of course, that things are not as simple as he supposed. But this is not the point. It would be absurd to criticize Anaximenes for not being a modern scientist. It is more to the point to see that his kind of thinking laid the basis for modern scientific practice. For, in the first place, Anaximenes' was the kind of account, unlike Homer's or Hesiod's, that can be tested. This is why it has been stated that with the Milesians we come to a type of thinking about the world that is fruitful instead of barren. In the second place, though the Greeks on the whole failed to see the enormous significance of his idea, Anaximenes laid the basis for a quantitative description of the world.

Even those Greeks who recognized the value of mathematics as an exact science failed for the most part to see that mathematics could be applied to the description of the physical world by means of measurement. The Greeks who came nearest this concept were, as we shall see, the Pythagoreans, but their ideas in this respect were not followed up. Indeed, it was in the Renaissance that techniques were first developed for the "quantification" of experience. That is to say, we have to wait until the Renaissance for the appearance of the modern scientific method of investigating nature.

## Heraclitus

Heraclitus[7] was another Ionian Greek who proposed an answer to Thales' question, "What is the stuff out of which the world is made?" According to Heraclitus, this stuff is fire—"This world . . . was ever, is now, and ever shall be an everlasting Fire." At first sight this seems merely a variant of the Milesian answer, but though Heraclitus was obviously influenced by the Milesian thinkers, his views were more subtle. He seems to have been much occupied with the problem that, as we have seen, Anaximenes discovered hidden in the formulations of Thales and Anaximander: How can the one change into the many? As long as the world is one (that is, one thing) it would seem to be impossible for it also to be many things. And if it is many, how can it be one? Anaximenes had not cleared up this puzzle. At most his theory merely gives the *conditions* under which something

7 Heraclitus was a citizen of Ephesus. He lived during the latter part of the sixth and the early part of the fifth centuries B.C. (Burnet, *op. cit.*, pp. 130–31). G. S. Kirk and J. E. Raven (*The Pre-Socratic Philosophers* [Cambridge University Press, 1962], p. 182) think that 480 B.C. is the terminal date. Of Heraclitus' writings, about 130 "fragments" have survived. Some are sentences; some are only phrases. The task of putting these isolated bits into a meaningful mosaic is so difficult that almost every student of Greek thought has ended with his own Heraclitus.

(air) becomes something else (fire, earth, water). It does not explain what it means to say that air *becomes* water. Unless air remains air throughout the process of rarefaction and condensation, we cannot say it is the "one"; but if it does remain the same, what do we mean by saying that it *becomes* water?

Heraclitus seems to have held the problem to be insoluble as long as the "one" is taken to be a material thing. But what if the oneness of the world consists in the orderliness with which things change? Then the world would have a unity—not the unity of a material underlying the diversity, but rather the unity of pattern. The universe would be one in the sense of being an ordered cosmos, capable of being explored and understood by the human mind, instead of the chaos of conflicting wills that the old theologians had seen at the heart of things. Thus the central purpose of the Milesian philosophers would be satisfied by abandoning their basic concept of "stuff" and substituting for it the concept of process, that is, ordered change, or, as Heraclitus would say, "change according to the measures." Here, then, is another modification of theory produced by the recognition of logical deficiencies in earlier formulations.

The Heraclitean world view, thus stated, may sound very "modern." It is true that, like Heraclitus, contemporary scientists look for the measures—for regular relations among varying events—rather than for self-identical, enduring "things." But we have formulated what seems implicit in Heraclitus' view, not what Heraclitus himself stated unambiguously. What is involved is the abstract concept of process, and, since nothing is more difficult—even for modern men—than to think abstractly, it is not surprising that Heraclitus failed to think about this with complete clarity. We say, for instance, "My head is full of ideas," using a spatial metaphor for a relationship that is not spatial. Or we say that such-and-such a conclusion "follows from" such-and-such evidence, using another mistaken metaphor, for though our enunciation of the conclusion may follow in time the presentation of the evidence, the relationship we are really talking about is logical, not temporal. We do not mean that the conclusion literally follows the evidence, but that if one accepts the evidence one cannot, logically, reject the conclusion.

It might be said that these are merely verbal conventions that everyone understands. But though we "know better," we are likely to draw conclusions about the mind, say, that are not warranted and that seem plausible only because our language suggests that the mind is a box into which ideas fit.

This seems to have happened to Heraclitus. Unable to think abstractly about process, he slipped into using an image that represented process. What would do better for this purpose than "fire," which is always changing yet somehow is always the same? Hence, though he ought to have denied that the world is one *thing*, he ended by identifying it with fire.

The logical development of Thales' initial premise thus gradually led philosophers to a point very far from common sense. Thales and the other Milesians were naturally aware of change (day follows night; summer, winter; wet, dry; and so on). Their problem, indeed, was to reconcile the fact of change with their belief in unity. But the kind of change they were thinking of is very different from the kind of change Heraclitus' theory required him to postulate. For this theory committed him to assert that everything changes all the time. This is far more change than experience furnishes evidence for. For if experience discloses change, it also discloses permanence. Things endure, says experience. The desk, the chairs, in my study remain the same, as far as perception goes, for an appreciable length of time—years, I hope. But such permanence Heraclitus had to deny: "One cannot," he said, "step into the same river twice,"[f] for the river is constantly flowing and no matter how quickly one puts one's foot in again, one puts it into different water. Similarly, the desk and chairs are in a state of flux; their appearance of permanence results from the fact that their rate of change is constant. It is as if water were running into and out of a swimming pool at a constant rate: Because the level remains constant, we might suppose that the water is the same. Thus the requirements of theory forced Heraclitus to make a new kind of distinction. In addition to the distinction between the one and the many, we now have a distinction between the world as it *appears* to common-sense perception and the world as theory says it *really* must be.

## MORAL AND SOCIAL THEORY

What we know about the Milesian philosophers suggests that their interest was focused on the physical world. But when questions of the sort the poets had asked—What is man? What is his destiny?—were once more raised, new answers became necessary. New theories about the physical world and the substitution of natural for divine causality obviously required adjustments in the old Greek view of man and his role in the universe.

With this larger question Heraclitus, unlike the Milesians, was concerned. We are told that he wrote two treatises besides the one dealing with the physical universe. These were devoted to theology and to politics, and a few fragments of them have survived. As regards politics, it would seem that he transferred his conception of universal flux from the physical world to the social. Thus the famous passage in which he spoke of the Milesian opposites as "an attunement of opposite tensions, like that of the bow and the lyre" could equally apply in the field of politics. In other words, social and political stability rests on, and is an appearance of, opposing tensions. The bent bow seems at rest, but only because the string and the bow pull equally against each other. So everywhere in nature rest is the appearance of equal and opposite forces. Thus, "War is the father and King of all" and "Strife is Justice." It follows that "The people must fight for its law as for its walls."

In the turbulent era during which Heraclitus lived this must have seemed only too true. In the city-state of his day internal peace was only a sign that neither the downtrodden people nor the nobles were strong enough to seize power. When one side became strong enough to "fight for its law," the unstable equilibrium was destroyed until an approximate equality of forces again restored "peace." Thus, without strife peace could not exist. This may sound like a paradox, but Heraclitus meant that without a balance of opposing forces society would disappear in civil war. Hence, according to Heraclitus, "Homer was wrong in saying: 'Would that strife might perish from among Gods and men!' He did not see that he was praying for the destruction of the universe; if his prayer were heard, all things would pass away."

Of course, as a matter of fact, Homer and Heraclitus used the term "strife" in different senses. The strife Homer objected to is an open outbreak of violence, which—in Heraclitus' terms—is a sign of inequality of forces; the strife Heraclitus praised is what may be called the hidden, or underlying, tension of opposites. This is perhaps what he meant when he said in another place that "the hidden attunement is better than the open."g

In the struggle he envisaged political life to be, Heraclitus' sympathies were on the side of the nobles. He is said to have been a member of the royal house of Ephesus, and his views are those we might expect from his class during a time when political power was passing into the hands of the masses.

With a keen sense of his own intellectual (and doubtless also social) superiority, he rejected the equalitarian theories of the democrats. "The Ephesians," he said, "would do well to hang themselves, every grown man of them, and leave the city to beardless lads, for they have cast out Hermodorus, the best man among them, saying, 'We will have none who is best among us; if there be any such, let him be so elsewhere and among others.'"h

His contempt for the masses is perhaps also expressed in the aphorism, "Asses would rather have straw than gold." Over and over, even in these few fragments, we find him attacking the folly of the masses. They did not appreciate him, it is clear, any more than they appreciated Hermodorus. "Fools when they do hear are like the deaf: of them does the saying bear witness that they are absent when present." That is, the masses did not understand his theory; they believed what they saw—that the world consists of relatively permanent, slowly changing things—not the "Truth," as taught by Heraclitus, that everything flows.i

## RELIGION

The masses were no better, Heraclitus thought, when it came to religion. "They pray to images, as if one were to talk with a man's house." Their beliefs were a farrago of superstitions, because in religion as in everything else they relied on benighted teachers. Fools listen to fools: "Hesiod is most men's teacher. Men are sure he knew very many things, a man who did not know day or night!"8 As for Homer, he "should be turned out of the lists and whipped." It is obvious, of course, that anyone who accepted Milesian science, as Heraclitus did, neces-

8 In the *Theogony* Hesiod had taught that Day is the child of Night.

sarily rejected the old religion. But it does not follow that Heraclitus was an atheist. On the contrary, he believed "the wisest man is an ape compared to God, just as the most beautiful ape is ugly compared to man." Indeed, Heraclitus seems to have identified god (in some passages at least) with the world process itself. "God is day and night, winter and summer, war and peace, surfeit and hunger; but takes various shapes, just as fire, when it is mingled with spices, is named according to the savour of each."j

But if god is the process taken as a whole, how can he have that concern for men that poets like Hesiod insisted on? This conclusion, which would have shocked most of his contemporaries, Heraclitus accepted. "To God all things are fair and good and right, but men hold some things wrong and some right."k This seems to mean that god (the world process) is indifferent to human notions of right and wrong, justice and injustice.[9]

Here Hesiod's universal law is being stripped of its divine and moral associations and is becoming neutral and amoral like that old fate from which, as we have seen, it was descended. But in reverting to the notion of an amoral force, philosophers like Heraclitus did not lose the notion of universality and necessity that had been contributed by such thinkers as Hesiod. What we have in fact is the gradual emergence of the concept of natural law—of a neutral, regular, and pervasive interrelationship of all things in nature. Once this concept became firmly fixed, only the development of techniques for exploring these natural relationships was needed for the emergence of science in the modern sense of the word.

But, of course, the development of such techniques was long in coming. And there were other elements in Heraclitus' doctrines that could be, and were, developed in a very different direction. One of the terms Heraclitus used to describe the world process is "logos,"[10] and some of the fragments suggest that man's chief good is to "listen to," to become attuned to, even to become absorbed into, this logos. This line of thought emphasizes the religious, rather than the scientific, implications of there being a universal order in the world. It is difficult to state clearly, but nonetheless it greatly appeals to some minds—sometimes because it *is* obscure. At least, both the Stoics and the Christians later made much of this theological strain in Heraclitus' views. If it be asked which was the real Heraclitus—the religious or the scientific—the answer must be, both. The question implies a clear-cut distinction that thinkers in that age did not make.

---

9  Although it is true that human law has its source in ("is fed by") the world process, the latter "prevails as much as it will," that is, has no significant moral relation to human law.

10  Not all modern critics by any means agree on what Heraclitus meant by "logos." But whatever he himself meant, the Stoics and the Christians attributed metaphysical and theological implications to Heraclitus' logos. From the point of view of the history of philosophy, what Heraclitus himself thought is perhaps less important than what later thinkers thought he thought. For a judicious discussion of the current status of the dispute over what the term meant to Heraclitus, see P. Wheelwright, *Heraclitus* (Princeton University Press, 1959), pp. 19–25.

# Xenophanes

Much the same attitude toward religion is seen in the views of Xenophanes,[11] another Ionian, from whose writings a few fragments survive. Like Heraclitus, he attacked the old theology. "Homer and Hesiod," he held, "have ascribed to the Gods all things that are a shame and a disgrace among mortals, stealings and adulteries and deceivings of one another." Like Heraclitus, too, he realized that the old mythology was not only immoral; it was also untrue: "She that they call Iris is likewise a cloud. . . ." The "likewise" is, as Burnet observes, significant. Xenophanes had been enumerating other phenomena and pointing out that they are all natural processes, not anthropomorphic deities. Like Heraclitus again, Xenophanes believed that god is called different names by different men: "Yes, and if oxen and horses or lions had hands, and could paint with their hands, and produce works of art as men do, horses would paint the forms of the gods like horses, and oxen like oxen, and make their bodies in the image of their several kinds."[12] But, again like Heraclitus, he was not led by this to reject religion; on the contrary, he believed he had found a better religion than the old mythologies. There is, he said, "one God . . . neither in form like unto mortals nor in thought. . . . He sees all over, thinks all over, and hears all over. . . . Without toil he swayeth all things by the thought of his mind."[1]

Though this may sound as if Xenophanes were a monotheist who anticipated some of the doctrines of Christianity, he was probably a pantheist like Heraclitus. But actually, terms like monotheism, polytheism, pantheism, are misleading here; they imply distinctions that thinkers like Xenophanes and Heraclitus had not yet made. It is more to the point to see that the old religion was being undermined and that, while rare spirits like Heraclitus and Xenophanes could worship a "world process" or a "material one," most men were incapable of such rarefied abstractions. In destroying the old, these philosophers provided no satisfactory substitute on which the emotions of man could fix. Thus, as the "man in the street" gradually became aware of the new science, a serious problem developed. The reaction was doubtless similar to the one that occurred in Europe and America during the second half of the last century when the old fundamentalist faith in a literal Bible was undermined by Darwinism.

Since, however, religion played a much more prominent role in Greek life than it did in nineteenth-century Europe and America, its loss was a more acute blow to the structure of Greek society. Among our grandfathers, religion was doubtless important, but in a sense it was a luxury. During the preceding two centuries life had been growing increasingly secular, and by the nineteenth

---

11 For a discussion of the probable dates of Xenophanes' life, see Burnet, *op. cit.*, pp. 112–15; Kirk and Raven, *op. cit.*, pp. 163–64.

12 Compare Fragment 16: "The Ethiopians make their Gods black and snub-nosed; the Thracians say theirs have blue eyes and red hair."

century a duplicate set of sanctions had been worked out that continued to operate when the religious motive disappeared.[13] For the Greeks, in contrast, all the major sanctions that held society together and moved men to conform to the law and to act with restraint and moderation were ultimately religious. Hence the collapse of religious belief had very serious repercussions on Greek society.

## Axiomatic Geometry

While these theories about the ultimate stuff of the world were being worked out, there was a development of great importance in geometry. This was the invention of the axiomatic method of proving and systematizing a set of conclusions. Sixth-century Greeks were familiar with the rules used by the Egyptians to measure land. The Egyptians seem to have been motivated in developing these rules chiefly by urgent practical considerations; for instance, the yearly flooding of the Nile washed away landmarks in the fertile fields near its banks. It was characteristic of the Greeks not to be content to use the rules. They wanted to understand *why* the rules worked.

At first, their attempts were limited to finding separate proofs for each geometric truth. But late in the sixth century and early in the fifth century efforts were made to combine known geometric theorems into a single axiomatic system, so called because all the conclusions were proved by logical reasoning from a set of first premises (axioms), which were simple statements believed to be self-evidently true.

It is not known who first succeeded in systematizing geometry into one axiomatic system. The oldest extant text that does it is Euclid's *Elements*, written about 300 B.C. In Euclid's book, the first theorems are proved by showing that they follow directly from the axioms; then, by judicious combinations of already proved theorems with the axioms, more complex theorems are derived. In this systematic way Euclid was able to "demonstrate" a large body of geometrical knowledge.

Not until the nineteenth century were any of Euclid's axioms or theorems challenged. So impressive is Euclid's achievement that most Western philosophers have regarded it as the paradigm of human reasoning. It is not surprising, then, that Greek thinkers came to rely on reasoning rather than on sense perception in their pursuit of natural knowledge.

---

13 For instance, a good Utilitarian might continue to follow the Ten Commandments even after becoming convinced that God had not addressed Moses in person out of a cloud, because he believed that obeying the Commandments tends to produce "the greatest happiness for the greatest number."

# Parmenides

It may well be that the achievements of Greek geometers influenced the next development in physical theory. For this development emphasized logical reasoning from premises regarded as self-evident. But whereas the geometers reached conclusions that agreed with sense experience, the physicists and cosmologists who first used the geometric method reached conclusions that collided head-on with perception. Parmenides[14] is an example. He saw more clearly that any of his predecessors that the principle problem resulting from Thales' original formula was the problem of change. How does that basic one, whose existence every thinker had assumed, change into the many encountered in ordinary experience? This was the problem Parmenides set himself to solve. A modern scientist would be primarily interested in showing by experimental means the conditions under which transformations in color, volume, or density, for instance, occur; Parmenides was concerned only to analyze the concept of change itself.

Starting from the basic premise of monism, that reality is fundamentally one, and adding two additional premises that seemed self-evident, he reached the conclusion that the very notion of change is self-contradictory and hence that the change that we think we perceive simply does not occur: When we think we see things changing, we are victims of an illusion.

The two new premises were, first, "What is, is" and, second, "What is not, is not." Understood in one way, these are tautologies (like "A is A"); it is this that led Parmenides to take them to be self-evidently true. But he understood them to be making complex statements about the world, and they are not self-evidently true when loaded with all the meaning Parmenides made them bear.

According to Parmenides, "What is not, is not" means that there is no nothing, that is, that the word "nothing" does not name anything. He seems to have reasoned in the following way. You can try to think, for instance, about a unicorn; if you succeed, you are thinking about something, if only about a fictitious animal. But now try to think about nothing. You may believe that you are succeeding in doing so, but as far as you are thinking at all, you are thinking about something (that is, there is some object of thought before the mind), not about nothing. You may *call* the object about which you are thinking "nothing," but that is just a name. There is, and can be, no object, no nothing, named by the name "nothing." This apparently is what Parmenides meant when he wrote, "Thou canst not know nor utter what is not—that is impossible." It follows, according to Parmenides' reasoning, that the sentence "Nothing exists" is self-contradictory—there is no nothing that can be the subject judged in this sentence.

From these two premises and the underlying assumption of monism, to

14 Parmenides was probably born about 515 b.c. in Elea, a Greek colony in southern Italy. It is likely that he lived until at least 450 b.c. He was thus a younger contemporary of Heraclitus, whose work Parmenides seems to have known and criticized.

Parmenides it seemed to follow that whatever is, is (1) uncreated, (2) indestructible, (3) eternal, and (4) unchangeable. His arguments can probably be reconstructed as follows.

(1) *What is, is uncreated.* In order to prove this let us assume its opposite, namely, that what is was created. If what is was created it must have been created either (*a*) out of nothing or (*b*) out of something. But (*a*) it could not be created out of nothing, for there is no nothing; and (*b*) we cannot say that it was created out of something, for, on the assumption of monism, there is no "something else"—there is only what is. This exhausts the possibilities: Since something is neither created (*a*) out of nothing nor (*b*) out of something, it is uncreated.

Again (2) *what is, is indestructible.* Destruction of anything would involve its disappearance (change into nothing), and there is no nothing.

It follows that (3) *what is, is eternal,* for what is uncreated and indestructible is obviously eternal.

(4) *What is, is unchangeable.* This follows, in the first place, from the argument about indestructibility. What we mean by change is transformation into something else. When a thing is transformed into something else, it becomes what it was not (the old thing disappears; the new thing appears). But there is no nothing for the old thing to disappear into.

Another consideration leads to the same conclusion. If something changes, it changes at some particular time. There must be a reason, therefore, why it changes at *this* time rather than at some other time. But this reason must have come into being (for had it existed earlier, the change we are discussing would itself have occurred earlier). What made the reason for our change occur *now?* Obviously the only answer is that something else has occurred, and this something else's occurring clearly depends on some other thing's occurring. When we try to explain a change that occurs here and now, we can do so only by assuming another change to have occurred somewhere else, and when we try to explain this other change, it eludes us and leads us on to some other and equally elusive change. So we may as well return to the original case of change that was to be explained. As Parmenides said, "What need could have made it arise later rather than sooner? Therefore must it either be altogether or be not at all." Hence change does not occur.

### ZENO'S PARADOXES

These arguments of Parmenides' were supported by one of his pupils, Zeno, in a dramatic fashion. Zeno was the author of a number of famous paradoxes intended to show that motion, a special case of change (that is, change of place), cannot occur, because it is "impossible"—that is, because the concept is self-contradictory. Let us examine two of these paradoxes.

(1) Aristotle's version of one argument runs as follows: "Before any distance can be traversed half the distance must be traversed. These half-distances are infinite in number. It is impossible to traverse distances infinite in number."[m]

For instance, suppose you want to get up from your chair and walk to the door. You may try to do this and believe that you succeed, but you are mistaken. Your senses deceive you; you have never left your chair. For you must traverse *half* the distance from chair to door before you traverse the whole. But before you can traverse that half you must traverse half of it, that is, a quarter of the distance. And before you traverse that quarter you must traverse half of *it,* and so on. No matter how short a length you take, it consists of an infinite distance; that is, there are an infinite number of points to be traversed. Since the time at your disposal is finite, it is obvious that you cannot get to the door, or even for that matter move from your chair, for the slightest movement involves an infinite number of points.

(2) This argument concerns "swift Achilles and the tortoise." It purports to show that, contrary to all the evidence of the senses, no matter how fast Achilles runs he never overtakes the tortoise, no matter how slowly the tortoise crawls. Let the tortoise be at *T* at the moment Achilles, who is at *A,* begins to pursue him. Thus

No matter how fast Achilles runs, it takes him some finite amount of time, however small, to reach *T* from his starting point *A.* During this time the tortoise will have moved some distance, however small, to *T'.* Hence Achilles, who is now at *T,* has not yet overtaken him.

But while Achilles is running from *T* to *T'* (which takes some time, however little) the tortoise will have moved on to *T''.*

It seems clear that, although the distance becomes shorter and shorter, some distance, however short, will separate them. Hence Achilles will never overtake the tortoise.

These contentions, which still worry philosophers and mathematicians, are even more obviously at variance with common sense than was Heraclitus' position, for surely the most universal impression we have is of multiplicity, change, and motion. Here, then, is a head-on collision between experience and conclusions reached by what seemed logical reasoning from self-evident premises. Moreover, Heraclitus and Parmenides, both of whom depended on reasoning instead of perception, were led by their reasoning to directly contradictory conclusions. Even philosophers who cared nothing for sense experience had to admit that something was wrong, and it is obvious that the fault lay with reason itself. This at least was the conclusion the Greeks themselves were to reach. The exaggerated confidence some of these early thinkers had in the power of the human mind led others to profound scepticism about its capacities.

### RATIONALISM AND EMPIRICISM

It may be asked why Parmenides, Heraclitus, and Zeno themselves did not become sceptics. Parmenides put the case for rationalism (as we may call the conviction of these early thinkers that reason is more reliable than sense perception) clearly and explicitly: "It is the same thing that can be thought and that can be. It must needs be that what can be spoken and thought *is*."[15,n] But how could Parmenides be so confident that the test of knowledge and existence is logical consistency?

The answer is that the test of logical consistency has a number of advantages as compared with perception. It is indubitable, whereas perception often turns out to be false (for example, the mirage in the desert). It is universal, whereas perception at best gives only information about particulars. For instance, if I know that A is to the right of B and also that B is to the right of C, I can indubitably conclude that A is to the right of C. This is a universal relationship, holding for all A's, B's, and C's whatever. I can *know* that this is true prior to perceiving the actual spatial relation between a particular A and a particular C; and, in any case, perception would only give me information about this A and this C, not about all A's and all C's. Thus the test of logical consistency yields a kind of knowledge that does not have to wait for an often tardy and always uncertain confirmation by observation.

Suppose the question arises of whether round squares exist anywhere in the world. I do not look around in a random sample of places, fail to find a round square, and then conclude that there is a high probability that round squares do not exist. I know, antecedently to any such test by experience, that the world cannot anywhere contain a round square, for the concept of a round square is contradictory. I can think of round and of square, and I can indeed say the words "round square"; but I cannot *think* of a square that is round, for round and square are contradictory concepts. According to Parmenides' way of thinking, if what can be thought is and what cannot be thought is not, it follows that the world contains no round squares.

Because the knowledge obtained by logical thinking seems so superior, it has appealed to countless philosophers, who may be called, for want of a better name, "rationalists." Like Parmenides, these early Greeks held that knowledge of reality is reached by reasoning rather than by sense-perceiving.

In contrast, the name "empiricists" may be given those who take sense

---

15 Or, as Hegel was to formulate it many centuries later, "the real is rational and the rational is real."

experience[16] as their ultimate criterion. Most philosophers take a stand on one side or the other of this dispute, but, just to make matters more complicated, few are either "pure" empiricists or "pure" rationalists. It will, in fact, become increasingly clear as we proceed that neither extreme position is satisfactory. The real problem, therefore, is not how to choose between them but how to combine the use of reasoning and the use of the senses in a fruitful method of inquiry. This is a problem of great difficulty. It is because Parmenides stated the rationalistic alternative in such an uncompromising form that so much time has been devoted to his view.

## The Pluralists

Though Parmenides did not recognize it, his argument was hypothetical. Its form was: *If* the Milesians' basic assumption that there is one underlying material substance is correct, then there is no change. Since it seems never to have occurred to him to question this assumption, he failed to see the hypothetical character of his reasoning. The next generation of scientist-philosophers rightly concluded that since change is obviously real, the premise must be false.[17] They saw that Parmenides' argument was, in effect, a *reductio ad absurdum* of Milesian monism.[18] Though we shall from time to time meet other types of monism in the history of philosophy, we shall never again come across a materialistic monism of the Milesian type. Pluralism now succeeds monism as the basic assumption of Greek thought. As the development of Greek philosophy before Plato is pursued, we shall see how the implications of this new assumption were gradually revealed.

## Empedocles

The first of the pluralists about whom we know anything is Empedocles.[19] He accepted the Parmenidean thesis that nothing is created or destroyed: What is,

16 These two alternatives do not, obviously, exhaust the possibilities. One could take as one's criterion, for instance, neither sense experience nor logical reasoning but some kind of mystical experience, or the authority of some allegedly divine book, or some combination of these.
17 Another option, of course, would have been to retain the premise and to show that Parmenides' reasoning was fallacious. But it was a long time before anybody was able to prove Parmenides' logic wrong.
18 Parmenides of course did not recognize that his argument was a *reductio ad absurdum*.
19 Like Parmenides, Empedocles was a citizen of one of the western Greek colonies—of Acragas in southern Sicily. For a discussion of the evidence on Empedocles' dates, see Burnet, *op. cit.*, pp. 197–98; Kirk and Raven, *op. cit.*, pp. 320–21. About all that can be said is that the greater part of his life probably fell in the first half of the fifth century B.C.

is.[20] But he denied Parmenides' contention that motion cannot occur. Parmenides had assumed that because "there is no nothing," there is no empty space. This assumption Empedocles also accepted. For him, as for Parmenides, the argument about the nonexistence of nothing proved that reality must be a plenum; that is, it must be completely full, without any holes or pockets in it. But Empedocles saw an ingenious way of reconciling Parmenides' logic with the obvious facts of experience. Since, as Parmenides had proved, monism and motion are contradictory, reality must be plural. Let us suppose, then, that the "many" that fill the plenum are capable of motion—not movement *into* empty space, of course, but a movement whereby one of the many takes the place of some other one of the many.

Empedocles thought that he had empirical evidence to support this theoretical solution of the difficulty. He had observed that if you put one end of a tube in water while holding a finger over the other end, water will not enter the tube. But as soon as you release your finger, water enters. This is an instance of motion in a plenum, he argued: The water does not wait for the tube to become empty; it flows in at one end as the air flows out at the other. Though there is no empty space, motion occurs. Hence motion in a plenum is possible, provided that reality is a plurality, not a unity.

Having thus got (1) a many that (2) moves, Empedocles turned his attention to the world process. He proceeded as follows: First he assumed that the many are four in number—earth, air, fire, and water.[21] Each of these "roots," he held, is eternal, uncreated, indestructible, and unchanging—that is, a Parmenidean "one." Second, he assumed that there are two types of motion, which he called Love and Strife. Love he defined as a motion uniting different things (forming a mixture). Strife is its opposite; it separates a mixture into its component elements. It is clear that Empedocles was on the way to the notion of "force" but that, like Heraclitus, he had difficulty in thinking abstractly. Hence Love and Strife appear in his thought as material. In a way, there are thus six, not four, basic elements in Empedocles' system; four of them are definitely corporeal since they are elements that are moved, and two are conceived (on analogy, doubtless, with human behavior) to be "movers."

The world process as Empedocles conceived of it is a continuous cycle in which, at the outset, the four basic elements are completely mixed up, as in a well-tossed salad. At this stage in the process Love is dominant. Then, gradually, Strife replaces Love, as water replaces air in a tube, until finally the mixed elements are separated out and the "salad" becomes untossed, with all the air collected in one place, all the fire in another, and so on. Now Strife is completely

---

20  Empedocles' formula was "Fools . . . deem that what before was not comes into being [and] that aught can perish and be utterly destroyed. For it cannot be that aught can arise from what in no way is, and it is impossible and unheard of that what *is* should perish." The influence of Parmenides is obvious.

21  Empedocles seems simply to have taken over a traditional view that there are two basic pairs of opposites—hot-cold, wet-dry. See p. 12.

dominant, and the reverse process at once begins. Eventually there is the mixture as before, and alternation continues indefinitely.

To Empedocles it seemed obvious that our world is neither a complete melange nor its opposite. It is a mixture, constituted of entities that we loosely call "things." But, strictly speaking, the only real things are earth, air, fire, and water. The objects of this world—rocks, plants, animals, and men—are simply unstable combinations of these primary elements.[22] If, then, our world is "in process," are we moving in the direction of complete mixture or complete separation? Empedocles seems to have held that Strife is becoming ascendant and Love is being forced out. In any case, he thought that the world as we know it will disappear and be succeeded eventually by other worlds like it, which in their turn will disappear.

The fragments of Empedocles' writing that have survived show that, like Anaximander, he anticipated such modern evolutionary doctrines as the survival of the fittest. Consider, for instance, his description of the period after Strife's dominance when Love again begins to enter. At this time the various parts of animals arise in a hit-or-miss way, as Love bit by bit mixes the elements that Strife has separated: "heads spring up without necks and arms wander bare and bereft of shoulders. Eyes stray up and down in want of foreheads." As Love continues to mix things up, these parts get united in a completely haphazard way: "these things joined together as each might chance, and many other things besides continually arose." Eyes might, for instance, "mix" with hands, feet with shoulders. Such mixtures obviously cannot survive, but in the course of random combinations a successful relationship sooner or later occurs. An eye mixes with a forehead, a hand with an arm, and there is a mixture that can see, walk, reproduce, think. All this happens by chance. There is no god who plans it "for the best." The fact that men, with the faculties they have, exist at all is the temporary and accidental result of a casual mixture of elements.

This is at least the implication of Empedocles' evolutionary theory. But when he wrote of the world process as a whole, his point of view changed. He called the process "god" and worshiped it just as Xenophanes worshiped his world process. As did Xenophanes, he held that this god who is a process cannot have human characteristics. "He is not furnished with a human head on his body, two branches do not sprout from his shoulders, he has no feet, no swift knees, nor hairy parts." ° How, then, could Empedocles in the same passage attribute a mind to the whole?—"He is only a sacred and unutterable mind flashing through the whole world with rapid thoughts." How could Empedocles reconcile this thinking mind with the purely chance operation of the world process just described? We have to conclude that he was not entirely aware of the implications of either his scientific theories or his religious attitude. Not until we reach

22 "There is no substance of any of all the things that perish, nor any cessation for them of baneful death. They are only a mingling and interchange of what has been mingled. Substance is but a name given to these things by men"—Fragment 8 (Burnet).

Plato do we find a full recognition of the problem of reconciling a purposive and valuational conception of man with the notion of a mechanistic universe.

Empedocles was the first of the pluralists. After him, the pluralistic hypothesis underwent radical alterations as the result of a critical study similar to the one that changed Thales' version of monism into Parmenides'.

## Anaxagoras

Empedocles' first critic was Anaxagoras, an Ionian Greek.[23] Let us remind ourselves that what had troubled Thales' successors about his monism was his reduction of all the variety of the sense world to one ultimate stuff. But we are hardly better off with Empedocles' four ultimate stuffs than with the Milesians' one. How can water—or any mixture of water with earth, air, and fire—become a cabbage or a lion?

Anaxagoras seems to have recognized this difficulty. "How," he asked, "can hair come from what is not hair, or flesh from what is not flesh?"[p] This question implies that he accepted Parmenides' thesis that change (in the sense of the transformation of one thing into another) is an illusion. But Anaxagoras was not content to leave unsolved the conflict between the world as reason reveals it "really" is and the world as it "appears" to the senses. In order to solve this problem he made the following assumptions:

(1) The stuff of the world is eternal. (2) There is a many, each one of which is a Parmenidean "one." (3) There is motion (that is, change of relative spatial position of the parts of a plenum).

These three presuppositions are of course identical with those made by Empedocles. Anaxagoras' problem was to explain the existence of ordinary sense objects without falling back (as Empedocles had done) on the seemingly contradictory view that things can change and yet remain the same. Since "nothing comes into being or passes away," sense objects must result from "a mingling and separation of things that are."[q] But how can the qualitatively unchanging many become the changing many of the sense world?

To begin with, since Anaxagoras had ruled out change in the sense of transformation, it seemed to him that "in everything there is a portion of everything."[r] Every visible sense object is a mixture containing bits of all the real stuffs in the world. In what we call "hair" (that is, the stuff of this sense world) there are bits of cabbage stuff, bits of lion stuff, and so on—bits of all the infinitely

---

23  The fact that we have yet to study the views of a single Greek mainlander testifies to the intellectual predominance of the colonials. But it is significant of the change that occurred toward the middle of the fifth century B.C. that Anaxagoras went to Athens to live. From this time on, the mainland, and especially Athens, became increasingly the philosophical center of Greece.

various stuffs that we see about us.[24] Similarly, in "flesh" (the stuff of this sense world) there are bits of hair stuff, cabbage stuff, sealing-wax stuff, and, of course, flesh stuff. But flesh stuff happens to predominate in the latter, and, because our vision is gross and inadequate,[25] we see it as being all flesh and call it by the name of what is only the predominant element in the mixture. Since, similarly, hair stuff predominates in the other mixture, we see only the hair stuff and so call the mixture by that element's name. In other words, Anaxagoras replaced Empedocles' four "roots" with an infinite diversity of qualitatively different "seeds."

So much for Anaxagoras' "many." As regards the motion by which the many real stuffs become mixed in the various proportions found in the objects of the sense world, Anaxagoras replaced Empedocles' Love and Strife with a single motion, which he called "Mind." Like Love and Strife, Mind is material; no more than Heraclitus or Empedocles was Anaxagoras able to think abstractly of "process" or "force." It is possible that Anaxagoras' motion was derived from Empedocles' "sacred and unutterable mind flashing through the whole world with rapid thoughts."[26] There is a corresponding difficulty, at any rate, in reconciling the various assertions Anaxagoras made about the nature of motion. On the one hand, he held that Mind "sets all things in order," which seems to imply purpose. On the other hand, in his detailed description of what Mind does, the process appears to be purely mechanical.

According to Anaxagoras, at the outset of the world process all the multitudinous real stuffs of the world were in such homogeneous distribution that, even if human sense organs had existed (of course they did not), the world would not have been recognizable as the familiar world of our experience. "Before they were separated off, when all things were together, not even was any colour distinguishable, for the mixtures of all things prevented it."

This mixture has an obvious relationship to Anaximander's "boundless." Like the boundless, the initial state of Anaxagoras' world process is nothing in particular. But this was impossible to conceive of on Anaximander's principles (for how could one particular stuff be nothing in particular?). Anaxagoras got around

---

24 The question of whether the ultimate reals (Anaxagoras called them "seeds") are qualitative mixtures or qualitative simples has been much debated. Most commentators now accept the former view (see Burnet, *op. cit.*, pp. 262–65). Here I have adopted what Burnet rejects as "the old view," because (1) it seems to me more consonant with what Anaxagoras actually said and (2) the objections to it that Burnet and others state are inconclusive. Even if "infinite divisibility" and "qualitative simples" are incompatible as Burnet maintains, this would not prove that Anaxagoras rejected the latter. It would have to be shown that he knew them to be incompatible. Since Anaxagoras did not clearly distinguish between "qualities" and "things" (even though he had a word for quality), he is unlikely to have limited his seeds to the old "qualitative" opposites. If he talks in one place about "opposites" (hot-cold, moist-dry), he talks in another about "things" (hair and flesh, for instance). And there is no evidence that he did not think of them in the same way.

25 Fragment 21: "From the weakness of our senses we are not able to judge the truth," and Fragment 21a: "What appears is a vision of the unseen."

26 See p. 27.

the difficulty by assuming a plurality of stuffs. According to him, each stuff has its own particular nature, and it is the totality that is nothing in particular, precisely because, being a uniform mixture, no one of its particular stuffs predominates to be "picked out" by sense organs like ours.

Gradually, into this complete mixture Mind enters (just as in Empedocles' system Love and Strife alternately enter the plenum). As it enters, Mind sets up a circular motion like a vortex, causing the various stuffs to "separate off."

> Mind began to revolve first from a small beginning; but the revolution now extends over a larger space, and will extend over a larger still. [In] this revolution . . . now revolve the stars and the sun and the moon, and the air and the aether that are separated off. And this revolution caused the separating off, and the rare is separated off from the dense, the warm from the cold, the light from the dark, and the dry from the moist.[8]

Thus Mind produces a kind of shuffling. If one thinks of a deck of cards as a completely random distribution, one has a picture of the plenum at the start of the world process. Shuffling (the introduction of motion by the entrance of Mind) causes the deck to lose its random character. Various sequences appear. Spades, clubs, hearts, and diamonds are separated out into varying combinations; groupings occur. If this shuffling were to go on long enough, each of the suits would be completely separated out. (This would be equivalent to the stage in Empedocles' system in which Strife is dominant.) But in the world process as conceived by Anaxagoras, this has not yet occurred. At present "there are many portions in many things. But no thing is altogether separated off nor distinguished from anything else." This is why what we call hair contains not only hair stuff but also flesh stuff, cabbage stuff, and so on.

Since there are seeds of every kind of stuff in every sensible thing, there must be an infinite number of seeds. And it follows that the seeds must be infinitely small. Otherwise there would not be "room" in a very small, sensible thing for the requisite diversity of real stuffs that it contains.[27]

## ESTIMATE OF ANAXAGORAS' THEORY

In some respects Anaxagoras' views marked an advance. His concept of motion, for instance, was simpler than Empedocles'. Anaxagoras held that there is a single circular motion instead of two alternating forces. But Anaxagoras' account of the many was not helpful. Obsessed with the difficulties inherent in the notion of transformation, he introduced the idea of an infinite plurality of irreducible stuffs. This amounted almost to a denial of the scientific spirit that had imbued all the Greek thinkers since Thales. All of them had felt that under-

---

27 The argument for infinite diversity and infinite smallness is contained in Fragments 1 and 3.

lying the apparent chaos and multiplicity of the sense world there must be some sort of unity that the human mind can fathom. Yet if flesh is nothing but flesh or hair nothing but hair, it is meaningless to try to find the basic elements that these diverse "things" have in common. To erect the apparent diversity of the world into a philosophical principle, as Anaxagoras did, puts an end to the scientific enterprise, which must be guided by a kind of Milesian belief in still simpler simples, still more unified unities.

At this point in our study, then, the basic problem remains intact, though Empedocles and Anaxagoras have helped formulate it more clearly: How can we get to the world of various sense things from qualitatively single but quantitatively plural real things?

The next step in the development of pluralism will take us to Atomism, a school of thought that spanned the centuries from Socrates' youth until the beginnings of Christianity. Study of the Atomists will be postponed until we have examined certain philosophical movements that grew up side by side with those we have been tracing. Since thinkers of these other schools raised questions the later pluralists felt called upon to answer, it will be necessary to consider their views before passing on to the pluralists themselves.

## Pythagoras and the Pythagoreans

About the life of Pythagoras we know almost nothing; we know even less about his views, as distinguished from those of his followers. He is mentioned by Heraclitus in two surviving fragments, which at first sight appear contradictory. In one it is said that Pythagoras "practiced scientific inquiry beyond all other men"; in the other he is linked with Hesiod and Xenophanes, who were religious teachers, not in any sense scientists.[28],t Other reports about Pythagoras suggest that this dual characterization is correct. There is good evidence that Pythagoras was born on the island of Samos just off the coast of Asia Minor opposite Ephesus and that he emigrated to southern Italy about 530 B.C., where he founded a society at Croton. This society was primarily a religious fraternity, but it also conducted scientific research and for a time it dominated the political life of Croton and nearby communities. Perhaps the Pythagorean order was not unlike a medieval monastery, where the exercise of political power was joined with the worship of God and the pursuit of learning. And just as in the mind of the monks these varied activities combined for the greater glory of God, so the Pythagoreans seemed to think of their science as a part of their worship.

---

28 Heraclitus, of course, had nothing but contempt for Pythagoras in either role.

## THE MYSTERY CULTS

Let us begin our discussion of the Pythagoreans, therefore, with an account of their religious views. During the seventh and sixth centuries B.C. a new religious feeling appeared in Greece, a feeling that hardly touched the Milesians but of which there are echoes in Xenophanes and Heraclitus. This was very different in tone from the Olympian religion of Homer, in which man's relation to the gods was largely commercial. In Homer, man shows little wish to become like the gods or to be joined to them; there is no evidence, for instance, of a desire for immortality. In the *Odyssey* Homer describes a visit that the gods permit Odysseus to make to the dwelling place of the spirits of the dead. There the pale, bloodless ghosts of the dead sit all day longing for the earth and the warmth of the sun. When Odysseus urges Achilles not to grieve because he is dead, the latter replies, "Nay, speak not comfortably to me of death, oh great Odysseus. Rather would I live on ground as the hireling of another, with a landless man who had no great livelihood, than bear sway among all the dead that be departed."[u] The fact that a great noble would prefer enslavement—and enslavement to a *poor* man at that—to immortality shows the extent to which the Homeric ideal was conceived in terms of the good things of this life—fighting, chariot racing, drinking, debating in counsel. To lead this life, to be a man, above all to be a Hellene, seemed to Homer so fine a thing that no reasonable person could ask for more; an afterlife could only be an anticlimax.

The new religious movement, introducing the worship of Dionysus, sounded a very different note. Here the primary motif was a yearning for immortality, motivated by a profound discontent with what was felt as the finitude, the defeats, and the inadequacies of this earthly life. This was a religion of redemption—the religion of a savior god who draws his worshipers to him in complete and joyful union.

The new worship was organized into cults whose rituals were regarded as precious secrets. For this reason there is much uncertainty about the details of the worship and about its origins, but it is known that Dionysus was worshiped under various animal forms and invoked by wild dance and song. The ceremonies took place, often at night, in remote places, and women—to the scandal of conservative males—took a prominent part in them. In a frenzy of intoxication the worshipers tore living animals apart, drank their blood, and danced to the point of exhaustion. They felt the spirit of the god pass into their bodies; the union so passionately desired was consummated, and the worshipers exulted in a supreme happiness and utter freedom from any sort of restraint.

The chorus in Euripides' play, the *Bacchae*,[29] represents women worshipers of Dionysus, and a few lines from one of their hymns will give some idea of this religion and of its powerful effects on the human personality.

29  See pp. 61–63.

—Blessèd, blessèd are those who know the mysteries of god.

—Blessèd is he who hallows his life in the worship of god,
    he whom the spirit of god possesseth, who is one
    with those who belong to the holy body of god.

—Blessèd are the dancers and those who are purified,
    who dance on the hill in the holy dance of god. . . .

—Blessèd are those who wear the crown of the ivy of god.

—Blessèd, blessèd are they: Dionysus is their god. . . .

He wears the holy fawn-skin. He hunts the wild goat
    and kills it.

He delights in the raw flesh,

He runs to the mountains of Phrygia, to the mountains
    of Lydia he runs!

He is Bromius who leads us! *Evohé!*

Flames float out from his trailing wand
    as he runs, as he dances,
    kindling the stragglers,
    spurring with cries,
    and his long curls stream to the wind!

—And he cries, as they cry, *Evohé!*—
    On, Bacchae!
    On, Bacchae! [v]

In its early stages, at least, this type of worship was certainly no moral advance over Homeric religion. If the latter urged the performance of certain acts lest the gods hurl a thunderbolt in man's direction—a negative injunction, certainly—the former recommended for the sake of a pleasant reward, a life of permanent leisure and security. In both cases the acts prescribed were ritualistic rather than moral.

The Pythagoreans, obviously deeply affected by this religious movement, did much to elevate its tone. That some of their precepts, however, had originated in magic and taboo is evident from instructions to members of the order not to eat beans, not to stir the fire with iron, not to leave the impress of their body on the bed upon rising from it, and so on. But instead of using wine to intoxicate the body, the Pythagoreans used music to purify the soul; their emphasis was on a way of life rather than simply on the performance of certain rites. They were deeply concerned for the well-being of the soul, which they believed to be immortal and to pass through a cycle of births, appearing on earth in various guises, each determined by the kind of life led by the soul in its preceding existence. For them the moral goal was to obtain release from this cycle of birth and death. This could be accomplished by attaining wisdom. Men, the Pythagoreans thought, fall into three classes that correspond to the three types of people who frequent the Olympic games. Lowest are the "lovers of gain"—those who set up booths and sell souvenirs. Next are the "lovers of honor"—the competing athletes. Highest are the "lovers of knowledge"—the spectators who contemplate, without participating in, the vulgar competition for money or fame. In the same way, contemplation of the eternal truths to which their science gave them access lifted the Pythagoreans out of the tensions and conflicts of the "wheel of birth" and projected them into a higher sphere. Hence the importance to them of "science." For the Milesians, science was good in that it satisfies the natural human appetite of curiosity. They also saw that a knowledge of the processes of nature has a practical application.[30] But to the Pythagoreans this was inconsequential; they cultivated science, as they cultivated music, as the means to spiritual redemption.

### PYTHAGOREAN SCIENCE

This conception of the end and purpose of science had a profound effect on the Pythagoreans' conception of the nature of science. It meant that they were more interested in mathematics than in physics and still more interested in the application of mathematics to large-scale cosmological speculation. Fascination with this latter type of inquiry has been recurrent in the history of culture; there are still "Pythagoreans" among scientists, and probably there always will be.

In mathematics the Pythagoreans made many notable advances, including the invention of a new notation. Since they used arrangements of pebbles to represent numbers, it was natural for them to give spatial names to their numbers. Suppose, for instance, that one wants to describe the sequence of the sums of successive odd numbers. Today this would be written in the following way: 1, 4, 9, and so on. The Pythagoreans represented this sequence as follows:[w]

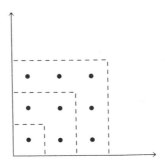

---

30  There is an old story to the effect that Thales applied his theoretical knowledge of astronomy to weather forecasting and, predicting a bumper olive crop for the coming year, bought up all the olive presses and made a killing. Whether the story is true is unimportant. It shows an appreciation of the practical advantages of theoretical science.

This led them to call the numbers making up this sequence "square numbers." (The dotted lines and the arrows have been inserted to show how the Pythagoreans added successive odd numbers together: 1, 1 + 3, 1 + 3 + 5, . . . .)

Similarly, today the sequence of the sums of successive even numbers would be written as 2, 6, 12, and so on. The Pythagoreans represented this sequence of sums as

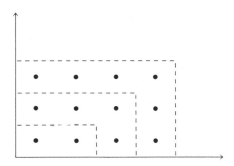

and called the numbers in this sequence "oblong numbers."

The Pythagoreans were most pleased by the *tetraktys*, the formula for "triangle numbers":

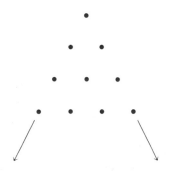

This is the formula for the sums of natural integers, 1, 3, 6, 10, and so on (that is, 1, 1 + 2, 1 + 2 + 3, 1 + 2 + 3 + 4, . . .). The *tetraktys* shows that the Pythagoreans conceived of the number series as being generated from the unit by a process of division. This was to have an important bearing on their cosmological theory.

The Pythagoreans made some interesting applications of mathematics to natural phenomena. Of these the most striking is their study of harmonics. They found that the relationships between the lengths of the strings of a tuned lyre were simple proportions. The lyre was a seven-stringed instrument of which four strings—the first, fourth, fifth, and seventh—were harmonically basic. Since it was tuned by tightening or relaxing the tension of strings of equal length, the Pythagoreans could not simply look at the strings of the tuned lyre and observe the mathematical relationships. They must have performed an experiment in the modern sense of the term: They had to find a way of measuring indirectly what they could not measure directly. This, of course, was not difficult. But the point is that since they could not have reached their conclusion by direct observation, they must first have formed an hypothesis and then found a way, however simple, to check it. Perhaps they stopped a string at various points and measured the length of the segments whose notes corresponded to those of the tuned lyre. Such measurement would show that the section of string sounding the note an octave above the low note is half as long as the section of string sounding the low note. If the latter is 12 units long, the former is 6 units long, a ratio of 2 : 1. When the fourth string is put in accord, it is found to be sounded by a section of string 9 units long, and the fifth, by a section 8 units long. These measurements give ratios of 4:3 (12 units to 9 units) and 3:2 (12 units to 8 units) respectively for the relation between these strings and the low-note string.

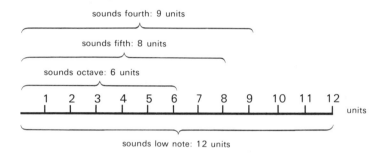

Further, the fourth and fifth strings each stand in a mathematical relationship as a mean between the low and high strings. The length of the fourth is 9 units when the low is 12 and the high 6; $12 - 3 = 9$ and $6 + 3 = 9$. In other words, 9 is a mean which is exceeded by one extreme by the same amount that it exceeds the other extreme. This is called the "arithmetic" mean. Again, the length of the fifth is 8 units when the low and high strings are 12 and 6 respectively; and 8 exceeds and is exceeded by the same fraction of the extremes: $12 - 12/3 = 8$ and $6 + 6/3 = 8$. This is called the "harmonic" mean.

The Pythagoreans applied this idea of the mean to the conflict of opposites that, as we have seen, Milesian physics had proved incapable of resolving. The wet and the dry, the hot and the cold, far from being in irreconcilable conflict, might be "harmonized" just as the high and low notes are. And if the mean that harmonized them were similarly capable of mathematical statement, it would follow that the relation between the opposites is thoroughly intelligible.

The idea of the mean was also used by the Pythagoreans in medicine and in morals. Health they conceived to be an attunement and harmony of opposites; the body is healthy, for instance, when it is neither too hot nor too cold but is in a mean between having a chill and having a fever. It was easy to define the good generally as the mean. Thus the traditional notion of *sophrosyne*, or moderation, received a precise and formal statement.

The Pythagoreans also pursued cosmological studies similar to those of the Milesians. But instead of taking some physical material (water, air, or fire, for instance) as their basic concept, they derived everything from numbers. This paid handsome dividends in astronomy. The Pythagoreans argued that the earth is a sphere, instead of a disk or a drum as the Milesians had variously supposed. They held that it and the other planets (including the sun) revolve about a "central fire" that we do not see because the earth turns on its axis as it revolves and so always presents the same surface to the fire. It was, in fact, Aristotle's reaffirmation of the geocentric theory and the weight of his prestige that necessitated the "discovery" of Copernicus, who was well acquainted with the Pythagorean view, in the sixteenth century.

When we turn, however, from the Pythagoreans' astronomical theories to their accounts of the cosmological process, we find that we have passed from exact, mathematical science to murky mysticism. According to Aristotle, the Pythagoreans held that there are two basic principles: the Limit and the Unlimited. Thus they were neither monists like the Milesians nor pluralists like Empedocles and Anaxagoras, but dualists.

The Unlimited they conceived to be a "boundless breath"—a mass of indeterminacy and indefiniteness. This suggests that they were acquainted with the views of Anaximander and Anaximenes. The Limit they thought of as fire, which sounds like Heraclitus. But—more fruitfully—they also conceived of it as number. That they could think of it in both ways is but another example of the difficulty of thinking abstractly. Since numbers are the most abstract of all abstractions, it is not surprising that the Pythagoreans found it easier to picture them as material.

All numbers, they believed, are generated by partition from the unit.[31] Consequently, the "principles" of the world are the infinite and the unit. But how do the unit and the infinite combine to form the material things of this world? To this question, of course, we get no firm answer. "Fire," the Pythagoreans maintained, "is composed of twenty-four right-angled triangles surrounded by four equilaterals. . . . Air is composed of forty-eight triangles surrounded by eight equilaterals," and so on.[x]

Unlike the case of the lyre, for which there was empirical evidence, this is sheer speculation. However, the analogy of the lyre will help us to understand at least the general lines on which Pythagorean thought was operating here. We can think of the mathematical ratios $12:6$, $12:8$, $12:9$, as being, quite literally, imposed on the various strings by the musician as he tunes his lyre. And these ratios, when imposed, create a significant concord—a particular something—out of a jumble of noises and discords that was previously nothing in particular.[32] Out of boundless noise, as it were, a concord of notes is formed by *limiting* the

31 See p. 35.
32 Compare the difference between the noise an orchestra makes as it tunes and the music it makes when the conductor leads it.

strings to certain designated lengths. As an account of how the world comes to be, this is, of course, nothing but a weak analogy that suggests a human agent. Who imposes the limit? How does he impose it? Why? These questions are enough to show that, conceived as a process in time (as the Pythagoreans undoubtedly thought of it), the notion of a limit is not particularly helpful. But after the Parmenidean bombshell was exploded[33] and the whole idea of process underwent criticism, Plato was to take up this notion of a limit and employ it in a novel way.

The Pythagoreans conceived of the cosmic order as having a unity that is mathematical in character. The discovery of the mathematical relationships underlying the harmonies of the tuned lyre led them to extrapolation on a cosmic scale. Why, if numbers underlie and express the musical harmonies of the tuned lyre, do not similar mathematical relationships lie at the heart of all the qualitative variety of the sense world? Why not indeed? The thought was father to the assertion, and what would be merely a daring hypothesis to a modern scientist became a statement of fact to the Pythagoreans.

Accordingly, they declared that everything has its number. Since they did not experiment to discover (as they had with the tuned lyre) what the numbers actually are, an enterprise that was at first truly scientific in spirit soon collapsed into an esoteric mystery: They said that justice is four, marriage is seven, and so on. This is, of course, nonsense; but even when the Greeks talked nonsense it was on so grand a scale as to contain ideas on which future generations could work with profit. And so it was with the Pythagorean notion that number is at the heart of the universe.

### ESTIMATE OF PYTHAGOREANISM

To characterize Pythagoreanism as a whole, one can say that it was an extraordinary mixture of mysticism and brilliant insight. The Pythagoreans' most notable achievement, certainly, was the concept of "cosmos"—the notion that the universe is not a chaotic hodgepodge but a thoroughly ordered system in which every element is harmoniously related to every other. Of course, this idea had been implicit in Greek thought almost from the start; for instance, there were signs of it in theological dress in Hesiod. It appeared too in the Milesians, but for them, as for Hesiod, order was something imposed on a basic chaos. The opposites, Anaximander thought, had to "make reparation for their injustice" to one another. So, too, Heraclitus: The logos, the eternal process, "will not overstep its measures; if it does the Erinyes, the handmaidens of justice, will find it out."[y]

What had long been implied was finally stated emphatically by the Pythagoreans. The universe, they held, is well ordered because all its parts are related to one another mathematically (on analogy with the lyre). Since the kind of

33 See pp. 21–24.

knowledge we have in mathematics is knowledge par excellence, the universe must be thoroughly intelligible. To say that it is well ordered and that it is intelligible is simply to express the same idea two ways. This idea, taken up by Plato and passed on to Christian theology, is one of the great heritages of the modern mind. How could science with its technique of experimentation and measurement ever have made a beginning, let alone have had the fixity of purpose to continue its researches, without the Pythagorean conviction that the universe constitutes a cosmos pervaded by a single intelligible order?

Pythagoreanism and Atomism[34] complement each other in a remarkable way. The Pythagoreans conceived of a world that, when measured, shows simple mathematical relationships, but they never thought their way through to a clear concept of what must be the nature of a world capable of being measured. The Atomists, in reducing the world to spatial and temporal relations of particles, conceived of a world that is in essence measurable, but they never conceived of the utility of measuring those relations and so discovering the mathematical relationships that obtain. If we combine Pythagorean emphasis on mathematics and measurement with the Atomists' view that reality consists in entities varying only in shape, size, and velocity, we have the conception from which modern physical theory began its great career.

Only the dominance first of Platonism, with its emphasis on other aspects of Pythagoreanism and its lack of interest in Atomism, and then of Christianity, with its extreme otherworldliness, prevented the possibilities of this combination from being immediately seen. As it was, the world had to wait until the seventeenth century for the combination to be effected.

The puzzles about the nature of reality and about the possibility of change, which the earliest thinkers had uncovered in Thales' original formulation and which they themselves had been unable to resolve, form the main topics of Plato's philosophy. Pythagoreanism furnished him with some of the leading concepts in which his answer was formed. But examination of this answer must be postponed until we have considered some of the other elements, drawn from the general culture rather than from the specifically philosophical tradition, that entered into his theories.

34 See Chapter 3.

# CHAPTER 2

# Education
# Through
# Violence

So far, in preparation for studying Plato's theory and the other great syntheses of the late fifth and fourth centuries, we have been reviewing the emergence of metaphysical and epistemological speculation in Greece. But we cannot understand Plato if we concentrate entirely on philosophical issues. We need to understand the mood of Athens, and of Greece generally, in his day. Plato grew up during the latter years of the Peloponnesian War (431–404 B.C.). According to Thucydides, a Greek historian in the fifth century B.C., "War is a teacher who educates through violence; and he makes men's characters fit their condition."[1,a] How true this hard saying is we shall see in the following pages; and we shall see, too, the extent to which Plato reacted to this education for violence. His thought, indeed, was largely oriented by the impact of the war and the cultural malaise that it produced.

1 For the full passage from which this sentence is taken see p. 53.

About the Peloponnesian War and the events leading up to it, a few words should be said. Though economic rivalries underlay the struggle, it was greatly exacerbated by ideological conflicts. It is necessary therefore to give some account of the differing political institutions of Sparta and Athens, who were the chief opponents.

## Sparta: An Athenian Estimate[2]

I recall the astonishment with which I first noted the unique position of Sparta among the states of Hellas, the relatively sparse population, and at the same time the extraordinary power and prestige of the community. . . .

Take for example—and it is well to begin at the beginning—the whole topic of the begetting and rearing of children. Throughout the rest of the world . . . we, the rest of the Hellenes, are content that our girls should sit quietly and work wools. . . .

Lycurgus[3] pursued a different path. . . . Believing that the highest function of a free woman was the bearing of children, in the first place he insisted on the training of the body as incumbent no less on the female than the male; and in pursuit of the same idea instituted rival contests in running and feats of strength for women as for men. . . .

And so again after marriage. . . . He laid it down as an ordinance that a man should be ashamed to be seen visiting the chamber of his wife, whether going in or coming out. When they did meet under such restraint the mutual longing of these lovers could not but be increased, and the fruit which might spring from such intercourse would tend to be more robust than theirs whose affections are cloyed by satiety. By a farther step in the same direction he refused to allow marriages to be contracted at any period of life according to the fancy of the parties concerned. Marriage, as he ordained it, must only take place in the prime of bodily vigour, this too being, as he believed, a condition conducive to the production of healthy offspring. Or again, to meet the case which might occur of an old man wedded to a young wife . . . he made it incumbent on the aged husband to introduce some one whose qualities, physical and moral, he admired, to beget him children. . . .

[Next, as regards education,] instead of leaving it to each member of the

---

2 Xenophon, who wrote this account between 378 and 375 B.C., was an Athenian. The interest of Athenians in the Spartan constitution was natural. Dissatisfied with their own political system, they looked abroad for models, especially to the power that had been strong enough to defeat them. Similarly, in Europe, in the aftermath of the Napoleonic wars there was an outbreak of constitutional monarchies modeled on the British pattern and, after World War I, the creation of a great number of political democracies patterned after those of Britain and the United States.

3 [According to Spartan legend, Lycurgus, about whom nothing is now known and who may not even be a historical personage, gave Sparta its laws—AUTHOR.]

state privately to appoint a slave to be his son's tutor, he set over the young Spartans a public guardian, the Paidonomos, to give him his proper title, with complete authority over them. This guardian was selected from those who filled the highest magistracies.

· · · · · · · · · · · · · · · · · · · · · · · · · · · · · · · · · · · · · · · · · · · ·

I ought, as it seems to me, not to omit some remark on the subject of homosexuality, it being a topic in close connection with that of boyhood and the training of boys.

· · · · · · · · · · · · · · · · · · · · · · · · · · · · · · · · · · · · · · · · · · · ·

Lycurgus adopted [the following] system . . . . Given that some one, himself being all that a man ought to be, should in admiration of a boy's soul endeavour to discover in him a true friend without reproach, and to consort with him—this was a relationship which Lycurgus commended, and indeed regarded as the noblest type of bringing up. But if, as was evident, it was not an attachment to the soul, but a yearning merely towards the body, he stamped this thing as foul and horrible; and with this result, to the credit of Lycurgus be it said, that in Lacedaemon the relationship of lover and beloved is like that of parent and child or brother and brother where carnal appetite is in abeyance. . . .

It remains that I should endeavour to describe the style of living which he established for the whole body [of citizens], irrespective of age. It will be understood that, when Lycurgus first came to deal with the question, the Spartans, like the rest of the Hellenes, used to mess privately at home. Tracing more than half the current misdemeanours to this custom, he . . . invented the public mess-rooms. . . .

As to food, his ordinance allowed them so much as, while not inducing repletion, should guard them from actual want. . . .

There are yet other customs in Sparta which Lycurgus instituted in opposition to those of the rest of Hellas, and the following among them. We all know that in the generality of states every one devotes his full energy to the business of making money: one man as a tiller of the soil, another as a mariner, a third as a merchant, whilst others depend on various arts to earn a living. But at Sparta Lycurgus forbade his freeborn citizens to have anything whatsoever to do with the concerns of money-making.

· · · · · · · · · · · · · · · · · · · · · · · · · · · · · · · · · · · · · · · · · · · ·

That too was a happy enactment, in my opinion, by which Lycurgus provided for the continual cultivation of virtue, even to old age. By fixing the election to the council of elders as a last ordeal at the goal of life, he made it impossible for a high standard of virtuous living to be disregarded even in old age. . . .

And was not this a noble enactment, that whereas other states are content to inflict punishment only in cases where a man does wrong against his neighbour, Lycurgus imposed penalties no less severe on him who openly neglected to make himself as good as possible? . . .[b]

This is obviously a highly sympathetic account of the oligarchy (or rather, timocracy) that ruled Sparta. Such a life was likely to produce a stern, warlike race, and indeed the Spartans were regarded as the best soldiers in Greece. They needed to be good soldiers, for this small company of nobles ruled a mass of serfs who were without any political rights. During the Peloponnesian War, for instance, the oligarchs lived in constant uneasiness lest the Athenians foment a rebellion among the serfs, and even in peacetime they had constantly to be on the alert lest their serfs get out of hand. Eternal vigilance is said to be the price of liberty; it is equally, but in another sense, the price of tyranny.

## Athens

The Athenian solution to the problem of how to deal with the disaffection of the lower classes was radically different from that adopted at Sparta. From the beginning the history of Athens was a succession of expansions of the franchise, until by the middle of the fifth century B.C. the Assembly of Athenians—all the male adult citizens who chanced to be present at any meeting—was the final authority in the state. This democracy was in some respects more complete than ours and in others more limited. It included only male citizens. Women, a large body of foreigners,[4] and slaves were excluded from the Assembly. Of the 400,000 inhabitants of Athens it is estimated that only 40,000—one in ten—were eligible for the Assembly. On the other hand, the Assembly was completely sovereign, even though only a fraction of those eligible attended. Any particular sitting of the Assembly could rescind or amend any earlier law; it could pass any new law that struck its fancy, though this might remain on the statute books only until the next meeting of the Assembly. The Assembly was at once legislative, executive, and judiciary. Even more important, it was a direct democracy, not a representative democracy like the United States today. In this respect it was like a New England town meeting, where all the citizens vote on all measures instead of merely electing representatives to make decisions for them. But what was to work satisfactorily on a small scale in New England was open to serious objections when a large, uneducated, urban proletariat was exposed to the operations of clever and unscrupulous demagogues.

Some contemporary criticisms of this regime will be examined later. For the moment it may be noted that Athenian democracy did not exclude great differences of wealth and social status. Indeed, during the first three-quarters of the fifth century B.C. the old aristocratic families still managed to rule—not directly as in former years, but by managing and controlling the votes in the Assembly, somewhat like modern political bosses.

---

4 Citizens of neighboring city-states only a few miles away were, of course, foreigners.

Athens was in fact a vigorous, commercial democracy. Unable to support its population from its own agricultural resources, it developed manufacturing and paid for necessary food importations by supplying agricultural states with industrial products. During the fifth century B.C., as they built up their expanding trade, the Athenians acquired an "empire"—a loose union of lesser and dependent states, chiefly on the Aegean islands—which paid an annual tribute in return for "protection" by the Athenian fleet and whose dependence on Athens was a source of economic strength for the imperial city. These tributary powers were, however, a source of weakness in time of war. Just as the Spartans had constantly to fear an uprising at home on the part of their serfs, the Athenians had constantly to cope with the defection, often aided and abetted by the Spartans, of some of their far-flung dependencies.

## The Peloponnesian War

It was all but inevitable that Sparta and Athens would clash. The Spartans had long regarded themselves, and been regarded by the rest of Hellas, as the primary power in Greece; but all during the fifth century B.C. (since the defeat of Persia, in which the Athenian fleet had played a great part) Athens had been growing in power, until it was not only challenging but surpassing Sparta. Moreover, the lesser commercial states, like Corinth, felt themselves outclassed by Athens and feared losing out in the competition for trade. The Corinthians found Athenian policy toward the small city of Megara an instructive example of what Athens was able to do to its rivals. By embargoing Megarian goods and forbidding Megara to trade in any ports of the Athenian empire, Athens had virtually destroyed that prosperous city's business.

With this and other examples of Athens' power and policy before them, the Corinthians and their friends went to the Spartans, urging a combined campaign against "the tyrant city which . . . is a standing menace to all alike; she rules over some of us already, and would fain rule over others. Let us attack and subdue her, that we may ourselves live safely for the future and deliver the Hellenes whom she has enslaved." [c] This argument appealed to the Spartans, and an agreement was reached to put an end to Athenian hegemony.

The Athenians were well aware that their expansionist policy was causing opposition.

> For some time past [Pericles told the Athenian Assembly] the designs of the Spartans have been clear. . . . They tell us to . . . rescind the decree respecting the Megarians. . . . I would have none of you imagine that he will be fighting for a small matter if we refuse to annul the Megarian decree, of which they make so much, telling us that its revocation would prevent the war. You should have no lingering uneasiness about this; you are not really

going to war for a trifle. For in the seeming trifle is involved the trial and confirmation of your whole purpose. If you yield to them in a small matter, they will think you are afraid and will immediately dictate some more oppressive condition. . . .

Wherefore make up your minds once for all, either to give way while you are still unharmed, or, if we are going to war, as in my judgment is best, then on no plea great or small to give way at all. . . .[d]

As Pericles said, there was nothing to arbitrate. The whole destiny of each state depended on its pursuit of a policy diametrically opposed to that of the other. The lives the states had chosen to lead, determined by economic, geographic, temperamental, and other differences, had brought each to a point from which it could not turn back without destroying its whole life and could not go forward without destroying the life of the other.

The war, which was to last twenty-seven years, began almost casually early in the summer of 431 B.C. with an attack on Plataea, a rather minor ally of Athens. Pericles realized that Athens' strength lay on the sea and that it could not hope to prevent invasion of its territory. He proposed, therefore, to withdraw all the inhabitants of Athenian territory behind the fortifications of the city and to allow the countryside to be overrun and laid waste, while he used his command of the sea to make what today would be called commando raids along the coast of the Peloponnesus, harassing the Spartans and their allies at will. He planned, indeed, a war of attrition, for he believed that time and money were on the Athenian side. This strategy might have worked but for a series of misfortunes. A plague broke out in Athens that first hot summer and the population, which Pericles' policy had crowded within the walls of the city without adequate housing facilities, was virtually decimated.

Moreover, though Pericles had expected some dissatisfaction on the part of the country people upon seeing their fields and crops laid waste, "the popular indignation actually was not pacified until they had fined Pericles; but, soon afterwards, with the usual fickleness of the multitude, they elected him general and committed all their affairs to his charge."[e]

Even if Pericles had lived, it is doubtful that he would have been able to control Athenian policy. As it was, he died in the second year of the plague and Athens was left without any person of long-range vision who had the confidence of the Assembly. Power passed into the hands of rabble-rousing demagogues who were incapable of deciding on a competent policy and whose control of the Assembly in any case depended on their making all sorts of unsound concessions—even against their own better judgment—to the momentary whims of the populace.

In spite of these misfortunes, the war did not go badly for the Athenians. There were occasions in the early years when the Spartans would gladly have come to an understanding. These opportunities were thrown away by the Athenians because the demagogues in control of Athens judged (as Thucydides said specifically of the demagogue Cleon) that "in quiet times [their] rogueries would be transparent and [their] slanders less credible. . . ."ᶠ

In 415 B.C. the Athenians made their fatal mistake. Not content to fight a defensive war, which would have been the wisest policy for Athens in its weakened condition, the Assembly allowed itself to be persuaded by the oratory of Alcibiades, a brilliant but unprincipled young general and politician who was motivated primarily by private ambition, into the foolhardy Sicilian expedition. Athenian manpower and financial resources were drained to carry the war to a distant area where the army could be supplied only at great cost and hardship. Two years later the whole force, naval and military, had been wiped out, and Athens had gained for itself nothing but new and formidable enemies.

Though it must have been obvious at this point that the war was lost, Athens continued the struggle for almost ten years. Bitterness over the continuance of a hopeless struggle grew as the years went on, and a peace party emerged in Athens, constituted—as peace parties often are—by those who had the most to lose by further fighting. The wealthy and noble families in particular, who had seen their crops destroyed year after year, faced terrible financial losses with no prospect of recovery. They had certainly never been enthusiastic democrats, and now the disasters of the war seemed to them the result of mistakes made by the Assembly. Moreover, they knew themselves to be acceptable to the Spartans and probably saw the prospects of a return to oligarchical rule with the final triumph of Sparta.

## The Old Oligarch

The gradual change in the conservatives' attitude toward the Athenian democracy is evident when we compare a criticism written early in the war, about 424 B.C., with the increasingly bitter and violent attacks made as it became clear that mass democracy was proving unequal to the strain of conducting the war.

The tone of the earlier criticism was slightly ironical; though it is clear that the author[5] thought it an inefficient form of government, he was capable of a reasonably objective appraisal of Athenian democracy: "For my part, I pardon the People its own democracy, as, indeed, it is pardonable in anyone to do good to himself."

This is the principal note of the Old Oligarch's essay: a realistic, almost cynical, recognition that it is natural for everyone to aim at his own good. The people naturally wanted a constitution that would be to their advantage; since they were in power the only relevant question was whether the constitution did what it was intended to do. It was designed to promote "the welfare of the 'baser

---

5  His name is unknown. He is called the Old Oligarch because of his evident political sympathies.

folk' at the expense of the 'better sort.'" This "is not my taste," but "given the fact that this is the type of constitution Athens desires," the Old Oligarch argued that certain of "those characteristics [of the constitution] which are looked upon as blunders by the rest of Hellas are in fact the reverse."

On other points, however, he agreed fully with critics. It is true, according to him, that the Athenian government was bogged down in red tape: "It not seldom happens that a man is unable to transact a piece of business with the senate of the People, even if he sit waiting a whole year." It is also true that the government was irresponsible. If oligarchies

> . . . fail to abide by their contracts, the offense, by whomever committed, lies nominally at the door of the oligarchs who entered upon the contract. But in the case of engagements entered into by a democracy it is open to the People to throw the blame on the single individual who spoke in favour of some measure, or put it to the vote, and to maintain to the rest of the world, "I was not present, nor do I approve of the terms of the agreement." . . . If any mischief should spring out of any resolutions which the People has passed in council, the People can readily shift the blame from its own shoulders. . . . But if any good result ensue, they, the People, at once take the credit of that to themselves.

In a word, the Old Oligarch concluded, a state has to choose between freedom and good government.

> What it comes to, therefore, is that a state founded on democratic institutions will not be the best state; but . . . the People does not demand that the city should be well governed and itself a slave. It desires to be free and to be master. As to bad legislation, it does not concern itself about that. In fact, what you [the "better sort"] call bad legislation is the very source of the People's strength and freedom. If you seek for good legislation [it will be necessary to let] the . . . better class . . . deliberate in behalf of the state and not suffer crackbrained fellows to sit in council, or to speak or vote in the assemblies. No doubt; but under the weight of such blessings the People will in a very short time be reduced to slavery.[g]

## Aristophanes

When we turn from the Old Oligarch to Aristophanes[6] we find many of the general criticisms of democracy repeated—inefficiency, indecision, irresponsibility. But Aristophanes was not as urbane, balanced, and objective as the Old Oligarch had been. Unlike the latter, he did not allow that democracy, though

6 Aristophanes lived from about 448 B.C. to about 388 B.C.

not a good state per se, is best for the "baser folk." In Aristophanes' opinion, democracy was destroying the state; the baser sort, along with "the cream of society," were doomed unless the framework of the constitution could be altered. This was not merely a temperamental difference. It was easy when the Old Oligarch wrote, while the war was still young, to be tolerant and ironically amusing about the deficiencies of the Assembly; but as more and more blunders were committed, feelings naturally became more and more exacerbated.

In the *Acharnians* (425 B.C.), an Athenian citizen sits at the Pnyx, the place where the Assembly meets, waiting for the other citizens to arrive and brooding over the hardships of life:

> It is the day of assembly; all should be here at daybreak, and yet the Pnyx is still deserted. They are gossiping in the market-place. . . . The Prytanes even do not come; they will be late, but when they come they will push and fight each other for a seat in the front row. They will never trouble themselves with the question of peace. Oh! Athens! Athens! As for myself, I do not fail to come here before all the rest, and now, finding myself alone, I groan, yawn, stretch, fart, and know not what to do; I make sketches in the dust, pull out my loose hairs, muse, think of my fields, long for peace, curse town life and regret my dear country home. . . . Therefore I have come to the assembly fully prepared to bawl, interrupt and abuse the speakers, if they talk of anything but peace. . . .[h]

The speaker, like the heroes of many of Aristophanes' plays, is a countryman. Aristophanes always preferred the old-fashioned farmer to the urban industrial worker. It is not that he thought farmers more intelligent than city-dwellers; he had nothing but contempt for the intelligence of the uneducated masses wherever they lived. But he thought that the countryman at least knew his place, whereas the city-dweller was without loyalty and without piety, was simply "on the make" in opposition to all the traditions that had formerly held society together. As long as the Assembly of city-dwellers, dominated by its crooked politicians, ruled Athens, there was no hope of peace.

### ARISTOPHANES' ATTACK ON DEMOCRACY

The basic trouble, of course, in Aristophanes' opinion, was the series of so-called reforms that had gradually transferred political power to the hands of the mob. He never tired, for instance, of attacking the policy, inaugurated as early as 493 or 492 B.C., of paying citizens for attending to their duties as jurors. This measure, doubtless popular with the mass of poor citizens and instituted for that reason, had made a travesty of justice. Juries of the time were filled by men interested primarily in the pay—the lazy and the shiftless, the ignorant and the incompetent.

In the *Wasps* (422 B.C.), Philocleon, a democratic supporter of the demagogue Cleon, enumerates the delights of jury service:

Is there a pleasure, a blessing comparable with that of a juryman? Is there a being who lives more in the midst of delights, who is more feared, aged though he be? From the moment I leave my bed, men of power, the most illustrious in the city, await me at the bar of the tribunal; the moment I am seen from the greatest distance, they come forward to offer me a gentle hand . . . ; they entreat me, bowing right low and with a piteous voice. . . .

Am I not equal to the king of the gods? . . . If I let loose the lightning, the richest, aye, the noblest are half dead with terror and crap for fright. You yourself are afraid of me, yea, by Demeter! you are afraid.[i]

Aristophanes' reply, put in the mouth of Cleonphobe, an antidemocrat, is that the poor Athenian citizen who thinks himself all-powerful is really nothing but a slave of the demagogues who lead his party.

The cure of a disease, so inveterate and so widespread in Athens, is a difficult task and of too great importance for the scope of comedy. Nevertheless, . . . listen to me . . . unruffle that frowning brow and reckon, you can do so without trouble, not with pebbles, but on your fingers, what is the sum-total of the tribute paid by the allied towns; besides this we have the direct imposts, a mass of percentage dues, the fees of the courts of justice, the produce from the mines, the markets, the harbours, the public lands and the confiscations. All these together amount to nearly two thousand talents. Take from this sum the annual pay of the jurymen; they number six thousand, and there have never been more in this town; so therefore it is one hundred and fifty talents that come to you.

PHILOCLEON. What! our pay is not even a tithe of the state revenue?

CLEONPHOBE. Why no, certainly not.

PHILOCLEON. And where does the rest go then?

CLEONPHOBE. To those who say: "I shall never betray the interests of the masses; I shall always fight for the people." And it is you . . . who let yourself be caught with their fine talk, who give them all power over yourself. They are the men who extort fifty talents at a time by threat and intimidation from the allies. "Pay tribute to me," they say, "or I shall loose the lightning on your town and destroy it." And you, you are content to gnaw the crumbs of your own might.

Is it not the worst of all slaveries to see all these wretches and their flatterers, whom they gorge with gold, at the head of affairs? As for you, you are content with the three obols which they give you and which you have so painfully earned in the galleys, in battles and sieges. . . . You have only eyes for the public pay-clerk, and you see nothing.

In the *Knights* (424 B.C.) Aristophanes discusses in detail the follies of the masses, personified as Demos (or, as we might translate, John Q. Public). Nicias and Demosthenes, two prominent Athenians and men of high birth and wealth, are brought on the stage and represented as "slaves" of Mr. Public. Once his favorites, they have been replaced in Mr. Public's fickle taste by a new slave.

> We have a very brutal master [Demosthenes complains to Nicias], a perfect glutton for beans, and most bad-tempered; it's Demos of the Pnyx, an intolerable old man and half deaf. The beginning of last month he bought a slave, a Paphlagonian tanner,[7] an arrant rogue, the incarnation of calumny. This man of leather knows his old master thoroughly; he plays the fawning cur, flatters, cajoles, wheedles, and dupes him at will . . . . The Paphlagonian . . . keeps us at a distance and suffers none but himself to wait upon the master; when Demos is dining, he keeps . . . singing oracles to him, so that the old man now thinks of nothing but the Sibyl. Then, when he sees him thoroughly obfuscated, he uses all his cunning and piles up lies and calumnies against the household; then we are scourged and the Paphlagonian runs about among the slaves to demand contributions with threats and gathers them in with both hands. . . . There must be an end to it, friend. Let us see! what can be done? Who will get us out of this mess?[j]

Happily, Demosthenes and Nicias discover an oracle that foretells that the tanner is shortly to be succeeded as favorite by a sausage-seller. When the sausage-seller turns up, they inform him of the brilliant future in store for him. He fears he is ill-equipped to guide the destinies of the state, but they point out that in a democracy lack of competence is actually an advantage:

> DEMOSTHENES. According to the oracle you must become the greatest of men.
> SAUSAGE-SELLER. Just tell me how a sausage-seller can become a great man.
> DEMOSTHENES. That is precisely why you will be great, because you are a sad rascal without shame, no better than a common market rogue. . . . Spoilt child of fortune, everything fits together to ensure your greatness.
> SAUSAGE-SELLER. But I have not had the least education. I can only read, and that very badly.
> DEMOSTHENES. That is what may stand in your way, almost knowing how to read. . . .[k]

Cleon now rushes on the stage to defend his interests. After a yelling match, which the sausage-seller wins, the two compete for Mr. Public's favor by paying him all sorts of extravagant homage ("When you wipe your nose, clean your fingers on my head," Cleon invites him; "No, on mine," the sausage-seller urges; "On *mine,*" Cleon insists) and by making him all sorts of extravagant promises. "Mind you keep your promises," Mr. Public says. "To whichever of you shall beat me best will I hand over the reins of state."

---

7 This is Cleon, one of the demagogues who succeeded to power after the death of Pericles. See pp. 45–46.

## ARISTOPHANES' "SOLUTION"

That Aristophanes did not expect the sausage-seller to be better than the tanner is clear from the *Ecclesiazusae* (392 B.C.). Aristophanes' sense of the hopelessness of the situation as long as Athens remained a mass democracy is reflected in the fantastic "solution" he proposed—a solution that (as we shall later see) anticipated in an interesting way the utopian proposals Plato was to make a few years later.

In the *Ecclesiazusae,* the women of Athens by a ruse get themselves appointed to govern the state. The program of Praxagora, their leader, is nothing less than communism:

> I want all to have a share of everything and all property to be in common; there will no longer be either rich or poor; . . . I intend that there shall only be one and the same condition of life for all. . . . I shall begin by making land, money, everything that is private property, common to all. . . . I intend that women shall belong to all men in common, and each shall beget children by any man that wishes to have her. . . .
>
> BLEPYRUS. But if we live in this fashion, how will each one know his children?
>
> PRAXAGORA. The youngest will look upon the oldest as their fathers. . . . Athens will become nothing more than a single house, in which everything will belong to everyone; so that everybody will be able to go from one house to the other at pleasure.
>
> BLEPYRUS. And where will the meals be served?
>
> PRAXAGORA. The law-courts and the porticoes will be turned into dining-halls.
>
> BLEPYRUS. And what will the speaker's platform be used for?
>
> PRAXAGORA. I shall place the bowls and the ewers there; and young children will sing the glory of the brave from there, also the infamy of cowards, who out of very shame will no longer dare to come to the public meals.[1]

We can see the effect of the war in the increasingly severe criticisms of democratic institutions and in the corresponding search for alternatives, either in Sparta and other contemporary models or in fantastic utopias. As the conflict went on, political criticism became less and less objective, party spirit more violent.

The ideological struggle between Sparta and Athens broke out internally in every city. Athens itself became divided into mutually suspicious groups. The democratic masses feared the well-to-do and on the slightest grounds purged suspected traitors. Only too often this suspicion was justified; frequently, however, unjust suspicion was the cause of treasonable activity. The upper classes, despairing of their lives and property in the atmosphere of hatred and mistrust, did indeed begin to plot against the regime.

## What War Does to Man

What happened during wartime to the internal unity of the Greek city-state is starkly revealed by Thucydides' description of the events in Corcyra, a Corinthian colony sympathetic to Athens. As in many other states, there was a strong aristocratic party in Corcyra whose interests lay rather with the Spartans and their allies and who sought to bring the city over to the other side. To this end they began maneuvering against

> . . . a certain Peithias, . . . the popular leader, . . . affirming that he wanted to bring Corcyra under the yoke of Athens. He was acquitted and then he in turn summoned their five richest men, declaring that they were in the habit of cutting poles for vines in the sacred precinct of Zeus and Alcinous; now for each pole the penalty was fixed at a stater [a huge fine]. They were condemned . . . and perceiving that Peithias, as long as he remained [in power], would try to induce the people to make an alliance . . . with Athens, conspired together, and rushing into the council chamber with daggers in their hands, slew him and others to the number of sixty. . . .[m]

The oligarchs failed to win the people over to their point of view. But the opportune arrival of a Corinthian warship provided the necessary backing for them, and they

> . . . attacked and defeated the people, who at nightfall took refuge in the Acropolis. . . . On the following day . . . both parties sent messengers around the country inviting the slaves to join them, and promising them liberty; the greater number came to the aid of the people. . . . They fought again, and the people, who had the advantage in numbers and in the strength of their positions, gained the victory. . . . The oligarchy . . . set fire to the private houses which surrounded the Agora, as well as to the larger blocks of buildings . . . . Much merchandise was burnt, and the whole city would have been destroyed if the wind had carried the flame in that direction. Both parties now left off fighting, and kept watch in their own positions during the night. . . .
>
> On the following day, Nicostratus . . . an Athenian general, arrived from Naupactus with twelve ships and 500 Messenian hoplites. He tried to effect a reconciliation between the two parties . . . , but [the oligarchs] would not trust him; whereupon the people armed themselves, arguing that their mistrust . . . was a proof of their evil designs. . . .
>
> At this stage of the revolution . . . fifty-three Peloponnesian ships . . . arrived on the scene. The whole place was in an uproar; the people dreaded their enemies within the city no less than the Peloponnesian fleet. . . .

Meanwhile the Athenians, who had got wind of what was going on, sent a larger fleet, and the Peloponnesians were obliged to retire. Reinforced by the

Athenian support, the people now decided to destroy the oligarchical party. In the seven days during which the Athenian fleet was in the port

> . . . they killed any of their enemies whom they caught in the city. . . . They also went to the temple of Hera, and persuading about fifty of the suppliants[8] to stand their trial, condemned them all to death. The majority would not come out, and, when they saw what was going on, destroyed one another in the enclosure of the temple where they were, except a few who hung themselves on trees . . . . The Corcyraeans continued slaughtering those of their fellow-citizens whom they deemed their enemies; they professed to punish them for their designs against the democracy, but in fact some were killed from motives of personal enmity, and some because money was owing to them, by the hands of their debtors. Every form of death was to be seen, and everything, and more than everything that commonly happens in revolutions, happened then. The father slew the son, and the suppliants were torn from the temples and slain near them; some of them were even walled up in the temple of Dionysus, and there perished. To such extremes of cruelty did revolution go; and this seemed to be the worst of revolutions because it was the first. . . .
>
> In peace and prosperity both states and individuals are actuated by higher motives, because they do not fall under the dominion of imperious necessities; but war which takes away the comfortable provision of daily life is a hard master, and tends to assimilate men's characters to their conditions.
>
> When troubles had once begun in the cities, those who followed carried the revolutionary spirit further and further, and determined to outdo the report of all who had preceded them by the ingenuity of their enterprises and the atrocity of their revenges. The meaning of words had no longer the same relation to things, but was changed by them as they thought proper. Reckless daring was held to be loyal courage; prudent delay was the excuse of a coward; moderation was the disguise of unmanly weakness; to know everything was to do nothing. Frantic energy was the true quality of a man. A conspirator who wanted to be safe was a recreant in disguise. The lover of violence was always trusted, and his opponent suspected. He who succeeded in a plot was deemed knowing, but a still greater master in craft was he who detected one. On the other hand, he who plotted from the first to have nothing to do with plots was a breaker up of parties and a poltroon who was afraid of the enemy. In a word, he who could outstrip another in a bad action was applauded, and so was he who encouraged to evil one who had no idea of it. The tie of party was stronger than the tie of blood, because a partisan was more ready to dare without asking why. . . . The seal of good faith was not divine law, but fellowship in crime. . . . Revenge was dearer than self-preservation. Any agreements sworn to by either party, when they could do nothing else, were binding as long as both were powerless. . . .
>
> The cause of all these evils was the love of power, originating in avarice

---

8 [The oligarchs who had taken refuge in the temple were supposedly inviolate as long as they remained there—AUTHOR.]

and ambition, and the party-spirit which is engendered by them when men are fairly embarked in a contest. . . . Striving in every way to overcome each other, [the leaders of the parties] committed the most monstrous crimes; yet even these were surpassed by the magnitude of their revenges which they pursued to the very utmost, neither party observing any definite limits either of justice or public expediency, but both alike making the caprice of the moment their law. . . . And the citizens who were of neither party fell a prey to both; either they were disliked because they held aloof, or men were jealous of their surviving.

Thus revolution gave birth to every form of wickedness in Hellas. The simplicity which is so large an element in a noble nature was laughed to scorn and disappeared. An attitude of perfidious antagonism everywhere prevailed; for there was no word binding enough, nor oath terrible enough to reconcile enemies. Each man was strong only in the conviction that nothing was secure; he must look to his own safety, and could not afford to trust others. Inferior intellects generally succeeded best. For, aware of their own deficiencies, and fearing the capacity of their opponents, for whom they were no match in powers of speech, and whose subtle wits were likely to anticipate them in contriving evil, they struck boldly and at once. But the cleverer sort, presuming in their arrogance that they would be aware in time, and disdaining to act when they could think, were taken off their guard and easily destroyed.

## IMPORTANCE OF POLITICAL UNITY

What shocked Thucydides was not only the brutality and savagery of the struggle but the fact that it was *civil* war. The Greeks had a far higher regard for political unity than most of us have, and for them, of course, political unity meant the unity of a city. To us, used to the problems of great national states, it may seem that so small a union would be easy to achieve and to maintain. But for the Greek cities it had been no mean task to forge a real spirit of unity. Family loyalties, and loyalties to clan and tribe, which were survivals of more primitive times, were deep-seated; and the bitterness of the poor with regard to the rich was another divisive factor. There can be no doubt that the chief purpose of the constitution reformers was to achieve a real national unity in which all the lesser loyalties were submerged in a profound love for the city itself. Democracy was, of course, a powerful instrument to this end, and the reformers probably used the broadened franchise deliberately to give the mass of the people a sense of belonging to the state.

Unity was precious not only because it had been won with difficulty but because it had been achieved only recently. And it was important because the city played so large a role in the life of the citizen. The state was not merely the passive guarantor of his political freedom, as it often is for us; it was an active force molding his whole life. If, in Pericles' noble phrase, Athens was the school of Hellas, it was also in the literal sense the school of every Athenian citizen, regulating his dress and his behavior, furnishing his amusements, and serving as the focus of his religious and moral life.

> Who is not bad . . . , who knows
> the right that makes the city stand—
> a sound man he

declared Simonides of Ceos,[n] summing up the relation all Greeks felt between private morality and public virtue.

### THE "NEW" MAN

All this was now being lost in the partisan dissensions the Peloponnesian War had engendered. The old ideal, which conservatives like Aristophanes still admired, of a life of simple piety, of respect for law and religion and custom, and of patriotic devotion to one's city as the completion and fulfillment of one's own life, had largely lost its force. The new type of man developing under the pressures of war was a cynic who believed that might makes right, who rejected all the old loyalties and the old virtues unless they were expedient, that is, unless they helped him accomplish his private ends. He was, in fact, the type of the Athenian representative whose negotiations with the Melians Thucydides described.

Melos was one of the few Aegean islands the Athenians had not managed to bring into their empire. Up to 416 B.C., Melos had successfully remained neutral, but in that year the Athenians, according to Thucydides' account, sent an expedition to "persuade" the Melians to join them.

> ATHENIANS. . . . We Athenians will use no fine words. . . . We should not convince you if we did; nor must you expect to convince us by arguing that . . . you have never done us any wrong. . . . For we both alike know that into the discussion of human affairs the question of justice only enters where the pressure of necessity is equal, and that the powerful exact what they can, and the weak grant what they must.
>
> MELIANS. Well, then, since you set aside justice and invite us to speak of expediency, in our judgment it is certainly expedient that you should respect a principle which is for the common good. . . . Your interest in this principle is quite as great as ours, inasmuch as you, if you fall, will incur the heaviest vengeance, and will be the most terrible example to mankind.
>
> ATHENIANS. The fall of our empire, if it should fall, is . . . a danger which you may leave to us. . . . We want to make you ours with the least trouble to ourselves, and it is for the interests of us both that you should not be destroyed.
>
> MELIANS. It may be your interest to be our masters, but how can it be ours to be your slaves?

ATHENIANS. To you the gain will be that by submission you will avert the worst; and we shall all be the richer for your preservation.

MELIANS. But must we be your enemies? Will you not receive us as friends if we are neutral and remain at peace with you?

ATHENIANS. No, your enmity is not half so mischievous to us as your friendship; for the one is in the eyes of our subjects an argument of our power, the other of our weakness. . . . They think that states like yours are left free because they are able to defend themselves, and that we do not attack them because we dare not. So that your subjection will give us an increase of security, as well as an extension of empire. . . .

MELIANS. . . . How base and cowardly would it be in us, who retain our freedom, not to do and suffer anything rather than be your slaves.

ATHENIANS. . . . The question is not one of honour but of prudence.

MELIANS. But we know that the fortune of war is sometimes impartial, and not always on the side of numbers. If we yield now, all is over; but if we fight, there is yet a hope that we may stand upright. . . . We know only too well how hard the struggle must be against your power. . . . Nevertheless we do not despair of fortune; for we hope to stand as high as you in the favour of heaven, because we are righteous, and you against whom we contend are unrighteous. . . .

ATHENIANS. As for the gods, we expect to have quite as much of their favour as you: for we are not doing or claiming anything which goes beyond common opinion about divine or men's desires about human things. Of the gods we believe, and of men we know, that by a law of their nature wherever they can rule they will. . . . You and all mankind, if you were as strong as we are, would do as we do. . . . You are showing a great want of sense. . . . Reflect once more. . . .

The Athenian envoys returned to the army; and the generals, when they found that the Melians would not yield, immediately commenced hostilities.

[They were unable to make any progress until] there was treachery among the citizens themselves. So the Melians were induced to surrender at discretion. The Athenians thereupon put to death all who were of military age, and made slaves of the women and children. They then colonized the island, sending thither 500 settlers of their own.°

## Euripides

### HORRORS OF WAR: THE *TROJAN WOMEN*

This barbarous act of the Athenians caused a revulsion of feeling that was clearly reflected in Euripides' tragedy, the *Trojan Women,* produced the next year. In the early years of the war, Euripides[9] had written plays glorifying

---

9 Euripides was born in 480 B.C. and died in 406 B.C.

Athens (the *Heraclidae* and the *Suppliants*), attacking the Spartans (*Andromache*), and generally evincing patriotism and optimism. When he wrote the *Trojan Women*, however, Euripides no longer hoped for victory and saw only the cruelty and futility of war. To express his feelings, he hit upon events analogous to those that occurred at Melos.

The scene is Troy, a few days after its capture by the Greeks. The city is in ruins and the men have been killed; the women and children are huddled together awaiting the decision of the victors. But even now, in the moment of their triumph, a bitter future is preparing itself for the Greeks:

> How are ye blind,
> Ye treaders down of cities, ye that cast
> Temples to desolation, and lay waste
> Tombs, the untrodden sanctuaries where lie
> The ancient dead; yourselves so soon to die!ᵖ

The goddess Pallas, who guided and supported the Greeks in their long war against the Trojans and whom Euripides' Athenian audience recognized as the special protector of their own city, has been offended by the impiety of the victors[10] and now plots their destruction.

Euripides' thesis at this point in the play seems to be that there is a moral order in the world—personified for dramatic purposes by gods and goddesses—that rights wrongs and metes out punishment for injustices. This moral order is a *natural* order: An act of injustice or of impiety carries in it, as it were, seeds of destruction, and with the unfolding of time these inevitably bear fruit. (As a matter of fact, the sack of Melos was followed the next year by the launching of the disastrous Sicilian expedition,[11] preparations for which were under way when Euripides' play was performed.)

After this prologue, the Trojan women are apportioned to the victors, and Cassandra is dragged away crying, "Would ye be wise, ye Cities, fly from war." Attention then shifts to Helen, the wife of the Greek chief, Menelaus. It was her elopement with Paris, the son of the Trojan king, that caused the bitter ten-year siege. Menelaus appears, prepared to revenge himself on Helen for the wrongs she has done him and for the suffering her conduct has caused Greeks and Trojans alike. But when he sees her he once again falls under the spell of her beauty, and it is clear before the play ends that he will take her back. Thus Euripides declares that the Trojan war, like all wars, was doubly futile: futile because the suffering that war causes always exceeds the wrongs that led to the outbreak of the war; futile, also, because war solves nothing.

---

10 Among the crimes committed by the Greeks during the capture of Troy was an attempt by Ajax to ravish Cassandra. This would have especially offended Pallas since Cassandra had sought her aid.

11 See p. 46.

The main thesis of Helen's defense is worth noting: She is not to blame for eloping with Paris; "passion" mastered her and she was not herself.

> I ask not thee; I ask my own sad thought,
> What was there in my heart, that I forgot
> My home and land and all I loved, to fly
> With a strange man? Surely it was not I,
> But Cypris, there! Lay thou thy rod on her,
> And be more high than Zeus and bitterer,
> Who o'er all other spirits hath his throne,
> But knows her chain must bind him. My wrong done
> Hath its own pardon. . . .

This note of a conflict between reason and passion, in which the former is worsted, appears again and again in the play. Reason (Aristophanes' "common sense") should have told the Greeks to conduct themselves with piety and probity when they finally captured Troy, but lust and revenge sweep them off their feet. Reason has told Menelaus the prudent course would be to have nothing to do with Helen and her fatal beauty, but it has no chance against the passion she inspires in him. Men, Euripides observes, no longer act from a calm and reasoned calculation of their own and their community's interest; passion moves them to deeds of violence that can destroy both themselves and their cities.

Nothing is left to Hecuba, not even the sweetness of revenge. In the closing lines of the play she gives expression, surely, to the poet's own despair:

> O vain is man,
> Who glorieth in his joy and hath no fears:
> While to and fro the chances of the year
> Dance like an idiot in the wind! And none
> By any strength hath his own fortune won. . . .
> Lo, I have seen the open hand of God;
> And in it nothing, nothing, save the rod
> Of mine affliction. . . .

> God! O God of mercy! . . . Nay:
> Why call I on the Gods? They know, they know,
> My prayers, and would not hear them long ago. . . .
>
> (The Greek trumpet sounds.)
>
> Farewell!—O spirit grey,
>         Whatso is coming,
> Fail not from under me.
> Weak limbs, why tremble ye?
> Forth where the new long day
> Dawneth to slavery!

CHORUS (*singing*).  Farewell from parting lips,
Farewell!—Come, I and thou
Whatso may wait us now
Forth to the long Greek ships
And the sea's foaming.

The war had brought Euripides to a point at which belief in a moral order, which is shown in the beginning of the play, was no longer possible. There are no gods; or if there are, they are utterly helpless. Many of his plays—*Alcestis, Helen, Andromache, Medea,* the *Bacchae*—conclude with the same lines:

There be many shapes of mystery.
And many things God makes to be,
    Past hope or fear.
And the end men looked for cometh not,
And a path is there where no man thought.
So hath it fallen here.q

Euripides must once have been a deeply religious man—at least in the sense of believing in a moral order of the universe—and the loss of his faith was obviously painful to him. The old world of simple piety and natural religion was gone forever as far as he was concerned, yet he could not reconcile himself to a world without religion, and therefore without ultimate meaning. The real tragedy of his position was that, like Hecuba, he cried aloud to the gods without believing in them.

Ye Gods—Alas! Why call on things so weak
For aid? Yet there is something that doth seek,
Crying, for God, when one of us hath woe.

## EURIPIDES CONTRASTED WITH SOPHOCLES

Euripides' despair is all the more poignant when contrasted with the deep religious certainties, and the corresponding assurance, poise, and balance, of the prewar generation.

Aeschylus, who was born in 525 B.C. and fought against the Persians at Marathon, conceived of religion as having a benign and enlightening influence on human affairs. His trilogy, the *Oresteia*, recounts the terrible deeds done by Agamemnon and his family—cannibalism, infanticide, adultery, murder, matricide. There seems no end to the blood-letting, as each crime calls forth another to avenge it. This is the situation as the last of the three plays opens: The Furies, who represent a primitive, eye-for-an-eye level of religion as well as something deeply irrational and savage in human nature, are pursuing Orestes to punish him for the murder of his mother, Clytemnestra. But the "younger gods," Apollo and Athena, intervene. The case against Orestes is taken out of the hands of the Furies and transferred to the Areopagus, a human court in Athens. There Apollo acts as Orestes' counsel, and Athena casts the deciding vote in favor of justice tempered with mercy. Still, Aeschylus was no facile optimist: He did not believe that the "furies" could be eradicated from human nature, even by the younger gods; he believed that they could be tamed, and at the end of his play Athena leads them to the cave that is to be their new home.

Sophocles, another Athenian playwright, was born about 495 B.C., only fifteen years before Euripides; yet his outlook on life was wholly different. For if Euripides expressed the doubts engendered by Athens' defeat, Sophocles reflected the confidence born of the period of Athens' greatness—the fifty years between the great victory over the Persians and the death of Pericles. Serenity is a word that is often used to describe the mood of Sophocles. That the world is one and well ordered, that every part, however discordant, ugly, or inharmonious it may appear, fits into the whole and forms a perfect picture, he never doubted. Men may, and do, err; but over man is a divine law that is the fulfillment of all human striving.

This is the theme of Sophocles' *Antigone* (442 B.C.). The play is concerned with a conflict between man-made law and divine law. In an attempt to seize the city of Thebes, Polyneices, the brother of Antigone, is killed. Their uncle, Creon, the ruler of Thebes, forbids the burial of the rebel's body—a particularly painful punishment since the religion of the Greeks laid special emphasis on proper funeral rites. Antigone disobeys this edict, even though she knows it means her death, because she believes that her deepest loyalty is to the higher, religious law with which Creon's decree is in conflict. When Creon finds her at the work of burial, she says,

> Nowise from Zeus, methought, this edict came,
> Nor Justice, that abides among the Gods
> In Hades, who ordained these laws for men.
> Nor did I deem *thine* edicts of such force
> That they, a mortal's bidding, should o'erride
> Unwritten laws, eternal in the heavens.
> Not of today or yesterday are these,
> But live everlasting, and from whence
> They sprang none knoweth. I would not, for the breach
> Of these, through fear of any human pride,
> To heaven atone. I know that I must die:
> How else? Without thine edict that were so.
> And if before my time, why, this were gain.
> Compassed about with ills, who lives, as I,
> Death, to such life as his, must needs be gain.
> So is it to me to undergo this doom
> No grief at all: but had I left my brother,
> My mother's child, unburied where he lay,
> Then I had grieved; but now this grieves me not.[r]

It is instructive to contrast this conclusion with one of Euripides' last plays, the *Bacchae*,[12] which is concerned with a theme analogous to that of *Antigone*. Pentheus, the ruler of Thebes, opposes the introduction into his city of the wild rites of Dionysus and suffers, as Creon eventually did, a terrible penalty for opposing the divine command. But whereas Sophocles made Creon recognize the ultimate justice of his punishment ("All, all on me this guilt must ever rest, and on no head but mine," Creon exclaims as *Antigone* draws to its tragic denouement), Euripides portrayed the death of Pentheus as a brutal murder plotted by the god Dionysus himself. Moreover, the religious practice that Creon forbade was a dignified act of burial, opposition to which could only be considered unreasonable by Sophocles' audience. By contrast, the rite that Pentheus forbade was pictured by Euripides as so wild and savage that he must have intended the audience to approve Pentheus' decision to forbid it.

Again, in Sophocles' play the tragic climax develops through the characters of the protagonists: Divine law, in a word, does not operate like a fiat out of the blue but in the self-will and stubbornness of Creon. In Euripides' play, however, the protagonists are passive victims. Dionysus hypnotizes his victim and leads him in this state to the place where the rite is celebrated. There Pentheus' mother, a member of the sect, in a frenzy induced by the orgiastic ritual, unknowingly tears her own son limb from limb. The impression the play makes is that religion is a wild and violent passion; and, like every other passion—the one that leads men to make war on one another, for instance—it can only issue in pain and suffering for mankind.

## THE DISSOLUTION OF THE OLD IDEAL

Those men are fortunate, Euripides felt, who are able to develop a callous indifference to the truth about humankind. A sensitive man—one like Euripides himself—suffers more; he experiences not only his own pain but also, sympathetically, that of other men. Thus, in *Medea*, one of the characters says,

> Long ago
> I looked upon man's days, and found a grey
> Shadow. And this thing more I surely say,
> That those of all men who are counted wise,
> Strong wits, devisers of great policies,
> Do pay the bitterest toll. Since life began,
> Hath there in God's eye stood one happy man?
> Fair days roll on, and bear more gifts or less
> Of fortune, but to no man happiness.[s]

This play is symptomatic of the change that had come over Greece. Jason, a Greek, has effected a morganatic marriage with a barbarian, Medea, by whom he

12 See p. 33.

has two children. As the play opens, Jason has decided to abandon Medea in order to make an extremely advantageous match with a proper Greek lady, the only child of the ruler of Corinth. Like the Helen of the *Trojan Women*, Medea is a woman ruled by passion, and the play is concerned with the terrible revenge that she exacts. Thus the primary motif of the play is the appearance in the settled life of a Greek community of a soul utterly abandoned to passion.

In words that might almost stand as a summary of the Greek ideal of community life, Jason describes to Medea the advantages she has gained from her association, through him, with Greek culture.

> A good Greek land hath been
> Thy lasting home, not barbary. Thou hast seen
> Our ordered life, and justice, and the long
> Still grasp of law not changing with the strong
> Man's pleasure.[t]

This noble ideal of order and reason, which may have been realized to a considerable extent during the middle years of the fifth century B.C., was destroyed by the eruption of the war, just as, in the play, the ordered life of Corinth is disrupted by Medea's frenzy. And, as the passion released by the war so debased the Corcyraeans that they forgot their civic duties and fell into fratricidal strife, so the intense hatred Medea feels leads her to kill her own children in order to strike at their father. "I understand," she says, "the awful deed I am to do; but passion, that cause of direst woes to mortal man, hath triumphed o'er my sober thoughts."[u]

Though Medea's hatred is directly responsible for the deaths, the poet makes it clear that Jason's cold and calculating egoism is indirectly also a cause. He tries to argue with her as if she were capable of the same calculation of self-interest that he himself habitually employs. Indeed, he is pictured as so intent on his own advancement as to be quite incapable of understanding what goes on in the minds of other people. Because he is utterly indifferent to the fortune of anyone but himself, Medea finds it easy to dupe him into believing that she meekly accepts his desertion.

Thus Euripides seems to be saying that the destruction of that ordered life of justice that had been the achievement of Hellas was the result of a marriage of narrow egoism with violent passion. This at any rate is the theme reiterated by the chorus. It sympathizes with Medea in the wrong done her, but it constantly counsels her to "lay aside the fierce fury of her wrath" and to leave "Zeus to judge twixt thee and him." In other words, the chorus begs Medea to avail herself of the "still grasp of law" (especially that "higher law" Antigone obeyed) instead of "the strong man's pleasure." Again and again there is an appeal for moderation. "Moderation," Medea's old nurse says, "wins the day first as a better word for men to use, and likewise it is far the best course for them to pursue."[v]

The Greek word rendered as "moderation" in this passage is *sophrosyne*. It is one of the major clues to the Greek conception of life. The idea goes back at least as far as Homer: As we have seen, the whole story of the *Iliad* turns on the consequences of immoderation—for instance, the consequences of Agamemnon's excessive pride and of Achilles' excessive wrath. What the Greeks admired was not simply moderation, but a kind of internal, self-imposed discipline that keeps the passions in check and so permits a balanced and all-round development. Emotion per se, it should be noted, was not considered bad. There are two loves, Euripides' chorus sings, and only one is bad:

> Alas, the Love that falleth like a flood,
> Strong-winged and transitory:
> Why praise ye him? What beareth he of good
> To man, or glory?
> Yet Love there is that moves in gentleness,[13]
> Heart-filling, sweetest of all powers that bless.[w]

It is clear that the opposite of *sophrosyne* is not emotion but excess. Excess of any kind—the excessive egoism of Jason as well as the excessive passion of Medea—is bad because it interferes with the other activities of a full, well-rounded life. Thus Medea's excessive hatred of Jason conflicts with a mother's normal affection for her children. Since a man or a woman who goes to excess in anything inevitably loses much, the Greeks thought that moderation is the key to the good life.

Sophrosyne therefore implies order, discipline, and restraint. To say that excess is the opposite of *sophrosyne* is simply to say that it is the opposite of that "ordered life, and justice, and the long still grasp of law" that was the Greek ideal.

From this point of view the whole play is Euripides' condemnation of "contemporary" fifth-century values:

> Life, life is changed and the laws of it o'ertrod. . . .
> Man hath forgotten God. . . .[x]

## The Sophists

One of the products of this world of disintegrating moral standards and decaying religion was the movement known as Sophism. The Sophists were neither scientists nor philosophers. They were educators who traveled through Hellas from city to city, stopping wherever they could find pupils. And like modern teachers

13 [In this passage "gentleness" is the translator's choice to render the meaning of *sophrosyne*—
AUTHOR.]

they expected to be paid for their services. The fact that there was now room in Greek life for paid teachers is significant of the change in conditions. In the old days the sons of noble houses had been brought up—as Achilles had been brought up by Phoenix—on stirring accounts of their illustrious and divine ancestors, whose deeds furnished models to be emulated. But gradually a class of "new rich" arose—persons who lacked the legendary heritage of the old nobility and who had made their money in "trade." This new aristocracy wanted to learn how to live well and could afford to pay for what it learned.

Moreover, as the franchise broadened in cities like Athens, political leadership was no longer an inevitable birthright; it now entailed being able to please the electorate. And with a juridical system that put the courts' decisions in the hands of the masses, success in lawsuits depended on being able to move the jury's emotions.

Accordingly, the emphasis in education shifted radically from the knightly virtues of courage, loyalty, personal honor, and moderation to the more worldly talents of facility in debate and oratorical skill. Educational practice always conforms to the dominant cultural pattern: Educators teach the young how to do, or to get, the things their parents value. In the fifth century B.C. the old values of the warrior class were no longer highly regarded because they no longer brought men the preeminence they had once assured. The new values were essentially political and secular, and the new education reflected this change.

The Sophists said that they taught "virtue"; the virtue they taught was the technique of success in the contemporary democracy. "How to Win Friends and Influence People" was the substance of their morality. Beyond this it is impossible to generalize. What specifically they taught—what they believed to be the rules for success—depended to a considerable extent on their individual temperaments. Whereas a conservative like Protagoras[14] maintained that the way to success was prudent acceptance of the laws and customs of the community one lived in, a radical like Thrasymachus[15] openly advocated that might is right and the devil take the hindmost.

Though the Sophists did not teach a common doctrine, they were united by a common hostility toward traditional Greek beliefs. They felt themselves to be "enlightened." By this they meant that they had liberated themselves from the superstition and ignorance that still bound less fortunate men and that they would be glad—for a price—to set others free.

The Sophists naturally met with a mixed reception. The avant-garde received them with open arms, and bright young men sat at their feet in rapt attention. But the bulk of the population was still devout and superstitious. This was true even in Athens, where "society" was doubtless sceptical and progressive but the mass of the citizenry was as conservative intellectually as it was radical politically. Since most of the Sophists' pupils were opponents of the people's rule,

14 See p. 67.
15 See p. 71.

opposition to the Sophists' teachings came to be associated with the defense of political democracy. Hence it was easy, even in Pericles' day, and still more so in the period of mob rule following his death, to try innovators for atheism and treason at the same time, making no distinction between the two charges.

### ESTIMATE OF THE SOPHISTS

It is hard even today to make a fair assessment of the Sophists, especially since our principal source for their views is Plato—a very prejudiced observer. One thing it is certainly possible to say: Their interest in rhetoric and oratory led them to pay attention—much more attention than anyone before them had paid—to the nature of language. They realized that language could be used to mislead the unwary, and they sometimes employed it to entangle their opponents. They taught Plato—if only by force of negative example—that the language in which a problem is framed enormously affects the solution of the problem. Indeed, from their time to our own, linguistic analysis has always been an important part of philosophy.

It is also possible to say that they helped turn attention away from physical nature to man, and to man as an empirical being with the practical problem of making a life for himself in this world. They certainly performed a useful social function in helping to sweep away superstition. But even their greatest admirers must admit that they had little that was positive to put in its place. For the most part, they merely made explicit, and passed on to the next generation, the negativism implicit in the contemporary intellectual structure. It makes less sense to condemn—or to praise—the Sophists as a destructive force than to take them as "signs of the times" and to ask why they and such a large part of Greek society came to be so sceptical about beliefs the masses still held dear.

Partly it was a result of social changes that made the old values no longer significant in achieving success. Partly it was the result of the thinking of the natural scientists. In Hesiod's time, as we have seen, there was a deep-seated conviction that law has its source in divine authority. Zeus, the son of Cronos, had decreed a line of conduct for men to follow, and, sooner or later, those who failed to live up to these rules would be punished. Moreover, these rules were by implication absolute. Since there was but one Zeus, there was but one justice. Justice, as Zeus's decree, must be everywhere the same.

These admirable but naïve notions could hardly survive in a period of scientific study. If the "goddess" Iris turned out to be a natural phenomenon like a rainbow, a similar explanation would inevitably be given for Zeus himself. And once Zeus was no more, what would happen to the law of justice he was supposed to have promulgated? As Aristophanes remarked, when Zeus is uncrowned, chaos succeeds to his place, and whirlwind rules.

Furthermore, though Xenophanes' discovery that every man makes god in his own image had led him to conclude that god transcends all human grasp, it led others to the conclusion that god is only a figment of the human mind.

If the Ethiopians judged god to be black because they were so, and the Thracians said that god is fair because they were fair, did it not follow that the Greek god was but a reflection of the Greek mind?

The same line of reasoning seemed to apply to supposedly god-given moral codes. The more the Greeks traveled in other lands, the more they realized that in the diversity of men's customs and laws there is only one common element— the conviction of each group that its own set of rules is god-given. Obviously, they all cannot be divinely inspired; if some are not, why should any be?

The Greek historian Herodotus, a great traveler, was enormously impressed by the variety of laws he found in the different countries he visited:

> If one were to offer men to choose out of all customs in the world such as seemed to them the best, they would examine the whole number, and end by preferring their own; so convinced are they that their own usages far surpass those of all others. . . . That people have this feeling about their laws may be seen by very many proofs: among others, by the following. Darius, after he had got the kingdom, called into his presence certain Greeks who were at hand, and asked what he should pay them to eat the bodies of their fathers when they died. To which they answered that there was no sum that would tempt them to do such a thing. He then sent for certain Indians, of the race called Callatians, men who eat their fathers, and asked them, while the Greeks stood by, and knew by the help of an interpreter all that was said, what he should give them to burn the bodies of their fathers (as was the Greek practice) at their decease. The Indians exclaimed aloud, and bade him forbear such language.[y]

It is clear that Herodotus did not share the simple faith of the Spartan who proudly declared to Xerxes: "Though the Spartans be free men, they are not in all respects free; Law is the master whom they own, and this master they fear more than your subjects fear you. Whatever it commands they do; and its commandment is always the same: it forbids them to flee in battle, whatever the number of their foes, and requires them to stand firm, and either to conquer or die."[z]

Even allowing for the bombast that might well have crept into a provincial Greek's address to the Great King, these are noble words; but they are not the kind of words, nor is Antigone's the kind of choice, that appealed to the new, enlightened generation. Religious sceptics had to find new sanctions to enforce the self-discipline and moderation that the best Greek conception of the good life had involved. This search was complicated by the fact that, although the activity of the scientists had successfully undermined the old religious view of life, it had failed to give convincing evidence of its own intellectual authority. Hence scepticism was not confined to the sphere of religion but became a pervasive attitude of mind.

It is not difficult to see why this came about. The diversity of scientific explanations of the universe was as great as the diversity of moral codes, and, like the latter, these various explanations had nothing in common save a conviction of omniscience on the part of their inventors. The succession of rival theories that had been evolved in the century and a half since Thales' day seemed evidence of the incapacity of the human mind to fathom the nature of the universe.

Further, the paradoxes of Parmenidean logic must have led many to the same conclusion—that reason is a hopelessly inadequate instrument for understanding the world. What, then, was a man to do? Fall back on sense perception as the criterion of truth?[16] Alas, the unaided senses are obviously fallible (straight sticks look curved in water, square towers look round at a distance, and so on). And it was not possible for a fifth-century Greek to reply, as a modern empiricist might, that controlled experiments can check on and refine the information that the senses present. The Greeks lacked such safeguards.

## PROTAGORAS

Protagoras, one of the earliest of the Sophists,[17] worked out a theory of sense perception, based on Heraclitean physical theory, that led to the same sceptical conclusion. Everything, according to Heraclitus, is in a constant flux. We say, for instance, that you and I are looking at the same brown horse. But the horse out there is continuously changing. So are my eyes, and so are yours. The brown that we say we see is not out there in the horse; it is a product of two motions—a motion out there that we call the horse and a motion in here in the sense organ. But if the sensed color is a product, one of whose factors is the motion in a sense organ, it follows that each different sense organ experiences a different color. The brown I see is different from the brown you see. There are two browns, and each is a private, subjective state.[18]

If neither reason nor perception yields the truth about the world, Protagoras argued, objective knowledge of a public reality is quite impossible. "Man," he said, "is the measure of all things, of things that are that they are and of things that are not that they are not." This was, of course, a complete rejection of the whole philosophic and scientific enterprise as it had been conceived since Thales. For everyone since Thales' day had held that (1) there is a public, objective reality and that (2) this reality is intelligible, that is, it can be understood by the human mind. All this Protagoras in effect denied.[19]

---

16 See pp. 24–25.
17 Burnet thinks Protagoras was born about 500 B.C. This would make him somewhat older than Empedocles and Anaxagoras and a few years younger than Parmenides. [*Greek Philosophy: Thales to Plato* (Macmillan, New York, 1932), p. 111.]
18 For a further discussion of this theory see pp. 149–50.
19 A somewhat younger Sophist, Gorgias, is said to have maintained that there is nothing, that even if there were something we could not know it, and that even if we could know it we could not communicate our knowledge about it. In making this assertion Gorgias contradicted himself, for he was communicating something he believed he knew. But, contradictory though it is, it shows the extent to which the Sophists were reacting against the investigations of the cosmologists.

The formulation Protagoras used suggests acquaintance with Parmenides' views. Parmenides had maintained that logical consistency is the measure (or test) of reality, of what is and of what is not. To this Protagoras replied that not logic but human opinion is the test. Since we cannot reach an objective truth about things, we should rely on common sense. If logic forces us to the conclusion that the world is one and immovable, when common sense knows it is diverse and changing, so much the worse, Protagoras said, for logic. Instead of pinning our hopes on the discovery of an elusive Reality, let us take as real what we see about us and operate on that basis.

Protagoras also applied this point of view to questions of conduct. As regards religion, he held that we will do well, since we cannot know the absolute truth, to follow the ceremonies and accept the practices of the community in which we live. And the same holds for our social relations: We can never discover the absolute ideal of justice, about which Hesiod wrote so movingly. Let us therefore accommodate our behavior to the pattern established for us by our own city. These customs and traditions perform a vital social function by producing a cohesive and orderly community, even though they are not "true" in the sense in which the masses believe. To conform to them will be best for us, and this, therefore, was the "goodness" that Protagoras taught.

## THE YOUNGER SOPHISTS

Obviously, such conclusions would appeal only to the socially conservative. The younger Sophists, starting from a similarly sceptical basis, were soon advocating an entirely different program. The question, they said, was whether law is reality or "mere" convention. The Greek words they used to express this disjunction are *physis* and *nomos*. *Physis* is the word that the scientists had used when they asked, "What is the stuff (or *physis*) out of which the world is made?" Because they thought that this *physis* was real, the word *physis* gradually came to mean generally what is real in contrast to what is not. Hence, in asking whether or not law is *physis*, the Sophists did not mean to ask whether law is material, but whether it is real in the way in which the scientists held matter to be real, that is, whether it is a public object that men can come to know. It seemed obvious to the younger generation of Sophists that law is not real in this sense. Protagoras himself had admitted that we could never know it, and if we cannot know it, what is the point of asserting its existence? Moreover, no one—that is, no "enlightened" man—believed any longer in the gods as a possible source of law's reality. Every "enlightened" man knew that laws were, as a matter of fact, the product of the activities of men—either individuals like Lycurgus or groups of men in assemblies. Hence, how was it possible to maintain that law is anything more than "mere" convention? And why, if it is merely convention, should it have any claim on us? Why obey it if it is not to our advantage to do so?

This is not a rejection but merely a reinterpretation of Protagoras' basic position. Protagoras argued in favor of obedience to the law not because obedience is "right" but simply because it is advantageous. Protagoras' version of the argument might well have appealed to those who, like Protagoras, had much to lose in a time of civil disorder, but it would not have attracted "have-nots" who hoped to become "haves." To disobey the law, as long as they were not found out or as long as they were strong enough not to fear punishment, would have been very much to *their* advantage.

The younger Sophists' more radical version of the argument was calculated to appeal particularly to a special class of "have-nots"—the "enlightened" few whose new knowledge had liberated them from superstition. The sons of wealthy men and of the old nobility, men of real or fancied ability whose families had once ruled by birthright but who were now excluded from power unless they could please a democratic electorate—men made sceptical by the kind of attack on natural science that has just been discussed and made cynical by the corruption and venality of the democratic electorate—would have seen that *their* advantage lay not in a modest conformity with the law of their city but in a ruthless egoism.

Such men were the pupils of the later Sophists, from whom they learned what they doubtless wanted to know: that there is no real "justice" or "right," that these are only names applied to local and changing conventions, and that the only real authority in the world is force. The views of these later Sophists may be represented fairly by Callicles and Thrasymachus.[20]

In Plato's dialogue called the *Gorgias,* Callicles maintains that what men call "right" is always an expression, whether they know it or not, of what they believe to be to their advantage. Hence, in democracies, where majorities rule, the law is merely an expression of the interests of the masses. Promise-keeping, telling the truth, paying "just" debts, living honorably, and the other alleged virtues that "right living" prescribes merely reflect the interests and preoccupations of the weak, the ineffectual, and the cowardly.

When Socrates argues that it is "wrong to do injustice," Callicles replies:

> You, who pretend to be engaged in the pursuit of truth, are appealing now to the popular and vulgar notions of right, which are admirable by convention, not by nature. Convention and nature are generally at variance with one another. . . . The reason, as I conceive, is that the makers of laws are the majority who are weak; and they make laws and distribute praises and censures with a view to themselves and to their own interests; and they terrify the stronger sort of men, and those who are able to get the better of them, in order that they may not get the better of them; and they say, that self-interested ambition is shameful and unjust, meaning, by the word in-

---

20 We know of Callicles only as a character in one of Plato's dialogues, in which he is not a Sophist but a fluent pupil thoroughly indoctrinated with Sophistic ideas. Whether such a person actually existed is immaterial; he is typical of many Athenian politicians during the Peloponnesian War. By contrast, there is independent evidence that Thrasymachus was well known as a teacher in 427 B.C. Hence both men can be taken as representing the "enlightened" point of view in the closing years of the century.

justice, the desire of a man to have more than his neighbours; for knowing their own inferiority, I suspect that they are only too glad of equality. And therefore the endeavour to have more than the many is conventionally said to be shameful and unjust, and is called injustice, whereas nature herself intimates that it is just for the better to have more than the worse, the more powerful than the weaker; and in many ways she shows, among men as well as among animals, and indeed among whole cities and races, that justice consists in the superior ruling over and having more than the inferior. For on what principle of justice did Xerxes invade Hellas, or his father the Scythians (not to speak of numberless other examples)? Nay, but these men, I suggest, act in this way according to the nature of justice; yes, by Heaven, and according to the law of nature, though not, perhaps, according to that law which we enact; we take the best and strongest of our fellows from their youth upwards, and tame them like young lions,—enslaving them with spells and incantations, and saying to them that with equality they must be content, and that the equal is the honourable and the just. But if there were a man born with enough ability, he would shake off and break through, and escape from all this; he would trample under foot all our formulas and spells and charms, and all our laws which are against nature: the slave would rise in rebellion and be lord over us, and the light of natural justice would shine forth. . . .[a]

Nature, then, is a continuous struggle for survival, and the only qualities that count are those that enable us to "win out." "Justice" in the ordinary sense helps only the weak; therefore it is not a virtue for the strong but a misfortune. Power, not justice, is what matters in the ruthless competition of life. But if power is good because it enables us to survive in this struggle, we must *want* to survive. What is the good that all men aim at—the good that makes life worth living? Obviously, according to Callicles, it is only pleasure—the sensual pleasures of food, drink, sex. Having as many as possible of these, conceived of as separate, discrete items of enjoyment, is what any enlightened man aims at. Hence the old ideal of moderation is only for fools or weaklings:

On the contrary, I plainly assert that he who would truly live ought to allow his desires to wax to the uttermost, and not to chastise them; but when they have grown to their greatest he should have courage and intelligence to minister to them and to satisfy all his longings. And this I affirm to be natural justice and nobility. To this, however, the many cannot attain; and they blame the strong man because they are ashamed of their own weakness, which they desire to conceal, and hence they say that intemperance is base. As I have remarked already, they enslave the nobler natures, and being unable to attain full satisfaction of their pleasures, they praise temperance and justice out of their own cowardice. For if a man had been originally the son of a king, or had a nature capable of acquiring an empire or a tyranny or sovereignty, what could be more truly base or evil than temperance and justice—to a man like him, I say, who might freely be enjoying every good, and has no one to stand in his way, and yet has himself admitted convention and reason and the disapproval of other men to be lords over him?—must not these fine conceits of justice and temperance have brought him to a miserable plight, when he cannot favour his own friends above his enemies, even though he be a ruler in his city? Nay, Socrates, you profess to be a votary of the truth, and the truth is this:—that luxury and intemperance and license, if they be provided with means, are virtue and happiness—all the rest is a mere bauble, agreements contrary to nature, foolish talk of men, nothing worth.[21,b]

In the *Republic*, Plato describes a similar discussion between Socrates and Thrasymachus. The question they are examining is, "What is justice?" According to Thrasymachus, justice "means nothing but what is to the interest of the stronger party."[c] This, of course, is equivalent to saying that justice, in the sense of implying a morally binding way of life, is an illusion. The dispute is therefore not an argument about what specific acts are binding, as it might have been between two philosophers who agreed that there is a moral law. It is a dispute about whether there is anything at all that men *ought* to do. Thrasymachus holds there is not. Look about you, he says in effect; wherever you turn you see that, whatever men *say*, they always aim at their own interest, or at what they take to be their interest. Kings may say that they act in the interest of their people, but the laws they promulgate are those that they believe to be to their own advantage. And the same is true when the people rule. The laws differ because the interest differs, but what men call "justice"—the law as it appears on the statute book—is to the interest of whoever has sufficient authority to get it inscribed there. The whole dispute about justice, therefore, is merely verbal except insofar as justice is reducible to a struggle for power. The enlightened man knows this and acts accordingly. He thus has a great advantage over those who are naïve enough to believe in shibboleths like "justice," "honesty," and "loyalty." The enlightened man knows that these are mere words he can turn to his advantage. The only restraint on his conduct is set by his circumstances. Whatever ruthlessness and ingenuity can obtain, whatever he has strength or cleverness enough to secure—that is his by the "right" of the stronger.

> . . . in politics, the genuine ruler regards his subjects exactly like sheep, and thinks of nothing else, night and day, but the good he can get out of them for himself. You are so far out in your notions of right and wrong, justice and injustice, as not to know that "right" actually means what is good for someone else, and to be "just" means serving the interest of the stronger who rules, at the cost of the subject who obeys; whereas injustice is just the reverse, asserting its authority over those innocents who are called just, so that they minister solely to their master's advantage and happiness, and not in the least degree to their own. Innocent as you are yourself, Socrates, you must see that a just man always has the worst of it. Take a private business: when a partnership is wound up, you will never find that the more honest

21 As Callicles finishes, Socrates sadly compliments him on his frankness: "What you say is what the rest of the world think, but do not like to say."

of two partners comes off with the larger share; and in their relations to the state, when there are taxes to be paid, the honest man will pay more than the other on the same amount of property; or if there is money to be distributed, the dishonest will get it all. When either of them hold some public office, even if the just man loses in no other way, his private affairs at any rate will suffer from neglect, while his principles will not allow him to help himself from the public funds; not to mention the offence he will give to his friends and relations by refusing to sacrifice those principles to do them a good turn. Injustice has all the opposite advantages. I am speaking of the type I described just now, the man who can get the better of other people on a large scale: you must fix your eye on him, if you want to judge how much it is to one's own interest not to be just. You can see that best in the most consummate form of injustice, which rewards wrongdoing with supreme welfare and happiness and reduces its victims, if they won't retaliate in kind, to misery. That form is despotism, which uses force or fraud to plunder the goods of others, public or private, sacred or profane, and to do it in a wholesale way. If you are caught committing any one of these crimes on a small scale, you are punished and disgraced; they call it sacrilege, kidnapping, burglary, theft and brigandage. But if, besides taking their property, you turn all your countrymen into slaves, you will hear no more of those ugly names; your countrymen themselves will call you the happiest of men and bless your name, and so will everyone who hears of such a complete triumph of injustice; for when people denounce injustice, it is because they are afraid of suffering wrong, not of doing it. So true is it, Socrates, that injustice, on a grand enough scale, is superior to justice in strength and freedom and autocratic power; and "right," as I said at first, means simply what serves the interest of the stronger party; "wrong" means what is for the interest and profit of oneself.[d]

Thrasymachus and the Athenian generals besieging Melos were in complete agreement.[22] Both were convinced that might makes right; both rejected the old-fashioned notion of right as a rule independent of, and often in conflict with, power. The Athenians at Melos were simply putting into practice the Thrasymachian principle that the only restriction on the exercise of power is more power—the principle that every man takes what he wants if he can get it. This does not mean, of course, that these Athenian generals had necessarily studied at the feet of the Sophists and imbibed their teachings. Sophistic teaching was less a cause than a symptom.

By the end of the fifth century B.C. all aspects of the culture—economic, political, intellectual—had combined to produce an extremely dangerous situation. A widespread dissolution of the old beliefs that had held society together, coupled with a radical scepticism about the possibility of discovering new and better grounds for the old social formula, had resulted in the same narrow and ruthless self-seeking that the tensions of war and defeat had naturally and inde-

22 See pp. 55–56.

pendently engendered. Thus the very fabric of society seemed to be collapsing. The hard-won and only recently achieved political unity of the city-state had disappeared in divisive party conflict; the old ideal of *sophrosyne*, of moderation and self-discipline, had given way to deliberate and unrestrained seeking of extremes; the old probity, the high-mindedness, loyalty, and devotion to civic duty that had enabled a tiny state like Athens to defeat the great Persian empire less than a century earlier, had been replaced by licentious self-seeking and a concentration on sensual pleasures that was altogether incompatible with the health of the city.

These were facts, as it seems, that could hardly have been passed over by any serious or observant Athenian at the end of the fifth century B.C. We have already seen some of the varied reactions.[23] Behind Aristophanes' bitter satire lay a longing for the "good old days," which doubtless seemed much better, contrasted with the painful present, than they had really been. Euripides, for his part, could only writhe in a helpless sense of frustration.

We shall now examine two philosophical reactions to this cultural malaise and to the intellectual and moral scepticism that was partly a cause and partly an effect of the debacle at the end of the fifth century B.C. Atomism, the first of these reactions, was a continuation and development of the views of the early pluralists, the fruition of the materialistic point of view initiated by Thales. It will be examined in the next chapter. The second, which will be examined in greater detail, was the theory developed by Plato and carried forward by Aristotle.

23 See pp. 47–51 and 56–63.

# CHAPTER 3

# Atomism

## *The Later Pluralists*

The final development of pluralism, called "Atomism" for reasons that will shortly appear, can be represented by the writings of four philosophers: Leucippus, Democritus, Epicurus, and Lucretius. About the first almost nothing is known; some indeed have questioned whether he ever existed. Nothing remains of his work, and it is difficult, if not impossible, to distinguish his views from those of his successors in this school. Some fragments of the extensive writings of Democritus and more substantial portions of Epicurus' work are still extant, and it is possible to reconstruct their views with some accuracy; but the most complete single work remaining from the Atomists' school is Lucretius' poem, *On the Nature of Things*. Lucretius was not, however, an original thinker; he did not contribute anything to the evolution of the theory but was content to translate into Latin for the benefit of his Latin-reading contemporaries the views of Epicurus, who in Lucretius' opinion had said the final and definitive word on every conceivable subject.[1]

Leucippus, if he lived at all, was a contemporary of Anaxagoras, which places him in the middle of the fifth century B.C.; Lucretius was a contemporary of Cicero and Julius Caesar and lived during the first half of the first century B.C. During this four-hundred-year period the theory naturally underwent a considerable development. The most important of the changes occurred in the Atomists' ethical doctrines, which reflect in a striking way the relation between philosophical thinking and the cultural milieu from which it springs. On the other hand, the Atomists were in basic agreement as regards physical theory. It will be possible therefore to formulate a statement of the Atomists' conception of the physical world that is generally valid for the whole school. This chapter will describe this general theory, drawing for illustration on the writings of all the Atomists but chiefly on Lucretius' poetical textbook, because it is the most complete extant document. A summary of Democritus' view on ethics will then be given. An account of the moral theories of Epicurus and Lucretius will be reserved for a later chapter,[2] in which they will be considered in the light of the cultural changes that occurred after the fifth century B.C.

## Democritus

Some of the Democritean fragments might suggest that Democritus was just another Sophist—"Man . . . is cut off from truth." "In truth we know nothing about anything, but every man shares the generally prevailing opinion." "That we do not really know of what sort each thing is, or is not, has often been shown."[a]

In another fragment, however, Democritus maintains that we must distinguish between

> . . . two forms of knowledge, one genuine, one obscure. To the obscure belong all of the following: sight, hearing, smell, taste, feeling. The other form is the genuine, and is quite distinct from this. . . . Whenever the obscure [way

---

1 A characteristic passage showing how much Lucretius leaned on his master is this "invocation" to Epicurus at the opening of Book III: "Thou, who out of the deep darkness didst first avail to raise a torch so clear . . . 'tis thee I follow, bright star of the Greek race. . . . Thou art our father, thou discoverer of truth, thou dost vouchsafe to us a father's precepts, and from thy pages, our hero, even as bees in flowery glades sip every plant, we in like manner browse on all thy sayings of gold," and so on. [*On the Nature of Things,* translated by C. Bailey (Oxford, New York, 1936), p. 107.]

2 See pp. 317–25.

of knowing] has reached the *minimum sensible* of hearing, smell, taste, and touch, and when the investigation must be carried farther into that which is still finer, then arises the genuine way of knowing which has a finer organ of thought.[b]

This shows that, far from being a Sophist, Democritus believed the human mind is capable of understanding the world. But Democritus' view was more subtle than that of the earlier rationalists. He accepted the Sophists' arguments about the subjectivity and privacy of the sense world. At the level of perception, he allowed, each man is the measure for himself; at that level truth consists, as the Sophists had held, in "generally prevailing opinions." Nevertheless, though truth is more difficult to ascertain than the Milesians and their followers had supposed, Democritus held that there is an objective, public world and that it can be discovered by reason.

What, then, is the truth about the world? The universe, Democritus thought, is constituted by

> . . . atoms and empty space; everything else is merely thought to exist. The worlds are unlimited; they come into being and perish. Nothing can come into being from that which is not nor pass away into that which is not. Further the atoms are unlimited in size and number, and they are borne along in the whole universe in a vortex, and thereby generate all composite things— fire, water, air, earth; for even these are conglomerations of given atoms. And it is because of their solidity that these atoms are impassive and unalterable. The sun and the moon have been composed of such smooth and spherical masses [that is, atoms], and so also the soul, which is identical with reason. We see by virtue of the impact of images upon our eyes. All things happen by virtue of necessity, the vortex being the cause of the creation of all things.[c]

## ATTEMPT TO AVOID DIFFICULTIES OF EARLIER PLURALISTS

In order to understand what Democritus meant, let us review the position reached during the first stage of pluralism.[3] The early pluralists had hoped that asserting the existence of a real many would resolve the puzzle about change. But it was not settled at the outset whether this plurality was merely a numerical plurality or a qualitative diversity. The latter was the more natural assumption. The objects of ordinary experience are qualitatively diverse particulars, marked by great variety in color, texture, odor. It was hard to think away all this concreteness and variety and so reach the notion of a stuff without qualitative specificity. This is why the earliest monists had said that reality is "water" or "fire" or "air." It is also why Empedocles, the first pluralist, had presupposed a plurality of qualitatively diverse "roots," and why, when Empedocles' assump-

3 See pp. 25–31.

tion of *finite* qualitative diversity failed, Anaxagoras had tried an *infinite* qualitative diversity.

When this too failed and it began to be clear that qualitative diversity was a blind alley, it was time to try the other alternative, namely, a many that differ only quantitatively. The first principle of Atomism, then, asserts the existence of a plurality of entities that differ only in shape and size and that (unlike Empedocles' "roots" and Anaxagoras' "seeds") are therefore qualitatively indistinguishable.

Though the main weakness of early pluralism had been its acceptance of qualitative diversity, another problem was caused by Anaxagoras' assertion of infinite divisibility. Anaxagoras had argued, "Nor is there a least of what is small, but there is always a smaller; for it cannot be that what is should cease to be by being cut."[d] This may have seemed to Anaxagoras to follow from Parmenides' conclusion: Since Parmenides had shown that what *is* cannot be destroyed, "cutting" reality cannot destroy it. Hence there is no reason why cutting should ever come to an end, and what is, is infinitely divisible.

But Parmenidean reasoning also led, by a different route, to the conclusion that reality cannot be infinitely divisible. For if the real entities are infinitely divisible, it seemed to imply that they are composed of infinitely small parts, and this led to very odd conclusions. For instance, as Zeno pointed out, if anything infinitely small "were added to any other thing it would not make it any larger; for nothing can gain in magnitude by the addition of what has no magnitude."[e]

The way out of this dilemma, the Atomists thought, was a many, each one of which is eternal, indestructible, uncreated, and indivisible. Each of these entities, which they called "atoms"—in Greek, *a* (negative prefix, like the English *un*) + *tome* (cut)—was in fact conceived to be a complete Parmenidean one.

It may well be that a remark made by Melissus, who was, like Zeno, a pupil of Parmenides', had suggested this conception. Against Anaxagoras he had argued that "if there were a many, these would have to be of the same kind as I say that the one is."[f] Although Melissus had meant this as a general refutation of pluralism, it was only a refutation of Anaxagoras' version of pluralism. Since the argument was hypothetical in form, it was always open to the pluralists to adopt the hypothesis and so to accept the conclusion.

This is precisely what the Atomists did. They saw that the Parmenidean arguments did not exclude a many if each of the many were itself a solid, impenetrable plenum. The next question was how, from this position to which it seemed to them that logic led, they could account for the experienced world. Supposing the world is a many, each of which is a solid bit of matter, could a rational account be given of the visible variety of the sense world? In order to do this they needed motion. Motion *in* a plenum Empedocles and Anaxagoras had assumed, and the former at least had thought he could prove its occurrence with his water tube. But since each of the atoms is itself a plenum, it was necessary for the Atomists to assert the motion of these plena—that is, motion in empty space—and this Parmenides had declared impossible.

They had to assume the existence of empty space for another reason. For what makes the many a plurality? Empedocles and Anaxagoras, both of whom had adhered to the old qualitative notion of "stuff," had had no difficulty on this score. Their plenum was a plurality of qualitatively distinct stuffs. But qualitative differentiation had proven untenable. What then divides the plenum into a many? Parmenides had said that the plenum is one precisely because he could not conceive of a way it could be divided. There is nothing (for "there is no nothing") to make it more than one. Hence the Atomists needed something that would divide the Parmenidean plenum into a number of separate entities. Empty space, in addition to serving as the locus of motion, would perform this function, for space could separate each real from every other real.

It was necessary, therefore, for the Atomists to get around Parmenides' denial of empty space. This crucial stage in their argument is difficult to reconstruct, but one fragment suggests they may have reasoned in this way: Parmenides, after all, had shown only that "there is no nothing." Assuming, as he did, that empty space is nothing, he concluded that reality is full. If, however, space were something, Parmenides' attack on the concept of nothing would be irrelevant to the question of the fullness or emptiness of space. Accordingly, the Atomists seem to have reasoned that there are two kinds of reality—a full reality and an empty reality. Parmenides was correct in holding that "What is not, is not"; but "What is, is" is ambiguous. The verb "to be" means either (1) to be a material something or (2) to be the space in which material moves.[4]

## Lucretius' Version of Atomistic Physics

Atomism was thus an attempt to reformulate pluralism in a way that would avoid the difficulties into which Empedocles and Anaxagoras had fallen. Democritus thought he could resolve the dilemma about change by asserting that reality consists of (1) solid, indivisible, and qualitatively indistinguishable bodies (2) moving (3) in empty space.

Let us now examine these principles in a little more detail by turning from the scanty Democritean fragments to Lucretius' later and fuller account.

### NOTHING IS CREATED

Lucretius' account of atomistic physics began with the Parmenidean proposition that there is no creation out of nothing. Lucretius' version of this thesis and his arguments in support of it were, however, quite his own:

---

4 This, it should be noted, established only the existence of empty space, not of motion in that space. It thus met Parmenides' objections but not Zeno's. There is no evidence that the Atomists ever found a reply to Zeno's paradoxes.

This terror, then, this darkness of the mind,[5] must needs be scattered not by the rays of the sun and the gleaming shafts of day, but by the outer view and the inner law of nature; whose first rule shall take its start for us from this, that nothing is ever begotten of nothing by divine will. Fear forsooth so constrains all mortal men, because they behold many things come to pass on earth and in the sky, the cause of whose working they can by no means see, and think that a divine power brings them about. Therefore, when we have seen that nothing can be created out of nothing, then more rightly . . . shall we discern that . . . all things come to be without the aid of gods.

For if things came to being from nothing, every kind might be born from all things, nought would need a seed. First men might arise from the sea, and from the land the race of scaly creatures, and birds burst forth from the sky; cattle and other herds, and all the tribe of wild beasts, with no fixed law of birth, would haunt tilth and desert. Nor would the same fruits stay constant to the trees, but all would change: all trees might avail to bear all fruits . . . .

If [things] sprang from nothing, suddenly would they arise at uncertain intervals and in hostile times of year . . . little children would grow suddenly to youths, and at once trees would come forth, leaping from the earth. But of this it is well seen that nothing comes to pass, since all things grow slowly, as is natural, from a fixed seed, and as they grow preserve their kind . . . . Therefore, we must confess that nothing can be brought to being out of nothing, inasmuch as it needs a seed for things, from which each may be produced and brought forth into the gentle breezes of the air . . . .[g]

The argument here is very different from the purely logical considerations advanced by Parmenides. In the first place, it is clear that Lucretius was chiefly interested in excluding the gods from the world. Rightly or wrongly, he held that belief in the possibility of divine intervention—for example, punishment for sin—causes men much distress of mind. If it could be shown that the gods do not, and cannot, intervene in human affairs, he believed that a great cloud would be lifted from mankind. Hence, despite the way in which he phrased his argument, he was much less interested in proving that nothing is created than in proving that the course of nature is completely regular.

We may agree that if he had proved the uniformity of nature, he would have excluded the possibility of divine interference. But did he establish that nature is uniform? Not at all. He pointed to a number of actual uniformities, but it would have been easy for any defender of divine causality to point to many irregularities—sudden thunderstorms, unpredictable earthquakes, and the like. Earlier thinkers had attributed these irregularities to divine temper tantrums. How did Lucretius know that they have regular, natural causes that were as yet undiscovered? And, in any case, even if nature be completely uniform, this

---

5 Lucretius has just been discussing man's fear of death and other fears that he held to be engendered by religious superstition.

does not prove that it will go on being uniform in the future, still less that it must be uniform.

A modern descendant of Lucretius might reply in the following fashion: "The whole scientific enterprise, the whole effort to discover the precise causes of natural occurrences, depends on the assumption that nature is uniform. Without this conviction, no one would bother to study nature. I admit that uniformity cannot be demonstrated; it is simply a basic methodological principle." Though Lucretius, of course, did not say this explicitly, he would probably have found this defense congenial. For underlying all his examples, there is one basic thought: Our understanding of nature depends, Lucretius said in effect, on our being able, when, for instance, we see an acorn, to predict that it will grow to be an oak; it depends on our being able, when we see an oak, to say with confidence, "This has grown from an acorn." But if some god, like a magician making rabbits appear in empty hats, could simply decree, "Let there be an oak," so that, on command, oak trees materialized out of nothing—or sprang arbitrarily from anything other than an acorn—we could never know what was going to happen next. All our attempts to determine the course of nature would be in vain. Since all explanation of the physical world proceeds from the finding of some occurrence (say, an acorn) on which some subsequent occurrence (in this case, an oak) depends, it follows that divine intervention is incompatible with the basic presuppositions of natural knowledge. If gods intervened at will in natural processes, there would be no earlier occurrence to which the occurrence of the oak tree was systematically related.

But these considerations are quite compatible with the possibility that the world as a whole was created out of nothing by divine fiat. The gods might have chosen to create, or might have unintentionally created, a universe that acts in a completely uniform way. True, once they brought such a universe into being, they would not be able to alter it or to affect the course of its events in any way, and their power would thus be radically limited. The view that the world and the laws governing it were created by a God who does not interfere with the operation of those laws is called deism and was widely held in the eighteenth century. Though it is not without difficulties, it is certainly logically consistent with the uniformity of nature. Hence Lucretius' argument did not successfully exclude creation.

Would some version of deism have been acceptable to Lucretius? Possibly. He was less interested in denying divine causality as such than in repudiating divine interference in a going world, especially any intervention in human affairs. And he was not an atheist. That gods exist he and the other Atomists allowed. How else was it possible, they thought, to explain the visions and dreams in which the gods appear to men?[6] But the Atomists denied the main theses of popular theology, namely, that the gods operate causally in the physical world, that they can

---

6 Compare the Atomists' account of perception, pp. 88–91.

interfere in the affairs of men or distribute rewards and punishments. According to the Atomists, the gods are not immaterial spirits. Like everything else that is real, they are material, being composed of particularly small and fine atoms. For the rest, they live a life apart from the world, in solitary blessedness, indifferent to us and our affairs.

### NOTHING IS DESTROYED

Lucretius' second principle—"Nor does [nature] destroy aught into nothing"[h] —completed his version of Parmenides' dictum: Nothing is created and nothing is destroyed. Though, like the earlier pluralists, Lucretius adopted Parmenides' conclusion, here again his reasoning was different. Parmenides had argued simply that, since there is no "nothing," creation out of nothing and destruction into nothing do not occur. Lucretius, for his part, pointed out that if complete destruction, that is, disappearance into nothing, occurred at all, no matter how slowly, everything would sooner or later disappear. Suppose the rate of destruction of matter to be as slow as you like—one cubic centimeter every million years, for instance. It still follows that in an infinite time the whole sum of matter would disappear. Since, according to his argument, the world was not created, it must already have endured an infinite time. Hence, as he said, if there be any destruction at all, "infinite time and the days that are gone by must needs have devoured all things that are of mortal body." It follows, in a word, from the fact that matter exists *now*, that none has ever been destroyed. Thus Lucretius' argument is more empirical than Parmenides': Whereas the latter proceeds from an analysis of the concept of "nothing," the former appeals to a fact—the empirical fact that something exists now.

### THERE IS EMPTY SPACE

Lucretius' third principle was that "There is a void in things."[i] This of course is where the Atomists departed both from Parmenides and from the earlier pluralists, Empedocles and Anaxagoras. Lucretius' argument for the existence of empty space assumes the occurrence of motion. Like Democritus, Lucretius made no attempt to reply to Zeno's denial of the reality of motion; he merely pointed out that since motion is impossible without empty space, there must be empty space. Nor, unless we allow the existence of empty space, can we account for the perviousness of some materials. "Noises," for instance, "creep through walls . . . but were there no empty spaces, along which these bodies might pass, you would not see this come to pass by any means. Again, why do we see one thing surpass another in weight, when its size is no whit bigger? For if there is as much body in a bale of wool as in lead, it is natural it should weigh as much."[j] Here again we see the more empirical tone of Lucretius' reasoning.

### SPACE IS INFINITE

Fourth, Lucretius argued that the void is infinite. If it were finite it would have a boundary, "an extreme point." But

> . . . nothing can have an extreme point, unless there be something beyond to bound it, so that there is seen to be a spot further than which the nature of our sense can follow it. As it is, since we must admit there is nothing outside the whole sum, it has not an extreme point, it lacks therefore bound and limit. Nor does it matter in which quarter of it you take your stand; so true is it that, whatever place every man takes up, he leaves the whole boundless just as much on every side.[k]

Suppose, Lucretius continued, you are standing at the edge of a finite universe. If you were to hurl a dart "with might and main," would it fly towards its goal or would something "check and bar its way"? Whichever you say, you have to admit there is something beyond the point at which you stand. If you say that the dart "fares forward," obviously it is space into which it flies; if you say that the dart is checked, obviously something bars it and this something must be in space. In any case, it is clear that you are not at the final bound of space. Well, then, transport yourself still farther. "Wherever you shall set the furthest coasts, I shall ask what then becomes of the dart? . . . Nowhere can a bound be set, and room for flight ever prolongs the chance of flight." Hence you must "grant that the universe spreads out free from limit," that is, that space is infinite.

### THE NATURE OF ATOMS

So much for the void. Next, as regards matter, Lucretius argued that in addition to being (1) uncreated and (2) indestructible, it consists of (3) an infinite (4) plurality of (5) very small but (6) indivisible particles, that is, atoms. Let us take up the argument for plurality first. Lucretius' argument is that without a plurality of particles no solution of the old dilemma about change is possible; with such a plurality those difficulties are resolvable. Hence, in a way, his basic argument for the existence of a plurality is simply the success of the theory, taken as a whole, in explaining the phenomena it sets out to explain. But this argument would not have been convincing if stated at the outset, when first principles were still being introduced and proved. Accordingly, the actual argument offered at this stage is an appeal to such empirical facts as compressibility. If a sponge, say, were one solid, continuous piece of matter, it could not be squeezed. It must therefore consist of small bits of matter separated by empty space. "Squeezing" is simply forcing these bits of matter closer together. In other words, on the assumption of monism, such phenomena as compressibility are inexplicable and have to be written off as sheer illusion; on the assumption, however, of a plurality of particles, these phenomena can be explained.

The "many" as conceived by the Atomists is not the old plurality of various qualitatively different "kinds." The particles are qualitatively identical (rather, they have *no* qualities such as hot or cold, wet or dry, and so on) and differ only in shape and size.

As regards the number of particles, Lucretius held that it must be infinitely large. Since space is infinite (according to the argument that has been given), a finite number, however large, of particles would become lost in it and the chances of the occurrence of such a world as ours, formed by the collisions of groups of atoms, would be infinitely small. Imagine a number of billiard balls, however many you like, in motion on a billiard table. Now think of the table expanding in area. As the table gets bigger the chances of any of the balls colliding grow smaller, and if the table becomes infinitely large, the chances, Lucretius maintained, become infinitely small. But obviously, he went on, collisions have occurred, since the world does exist. Therefore the number of particles in existence must be infinitely large. This argument assumes, as Lucretius noted, that no "foreseeing mind" arranges the atoms, as an expert billiard player might arrange the billiard balls. The presence of such a player would, of course, increase the chances of collisions occurring, even on a very large table. But Lucretius had already rejected the idea of a "foreseeing mind" on the basis of the first principle of his physics.[7]

Next, Lucretius maintained that though the particles vary considerably in size, they are all very small. Wind, he reasoned, is real, and reality consists of particles; since we do not see the particles that constitute wind, they must be very small. Again, olfactory sensation occurs because a rose, say, gives off particles that, coming in contact with our noses, cause us to experience their scent. These particles must be very small since we do not see them. Similarly, since stones erode very slowly, the particles separating from the mass must be very small, and so on.

The last of Lucretius' basic principles was that though the atoms are very small, they are not infinitely so. Infinite divisibility he held to be ruled out by the arguments about indestructibility, for unless there was a "least part" at which division stopped, the particles would eventually vanish into nothingness. The following argument also shows the influence of Parmenides:

> Moreover, if there be not a least thing, all the tiniest bodies will be composed of infinite parts, since indeed the half of a half will always have a half, nor will anything set a limit. What difference then will there be between the sum of things and the least of things? . . . And since true reasoning cries out against this, and denies that the mind can believe it, you must . . . confess that there are those things which consist of no parts at all and are of the least nature.[1]

7 See p. 79.

Here, then, is Lucretius' version of the basic principles of Democritean physics. Assuming material particles and empty space, he proposed to show how the world of particular things undergoing all sorts of qualitative change could be explained. But for this he also needed motion: "All nature . . . is built of these two things: for there are bodies and the void, in which they are placed and where they move hither and thither." m

Before the Atomists' view of motion is discussed, one general comment must be made. The entities asserted to be real by Lucretius are "intellectual" in the sense that we are persuaded of their existence by a line of reasoning rather than by direct sense perception. (We never *see* atoms or empty space; they are "constructions" developed to account for what we do see.) Yet Lucretius constantly thought of them in terms of sense experience. Thus, according to him, body is that which can be touched, and space is that which cannot be touched. Or again, body is that which acts or is acted upon; space is the locus of this action. But body defined in terms of a sensation (the feeling of tangibility) is quite different from body defined in terms of the requirements of Parmenidean logic. Unfortunately, since Lucretius failed to see the clear difference between the bodies of ordinary experience and the specially defined "body" of his physical theory, he attributed to the latter characteristics of the former. This is an example of the tendency to slip from an abstract into a concrete imagistic way of thought that we have already encountered—in a much cruder form, of course—in Heraclitus' identification of abstract process with material fire. It was to cause Lucretius much trouble, for instance, in his account of motion, to which we now turn.

## The Motion of Atoms

So far, though we have been following Lucretius' account of Atomism, we have been traversing ground on which (with minor exceptions)[8] all the Atomists agreed. However, as regards the motion of the atomic particles, there was diversity of opinion. All the Atomists held, of course, that the qualitative world of sense perception arises from the motions of qualitatively neutral atoms. They also agreed that the immense qualitative variety results from "jostlings" of atoms—to use Lucretius' picturesque phrase—as they collide, bounce apart, and so constantly form new groupings. But how do these complex movements, the "jostlings," get started? On this point the Atomists were in major disagreement.

The question is complicated by the fact that, though there is little doubt about the views of Epicurus and Lucretius, commentators differ as to the opinions of Leucippus and Democritus. It seems likely, however, that Democritus, at least, assumed there never was a time at which the atoms were not "vibrating" in

---

8 The size of the largest atoms and the phenomenon of weight were the principal matters of disagreement.

diverse directions, that is, "jostling" one another in a complicated manner. Thus he avoided the problem of explaining the origin of the complex motions of the atoms by simply affirming that it is their nature to move so. But this left him with an irreducible diversity of motions, which is hardly more satisfactory than Anaxagoras' plurality of irreducible and qualitatively various "seeds." The Greek mind, thirsting always for unity, required an explanation that would somehow "reduce" these complexities to an original simplicity.

At any rate, Epicurus set himself to find some very simple motion from which the varied jostlings of the atoms could be generated. It is instructive to contrast Epicurus' way of going about this with the way a modern scientist—also a seeker after unity and simplicity—might proceed. Presumably, the latter would first measure everything that is measurable about the various motions—times, distances, directions—and then try to find a single mathematical formula (the so-called "law of gravity," for instance) that would describe all the particular motions observed. For him, that is, simplicity would lie in the single "law" found to describe all the diverse motions. But for Epicurus, who knew nothing about experiment and measurement, simplicity lay in an antecedent state of affairs out of which the diverse motions would develop. This antecedent could only be another particular motion, not a generalized description. Further, its simplicity was not the simplicity of a mathematical formula. It had to be a motion that, as it were, "looked simple." As we proceed we shall see that most of the difficulties in Epicurus' account of motion result from the fact that he derived it from sense perception.

At the level of perception, rest seems more "natural" than motion. We may drag ourselves to a lecture or run to first base as the occasion requires, but afterwards we gratefully return to bed or to bench. Surely, with us, who know weariness and sleepiness, it is motion, not rest, that requires an explanation. Similarly, rest seems the natural state of physical objects. A ball or a stone lies on the ground until someone picks it up and throws it; as soon as the impetus thus imparted to it dies away, it returns to its natural state of rest. Hence Epicurus (and Lucretius, who followed him faithfully) was committed to finding a cause that would keep things moving. "Will," whether divine or human, is not the kind of cause that was required. Divine teleology in any form had already been excluded, and human will, along with all the rest of our sense world, was to be explained in terms of motion, not motion in terms of human will.

Now, though a rock clearly does not pick itself up and throw itself through the air, but requires an outside agent to initiate its flight, it will *fall* if there is nothing to hold it up, and it will go on falling as long as there is empty space for it to fall through. Fall through space is the one motion that does not require an outside agent to initiate it; it is therefore just the kind of motion Epicurus was looking for. Moreover, space is something he had plenty of. Indeed, since there is nothing to keep his atoms from starting to fall, and nothing—except other atoms—to stop their fall (for space has no "bounds"), their fall is eternal. There never was a time at which they were not falling; there never will be a time at which they will have ceased to fall. Moreover, in ordinary experience a body falls "straight down" until it hits the ground or some other object. But when it hits another body—when a collision occurs—tangential motions occur. Both bodies may continue to fall, but no longer straight down. Deflected from the vertical, they may collide with other falling bodies and so set up a complex of motions—the sort of thing, to take a gruesome instance, that may happen on a highway when cars pile up on one another after an initial collision.

This is the empirical, common-sense idea of motion that Epicurus incorporated in his physics. He did so because it suggested to him a way of deriving the complex motions or "jostlings" of atoms that his theory required. Atoms and empty space he derived by logical analysis from what doubtless seemed to him "self-evident" premises. Motion he simply took over from exactly that kind of sense experience that the theory was being introduced to explain.

Most of the difficulties in Epicurus' account of motion result from a conflict between these two sources of his theory. First, in the infinite space that logical analysis led him to presuppose, there is no "up" and no "down." Up and down are meaningful directions only in the finite, bounded space of perception. Further, "fall" applies only to a "down" direction. This in itself is not, of course, a serious objection to Epicurus' theory. Instead of talking about "falling," we could say the atoms "travel in straight paths." This avoids the awkwardness of talking about a fall through infinite space. But it creates a difficulty of another kind. Eternal motion in a straight path is not a fact of experience and does not seem "natural" in the way that "fall" does.

But even assuming that all the atoms are moving (or falling) in straight paths, we still have to account for the initial collision that starts off the whole process of the formation of worlds. Once even a single collision occurs, it is possible to assume—the paths of the atoms lie close together—that the tangential paths of the first two atoms after their collision will result in new collisions with different atoms, and these in still more collisions, and so on. But what causes the first collision? Why do two atoms moving (or falling) freely through space ever collide? There must be *some* cause, for an uncaused collision would be creation out of nothing, exactly the kind of arbitrary event that Epicurus wanted to exclude.

If the atoms' paths were curved, collisions might occur, but this possibility was ruled out for Epicurus because he started from our ordinary experience of fall through space, which seems to be straight down. Or, again, if the atoms moved at different velocities, fast atoms might overtake slow ones, even if they traveled in straight paths, and collisions would then ensue. But why should their velocities vary—except, of course, as a matter of convenience to Epicurus' physics?

It could have been suggested that differences in weight cause differences in velocity and that heavy atoms fall faster than light ones. This is doubtless true of objects falling through air or water, because (as Lucretius pointed out) the "thin nature" of these media "gives place more quickly when overcome by heavier bodies." But it does not apply to fall through *empty* space. Since there is nothing in the void itself that could hinder the free fall of the atoms, they all, regardless of differences of weight, must fall at the same velocity. "The empty void cannot on any side, at any time, support anything, but rather . . . it continues to give place; wherefore all things must needs be borne on through the calm void, moving at equal rate with unequal weights. The heavier will not then ever be able to fall upon the lighter from above . . . ."[n]

In this impasse Epicurus fell back on a device even less satisfactory than some of the explanations that he had rightly rejected. This is his doctrine of the "swerve." Immediately after pointing out that differences of weight cannot explain the original collision, Lucretius (faithfully following his master) added: "It must needs be that the first-bodies [atoms] swerve a little; yet not more than the very least, lest we seem to be imagining a sideways movement, and the truth refute it. For this we see plain and evident, that bodies, as far as in them lies, cannot travel sideways, since they fall headlong from above, as far as you can descry. But that nothing at all swerves from the straight direction of its path, what sense is there which can descry?"

Lucretius' embarrassment is evident from the way in which the passage is phrased; it must have been clear to him that this explanation would not do at all. A swerve, if it were to occur, would doubtless account for the original collision, in much the same way that a swing of the hips would account for a man's bumping into someone walking beside him. But why should an atom swerve—except to get the atomic theory out of an insoluble difficulty? Unfortunately, the doctrine of the swerve extricated the theory from one difficulty only by plunging it into another, equally grave.

It will be noted that the swerve was said to be so slight that we cannot detect it. This was doubtless an attempt to reconcile the alleged occurrence of the swerve with the facts of perception, and it reflected Epicurus' (and Lucretius') empirical point of view. But the fact that something would not have been observed had it occurred is no evidence that it in fact occurred. Lucretius had ruled out the possibility of there being any empirical evidence for the swerve, and there was an overriding theoretical argument against it: The swerve was said to be a spontaneous and arbitrary event—a creation out of nothing—which Lucretius had already explicitly ruled out. Atomism claimed to give a complete, mechanistic account for everything, but a spontaneous, uncaused event is just the kind of event that cannot be explained at all.

This can be put another way. Since there is nothing in the past of any atom to cause it rather than any other atom to swerve, it follows that if any atom swerves *at all*, all atoms must have been swerving constantly throughout their fall. In other words, instead of the straight downward fall through all eternity, which Epicurus and Lucretius actually postulated, there would be completely random and erratic movements on the part of all the atoms. This clearly takes us back to the position of Democritus, and, since atoms moving at random might collide, it would solve the difficulty about an initial collision. But Epicurus and Lucretius could not accept this amendment of their theory, both because they were aiming at simplicity and because their conception of atomic movement was rooted in the ordinary perception of a straight downward fall through space. It does not matter how tiny the swerve they presupposed or how infrequent its occurrence. There was no way for them to account for it. In the end they had to admit that the swerve "just happens," that is, that it is an arbitrary and uncreated event.

## The Sensory World

Let us now pass over these difficulties and, for the sake of argument, allow Epicurus and Lucretius their swerve. Given even one swerve the system can develop, for it is plausible to suppose that colliding atoms react in different ways. "Some leap back at great space apart, others are thrust but a short way from the blow." In this way different kinds of groupings of atoms develop. For instance, "those which are driven together in close-packed union and leap back but a little space apart . . . make the strong roots of rock and the brute bulk of iron and all other things of their kind," while the "thin air and the bright light of the sun" are formed by atoms that "leap back far apart," and so on.°

But how, exactly, are the various qualitative particulars of sensation—sun, rocks, iron, and so forth—"made" (to use Lucretius' vague term) from groups of atoms? The atoms themselves do not possess the sense qualities that we experience, and though it is easy to say that out of the movements of atoms the world as we know it develops, what precisely does this mean? If the atoms themselves have only weight, shape, and size, why do we experience them as a world of qualities in which roses are red, violets are blue and any number of people are in love with other people?

On this important point, as on the nature of motion, the Atomists disagreed, and here again the problem is complicated by differences of opinion among commentators as to what the conflicting views were. In this case, however, it is Epicurus' view that is in doubt, and there is more general agreement about Democritus' position. In these difficult circumstances we must proceed as best we can. We shall begin with a brief description of what seems on the whole the most reasonable interpretation of Epicurus' view and then examine Democritus' view, which is not only considerably simpler but also more consistent with the basic principles of Atomism.

### EPICURUS' VIEW

That the atoms themselves lack sense qualities must have been hard for the average man to grasp. Accordingly, Lucretius devoted a good deal of space to explaining this aspect of Epicurus' view.

Come now, listen to [my] discourse . . . lest by any chance you should think that these white things, which you perceive shining bright before your eyes are made of white first-beginnings,[9] or that things which are black are born of black seeds; or should believe that things which are steeped in any other colour you will, bear this colour because the bodies of matter are dyed with a colour like it. For the bodies of matter have no colour at all, neither like things nor again unlike them. . . .

Moreover, if the nature of colour has not been granted to the first-beginnings, . . . you can most easily at once give account, why those things which were a little while before of black colour, are able of a sudden to become of marble whiteness; as the sea, when mighty winds have stirred its level waters, is turned into white waves of shining marble. For you might say that when the substance of that which we often see black has been mingled up, and the order of its first-beginnings changed and certain things added and taken away, straightway it comes to pass that it is seen shining and white. But if the level waters of the ocean were made of sky-blue seeds, they could in no wise grow white. For in whatever way you were to jostle together seeds which are sky-blue, never can they pass into a marble colour. . . .

Moreover, since colours cannot be without light nor do the first-beginnings of things come out into the light, you may know how they are not clothed with any colour. For what colour can there be in blind darkness? . . .

But lest by chance you think that the first-bodies abide bereft only of colour, they are also sundered altogether from warmth and cold, and fiery heat, and are carried along barren of sound and devoid of taste, nor do they give off any scent of their own from their body. . . .[p]

Though individual atoms are thus without color, taste, or other qualities, a group of atoms, brought together temporarily by jostlings, has color and other qualities. The color changes as the constituent atoms of the group change their positions as a result of jostling and blows from without. So, *mutatis mutandis,* for the other sense qualities. To use Lucretius' own terminology, they are "properties," not "accidents," of combinations or collections of atoms. A property is a characteristic that some entity necessarily has; an accident is a characteristic that is temporary and transient. Thus, in accordance with these definitions, color is a property of atomic collections (for all[10] such collections have *some* color or other), and "red" is an accident. Though a collection is necessarily colored, it is not necessarily red. It may have, indeed it will have, many different colors as the collection changes its formation. Again, size and tangibility are properties of *individual* atoms (just as color is a property of *collections* of atoms). Intangibility is a property of the void. On the other hand, it is an accident of the void

9 [Lucretius used this expression instead of the Greek term "atom." The argument here is, of course, directed against Anaxagoras—AUTHOR.]

10 To speak with absolute precision, it ought rather to be said, as Bailey would have it, that color is a property of all *visible* bodies.

that this or that particular part of it should be full or empty at any particular time. Similarly, it is an accident of any *individual* atom that it should be at any particular place at any particular time (just as it is an accident of any collection of atoms that it should have any particular color at any particular time).

There are many difficulties with this view. In the first place, although there is a clear distinction, logically, between what is and what is not a necessary characteristic, this distinction is not illuminating when applied to the relation of sense qualities to atoms. It is easy to see why Lucretius wanted to say that sense qualities are the "properties" of atoms: The term suggests that they really belong to the atoms, in the way, for instance, that a man's landed property belongs to him. But this is merely a metaphor, for properties obviously do not "belong" to atoms in the way that a piece of real estate belongs to its owner. Nonetheless, Lucretius never got beyond this metaphor to any precise account of the necessity with which a sense quality belongs to a group of atoms.

Second, the atoms are "out there" in space, apart from us. If the sense qualities are the properties of atoms, not properties of us, presumably they too are out there in space. But where exactly are they? They cannot occupy exactly the space that the atoms themselves occupy, for the atoms of course wholly fill that space. Do they occupy an adjoining space? Or do they perhaps fill the interstices between the atoms of the particular group that we experience as having such-and-such a color? Both alternatives seem very odd.

And there is an even graver difficulty: What sort of ontological status do sense qualities have? The answer is that they can have none in Epicurus' system, for in this system only atoms and the void are real. Is some property (for instance, color) an atom? Obviously not. Is it the void? Again, no. Is it a group of atoms? No, not exactly. It is a "property," or an "accompaniment" (to use Epicurus' equally vague term), of a group of atoms. But this explains nothing; it only sidesteps the issue and hides under a name. For an accompaniment, whatever it may be, is neither an atom nor a void; since these alone are real, an accompaniment is only a subjective phenomenon. It is not a part of the real world.

## DEMOCRITUS' VIEW

This, in fact, was the view of Democritus. Unlike Epicurus, he reduced the question of the ontological status of sense qualities to a problem in the physiology of perception. Put briefly, his theory amounts to this: We say, for instance, that a rose looks red, smells sweet, and so forth. This sensed rose, of course, is not real, for only atoms and the void are real. "Out there," in the space where we sense the rose, atoms are colliding and bouncing off one another and so forming a certain configuration. As this continues, some atoms are flung off from the group, and some of these fall on our sense organs—on our eyes, our nostrils, and so on. Now, of course, what we call a sense organ is, like the rose, only a number of atoms moving together (relatively speaking) and so forming another collection.

When we look at this particular collection or pattern we sense an eye, just as when we look at that other one we sense a rose.

When the atoms flung off by the pattern that we call a rose strike those other atoms that we call an eye, the former set up a motion in the latter (as a billiard ball flung into a group of stationary balls sets them in motion), and this motion, communicated to other atoms by way of the optic nerve (itself, of course, really another collection of atoms with another configuration), eventually produces the sensation that we know and experience as "rose." Thus, unlike Epicurus, Democritus drew a radical distinction between the world as it really is (that is, as it was known to be by atomistic physicists like Democritus) and the world as it appears to sense perception.

Though this type of view has been frequently revived since Democritus' day and is even held in some quarters today, it is full of paradoxes. For instance, ordinary people would be inclined to say that the world as it appears to sense perception *is* the real world. Of course they know about illusions and hallucinations, but they also know how to discount them. Sense perception, they might say, corrects sense perception: We find out that a mirage is a mirage because, when we get close enough to it, it disappears. So these people would say, first, that what we see when we are close enough and when lighting conditions are good is real and, second, that all viewers see the same world. Democritus, in contrast, maintained that *all* that each viewer sees is an illusion, in the strict sense that what we see is wholly different from what is real (atoms and the void). Further, Democritus held that sense perception never corrects sense perception: We never escape this illusion at the level of perception, but only in thought, by means of the atomic theory. Finally, according to Democritus, every viewer views a different illusion: There are as many appearances as there are viewers.

This is bad enough, but there is an even worse paradox. To whom is the world of sense perception an appearance? "Viewer" as used in the sentences above is so vague that it lends Democritus' theory a specious plausibility. A viewer turns out to be some particular sense organ, and a sense organ is a collection of atoms. So Democritus' position is that one set of atoms in motion out there appears as a rose to another set of atoms in motion over here. Read over the sentences two paragraphs above in which Democritus' theory is described and notice how the word "we" has crept in: ". . . this motion, communicated to other atoms by way of the optic nerve . . . eventually produces the sensation that we know and experience as 'rose.'" But it is quite illegitimate to introduce a "we" that is supposedly doing the experiencing. There is no "we"; there are only atoms in motion. Does it really make any sense to say that one set of atoms experiences another set as red, solid, and extended?

## ATOMISM'S REPLY TO SOPHISM

Passing over the grave problems in which their theories of sense perception are involved, we can appreciate that both Democritus and Epicurus were attempting to reply to the scepticism expressed in Protagoras' "every man is the measure" formula. According to Protagoras and the other Sophists, if I judge an object to be green and you judge it to be blue, we are both right because each of us, judging only by his own experience, is the measure of that experience for himself. The Sophists held that there is no more disputing about, say, colors than about tastes. In both cases, however much we may think we are judging about the same object, we are actually judging about different objects. All disagreements, therefore, result from an illusion, specifically from a failure to realize that each of us, shut inside the world of his own experience, is judging about objects in *that* experience. This radical scepticism led, as we have seen, to all sorts of difficulties and paradoxes, so that an account of the phenomena of sense perception that would have reinstated a public sense world was most desirable.

Epicurus' theory, if it were otherwise acceptable, would have done just this. According to Epicurus, greenness is "out there" along with the collection of atoms that we call, say, a cabbage. Hence, if you judge the cabbage to be blue, you are mistaken; you are saying that what is really green is blue. In a word, when we judge about the color of the cabbage we are not judging about our private experiences but about a public quality. It would follow from this (if only Epicurus' analysis of sense perception were correct) that a man is *not* the measure of all his experiences. Unfortunately, as we have seen, Epicurus' theory has to be rejected on other grounds, so his reply to the Sophists is ineffectual.

At first sight it may look as if Democritus' account of sense perception concedes everything to the subjectivists, and this is probably why Epicurus abandoned it. In Democritus' view the color of the cabbage is not out there in real space. He held, indeed, that there is no "the" color of the cabbage. What each of us calls "the" color is only the way in which each of us experiences a motion set up in us by atoms out there. It follows that each of us experiences a private color and that there are as many colors as there are experiencers of the cabbage. For each of these colors each experiencer is obviously the measure. All of this Democritus explicitly admitted. Using language made fashionable by the Sophists[11] he said: "By convention sweet is sweet; by convention bitter is bitter; by convention hot is hot; by convention cold is cold; by convention color is color. But in reality there are atoms and the void. That is, the objects of sense are supposed to be real and it is customary to regard them as such, but in truth they are not. Only the atoms and the void are real."[q]

It is the last sentence that distinguishes Democritus from the Sophists. Since, according to him, atoms and the void really exist, each individual is not, as the Sophists maintained, the measure of *all* things. Besides the *nomoi* of sense qualities, there is an underlying *physis*, and this *physis* is one of the factors involved

---

11 For a discussion of the Sophistic contrast between nature and convention see p. 68.

in perception. For perception—the sensory experience—is a product. Though the color I see is in part a result of motions in my eye and my optic nerve, it is also in part the product of something out there—the collection of atoms that, loosely speaking, we call the cabbage. This collection of atoms contributes in the same way, in conjunction with *your* eye and *your* optic nerve, to the formation of the private color that *you* see. Hence, over and above the private color each of us sees, there is a public reality—colorless to be sure, but nevertheless a common basis for our various private colors. The atoms, according to Democritus' theory, are what they are, independently of men and their judgments. They are the measure of every man, as it were, in the sense that they are a *physis* against which the truth or falsity of all our judgments can be weighed.

It follows that Democritus did not have to analyze the judgment, "That cabbage is green," in the same way that the Sophists analyzed it. According to the Sophists, this statement means, and can only mean, "I am now having a sensation of green." Since the judgment, so analyzed, is about my private state of mind, it is infallible; nobody can contest it. (Of course, by the same token, I cannot argue with you or prove that you are mistaken if you judge that the cabbage is magenta. I can only bash you over the head until you give in and cry, "Green!") Now, according to Democritus' view, when I judged that the cabbage is green, I may of course be merely reporting a private experience; but I am not necessarily doing so. I may be judging about the public objective component that is in both your experience and mine. Thus "That cabbage is green" is analyzable into: "The atoms in that part of space are in such-and-such a configuration, a configuration that, in conjunction with eyes like mine (more atoms, of course, in such-and-such another configuration), produces the experience of 'green,' and that, in conjunction with eyes like yours, produces the experience of 'magenta.'" Since this judgment is about public atoms, not about private sensations, it is either true or false. If you disagree with me, you are not contesting my private feeling (about which I am obviously infallible); you are rejecting my account of a public situation. One of us is mistaken.

So far this discussion of the Atomists' answer to Sophistic scepticism has been limited to the field of sense perception. But the Sophists did not confine their subjectivism to sense perception. They were equally sceptical, for instance, about the possibility of obtaining knowledge of a public reality by processes of thought. It is obvious that this was a crucial point for the Atomists. Their account of sense perception depends on there being atoms and a void, but these alleged realities are obviously not known by perception but by thought. Hence, unless they could validate thought as a means by which we have access to reality, their answer to the Sophists—even at the level of sense perception itself—remained incomplete.

The Sophists also denied the objectivity of values. For them ethics and politics were meaningless inquiries. Since all values, they said, are merely matters of taste, let everyone do what he likes. We shall therefore have to see whether the Atomists were able to give an account of values that met this sceptical attack.

## Psychology

These inquiries require us to turn from the Atomists' account of the world in general to their account of the nature of man. Obviously, to their minds, men—like everything else in the world—are really nothing but congeries of atoms. The mind is material; it is just as much a physical organ, Lucretius held, as are "the hand and foot and eyes." The only ontological difference between men and, say, billiard balls is the degree of complexity in the groups of the atoms involved. A billiard ball is being bombarded by atoms from the cabbage just as I am, but it does not perceive the cabbage. Why? Because none of its atoms happen to be grouped into that configuration of atoms that we call a mind. Because of this, the particular motions that we call (and experience as) "seeing the cabbage" do not occur in the billiard ball.

### NATURE OF THOUGHT

Thought—for instance, thinking about the high cost of cabbages, as distinct from perceiving some particular cabbage—is simply another motion. Like sensation, thought is a movement of mind-atoms; it is distinguished from sensation simply by the fact that it is a more direct movement. Sensation is a movement of mind-atoms via some sense organ; thought occurs when smaller and "finer" atoms pass through the pores of our bodies and strike directly on the mind-atoms. Thought, therefore, is truer, because it is more direct, than sensation. Thus when we sense an object out there we experience it, not as it really is, but as a colored, solid thing with all sorts of qualities. When, however, we think about it, we know that it really is atoms moving in empty space. This difference between the object as it appears to sense perception (*nomos*) and the object as thought comes to know that it really is (*physis*) is the difference between two motions of our mind-atoms.

> Come now, let me tell you what things stir the mind, and learn in a few words whence come the things which come into the understanding. First of all I say this, that many idols of things wander about in many ways in all directions on every side, fine idols, which . . . are far finer in their texture than those which fill the eyes and arouse sight, since these pierce through the pores of the body and awake the fine nature of the mind within, and arouse its sensation. . . .
>
> That these things come to pass as I tell, you may easily learn from this.

Inasmuch as the one is like the other, what we see with the mind, and what we see with the eyes, they must needs be created in like manner. Now, therefore, since I have shown that I see a lion maybe, by means of idols, which severally stir the eyes, we may know that the mind is moved in like manner, in that it sees a lion and all else neither more nor less than the eyes, except that it sees finer idols. . . .

And in these matters many questions are asked, and there are many things we must make clear, if we wish to set forth the truth plainly. First of all it is asked why, whatever the whim may come to each of us to think of, straightway his mind thinks of that very thing. Do the idols keep watch on our will, and does the image rise up before us, as soon as we desire, whether it pleases us to think of sea or land or sky either? Gatherings of men, a procession, banquets, battles, does nature create all things at a word, and make them ready for us? And that when in the same place and spot the mind of others is thinking of things all far different. . . . It comes to pass that in any time however small the several idols are there ready at hand in all the several spots. So great is the speed, so great the store of things. Therefore when the first image passes away and then another comes to birth in a different posture, the former seems then to have changed its gesture. Again, because they are fine, the mind cannot discern them sharply, save those which it strains to see; therefore all that there are besides these pass away, save those for which it has made itself ready. Moreover, the mind makes itself ready, and hopes it will come to pass that it will see what follows upon each several thing; therefore it comes to be. Do you not see the eyes too, when they begin to perceive things which are fine, strain themselves and make themselves ready, and that without that it cannot come to pass that we see things sharply? And yet even in things plain to see you might notice that, if you do not turn your mind to them, it is just as if the thing were sundered from you all the time, and very far away. How then is it strange, if the mind loses all else, save only the things to which it is itself given up?[r]

This account of the nature of thought is the only one possible based on the Atomists' premises. If nothing is real except atoms and the void, it is necessary either to deny that thought occurs or to identify it with the movements of atoms in the void.

But is this identification plausible? or even meaningful? If the Atomists' account of the nature of thought were correct, would they ever have been able to work out their atomic theory about the nature of thought? According to the theory, Democritus, Epicurus, and Lucretius came to the conclusion that the world is really nothing but atoms and the void because some atoms from "outside" happened to strike their mind-atoms directly, instead of mediately, via a sense organ. Because the motions of these atoms were not disturbed by intervening sense organs, they revealed themselves as they really are, not as they appear to eyes, ears, tongue. However, if the theory originated in this way, why did it not occur much earlier and to many more people? How did it happen that Democritus, Epicurus, and Lucretius were the first men in whom these motions were set up, when literally millions of these tiny atoms had been constantly falling on men's mind-atoms for literally thousands of years?

Even allowing this immense implausibility, the theory presents grave difficulties on other grounds. According to the theory, thought is essentially a kind of visual perception, but better than ordinary perception because it by-passes the eye and reaches the mind directly. Hence (if the theory is correct) thinking is like seeing. When we want to look at something small or obscure we try to move closer to it or get it into a better light. But does anyone suppose that the thinking by means of which the Atomists reached this theory was at all like what the theory holds thinking to be? When Democritus was trying to decide whether such-and-such a thesis of Empedocles' was correct, did he ask himself, "Is the light right?" or "Would I do better with a magnifying glass?" Of course not.

Even a superficial examination of the way the Atomists actually proceeded shows that their account of the nature of thought is mistaken. The Atomists in fact used the principle of noncontradiction. For instance, Lucretius argued that there must be an infinite number of atoms because, if there were not, the world would never have come into being. Such-and-such, he said in effect, cannot be the case because it contradicts something else. (Similar arguments have been used in this text in criticisms of Epicurus and Lucretius. For instance, the swerve has been rejected because it is inconsistent with other propositions previously accepted by Epicurus and Lucretius.) But the rules of logic (such as the rule of noncontradiction) are very different from mechanical laws of motion, and the logical relation between the premises and the conclusion of a valid argument is very different from the cause-and-effect relation that, according to the Atomists' theory, exists between successive states of mind-atoms. When the mind is reasoning well—when it is "moving" from premises to a valid conclusion in accordance with the rules of logic—the order of the propositions that are successively before it is determined by considerations of logic, not by the mechanical motion of atoms.

Consider any piece of reasoning. Suppose we know that (1) all men are mortal and that (2) all Greeks are men. From these two propositions we would conclude that (3) all Greeks are mortal. Why do we conclude that all Greeks are mortal? Surely it is because we recognize that the premises imply the conclusion—because we detect a logical relation of entailment connecting propositions (1) and (2) with proposition (3).

On the basis of the atomic theory of the nature of thought, an Atomist would have to give a very different account of the process of reaching proposition (3). He would have to hold that what has been called "understanding" propositions (1) and (2) is really just a complex motion and that what has been called "detecting a logical relationship" between these propositions and proposition (3) is just the further mechanical development of this motion. The Atomist would not (or rather, should not) talk about "evidence" or "implication" or "premises and conclusion." For he would hold that the motion we call "reasoning out the conclusion" differs in no way from the motion of a billiard ball crossing a billiard table. In both cases the sequence is mechanical; in both cases velocity and direction at any given moment are completely determined by antecedent states of the moving body. Hence, according to the Atomists' theory, if my mind proceeds from propositions (1) and (2) to proposition (3), it is not because I recognize that the premises imply this conclusion; it is just because the initial motions of my mind-atoms had the velocity and direction they happened to have.

If reasoning were such a purely mechanical movement, the Atomists could never have discovered it. If the thought that goes into the mathematical description of, say, a billiard ball's motion were not different in essence from the motion it describes, it would be impossible for scientists to work out such descriptions.

Of course, to reduce logic to psychology in refuting the Atomists' theory would be as much a mistake in its own way as their reduction of logic to physics. Rather, it should be said that mental processes cannot be exhaustively described in terms of mere mechanical relations. This applies to mental processes quite generally. Logical connections are but one example (an important one, of course) of such nonmechanistic relations.

### THE PROBLEM OF FREE WILL

There are still other difficulties involved in the Atomists' account of the nature of thought, but it will be convenient to postpone consideration of them until the Atomists' view of volition has been examined. The main question on this score is: Could the Atomists give a reasonable account of such phenomena as those we call "choosing" and "deciding"? Nothing seems more evident to ordinary men than their ability to make plans and act on them and, generally, to alter the course of events by choosing to do so. Thus, as you sit reading these lines you might feel that, had you so chosen, you could be elsewhere, playing golf or talking with friends. Though you cannot do *anything* that you will (you probably could not jump through the ceiling even if you willed very hard to do so), there are many things over which you feel you have control—whether you think now about the atomic theory, whether you get up for a lecture or sleep through it. These you feel you could either do or abstain from doing, depending on how you decide.

Is this feeling of freedom, of the power of willing "as you decide," mistaken? It is very difficult to see how, according to the Atomists' theory, it can be other than an illusion. For the atoms that make up what you call your body are in a certain configuration at the moment when you try to decide whether to stay in bed or to get up and struggle to an eight o'clock lecture. Your thought about getting up is really just a complex motion of a certain kind, according to the Atomists. If the motion were different, the thought would be different, just as different motions set up in your eye cause you to experience different colors, because the thought or the color is nothing but the way in which you experience the particular motion in question.

At this moment, while you lie in bed, a certain complex motion occurs (your mind-atoms are agitated and "jostled" in a certain way), and this motion is experienced by you as a dubiety about attending a lecture. But why does this particular motion occur? Obviously, because the atoms that form your mind have been bumped and buffeted in just this particular way, at just this velocity, and from just this direction, by some other atoms. And why were those other atoms moving at that velocity and in that direction at just that time? Because a moment earlier they were hit by other atoms moving at some particular velocity and in some particular direction, and so on. As far back as you choose to trace the course of events, you will find that the motions of the atoms at any particular time were determined to be precisely what they were by certain antecedent motions. And, since time extends infinitely into the past, there never was a time at which the motions occurring were not determined by antecedent motions. Hence the whole antecedent state of the universe has determined the motion of your mind-atoms at this moment; they could not be moving in any other way or at any other velocity.

Now consider the moment after this one. You get up, not because your roommate has literally dragged you out of bed, but because (as you might say) you "decided" to go to the lecture. You believe that you "chose" to get up and that you could just as well have chosen to stay in bed. But what, according to the atomic theory, is happening? Obviously, the activity of "deciding to get up" is simply another motion of your mind-atoms and is determined by the antecedent motions of those atoms. Hence, however much you may *think* that you "chose" and that you could have chosen otherwise, your getting up is the necessary result of antecedent events. Given those antecedent motions, which were themselves determined by still earlier motions, you have to get up at just this moment. Hence your feeling that you might have chosen to stay in bed is an illusion. But it is a necessary illusion. The whole course of past events has not only determined that you shall get up at this moment but also that you shall experience at this moment the feeling of being free to stay in bed.

Democritus accepted the conclusion that human behavior is completely determined. But Epicurus was characteristically loath to adopt a theory so opposed to ordinary beliefs. We do have freedom of choice, he held, and he attempted to utilize the swerve to account for it. There is not only, he argued, that initial swerve that started off the complex of motions by which a world is formed. Other swerves occur from time to time, and these occasions are precisely those on which, as we say, we make a free choice. Thus, for instance, there might be a sequence of motions of mind-atoms: $M_1$, $M_2$, $M_3$, and so on. Normally $M_3$ (lying in bed thinking about getting up) is followed by $M_4$ (getting up), but on one particular morning when the motions reach the $M_3$ stage, one of the mind-atoms suddenly swerves. As a result the mind-atoms are sent into stage $M_4'$ (rolling over and going back to sleep) instead of $M_4$. As Lucretius said,

> If every motion is always linked on, and the new always arises from the old in order determined, . . . whence comes this free will for living things all over the earth, whence, I ask, is it wrested from fate, this will whereby

we move forward where pleasure leads each one of us, and swerve likewise in our motions neither at determined times nor in a determined direction of place, but just where our mind has carried us? For without doubt it is his own will which gives to each one a start for this movement, and from the will the motions pass flooding through the limbs. . . . Do you not then now see that, albeit a force outside pushes many men and constrains them often to go forward against their will and to be hurried away headlong, yet there is something in our breast, which can fight against it and withstand it? And at its bidding too the store of matter is constrained now and then to turn throughout the limbs and members, and, when pushed forward, is reined back and comes to rest again. Wherefore in the seeds too you must needs allow likewise that there is another cause of motion besides blows and weights, whence comes this power born in us, since we see that nothing can come to pass from nothing. For weight prevents all things coming to pass by blows, as by some force without. But that the very mind feels not some necessity within in doing all things, and is not constrained like a conquered thing to bear and suffer, this is brought about by the tiny swerve of the first-beginnings in no determined direction of place and at no determined time.[s]

But the swerve is as inadequate as a psychological concept as it has been shown to be in physics. For the swerve is complete indeterminism, sheer chance, whereas "free choice" implies a particular kind of causality. Of course, we believe that some of our behavior *is* a matter of chance. When we miss a serious wreck because we travel on an earlier train than that we originally intended to take, we may say that it is "sheer luck." We believe that other acts, however, grow out of our character. Though these acts certainly do not seem to us mechanically caused, we refuse to admit that we could do otherwise. A man habituated to honest dealing might say (and mean) when he confesses to a misdeed, "I could not lie." Though he would claim that he "freely chose" to tell the truth, he would deny that this "just happened" as a result of the arbitrary swerve of an atom. Thus, though the swerve was brought into the Atomists' theory of human behavior to save us from a complete determinism that contradicts the felt facts of introspection, it is no more compatible with the facts of introspection than is the assertion of a closed causal system.

The examples given by Lucretius in the passages just quoted only serve to emphasize this difficulty in the Atomists' theory. Many people have had the experience of "something in our breast that can fight against and withstand" coercion or temptation. But this is quite different from a swerve of some mind-atom. A swerve is just a sudden bolt from the blue, and a bolt from the blue is not a satisfactory explanation of what is felt as decision and volition.

## FURTHER DIFFICULTIES IN THE ATOMISTS' ACCOUNT OF THOUGHT

This difficulty about volition naturally infected Epicurus' and Lucretius' account of the nature of thought. We are able, as Lucretius said, to "turn the mind" now to this, now to that. This phenomenon of the control of attention is of course familiar to everybody, but how could Atomism account for it? Suppose you are now thinking about the highest point in the United States. You are doing so, according to the theory, because atoms from Mount Whitney are now passing through the pores of your body and jostling your mind-atoms. But atoms from Mount Whitney must often jostle your mind-atoms when you are not thinking about the highest point in the United States (for it seems implausible to suppose that these atoms, which are constantly streaming away from the mountain, should suddenly begin jostling your mind-atoms when you begin thinking about the mountain and cease their jostling when you cease thinking about it). And, in any case, atoms from great numbers of other objects must be jostling your mind-atoms at the same time that you are thinking of Mount Whitney. Why do you think of Mount Whitney instead of these other objects? If the atomic hypothesis were correct, your thought at any moment would be a melange of images corresponding to the compound motions set up by all the different sets of atoms jostling your mind-atoms at that moment.

Lucretius tried to get around these difficulties about the nature of attention by appealing to the doctrine of the swerve. Out of all the atoms falling now on your mind-atoms, you choose to attend to those that come from Mount Whitney, and this is why you happen to be thinking of the highest point in the United States. It is as if you owned a searchlight that you can turn in any direction you choose and that, as you turn it, illumines some narrow segment in the rain of atoms constantly bombarding your mind-atoms. But, according to the swerve theory, the fact that you choose to train your searchlight of attention on this, rather than some other, group of atoms is pure chance. And once again, we do not believe our thought is as random and as hit-or-miss as this.

There are still more difficulties with the Atomists' account of the nature of thought. On this theory *all* thought is imagistic, for all thought is a product of atoms flung off by physical objects and striking and jostling our mind-atoms. This is plausible as long as we are thinking of physical objects—objects like Mount Whitney, or a childhood friend, or the roast of beef we had for dinner yesterday. But many so-called "objects of thought" are not physical objects at all. What if you are thinking about the Constitution of the United States? It is far-fetched to say that the object of your thought is a particular piece of parchment in the National Archives.

And what, according to the Atomists' view, is the source of abstract ideas? What if you are thinking, not of the United States Constitution, but of constitutions in general? The best the Atomists could do was to say that the source of this thought is still some physical object (for example, the document in the National Archives). But in this case, because of the buffeting the atoms receive as they pass through the air, the object reaches you with its outlines blurred and lacking specific detail. This explanation seems clearly inadequate. For one thing, it fails to draw a distinction between abstract thought and confused visual memory. For another, it fails to take account of the difference between the idea of a particular thing and the idea of a class of things. It is certainly very implausible to hold that when you are entertaining the abstract idea of constitutional, as opposed to arbitrary, government, your mind-atoms are being bombarded by atoms torn out of a lot of particular pieces of paper. Yet this, it would seem, is the nearest the Atomists could get to the notion of a genus or a class.

## Ethics

So far an attempt has been made to give a general account of the Atomists' views about the nature of the world and of man. Such a generalized discussion is possible because, though Epicurus and Lucretius made important changes in Democritus' physical theory, these modifications do not alter the fact that Atomism was a concerted attempt to solve the dilemma about change and the other problems that had led to Sophistic scepticism. The differences among the Atomists on ethical questions were much more fundamental. In this section, therefore, we shall confine ourselves to a consideration of Democritus' views.[12]

Though Democritus seems to have been much less interested in the problems of conduct than in general physical theory, it is possible from existing fragments to see that his ethical teachings were noble and exalted.

> If any one hearken with understanding to these sayings of mine many a deed worthy of a good man shall he perform and many a foolish deed be spared.
> If one choose the goods of the soul, he chooses the diviner [portion]; if the goods of the body, the merely mortal.
> 'Tis not in strength of body nor in gold that men find happiness, but in uprightness and in fulness of understanding.
> Not from fear but from a sense of duty refrain from your sins.
> He who does wrong is more unhappy than he who suffers wrong.
> Strength of body is nobility in beasts of burden, strength of character is nobility in men.
> Those who have a well-ordered character lead also a well-ordered life.
> Men achieve tranquillity through moderation in pleasure and through symmetry of life. Want and superfluity are apt to upset them and to cause great perturbations in the soul. The souls that are rent by violent conflicts are neither stable nor tranquil. One should therefore set his mind upon the things that are within his power, and be content with his opportunities, nor let his memory dwell very long on the envied and admired of men, nor idly

12 For an account of Epicurus' and Lucretius' ethical theories see pp. 317–25.

sit and dream of them. . . . Holding fast to this saying you will pass your life in greater tranquillity and will avert not a few of the plagues of life—envy and jealousy and bitterness of mind.

The end of action is tranquillity, which is not identical with pleasure, as some by a false interpretation have understood, but a state in which the soul continues calm and strong, undisturbed by any fear or superstition or any other emotion.[t]

These fragments suggest that Democritus' interest in ethics was practical rather than theoretical. He was chiefly concerned with what he called "practical wisdom," that is, with communicating his views on how to live well in a form calculated to induce others to follow them. And the practical wisdom he taught was essentially the old Greek ideal of moderation and reasonableness, coupled with a strong sense of the importance of motive and disposition as contrasted with mere external conformity.

There is certainly no reason why Democritus should not have interested himself in improving ethical practice. But it is surprising that one whose physical theory was largely designed to meet the Sophists' sceptical attack on the objectivity of the physical world did not also seek to deal with their parallel attack on the objectivity of value. And it is clear that Democritus did indeed hold, in opposition to the Sophists, that values are objective. When he said that moderation is better than violence and that happiness lies in leading a well-ordered life rather than in pleasure-seeking, he did not regard himself as merely expressing a private sentiment: He claimed that these are statements about a *physis*, not merely about *nomoi*. But the question is whether he was justified, in terms of his own physical theory, in making this claim. Since he did not work out a theory of value (or if he did, it has not survived), let us see what account of values can be given in a universe in which only atoms and the void are real.

On analogy with his theory of the physiology of sense perception, it would seem that Democritus could have argued that there are both objective and subjective elements in value experience. When I judge that the cabbage is green, I may be judging about only a private sensation, but I may also be judging about the motions of atoms out there in physical space—motions that are a causal component in producing those motions in my body that I experience subjectively as "green." Similarly, when I judge, "The cabbage is good" or "Cabbages are better than cauliflowers," I may be judging about only a private sentiment—the way these vegetables taste to me. But I may also be judging that cabbages are higher in vitamin C than cauliflowers and that vitamin C counteracts respiratory infection. Statements concerning the presence or absence of vitamin C in the vegetables and the effect that a given quantity of vitamin C has on my body are statements about the motions of atoms, out there in the object and in here in my body. What we call vitamin C is a certain characteristic motion of atoms, and the frequency of the occurrence of this configuration in cabbages can be ascertained.

Further, predictions about value experiences are possible according to a Democritean theory of values, just as predictions about sensory experiences are possible. If enough were known about your body and the particular configurations of motions that occur in it, it would be possible to predict that in the presence of cabbage, to take a previously mentioned example, motions would be set up in you that you would experience as "magenta," though in most bodies the motions produced by these stimuli are experienced as "green." In the same way, if we knew enough about your body and mine, we could predict that whenever the motions occurred that we call eating chocolate ice cream, you would experience the sentiment of liking and I would experience the sentiment of disliking. So, again, we could predict that you and I would judge, "Lying is wrong" and that Callicles and Thrasymachus would judge, "OK to lie, if you can get away with it." Thus the fact that different men make radically different evaluations of the same object or event does not support the Sophists' claim that values are *wholly* subjective. Granted, there is a subjective element in all such judgments. But there is also an objective element—the motion out there that causes those changes in our bodies that we experience as sentiments of approbation and disapprobation. We would expect the same motion out there to cause different motions in different bodies; if we knew enough about the motion out there and if we understood how one body differs from another, we could predict the differential effects that would occur in these bodies and so account for the fact that ice cream is variously liked and disliked, that lying is alternatively praised and condemned.

Since the atoms and their movements are objectively real, statements about them are verifiable in the ordinary way. It follows that knowledge about values is possible on the Atomistic hypothesis. Thus a science *about* ethics is possible. But is this a science *of* ethics? The Atomists made a place for knowledge in the field of ethics only by reducing values—that is, the felt, appreciated, enjoyed experiences themselves—to an illusion. A necessary illusion, it is true, but still an illusion. This exactly parallels the paradox already discussed about the ontological status of the sense world. In the Atomists' view an ethical judgment is analyzable into an objective component and a subjective component. A movement of atoms occurs that is the objective component. When it occurs, an appreciator—an evaluator—experiences a value. But who is the appreciator? Like the viewer of the sense world, an appreciator turns out to be only a collection of atoms; in the Atomists' view one set of atoms values another set of atoms. This, to say the least, is very odd. And apart from this puzzle, the value experienced (the enjoyment, the appreciation) is no more real than is the evaluator of this experience, for only atoms and the void are real. The goodness of moderation that Democritus experienced is as much an illusion (a necessary illusion) as the greenness of the cabbage he saw. To put this differently, what is objective in the Atomists' theory of value is not valuable, and what is valuable is not objective.

## Evaluation of Atomism

Some serious objections to certain aspects of Atomism have been raised here, but taken as a whole it was an immense achievement, vastly superior to anything that had preceded it as well as to much that was to follow it. It did not appeal to faith or authority, but to logic and evidence. All the major concepts in the theory—matter, void, motion, and so on—are defined in ways that enable us to comprehend their meanings. Since the theory does not deal with anything that is not matter in motion, we are always in a position to understand it, even if we disagree with it. Epicurus' account of the gods is a case in point. With other philosophers and theologians it is often extremely difficult to discover exactly what was meant by the term "god." There is no doubt, however, about what Epicurus *meant* by god: a complicated collection of very fine atoms. Whether gods, as he defined them, exist would therefore be theoretically possible to determine. Whether this definition would satisfy the requirements of religion is, of course, another question. The penalty of saying quite unambiguously what one thinks about the gods—or about anything else—is that some people are going to disagree violently. Since the virtue of clarity always has the consequence of exposing any weakness in a theory, we should be on our guard against assuming that Atomism contained more confusions and contradictions than philosophies that hide their inadequacies behind a mass of esoteric verbiage that each reader understands as he chooses.

Take the matter of contradiction. It is true that Epicurus and Lucretius contradicted themselves badly on the swerve. But the point is that they formulated the first principles of their physics so lucidly and developed them so systematically that latent contradictions are easy to detect. Accordingly, there is the possibility of removing them and so improving the theory. Indeed, this particular contradiction is not intrinsic. It resulted from assumptions resting on a naïve sense experience of motion. Thus, though the theory as it stands breaks down badly, it would probably be possible to recast it in a satisfactory form, free from contradictions. Details apart, the Atomists' conception of nature as a vast system of motions occurring in an absolutely regular way is identical with that which has dominated modern culture since the seventeenth century. To have sketched the general outlines of such a philosophy of nature was certainly a great accomplishment. More particularly, and of perhaps more importance in their own day, the Atomists finally gave a definitive answer to Thales' question.

Thales had believed that, in spite of all its diversity, the world is one, and this one he had assumed to be a particular material stuff. This way of putting the matter implied of course that what is one is also many and that one sort of stuff "becomes" another. It was the function of Parmenides to state clearly all the difficulties that the later Milesians and Heraclitus had felt in Thales' formulation and to show that his question was incapable of being answered in its original form. It is a testimony to the extraordinary tenacity of this Milesian point of view that, despite the contradictions Parmenides had exposed, the pluralists tried to reformulate Thales' position instead of simply abandoning it.

Their reformulation admittedly has taken us a long way from Thales. We end with a "many" instead of a "one"; atoms are very different from water, of which Thales vaguely thought all things are made. Even the concept of "cause" has radically altered. From the notion of a simple transformation of one thing into another (water into air or earth or ice), the Atomists advanced to the notion that only motion in the sense of change of place is real and that all other forms of change are reducible to, and so appearances of, this kind of change. How, then, in the face of such radical alterations, can Atomism be called a "reformulation" of Thales' position? It is not just because of the historical connection that has been outlined. It is also (and this is much more important) because all the thinkers from Thales to the Atomists made a common assumption—that reality is *material* and that what happens to this material, the natural process that it undergoes, is intelligible.

Of course the notion of material, or of "stuff," underwent an important development between Thales and the Atomists. Thales' conception of stuff was vague. Water, he thought, is a stuff; so are air and fire. If we asked what he meant by saying that they are stuffs, the answer probably would be in terms of such ordinary sense properties as being touchable, visible, tastable, and so on. By the time we reach the Atomists we have come a long way from this naïve notion. Atomic "stuff" is no longer simply a sense-stuff. It has lost all these sense qualities,[13] which were primary for Thales and the other early philosophers, and is now thought to consist of colorless, soundless, tasteless particles varying only in shape and size. In fact, the principal characteristics of stuff now are that it is impenetrable and that it occupies space. Nevertheless, this is simply a refinement of Thales' thinking. Stuff is still the basic concept, and the intent of the philosophers is still the same: to explain the world in terms of matter—not in teleological or supernatural terms, but in terms of natural processes. This is why it has been said at the outset that these early thinkers could as fairly be called scientists as philosophers.

The Atomists, then, managed to solve the problem of change and to solve it in materialistic terms without departing from the basic orientation of Thales and his successors. This problem had been one of the principal causes of scepticism. The repeated failure of successive thinkers to show how change could occur had brought the Sophists to the point of denying that it is possible to explain change, and this amounted, of course, to a denial of the possibility of natural knowledge. It can fairly be said, therefore, that the Atomists, by showing how matter can change, rehabilitated the philosophy of science. This too was a great accomplishment. Unfortunately the particular solution that the Atomists devised for the problem of natural knowledge was incapable of dealing satisfactorily with

13 Except tangibility.

Sophistic scepticism in other fields—in the fields of ethics and religion, for instance.

The Atomists' reformulation of Thales' materialism terminated in a conception of the universe that is remarkably satisfactory as long as we are operating at the level of *physics* and are concerned with such questions as the problem of change. But it is much less effective when we turn to the other subject of Sophistic scepticism—man.

According to the Atomists, man is no more than a collection of atoms suffering from some extremely odd illusions. Though the Atomistic theory can teach him that they are illusions, it cannot help him escape from them. He continues to see cabbages, which are not in the least green, as if they were green; he continues to experience moderation as good, though it too is only a movement of atoms. But surely it is pointless for a collection of atoms to ask itself, "Why be good?" "Why sacrifice oneself for friend or country?" "Why keep promises? do one's duty? live justly?"

The Atomists could only have replied that, given the whole past state of the world, the raising of such questions, even though they may be pointless, is necessary. Everyone must decide for himself whether he thinks this is an adequate reply (the Atomists, of course, would have held that this decision, too, is necessary). But some people at least will conclude that a universe consisting solely of atoms moving in the void excludes the objective reality of such values just as much as did the Sophists' and that Atomism was incapable of dealing with the critical questions about an individual's relation to his community and about the rival claims of freedom and authority that were reflected in the Melian debate. Democritus met the Sophistic denial of civic duty and communal responsibility only by reaffirming the old values in language calculated to move the hearts rather than the minds of his readers. This was hardly enough. A philosophy like Platonism, which claimed that the traditional ends could be proved (not merely reaffirmed, but proved) to be best, performed a social function in a period of cultural change that Atomism could not equal.

Ethics and politics both touch religion. How adequately could Atomism answer the questions that the religious mind asks? If the universe is a machine, it pursues a blind, irresponsible, and irresponsive course, indifferent to us and our fate. Not alone our cosmic fears, as the Atomists pointed out, but, more important, our hopes—our very questions—are illusions. Life, in the Atomists' view, has no significance; it is a brief candle flickering for a moment in an immense dark.

Religion is a complex matter, but whatever else it involves, it involves a belief that the universe means something and that this meaning has some relevance to man. This belief in a cosmic meaning, though difficult to define with precision, has been held by numerous people who are neither religious nor ignorant and superstitious in the conventional sense of these terms. As to what the universe means these people doubtless differ, just as their ways of formulating this belief differ. (They might or might not, for instance, use the term "god" in describing it.) But those who have held the universe as a whole to be meaningful have also usually held that this is the most important of all facts about it. Hence all such people have inevitably found Atomism unsatisfactory. This explains why Atomism virtually disappeared during the Middle Ages, when the religious outlook was in the ascendancy. It also explains why Atomism's great rivals, Platonism and Aristotelianism, have had a greater appeal, over the centuries, to a great many people.

But, as we shall see, these philosophies proved weak where Atomism was strong. Their problem was to give an intelligible account of nature, of natural processes, and of man as a part of nature—which he surely is. Here Democritus' theory is far more cogenial, both in general outlook and in detail, to most modern minds than is that of Plato or even that of Aristotle. But it is pointless today to attempt to choose between classical idealism and classical materialism. What is desperately needed is a philosophical theory that combines the strong points of both these ancient world views. Indeed, the central problem of culture is to reconcile the mechanistic, nonteleological view of nature, which Atomism first formulated and which modern science has largely adopted, with an ethical, religious, and humanistic conception of man. So much space has been given to the discussion of difficulties inherent in the Atomists' conception of thought, volition, and, generally, "mind," not to denigrate Atomism, but because, when the scientific outlook revived, these difficulties became and remained major preoccupations of philosophers. The whole history of philosophy since the seventeenth century is in fact hardly more than a series of variations on this central theme.

# CHAPTER 4

# Plato:
# The
# Theory
# of Forms

## Life and Times

Whether we like it or not, whether we know it or not, we are all more or less Platonists. Even if we reject Plato's conclusions, our views are shaped by the way in which he stated his problems. This applies to poets, politicians, and proles, as well as to technical philosophers. It will be worthwhile, therefore, to study his views; in doing so, we shall better our understanding of ourselves. But in order to understand his theories we must understand the problems that seemed to him important and that he sought to solve. To do this it is necessary to examine the facts that are known about his life.

One of the most significant things about Plato (as indeed about anybody) was the time in which he lived. Born in Athens in 427 B.C., Plato was old enough to have fought through the last four or five years of the war with Sparta; he grew up in those years of defeat and of economic, social, and moral dissolution that have been described. He must have experienced the dissatisfaction and the difficulty of "making an adjustment" that the returning veteran seems always to face—exaggerated when, as in Plato's case, it is a return to a defeated, rather than a victorious, home.

Another matter of importance in Plato's life (as in everyone else's) was the family he was born into. Plato could hardly have been "better" born. On his mother's side he was descended from Solon, the great Athenian statesman and reformer; on his father's side, from the god Poseidon, via (naturally) a long line of distinguished Athenians. His uncle, Charmides, and his cousin, Critias, were prominent nobles of the day and leaders of the oligarchical faction.

Political leadership was traditional in his family, and Plato's whole life, as will be seen, was deeply affected by this background of ambition and service. In the good old days, a leading political role would have been his as a matter of course. But even by the beginning of the Peloponnesian War it was no longer a "matter of course," and, during the years of strain and defeat, members of noble families found themselves at ever greater disadvantage in the competition for the electorate's favor. By the time Plato had reached the age when an ambitious young man might begin to think of his political career, only two courses were open to him—he could give himself over to flattery and cajolery of the people, or he could join in a plot to overthrow the democratic regime by a *coup d'état*. The former course involved a compromise of principles that Plato's perhaps overscrupulous moral sense rejected. An opportunity for the latter alternative came at the end of the war, when a number of nobles, including Critias and Charmides, set themselves up in power. This must have seemed to the young Plato a hopeful change from rule by the venal and bungling demagogues who had led Athens to defeat. But the excesses of The Thirty (as the oligarchs were called) showed him that the will of the few is no better per se than the will of the many. And the savagery of the revived democracy, which shortly afterwards overthrew the oligarchy, did nothing to convince him that *it*, for its part, had learned a lesson.

## Socrates

What made more impression on Plato than anything else, however, was Socrates and the example of his fate. Something therefore should be said about this extraordinary man. Socrates was over forty years old when Plato was born. Unlike Plato, who reached manhood in a time of defeat, he had grown up during the period of Athens' greatest power and success—the half-century following the victories over the Persians. Socrates was a contemporary of Thucydides and a member of the generation that made the war with Sparta and lost it. But though he fought bravely as a soldier and performed all those political duties that the democratic state expected of its citizens, Socrates was not a politician or a leader. He claimed to differ from his fellow Athenians only in knowing that he knew nothing, and he spent his days in the highly unpopular but thoroughly successful task of proving to the Athenians their ignorance of things about which they had hitherto believed themselves well informed.

He must have seemed to his fellow citizens more like a Sophist than anything else. But he had a profound, and entirely un-Sophistic, conviction of the reality of goodness and the goodness of reality. He combined an intensely realistic and down-to-earth common sense with a passionate mysticism, a cool and dispassionate scepticism about ordinary beliefs and opinions with a deep religious sense. Plato's dialogue, the *Symposium*, which describes a dinner party Socrates attended at a friend's house, gives a good account of him.[1] By way of entertainment, each guest made an extemporary oration in praise of love.[2]

> [As the last speech was finished] suddenly there was a knocking at the outer door, which had a noisy sound like that of revellers, and they heard notes of a flute-girl. "Go and see to it," said Agathon to the servants; "and if it be one of our intimates, invite him in: otherwise, say we are not drinking, but just about to retire."
> A few moments after, they heard the voice of Alcibiades in the forecourt, very drunken . . . : he stood at the door, crowned with a bushy wreath of ivy and violets, and wearing a great array of ribands on his head.

The assembled company decided that Alcibiades too must fulfill the contract to praise love. He agreed, providing he was permitted to praise Socrates instead of the god of love himself:

> "Were it not that I might appear to be absolutely tipsy, I would have affirmed on oath all the strange effects I personally have felt from his words, and still feel even now. For when I hear him I am worse than any wild fanatic; I find my heart leaping and my tears gushing forth at the sound of his speech, and I see great numbers of other people having the same experience. When

1 Agathon was the host, and Alcibiades, who arrived late and tipsy, a guest. Agathon (born about 447 B.C.) was a successful young playwright celebrating a recently won dramatic prize. The dinner party is supposed to have taken place in 416 or 415 B.C., shortly before the start of the Sicilian expedition (see p. 46), of which Alcibiades, then at the height of his popular success, was the designated leader. But readers of the dialogue (which of course was written long after these events occurred) knew that this brilliant, spoiled, and unscrupulous young man was soon to be charged with profanation of the Mysteries and to begin his tragic career of treason and intrigue against his country. Modern readers must remember that in the society for which Plato was writing and whose life he was describing, homosexuality was acceptable. What was remarkable about Socrates was not his affection for handsome young men but his refusal to allow it to develop into sexual relationships.

2 For Socrates' speech on this occasion, see pp. 139–42.

I listened to Pericles and other skilled orators I thought them eloquent, but I never felt anything like this; my spirit was not left in a tumult and had not to complain of my being in the condition of a common slave: whereas the influence of our Marsyas here has often thrown me into such a state that I thought my life not worth living on these terms. . . . For he compels me to admit that, sorely deficient as I am, I neglect myself while I attend to the affairs of Athens. . . . For he brings home to me that I cannot disown the duty of doing what he bids me, but that as soon as I turn from his company I fall a victim to the favours of the crowd. So I take a runaway's leave of him and flee away; when I see him again I think of those former admissions, and am ashamed. . . .

"Such then is the effect that our satyr can work upon me and many another with his piping. . . . [Next] observe how Socrates is amorously inclined to handsome persons; with these he is always busy and enraptured. . . . And believing he had a serious affection for my youthful bloom, I supposed I had here a godsend and a rare stroke of luck, thinking myself free at any time by gratifying his desires to hear all that our Socrates knew; for I was enormously proud of my youthful charms. . . . Yes, gentlemen, I went and met him, and the two of us would be alone; and I thought he would seize the chance of talking to me as a lover does to his dear one in private, and I was glad. But nothing of the sort occurred at all: he would merely converse with me in his usual manner, and when he had spent the day with me he would leave me and go his way. After that I proposed he should go with me to the trainer's, and I trained with him, expecting to gain my point there. So he trained and wrestled with me many a time when no one was there. The same story! I got no further with the affair. . . .

"Now all this, you know, had already happened to me when we later went on a campaign together to Potidaea; and there we were messmates. Well, first of all, he surpassed not me only but everyone else in bearing hardships; whenever we were cut off in some place and were compelled, as often in campaigns, to go without food, the rest of us were nowhere in point of endurance. Then again, when we had plenty of good cheer, he alone could enjoy it to the full, and though unwilling to drink, when once overruled he used to beat us all; and, most surprising of all, no man has ever yet seen Socrates drunk. Of this power I expect we shall have a good test in a moment. But it was in his endurance of winter—in those parts the winters are awful—that I remember . . . : we all preferred not to stir abroad, or if any of us did, we wrapped ourselves up with prodigious care, and after putting on our shoes we muffled up our feet with felt and little fleeces. But he walked out in that weather, clad in just such a coat as he was always wont to wear, and he made his way more easily over the ice unshod than the rest of us did in our shoes. . . .

"One day, . . . immersed in some problem at dawn, he stood in the same spot considering it; and when he found it a tough one, he would not give it up but stood there trying. The time drew on to midday, and the men began to notice him, and said to one another in wonder: 'Socrates has been standing there in a study ever since dawn!' The end of it was that in the evening some of the Ionians after they had supped—this time it was summer—brought out their mattresses and rugs and took their sleep in the cool; thus they waited to see if he would go on standing all night too. He stood till dawn came and the sun rose; then walked away, after offering a prayer to the Sun.

"Then, if you care to hear of him in battle—for there also he must have his due— . . . let me tell you, gentlemen, what a notable figure he made when the army was retiring in flight from Delium: I happened to be there on horseback, while he marched under arms. The troops were in utter disorder, and he was retreating along with Laches, when I chanced to come up with them. . . . I noticed, first, how far he outdid Laches in collectedness, and next I felt—to use a phrase of yours, Aristophanes—how there he stepped along, as his wont is in our streets, 'strutting like a proud marsh-goose, with ever a sidelong glance,' turning a calm sidelong look on friend and foe alike, and convincing anyone even from afar that whoever cares to touch this person will find he can put up a stout enough defence. . . ."

[When Alcibiades had finished his speech] a great crowd of revellers arrived at the door. . . . [Soon] the whole place was in an uproar and, losing all order, they were forced to drink a vast amount of wine. Then, as Aristodemus related, Eryximachus, Phaedrus, and some others took their leave and departed; while he himself fell asleep, and slumbered a great while, for the nights were long. He awoke towards dawn, as the cocks were crowing; and immediately he saw that all the company were either sleeping or gone, except Agathon, Aristophanes, and Socrates, who alone remained awake and were drinking out of a large vessel, from left to right; and Socrates was arguing with them. As to most of the talk, Aristodemus had no recollection, for he had missed the beginning and was also rather drowsy; but the substance of it was, he said, that Socrates was driving them to the admission that the same man could have the knowledge required for writing comedy and tragedy— that the fully skilled tragedian could be a comedian as well. While they were being driven to this, and were but feebly following it, they began to nod; first Aristophanes dropped into a slumber, and then, as day began to dawn, Agathon also. When Socrates had seen them comfortable, he rose and went away . . . ; on arriving at the Lyceum, he washed himself, and then spent the rest of the day in his ordinary fashion; and so, when the day was done, he went home for the evening and reposed.[a]

## SOCRATES' TRIAL

Though Socrates was extravagantly admired by a group of bright young men who enjoyed watching him trap their elders in contradictions, such a character was inevitably disliked and misunderstood by the general public. He set up his own moral convictions in opposition to those of the public—he was indifferent to "public opinion," in a democracy a most dangerous practice. It is not altogether surprising, therefore, that he should have been brought to trial. One of the principal charges was atheism. The evidence the prosecution could present was convincing to an Athenian jury, for Socrates certainly did not believe in the gods in the sense in which his accusers did. But one of the motives underlying the indictment was surely a political animus. We have already seen that the defense of democracy and of religious superstition went hand in hand,[3] and Socrates had offended not only by exploding ancient beliefs but by associating, as friend and mentor, with oligarchs like Critias and traitors like Alcibiades. Hatred of the enemies of democracy, as well as religious piety, must have moved his judges to condemn him to death.

Moreover, Socrates made no attempt to defend himself. Or rather, he refused to stoop to defend himself in the only way Athenian juries understood. Instead of throwing himself on the court's mercy and painting a pathetic picture of his wife and children, he lectured the jury on its ignorance, tactlessly informing it that he believed in the gods in a far nobler sense than it did. Indeed, his real defense, as Plato reported it, was directed to future generations.[4]

> How you, men of Athens. have been affected by my accusers, I do not know; but I, for my part, almost forgot my own identity, so persuasively did they talk; and yet there is hardly a word of truth in what they have said. . . .
>
> Well then, men of Athens, that I am not a wrong-doer according to Meletus's indictment, seems to me not to need much of a defence. . . . Great hatred has arisen against me and in the minds of many persons. And this it is which will cause my condemnation, if it is to cause it, not Meletus or Anytus, but the prejudice and dislike of the many. This has condemned many other good men, and I think will do so; and there is no danger that it will stop with me. . . .
>
> To fear death, gentlemen, is nothing else than to think one is wise when one is not; for it is thinking one knows what one does not know. For no one knows whether death be not even the greatest of all blessings to man, but they fear it as if they knew that it is the greatest of evils. And is not this the most reprehensible form of ignorance, that of thinking one knows what one does not know? Perhaps, gentlemen, in this matter also I differ from other men in this way, and if I were to say that I am wiser in anything, it would be in this, that not knowing very much about the other world, I do not think I know. But I do know that it is evil and disgraceful to do wrong and to disobey him who is better than I, whether he be god or man. . . . While I live and am able to continue, I shall never give up philosophy or stop exhorting you and pointing out the truth to any one of you whom I may meet, saying in my accustomed way: "Most excellent man, are you who are a citizen of Athens, the greatest of cities and the most famous for wisdom and power, not ashamed to care for the acquisition of wealth and for reputation and honour, when you neither care nor take thought for wisdom and truth and the perfection of your soul?" . . . This I shall do to whomever I meet, young and old, foreigner and citizen, but most to the citizens,

3 See p. 64.
4 The following passages from the *Apology,* the *Crito,* and the *Phaedo,* describing Socrates' trial and death, should be read not merely for their biographical interest but for the light they throw on the ethical doctrines of Plato (see pp. 153–74). Taken together these descriptions of Socrates' last days are an account of Plato's ideal of human nature.

inasmuch as you are more nearly related to me. For know that the god commands me to do this, and I believe that no greater good ever came to pass in the city than my service to the god. For I go about doing nothing else than urging you, young and old, not to care for your persons or your property more than for the perfection of your souls, or even so much; and I tell you that virtue does not come from money, but from virtue comes money and all other good things to man, both to the individual and to the state. . . . Therefore I say to you, men of Athens, either do as Anytus tells you, or not, and either acquit me, or not, knowing that I shall not change my conduct even if I am to die many times over. . . .

Perhaps it may seem strange that I go about and interfere in other people's affairs to give this advice in private, but do not venture to come before your assembly and advise the state. But the reason for this, as you have heard me say at many times and places, is that something divine and spiritual comes to me, the very thing which Meletus ridiculed in his indictment. I have had this from my childhood; it is a sort of voice that comes to me, and when it comes it always holds me back from what I am thinking of doing, but never urges me forward. This it is which opposes my engaging in politics. And I think this opposition is a very good thing; for you may be quite sure, men of Athens, that if I had undertaken to go into politics, I should have been put to death long ago and should have done no good to you or to myself. And do not be angry with me for speaking the truth; the fact is that no man will save his life who nobly opposes you or any other populace and prevents many unjust and illegal things from happening in the state. A man who really fights for the right, if he is to preserve his life for even a little while, must be a private citizen, not a public man. . . .[b]

## SOCRATES IN PRISON

Socrates was convicted and sentenced to death. While he was in prison awaiting execution his friends were busy arranging for his escape. But Socrates refused to flee. Note how, in the following passage, he makes short work of his friend Crito's emotional appeals. Note too that Socrates and Crito both assume that values are objective—that there is something that it is *right* to do in this situation. Further, they assume that these objective values can be ascertained by a process of reasoning. Finally, they assume that when these values have been discovered, all reasonable men will act accordingly.

CRITO. My dear Socrates, even now listen to me and save yourself. Since, if you die, it will be no mere single misfortune to me, but I shall lose a friend such as I can never find again, and besides, many persons who do not know you and me well will think I could have saved you if I had been willing to spend money, but that I would not take the trouble. . . .

SOCRATES. But, my dear Crito, why do we care so much for what most people think? . . .

CRITO. That may well be. But, Socrates, tell me this: you are not considering me and your other friends, are you, fearing that, if you escape, the informers will make trouble for us by saying that we stole you away, and we shall be forced to lose either all our property or a good deal of money, or be punished in some other way besides? . . .

SOCRATES. I am considering this, Crito, and many other things.

CRITO. Well, do not fear this! for it is not even a large sum of money which we should pay to some men who are willing to save you and get you away from here. . . . And moreover, I think you are abandoning your children, too, for . . . they will probably meet with such treatment as generally comes to orphans in their destitution. . . .

SOCRATES. My dear Crito, . . . we must examine the question whether we ought to do this or not; for I am not only now but always a man who follows nothing but the reasoning which on consideration seems to me best. . . . Now how could we examine the matter most reasonably? By taking up first what you say about opinions and asking whether we were right when we always used to say . . . that we ought not to esteem all the opinions of men, but some and not others, and not those of all men, but only of some? What do you think? Is not this true?

CRITO. It is.

SOCRATES. Then we ought to esteem the good opinions and not the bad ones?

CRITO. Yes.

SOCRATES. And the good ones are those of the wise and the bad ones those of the foolish?

CRITO. Of course.

SOCRATES. Come then, what used we to say about this? If a man is an athlete and makes that his business, does he pay attention to every man's praise and blame and opinion or to those of one man only who is a physician or a trainer?

CRITO. To those of one man only. . . .

SOCRATES. Then, most excellent friend, we must not consider at all what the many will say of us, but what he who knows about right and wrong, the one man, and truth herself will say. . . .

The question is whether it is right for me to try to escape from here without the permission of the Athenians, or not right. And if it appears to be right, let us try it, and if not, let us give it up. But the considerations you suggest, about spending money, and reputation, and bringing up my children, these are really, Crito, the reflections of . . . the multitude. . . .

Let us, my good friend, investigate in common, and if you can contradict anything I say, do so, and I will yield to your arguments; but if you cannot, my dear friend, stop at once saying the same thing to me over and over, that I ought to go away from here without the consent of the Athenians; for I am anxious to act in this matter with your approval, and not contrary to your wishes. Now see if the beginning of the investigation satisfies you, and try to reply to my questions to the best of your belief.

CRITO. I will try.

SOCRATES. Ought we in no way to do wrong intentionally, or should we do wrong in some ways but not in others? . . . Do we believe this or not?

CRITO. We do. . . .

SOCRATES. Well, then, is it right to requite evil with evil, as the world says it is, or not right?

CRITO. Not right, certainly.

SOCRATES. For doing evil to people is the same thing as wronging them.

CRITO. That is true.

SOCRATES. Then we ought neither to requite wrong with wrong nor to do evil to anyone, no matter what he may have done to us. And be careful, Crito, that you do not, in agreeing to this, agree to something you do not believe; for I know that there are few who believe or ever will believe this. . . .

CRITO. I do hold to it and I agree with you; so go on.

SOCRATES. Now the next thing I say, or rather ask, is this: "Ought a man to do what he has agreed to do, provided it is right, or may he violate his agreements?"

CRITO. He ought to do it. . . .

SOCRATES. Consider it in this way. If, as I was on the point of running away (or whatever it should be called), the laws and the commonwealth should come to me and ask, "Tell me, Socrates, what have you in mind to do? Are you not intending by this thing you are trying to do, to destroy us, the laws, and the entire state, so far as in you lies? Or do you think that state can exist and not be overturned, in which the decisions reached by the courts have no force but are made invalid and annulled by private persons?" What shall we say, Crito, in reply to this question and others of the same kind? . . . Shall we say to them, "The state wronged me and did not judge the case rightly"? Shall we say that, or what?

CRITO. That is what we shall say, by Zeus, Socrates.

SOCRATES. What then if the laws should say, "Socrates, is this the agreement you made with us, or did you agree to abide by the verdicts pronounced by the state? . . . We brought you into the world, nurtured you, and gave a share of all the good things we could to you and all the citizens. Yet we proclaim . . . that anyone who is not pleased with us when he has become a man and has seen the administration of the city and us, the laws, may take his goods and go away wherever he likes. . . . But we say that whoever of you stays here, seeing how we administer justice and how we govern the state in other respects, has thereby entered into an agreement with us to do what we command; and we say that he who does not obey does three-fold wrong, because he disobeys us who are his parents, because he disobeys us who nurtured him, and because after agreeing to obey us he neither obeys us nor convinces us that we are wrong, though we give him the opportunity and do not roughly order him to do what we command, but when we allow him a choice of two things, either to convince us of error or to do our bidding, he does neither of these things. . . ." What shall we say to this, Crito? Must we not agree that it is true?

CRITO. We must, Socrates.

SOCRATES. "Are you then," they would say, "not breaking your compacts and agreements with us? . . . Ah, Socrates, be guided by us who tended your infancy. Care neither for your children nor for life nor for anything else more than for the right, that when you come to the home of the dead, you may have all these things to say in your own defence. . . . Do not let Crito persuade you to do what he says, but take our advice."

Be well assured, my dear friend, Crito, that this is what I seem to hear . . . and this sound of these words re-echoes within me and prevents my hearing any other words. And be assured that, so far as I now believe, if you argue against these words you will speak in vain. Nevertheless, if you think you can accomplish anything, speak.

CRITO. No, Socrates, I have nothing to say.

SOCRATES. Then, Crito, let it be, and let us act in this way, since it is in this way that God leads us.[c]

### SOCRATES' DEATH AND ITS EFFECT ON PLATO

So the day of execution came, and Socrates' friends gathered around him for one last discourse.[5] When it was finished

. . . it was nearly sunset. . . . Socrates said, "Come, Crito, let . . . someone bring the poison, if it is ready; and if not, let the man prepare it." And Crito said: "But I think, Socrates, the sun is still upon the mountains and has not yet set; and I know that others have taken the poison very late. . . . Do not hurry; for there is still time."

And Socrates said: "Crito, those whom you mention are right in doing as they do, for they think they gain by it; and I shall be right in not doing as they do; for I think I should gain nothing by taking the poison a little later. I should only make myself ridiculous in my own eyes if I clung to life and spared it, when there is no more profit in it. Come," he said, "do as I ask and do not refuse."

Thereupon Crito nodded to the boy who was standing near. The boy went out and stayed a long time, then came back with the man who was to administer the poison, which he brought with him in a cup ready for use. And when Socrates saw him, he said: "Well, my good man, you know about these things; what must I do?" "Nothing," he replied, "except drink the poison and walk about till your legs feel heavy; then lie down, and the poison will take effect of itself."

At the same time he held out the cup to Socrates. . . . Looking up at the man with wide open eyes, as was his custom, [Socrates] said: "What do you say about pouring a libation to some deity from this cup? May I, or not?" "Socrates," said he, "we prepare only as much as we think is enough." "I understand," said Socrates; "but I may and must pray to the gods that my departure hence be a fortunate one; so I offer this prayer, and may it be granted." With these words he raised the cup to his lips and very cheerfully and quietly drained it. Up to that time most of us[6] had been able to restrain

---

5 For some of the discussion on this occasion, see pp. 143–45.
6 [Phaedo, who was present on this occasion, is relating the events of that day to Echecrates. another friend of Socrates', who was absent—AUTHOR.]

our tears fairly well, but [now] we could do so no longer, but in spite of myself my tears rolled down in floods. . . . Socrates . . . said, "What conduct is this, you strange men! I sent the women away chiefly for this very reason, that they might not behave in this absurd way; for I have heard that it is best to die in silence. Keep quiet and be brave." Then we were ashamed and controlled our tears. He walked about and, when he said his legs were heavy, lay down on his back, for such was the advice of the attendant. The man who had administered the poison laid his hands on him and after a while examined his hands and legs, then pinched his foot hard and asked if he felt it. He said "No"; then after that, his thighs; and passing upwards in this way he showed us that he was growing cold and rigid. And again he touched him and said that when it reached his heart, he would be gone. The chill had now reached the region about the groin, and uncovering his face, which had been covered, he said—and these were his last words—"Crito, we owe a cock to Aesculapius. Pay it and do not neglect it." "That," said Crito, "shall be done; but see if you have anything else to say." To this question he made no reply, but after a little while he moved; the attendant uncovered him; his eyes were fixed. And Crito when he saw it, closed his mouth and eyes.

Such was the end, Echecrates, of our friend, who was, as we may say, of all those of his time whom we have known, the best and wisest and most righteous man.[d]

Socrates loved life, but he had no fear of dying. And he certainly preferred death to weaseling out in some mean and ignoble way. He may also have felt that to die in this dramatic fashion would accomplish more for his purpose—the education and enlightenment of man—than anything he might do alive. If so, he was correct; for Plato was shocked into a philosophical career and so launched one of the greatest educational movements in history.

Plato was too young to have been one of Socrates' most intimate friends. He knew Socrates only during the last few years of the latter's life; but he set himself, in a series of biographical dialogues, to defend the good man's memory. And then, even after his own thought matured, he continued to use Socrates as the protagonist of his dialogues. The result was such a blending of opinions that nobody today can possibly tell where the historical Socrates in Plato's writings leaves off and the fictional mouthpiece for the theories of Plato begins. Probably Plato himself could not have told, and he would have regarded the question as unimportant. What matters, he deeply believed, is the truth itself, not who happens first to light on it. Besides, the discovery of truth is always, he thought, a joint work in which friends discuss together. That one of the friends in many of his discussions happened to be dead was for Plato probably a trivial detail. Happily, we can follow Plato in this indifference to the niceties of the "Socratic problem." Since we are concerned with the theory itself—the questions it was intended to answer, its success or failure, and its subsequent development in the hands of others—we need not attempt to separate Socrates' contribution from Plato's. Whenever "Plato's theory" is referred to, it may be taken to mean "the theory of Socrates-Plato."

## Plato's Later Life

Socrates' death, then, confirmed Plato's aristocratic biases and his judgment about the causes of Athens' defeat at the hands of Sparta. It convinced him that a bad state breeds only bad men; that a good man cannot live in such a state; and that a state ruled by the many is inevitably bad, because the many are ignorant, emotionally unstable, and narrowly self-centered. Hence he withdrew from active politics. But he did not abandon his interest in politics. On the contrary, he conceived it his highest duty to try to discover the basis for a good state, one in which a good man might be happy and live in peace. He began, he said in one of his letters, by studying every possible way in which the degeneration of public and private morals might be checked. As time went on, however, and as he came to realize that "modern" degeneracy was not just a peculiarity of defeated and democratic Athens but a widespread disease, his hopes for speedy reform diminished. Not until philosophers became kings or kings philosophers—not until supreme knowledge and supreme power were combined in the same person— would real improvement be possible. It seems likely, therefore, that when he was forced to abandon his plans for a positive reform of the Athenian constitution, Plato fell back on the hope of exercising a more indirect influence on politics through a process of education.

Meanwhile he had commenced writing on philosophical subjects. This production took the form, as has been said, of dialogues in which various theories are presented and criticized in conversations between Socrates and some other character, often a member of Plato's family or another well-known Athenian. The dialogues are not systematic; often they are inconclusive. Those that are conclusive usually reach only negative conclusions. For instance, the *Theaetetus*, which is concerned with theory of knowledge, rejects certain views as mistaken— "neither perception, nor true belief, nor the addition of an 'account' to true belief can be knowledge"—but fails to formulate a position that Plato himself regarded as acceptable.

But even negative conclusions are in a sense positive—insofar as they eliminate false views. In the dialogue mentioned above, Theaetetus says that Socrates' questions have enabled him to "give utterance to more than I had in me," and, characteristically, the party decides "tomorrow morning to meet again." The pursuit of truth has not run into a dead end but is an on-going affair.

We have to remember this conception of truth as involving a joint search when we find Plato criticizing in one dialogue views to which, in others, he seems to have committed himself. We have to remember also that these dialogues were written over a long period of time and in an order about which we cannot now be certain. Moreover, Plato was not writing for us but for a group of friends and pupils who could almost certainly rely on receiving a more detailed oral exposition of Plato's views.

Indeed, though he was a consummate literary artist, Plato was rather ambivalent toward the written word[7]. Stating his criticism of written exposition in a perhaps exaggerated way, he once remarked in a letter that he had never attempted to put down in writing his views "about the subjects which I seriously study. . . . There does not exist, nor will there ever exist, any treatise of mine dealing therewith. For it does not at all admit of verbal expression like other studies, but, as a result of continued application to the subject itself and communion therewith, it is brought to birth in the soul on a sudden, as light that is kindled by a leaping spark, and thereafter it nourishes itself."[e]

Thus, in one sense, Plato was a mystic. But he was also, as we shall see, a rationalist and a mathematician. Though he believed that the highest truths cannot be formulated in an explicit, rational language, he held that truths at a lower level can be and that their formulation is a necessary preparation for the experience of the vision that cannot be put into words.

Finally, he was an administrator and an executive with enough energy and ability to found a school that was not only the chief educational institution of its day but a training ground for statesmen. Through its alumni and through the work done by its staff in supplying constitutions and legal systems for Greek states, it exercised indirectly the kind of influence on politics and affairs that the young Plato had probably once hoped to exercise directly through a political career.

Plato, however, had at least one adventure in practical politics. When Dionysius, the ruler of Syracuse, died in 368 B.C. he left his brother-in-law, Dion, as regent for his young son and heir, Dionysius II. By this time Plato was well known as a writer on political subjects, and Dion (who had made Plato's acquaintance during a visit the latter had paid to Sicily some years earlier) conceived the idea of putting into practice the educational and political theories Plato had been working out in the Academy. If, as Plato argued, a really good state was unattainable until philosophers were kings or kings philosophers, here was an ideal opportunity to try to make a philosopher out of a king. Plato, apparently not altogether willingly, undertook the philosophical education of the young Dionysius. But theory shattered on the harsh rocks of *realpolitik* in Syracuse. Four months after Plato's arrival Dion's position had been undermined by rival groups around the throne and Dion was exiled; in 366 B.C. Plato himself returned to Athens. However, he seems to have maintained friendly relations with Dionysius, who apparently still cherished the hope of some day becoming a philosopher. In 362 B.C. Plato made another trip to Syracuse, this time at Dionysius' own request, but this visit, too, failed to achieve anything, and Plato returned to the Academy to remain its head until his death at the age of eighty in 347 B.C.

So much for Plato's life. As for his views, we shall first consider his attempt to work out a theory of knowledge that would meet the sceptical arguments

7 See p. 194.

of the Sophists. This will occupy the rest of the present chapter. The next chapter is a study of the special sciences, as Plato understood them—physics, ethics, politics, art, and religion. In a final section, as preparation for a study of Aristotle, some criticisms of the theory of forms, including a number of criticisms raised by Plato himself, and Plato's answers to these criticisms will be examined.

## Theory of Knowledge

It has already been stated that Plato's primary concern was to discover the basis for a good state, one in which a good man might be happy. But before he could set forth his answers to such questions as, "What is the best type of political organization?" "What is morality?" he had to demonstrate that these are questions that do have answers. For the Sophists had claimed that there is no truth in the spheres of morality and politics, but only private prejudice. Plato thus devoted a great deal of attention to epistemology—more than had any philosopher before him.

Like Democritus, Plato saw that to answer the Sophists he had to find solutions to the various apparently insoluble dilemmas, growing out of earlier theories, that suggested the hopeless inadequacy of human reason. It was easy to point out that the complete scepticism of a Gorgias was self-defeating and absurd, but until one could resolve the dilemmas that had led Gorgias to this conclusion and could justify the claims of reason as an instrument of knowledge, one could hardly hope to halt the descent into scepticism about moral standards that Plato viewed with so much alarm.

### THE PUZZLE ABOUT CHANGE

Like Democritus again, Plato realized that these dilemmas—the problem of the one and the many, the problem of appearance and reality, the problem of change—grew out of the questions asked by the earliest philosophers. All of these tricky problems were implied in Thales' apparently innocent question, "What is the one out of which everything comes?" For instance, on the assumption that everything is really one, say, water, it is obvious that things look different from what they are: What is *really* water *appears* to be ships, sealing wax, cabbages, and kings. Thus we get the "problem of appearance": How can reality appear to be different from what it is? Again, saying that everything is really one involves us in the problem of the one and the many, for we are saying that what is one (water) is a plurality (ships, cabbages, kings), which sounds like a contradiction.

Suppose we try to get around this by saying that the one changes into the many, that reality undergoes some sort of transformation in the course of which it becomes appearance. This is not helpful because change itself is a puzzle. For instance, when we say that in the course of time you have changed from a baby to an adult we are saying that an enduring something has altered. This sounds simple, but only because we do not stop to think what we mean. If we do stop to think, it appears that we are contradicting ourselves. We are saying that you are the same thing now that, years ago, was the baby—only different, of course, for you are not the baby now. But how can this be? How can you be both the same *and* different? If you are the same, then surely you are not different; if you are different, then you are not the same. There would be no difficulty if it were simply a matter of a fully grown adult's *replacing* a baby, as a rabbit might suddenly replace a spectator's watch in a magician's hat. In this instance, nobody, not even the magician, would claim that the watch has changed into the rabbit: One thing has left the hat and another thing has entered it. But we do claim that the baby has changed into the adult—that the adult, who is not the baby, is also (somehow or other) that very same baby.

What philosophy must do, according to Plato, is to give a rational account of that vague "somehow or other." Hence it will not do to try to answer the critique of change by roundly declaring, "Of course change occurs, and everybody knows it." This misses the point. Of course change occurs; nobody, unless he were as extreme a rationalist as Parmenides, would deny it. It is precisely the fact that change occurs, even though it is a puzzle, that created the dilemma. None of us is puzzled by the contradiction "round square," but it would be puzzling if, despite the contradiction, we kept encountering round squares. This is exactly parallel to what seemed to these early thinkers to be happening, and their puzzlement explains much of the history of Greek philosophy.

It explains why, since nobody had been able to give a reasonable account of the "somehow or other," the Sophists became sceptical of reason. It also explains why Heraclitus and Parmenides developed their peculiar theories. Each was concentrating on just one side of what has been called the dilemma of change. It has been said that things obviously change and that this seems to mean they must remain the same and yet become different. It would seem that both Heraclitus and Parmenides saw that this is a contradiction. Hence each tried to get away with explaining the universe in terms of one of the conflicting concepts. Heraclitus, since he saw that difference must be admitted, rejected identity (which seemed to him incompatible with difference) and tried to explain everything in terms of flux. But this is of course unsatisfactory. Parmenides, on the other hand, realizing that whatever changes must be identical throughout its change, took identity as the basic concept and was forced to deny change, since the two concepts seemed to him, too, incompatible. And in this conclusion he was, of course, reinforced by Zeno, who was thought to have proved that motion (a particular type of change—change of place) was impossible.

Plato realized that these problems about change, the one and the many, and appearance and reality had to be solved before he could satisfactorily answer the Sophists. As long as change was incapable of rational explanation, it did indeed look as if reason is, as the Sophists maintained, a hopelessly fallible instrument.

## THE TWO REALMS

The main lines of Plato's solution are quite simple; it is their development that is difficult and complex. What Plato said, in effect, was this: Both Heraclitus and Parmenides were correct, for they were talking about different types of objects. The Sophists had supposed, as indeed Heraclitus and Parmenides themselves had probably supposed, that they were both talking about the same type of objects, namely, the objects of sense perception in the physical world. And it is of course a contradiction to assert of the same object the completely different predicates that Heraclitus and Parmenides attributed to "reality." But what if reality is not single, as the Milesians had supposed? What if it is dual, as the Pythagoreans had maintained? We could then say that one of these realities is in a constant flux, as Heraclitus had asserted, and that the other is eternally one, as Parmenides had claimed. This would resolve the dilemma formally, for there is no problem about asserting contradictory predicates (for example, "round" and "square") of different objects. But *are* there two worlds, and, if so, what are they? There is no doubt, surely, about the world of sense perception—it obviously exists and, what is more, it seems to have Heraclitean characteristics. It is a flux, but a flux that conforms to the "measures." Acorns never remain the same: They are always changing, growing, decaying. But they grow into oak trees, not lions; and they decay into humus, not brass buttons. It may be that we can never step into the same river twice, but the ever flowing river in the main keeps within its banks.

So much, then, for Heraclitus. But of what world are we to assert the Parmenidean properties? Plato's reply was that beyond the world of physical objects in space and time, but standing in intimate relation to it, is another world—nonphysical, nonspatial, nontemporal. This world Plato called the world of *ideai*. Since "idea" is derived from this Greek word, people sometimes speak of Plato's "world of ideas" and call his account of this world his "theory of ideas." Though a natural usage, this is misleading, for an idea, in English, is something that exists only as a thought in somebody's mind. Take away the mind and you take away the idea. Thus we contrast one's idea of a hamburger with the independently existing hamburger and attribute much less reality to the former than to the latter. But, according to Plato, *ideai* are not only real but much more real than anything else. Hence, though both our word "idea" and Plato's word *idea* name something that is not a physical object, the difference in meaning between them is greater than the similarity. The English word "form" will therefore be used to translate *idea*, and Plato's "theory of forms," not his "theory of ideas," will be spoken of. The use of "form" in this connection has ample precedent, and though it may not suggest anything very positive, it at least does not suggest anything very false.

## The Forms

So far we have said only that Plato believed there is a world of forms, over and beyond the sensible world, and that these forms are nonphysical, nonspatial, and nontemporal, yet very real. But a nonspatial, nontemporal "something" cannot be seen (for anything visible is spread out in space), nor touched (space again), nor heard (for anything audible endures through some time, however short), and so on. If, then, the forms cannot be known in sense perception, how can they be known? Plato's reply is that they are known in thought; they are, in fact, *the* objects of thought. Whenever we are thinking, what we are thinking *about* are forms.

What, for instance, is a geometrician thinking about when he is proving, say, the theorem that the interior angles of a Euclidean triangle equal two right angles? It seems clear (Plato held) that the geometrician is not inventing, imagining, or making up this property of triangles. He is discovering a property that triangles possess quite independently of his, or anybody else's, thoughts or fancies. If, for instance, he were to conclude that the interior angles of a triangle equal three right angles, he would be mistaken. About triangles, if not about taste, there *is* disputing; every man is *not* the measure of triangles for himself. It follows, Plato argued, that there is a public entity, *triangle*, whose properties it is the function of mathematical thinking to reveal. But what sort of object can this mathematical entity be? Surely, Plato maintained, it is not the physical triangle drawn in chalk or ink that the geometrician looks at. The triangle that is the object of mathematical thought is a plane figure enclosed by three straight lines, but blackboards and pieces of paper are not perfect planes. The drawn lines of chalk or ink have some breadth, fine though they may be, whereas the mathematical line enclosing the mathematical triangle has only one dimension, length. It is obvious, therefore, that the physical object drawn in ink or chalk is not a triangle. Nevertheless, it is somehow "like" a triangle (which justifies us, when we speak loosely, in calling it one), and it stands in a significant relation to the real triangle, for looking at it helps us think mathematically about the real triangle. (What this relation, which Plato called "participation," is will be discussed later.) It is clear, also, that the object of the mathematician's thought is not a *particular*. The properties he is asserting hold, he believes, universally, not just here and now. Now this nonphysical, nonspatial, nontemporal object of thought, not of sense, is what Plato called a form (*idea*). Plato believed that whenever we are *thinking* (in distinction from daydreaming, imagining, or perceiving), what we are thinking about is a form, in the sense described.

Ethics is another field in which it seemed plausible to Plato (and to many others) to maintain that there are forms. Probably most people believe that moral evaluations are not just the expressions of private prejudice that the Sophists held them to be. Most people would acknowledge that there are borderline cases.

For example, sometimes it is difficult to decide whether or not one ought to keep a promise; it is often far from easy to decide whether some particular individual, Mr. A., is a good man or a bad one. But most people would say that nonetheless right and wrong, good and bad are public characteristics: Either Mr. A. is good or he is bad (just as the triangle either has interior angles adding up to 180° or to some other figure). If Mr. A. is a good man, then, however difficult this may be to establish, those who judge him to be a bad one are mistaken. This is the sort of thing most people believe, and the theory of forms gives them (as it gave Plato) a way of answering Sophistic scepticism. They can argue that "good" and "right," like "circle" and "triangle," are forms and that whether a particular man, Mr. A., participates in the form "good" or fails to participate in it is an objective fact.

Though ethical forms were Plato's primary concern, further consideration of them will be postponed until the general theory of forms has been examined in more detail. So far we have seen that Plato pointed out that if mathematics is a science (and everybody agrees that it is), then there must be forms to be the objects of mathematical knowledge. Generalizing, we can say that, according to Plato, a science is a body of universal and necessary truths. Accordingly, every science has for its objects, and must have for its objects, forms; nothing other than eternal, unchanging forms can qualify to be the objects of scientific knowledge. For instance, if botany, zoology, and chemistry are sciences, there must be botanical, zoological, and chemical forms, which are the true objects of inquiry in these sciences. The botanist may collect and compare different species of primroses; the zoologist may study horses. But these physical objects are merely aids that they use in thinking about the properties of the form "primrose" or of the form "horse," as the mathematician uses the drawn triangle to help him think about the properties of the mathematical triangle. Thus Plato would have allowed that the scientist may use perception, but the objects that he comes to know by this means are not the objects that he perceives.

If, for instance, I look at a horse and see only this particular horse, Old Dobbin, with a brown coat, a cast in his right eye, and a wicked dislike of dogs, I am only perceiving, and what I am perceiving is a world of Heraclitean flux. Old Dobbin never for a moment remains the same; he is getting older, blinder, and wickeder all the time. But a zoologist looking at Old Dobbin might grasp more than I grasp. What I see is just an old friend or enemy, or a mode of conveyance. What the zoologist contemplates is a set of universal properties that are (probably) only very poorly exemplified in Dobbin, just as the properties of "triangle" may be poorly exemplified in some hastily scrawled figure on a blackboard—the set of properties that distinguishes horses from all other animals. And the totality of these properties, the possession of which makes Dobbin a horse, is what Plato would have called the form "horse." These properties are what the trained zoologist discovers.

This world of universal forms, which the sciences discover, has the characteristics of the Parmenidean one. Whereas Dobbin is Heraclitean, "horse" is Parmenidean. Even if disease were to kill off Dobbin and all other flesh-and-blood horses, the properties that constitute horseness would be what they are, just as the property of having interior angles equal to 180° would belong to plane figures enclosed by three straight lines even if there were no physical triangles, drawn in chalk, stamped out of bronze, or incised in marble, anywhere in the world. In this physical world, then, everything is changing and nothing is ever exactly what it is; it is always becoming something different. In the world of forms, however, everything (as Bishop Butler said in another connection) is always what it is and not another thing. It is, Plato would have argued, just the fact of its being Parmenidean—of its being eternally and unchangeably itself—that makes it possible for us to know it.

So much for an introduction to the theory of forms. In his own exposition of the theory in the *Republic*, Plato used three images—the divided line, the sun, and the cave—to help explain his meaning.

### THE DIVIDED LINE

Take a line divided into two unequal parts, one to represent the visible order, the other the intelligible; and divide each part again in the same proportion, symbolizing degrees of comparative clearness or obscurity. Then (A) one of the two sections in the visible world will stand for images.[8] By images I[9] mean first shadows, and then reflections in water or in close-grained, polished surfaces, and everything of that kind, if you understand.

Yes, I understand.

Let the second section (B) stand for the actual things of which the first are likenesses, the living creatures about us and all the works of nature or of human hands.

So be it.

Will you also take the proportion in which the visible world has been divided as corresponding to degrees of reality and truth, so that the likeness shall stand to the original in the same ratio as the sphere of appearances and belief to the sphere of knowledge?

Certainly.

Now consider how we are to divide the part which stands for the intelligible world. There are two sections. In the first (C) the mind uses as images those actual things which themselves had images in the visible world; and it is compelled to pursue its inquiry by starting from assumptions and travelling, not up to a principle, but down to a conclusion. In the second (D) the mind moves in the other direction, from an assumption up towards a principle

---

8 [See the diagram on p. 128—AUTHOR.]
9 [Socrates is addressing Glaucon, one of Plato's elder brothers. Socrates refers to himself occasionally in the first person, for Plato has represented him as reporting his conversation with Glaucon to a third party—AUTHOR.]

which is not hypothetical; and it makes no use of the images employed in the other section, but only of Forms, and conducts its inquiry solely by their means.

I don't quite understand what you mean.

Then we will try again; what I have just said will help you to understand. (C) You know, of course, how students of subjects like geometry and arithmetic begin by postulating odd and even numbers, or the various figures and the three kinds of angle, and other such data in each subject. These data they take as . . . self-evident. Then, starting from these assumptions, they go on until they arrive, by a series of consistent steps, at all the conclusions they set out to investigate.

Yes, I know that.

You also know how they make use of visible figures and discourse about them, though what they really have in mind is the originals of which these figures are images: they are not reasoning, for instance, about this particular square and diagonal which they have drawn, but about *the* Square and *the* Diagonal; and so in all cases. The diagrams they draw and the models they make are actual things, which may have their shadows or images in water; but now they serve in their turn as images, while the student is seeking to behold those realities which only thought can apprehend.

True.

This, then, is the class of things that I spoke of as intelligible, but with two qualifications: first, that the mind, in studying them, is compelled to employ assumptions, and, because it cannot rise above these, does not travel upwards to a first principle; and second, that it uses as images those actual things which have images of their own in the section below them and which, in comparison with those shadows and reflections, are reputed to be more palpable and valued accordingly.

I understand: you mean the subject-matter of geometry and of the kindred arts.

Then by the second section of the intelligible world (D) you may understand me to mean all that unaided reasoning apprehends by the power of dialectic, when it treats its assumptions, not as first principles, but as *hypotheses* in the literal sense, things "laid down" like a flight of steps up which it may mount all the way to something that is not hypothetical, the first principle of all; and having grasped this, may turn back and, holding on to the consequences which depend upon it, descend at last to a conclusion, never making use of any sensible object, but only of Forms, moving through Forms from one to another, and ending with Forms. . . . And now you may take, as corresponding to the four sections, these four states of mind: *intelligence* for the highest, *thinking* for the second, *belief* for the third, and for the last *imagining*. These you may arrange as the terms in a proportion, assigning to each a degree of clearness and certainty corresponding to the measure in which their objects possess truth and reality.[f]

In order to better understand this complex system of relationships, let us set out the divided line in accordance with Plato's instructions.

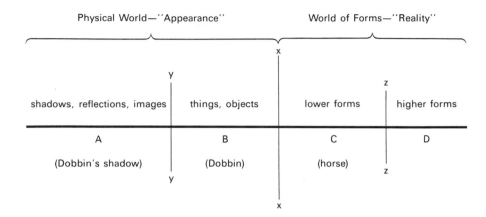

We divide a line unequally (at $x$) and then subdivide each part in the same ratio (at $y$ and $z$). It follows, of course, from this method of division that $A:B::C:D::(A + B):(C + D)$. Hence the physical world $(A + B)$ stands to the world of forms $(C + D)$, and the two sub-parts of the world of forms (C and D) stand to each other, as the two sub-parts of the physical world (A and B) stand to each other. This is fortunate from our point of view, for the relation between B and A is the familiar relation between an object and its shadow or reflection. We can say, therefore, that the physical world is a shadow of the world of forms (and that a lower form is a shadow of a higher form), just as the shadow cast by Old Dobbin is a shadow of Old Dobbin. A study of the relation between Dobbin and his shadow will thus bring out corresponding facts about the relation between higher and lower forms and the relation between the physical world as a whole and the world of forms as a whole.

Now, though no shadow tells us much about Dobbin, any shadow of him tells us *something* about him, and some shadows tell us more than others. Thus, though Dobbin's shadow in the morning or late afternoon hopelessly exaggerates the length of Dobbin's legs, it enables us (merely by seeing the shadow, without seeing Dobbin himself) to distinguish him from a table (which also has four legs), a cow, or a lion—all of which cast characteristically different shadows. So, too, though the cow's legs will be exaggeratedly long in the cow's shadow, by comparing Dobbin's shadow to the cow's we will be able to say whether the real Dobbin is taller than the real Bossy, for the elongation is not arbitrary but relative to the heights of the physical objects. Of course, not all shadows of Dobbin are equally reliable. Dobbin's shadow at noon and those of the table and of Bossy may be almost indistinguishable "blobs." Again, although an isolated shadow of Dobbin tells us *something* about Dobbin, a *collection* of Dobbin's shadows tells us more, if we are patient enough to study them. Suppose we collect the succession of shadows cast by Dobbin throughout the day. They constitute two series: There is a contracting series, then an expanding series, which is the mirror image of the first. Thus there is an order in the shadows—an order that is permanent, though the shadows are constantly changing, and that makes it possible for us, once we know it, to make predictions about the shapes and other characteristics of subsequent shadows. In other words, a crude science is possible entirely at the level of shadows. And this science is possible only because there is a real, though unseen, Dobbin who is casting the shadows. Dobbin, as it were, "makes" the order in which the shadows occur.

Now, the relation between one of the forms, say, the form "horse," and all *its* physical objects, is the same as the relation between one of these physical objects, say, Dobbin, and all *its* shadows. Thus (1) any physical horse will be a more or less adequate shadow of the form "horse," (2) some physical horses tell us more about "horse" than others, but (3) no one horse by itself tells us very much about "horse." Dobbin, a rather decrepit, ill-used beast, will probably tell us no more about "horse" than Dobbin's shadow-blob at noon tells us about him. Man o' War, or Traveller, on the other hand, being a more respectable shadow of "horse," tells us considerably more about the nature of "horse."

But rather than studying one particular horse, whether Dobbin or Man o' War, we should compare a number of horses. If we do so, even without ever passing beyond a purely empirical level, we shall be able to observe regularities and so make useful predictions. This is the kind of science the veterinarian or the racing fan has. I may have observed that, in general, a certain shadow follows another shadow, so I act on this observation. For example, I may have observed that a certain chest formation is an indication of speed, so I put my money on the horse with this chest formation. Similarly, the veterinarian, having observed the relation between certain bodily symptoms and certain drugs, proceeds to treat a diseased animal accordingly. He knows that the animal "responds" (that certain events are followed in general by others), but *why* that is the case he does not and cannot know until he passes beyond the physical to the form, any more than the student of Dobbin's shadows can know why the shadows follow one another in this orderly sequence without passing beyond the shadows to look at Dobbin himself. And, finally, just as Dobbin makes the order of his shadows, so the form "horse," which *is* a certain collection, or pattern, of properties, is the source of all the various particular horses and of their horsiness.

So far we have considered only a world made up of shadows of Dobbin, with Dobbin in the background, unknown and even unsuspected by the student of his shadows. Suppose, now, that after a long and careful study of, and generalization from, Dobbin's shadows, the student suddenly sees Dobbin himself. What a difference! And if the student had given the name "Dobbin" to this collection of shadows (for want of knowing better), would he not now exclaim, seeing for the first time the flesh-and-blood animal, "So that's what Dobbin really is!" Dobbin, the flesh-and-blood animal, when finally known, "illumines" the shadows hitherto called by his name and makes them more intelligible. In the same way, Plato would have had us think, the form "horse" when finally known illumines and makes intelligible the individual flesh-and-blood horses, which indeed we call "horses" (as the shadows were called "Dobbin") only because we do not know the form that is *really* horse and of which they, the flesh-and-blood animals, are only the inadequate shadows.

According to Plato, anything that, when known, makes something else intelligible is "higher." That which is illumined is "lower." Since he also held that it is the abstract and general that illumines the particular, he thought of forms as "higher" and physical objects as "lower." [10] The way in which successively higher (in this sense) and more general knowledge illumines the lower and less general may be seen if one thinks of what different people with different backgrounds of information "know" about the same object—say, the motor of my car. What I see when I look under the hood of my car is a jumble of wires and gadgets among which I can distinguish something called a carburetor from something called a spark plug. As to what these things do or why they do it I have only the vaguest idea, and as to *knowledge* of the engine, I have none. Plato would not have allowed that I even have "opinion." Let us say that I "recognize" the spark plug as a spark plug and the carburetor as a carburetor—I can call them by the right name, but that is all. Most of us, outside the one or two limited fields in which we happen to be especially proficient, never get much beyond recognition. A good mechanic, however, not only recognizes the various gadgets by name but he knows what they do and how to fix them. A certain squeak or rattle *means* something to him. What it means is a function of previous experiences of similar rattles or squeaks. He knows, for instance, that by tightening this nut or screw he can stop that squeak (which is more than I know), and so on. When a man knows what stops the squeak but does not know *why* it does so, he has "opinion" in Plato's terms. Such a man may be an extremely good mechanic in the sense that he has learned by trial and error that doing thus-and-so will correct such-and-such. But the mechanic does not have *knowledge* of the engine. This requires not only an empirical acquaintance with motor cars but a theory of heat engines in which the gasoline engine is seen to be an example of certain general laws of heat energy.

Each successively "higher" knowledge is higher because it makes the engine more intelligible. Each higher level is more abstract than the one below it, all the way from the almost bare particularity of my experience (of course if it were *wholly* bare I shouldn't even be able to recognize what I experience as an engine) to the very great generality of a theory of heat.

As regards the relation, within the realm of forms, between lower (C) and higher (D) forms, here again there is a correspondence, or an analogy, with the

---

10 "Higher" and "lower" are dangerous terms; they suggest a moral scale, but it does not follow, because *x* makes *y* more intelligible, that it makes *y* better. Unfortunately Plato constantly made this illegitimate inference. He also assumed that illumination always operates from the general to the particular. But sometimes generals are illuminated by particulars. (Thus an abstract, dictionary definition of "horse" may be made significant by our becoming acquainted with some particular horse, with the pleasures of riding him, the necessity of caring for him, and so on.) What illumines what in any given context depends on what we already know and what we want to know. But such considerations take us far beyond Plato's view.

relation between A and B. The higher still illumines the lower. When we have reached a knowledge of thermodynamics and a theory of heat, we still have not reached the knowledge that, if we had it, would completely illumine our experience of the car's engine. For thermodynamics is but a small part of physics, and in order fully to understand the phenomenon of heat we have to see how thermodynamics fits into the rest of physics, just as, in order to understand the engine, we have to see *it* in relation to thermodynamics. But, since no one scientist can ever actually cover all this ground, every special science puts up more or less arbitrary boundaries, at which there are signs reading in effect, "No need to go further (we hope!)." But we can never be sure. Euclidean geometry, for instance, was for millenia conceived to be an absolute and unconditioned science. It begins with certain definitions, axioms, and postulates: "A straight line is the shortest distance between two points," "Parallel lines will never meet," and so on. Plato called these *principles;* his point is that, whereas the geometer assumes them and, having assumed them, goes on to see what he can do with them, there is a kind of study that would begin from them and work upward, trying to *prove* the basic assumptions of the Euclidean geometer. That there is much sense to Plato's contention can be seen from the fact that when, more than two millenia later, mathematicians made a determined effort to prove one of these principles— the so-called postulate of parallels—whole new geometries undreamed of before were discovered, and the basis was laid for a completely new understanding of the nature of mathematics.

Every science, then, starts from certain assumptions. It must not forget that its starting point is only a set of assumptions and that study of them might radically alter the science's notion of itself. Another way of putting this is to say that all thinking—all knowing—is *conditioned.* Most American voters, for instance, merely decide between the Republican and the Democratic candidates for the Presidency. Very few of these voters—even those who think carefully about their decision—ever ask themselves whether the whole system of quadrennial elections is sound. Yet their decision to vote in the election is really conditioned on the validity of the principles of representative government as practiced in the United States. That is, if these principles were unsound and if a man came to know them to be unsound, he might decide to abstain from voting altogether, or he might vote for the Prohibitionist candidate as a symbol of protest. Now this does not mean that we should all wait to choose between the Democratic and Republican candidates until we have established the principles of representative government by means of a process of dialectic. It does mean that, though we are always having to decide and to act on the basis of conditioned knowledge, we ought never to forget that it is conditioned.

It is not just knowledge of politics that is finite and conditioned. So, as we have seen, is geometry. So is knowledge in the fields of physics, chemistry, and biology. All the sciences, for instance, attempt to discover natural causes in the physical world. This means that each starts from an assumption, for it has never been proved that every event has a cause.

The science of first principles, the knowledge that, if we possessed it, would prove the basic assumptions of the special sciences, belongs in section D of the divided line. As long as we remain at the level of conditioned knowledge (dependent on any assumptions whatever), we are in section C. Section D would illumine and make meaningful section C, in the same way that C illumines B, and B, A. Obviously, then, in this scheme knowledge forms a pyramid. The nearer we are to the base, the more conditioned our knowledge is. The higher we rise, the more we free ourselves from conditions, until finally—this seems to have been Plato's view—we reach a single point on which everything else depends and which itself depends on nothing else. If we could know *it*, it would illumine and throw into proper scale and perspective all the rest of our knowledge. Being completely knowable in itself, it could not be made more meaningful by our coming to know something else. Since it is unconditioned, we would know everything about it that there was to know; our knowledge of it would be final, immutable, complete. This summit to the pyramid of knowledge Plato called the "Form of the Good." This is unfortunately a very difficult, not to say an obscure, notion. Plato found it impossible to give a formal analysis of it; he could, he saw, only suggest it by analogy. Hence he presented it in the myth of the sun.

### THE MYTH OF THE SUN

Really, Socrates, said Glaucon, you must not give up within sight of the goal. We should be quite content with an account of the Good like the one you gave us of justice and temperance and the other virtues.

So should I be, my dear Glaucon, much more than content! But I am afraid it is beyond my powers. . . . However, I will tell you, though only if you wish it, what I picture to myself as the offspring of the Good and the thing most nearly resembling it. . . . First . . . let me remind you of the distinction we drew earlier and have often drawn on other occasions, between the multiplicity of things that we call good or beautiful or whatever it may be and, on the other hand, Goodness itself or Beauty itself and so on. Corresponding to each of these sets of many things, we postulate a single Form or real essence, as we call it.

Further, the many things, we say, can be seen, but are not objects of rational thought; whereas the Forms are objects of thought, but invisible.

Yes, certainly.

And we see things with our eyesight, just as we hear sounds with our ears and, to speak generally, perceive any sensible thing with our sense-faculties.

Of course.

Have you noticed, then, that . . . you may have the power of vision in your eyes and try to use it, and colour may be there in the objects; but sight will see nothing and the colours will remain invisible in the absence of a third thing peculiarly constituted to serve this very purpose.

By which you mean—?

Naturally I mean what you call light; and . . . of all the divinities in the skies is there one whose light, above all the rest, is responsible for making our eyes see perfectly and making objects perfectly visible?

There can be no two opinions: of course you mean the Sun. . . .

It was the Sun, then, that I meant when I spoke of that offspring which the Good has created in the visible world, to stand there in the same relation to vision and visible things as that which the Good itself bears in the intelligible world to intelligence and to intelligible objects.

How is that? You must explain further.

You know what happens when the colours of things are no longer irradiated by the daylight, but only by the fainter luminaries of the night: when you look at them, the eyes are dim and seem almost blind. . . . But when you look at things on which the Sun is shining, the same eyes see distinctly and it becomes evident that they do contain the power of vision.

Certainly.

Apply this comparison, then, to the soul. When its gaze is fixed upon an object irradiated by truth and reality, the soul gains understanding and knowledge and is manifestly in possession of intelligence. But when it looks towards that twilight world of things that come into existence and pass away, its sight is dim and it has only opinions and beliefs which shift to and fro, and now it seems like a thing that has no intelligence.

That is true.

This, then, which gives to the objects of knowledge their truth and to him who knows them his power of knowing, is the Form or essential nature of Goodness. It is the cause of knowledge and truth; and so, while you may think of it as an object of knowledge, you will do well to regard it as something beyond truth and knowledge and, precious as these both are, of still higher worth. And, just as in our analogy light and vision were to be thought of as like the Sun, but not identical with it, so here both knowledge and truth are to be regarded as like the Good, but to identify either with the Good is wrong. The Good must hold a yet higher place of honour. . . . I want to follow up our analogy still further. You will agree that the Sun not only makes the things we see visible, but also brings them into existence and gives them growth and nourishment; yet he is not the same thing as existence. And so with the objects of knowledge: these derive from the Good not only their power of being known, but their very being and reality; and Goodness is not the same thing as being, but even beyond being, surpassing it in dignity and power.[g]

Thus Plato held that the Form of the Good—the summit of the pyramid of knowledge, the point from which the whole of knowledge and of being is unified—is inexplicable to anyone who has not studied dialectic and traversed the long path through sections C and D of the divided line. This is probably correct. But it is true of any experience—not only of a great one like that of the Form of the Good. If you've never tasted an avocado, I cannot communicate the taste to you by a description. The best I can do is to say, "Well, it tastes a little like . . . ," and that is lame and inadequate. To take another example, there are only two ways of knowing what it is like to be under fire. One is by being under fire; the other is through a work of art, which is not a description but an imaginative re-creation.

This helps explain the role of *myth* in Plato's writings. Plato thought that none of the really important things—the real essence of goodness, nobility of spirit, humanity—could be condensed into neat copybook maxims. They elude these as the real flavor of Paris eludes a Baedeker guidebook. The best way, Plato thought, to learn the meaning of such concepts is to live close to someone who already knows them (just as the best way to get to know Paris is to go there, walk the streets and sit in the sidewalk cafés, stroll along the banks of the Seine and in the Luxembourg gardens). If one lives with such a great-souled man for a long time, one may pick up what he knows—not through formal lectures, nor even entirely through example, but through a kind of intellectual and moral osmosis. This would be direct experience. To those who are not fortunate enough to participate in such an experience directly, Plato offered a *myth*, which is, as it were, an imitation of the experience—not a description of it, but an artistic evocation of it. Hence, whenever in our reading of the dialogues we come to a myth, we can be sure we have reached a point of great importance for Plato. A good rule to follow is to take the myth seriously but not literally. It is not a fairy tale designed to amuse; it says in the language of poetry and art what is too subtle and elusive to be said in any other way.[11]

There is, unfortunately, a difficulty about this. If you've never tasted avocado, you have tasted other bland, pulpy foods; if you've never been to Paris, at least you've visited other large, many-faceted cities. Hence the artist who is seeking to communicate these experiences to you has something to go on. However, the philosopher (Plato in this case) who is seeking to communicate the nature of the Form of the Good has nothing to go on; his task is much harder. After all, we do know that Paris exists; we know that other people have eaten avocados. But nobody, unless he simply accepts what Plato said, even knows that there *is* a Form of the Good. Thus the sceptic who after listening to the myth replies, "Well, I'm sorry, I simply don't have any idea, really, what you're talking about," isn't necessarily to be pitied. Of course, it may be that Plato is right and that the sceptic is depriving himself of the opportunity to share in an all-important experience. However, it may be that Plato is deluded: There may be nothing there to be communicated about.

But assuming that Plato is correct, that there *is* something there, what can we learn about the Form of the Good from myth, in lieu of a direct experience through a study of dialectic? In the *Republic*, Socrates tries to bring out three points in his comparison of the Form of the Good with the sun. One is that, just as the sun makes physical things on the earth visible, the Form of the Good illumines and makes meaningful lower levels of knowledge and opinion. Enough, perhaps, has already been said on this point. Second, Socrates says that the sun

11 The role of myth in Plato's thought is discussed in greater detail on pp. 194–95.

nourishes plants and other living things. In an analogous way, we must suppose, the Form of the Good is not a cold, lifeless, and indifferent searchlight illumining our knowledge but is somehow an active and creative power.

Third, there is an "affinity" between our eyes and the sun. Here Plato probably had in mind a contemporary physiological theory according to which the eye contains fire (because it shines and is bright) just as the sun does. In order to bring Plato's analogy up to date one might state the affinity between eye and sun by saying that the eye is so constructed that it perceives at least a part of the range of light emitted by the sun. If this were not the case, we could not see. Thus it is an affinity between the sun and our eyes that makes visible things visible. In the same way there is an affinity between the Form of the Good and our minds, such that the Form of the Good satisfies the kinds of questions minds such as ours ask. The realm of forms might conceivably be indifferent to us, static and aloof. There might be an objective, public reality, but this reality might have no affinity with us. This is the reality Atomism revealed, and it is the kind of world modern science discloses: a world of energy that, by some curious coincidence, behaves in ways our mathematical minds can understand but that is utterly indifferent to the questions our moral natures ask— a world in which our cosmic hopes and fears get no answer.

This conception of reality Plato denied. Man is not merely, he thought, a neutral knower, merely curious about the world; he is not indifferent to everything except knowing what reality is. He is a moral, esthetic, social, and religious creature as well. For his final satisfaction, therefore, the world in which he lives must be one that can satisfy the demands his complex nature makes. This is why Plato called the highest reality the Form of the Good; it is something that, when known, answers our ultimate questionings. In other words, Plato was affirming the old Greek notion of cosmos. The world and man form an organic unity. The reality out there waiting to be known is somehow consonant with the moral knower. The world of forms, then, satisfies not merely our demands for knowledge but also, Plato maintained, our demands for justice, for beauty, and for religious and moral meaning. Since what truly satisfies is truly good, it is quite correct to describe the highest of all forms as the Form of the Good.

These notions, and many others, are brought out finally in the myth of the cave.

### THE MYTH OF THE CAVE

Next, said I,[12] here is a parable to illustrate the degrees in which our nature may be enlightened or unenlightened. Imagine the condition of men living in a sort of cavernous chamber underground, with an entrance open to the light and a long passage all down the cave. Here they have been from

12 [Socrates is still relating his conversation with Glaucon to a third party. See p. 126, note 9 —AUTHOR.]

childhood, chained by the leg and also by the neck, so that they cannot move and can see only what is in front of them, because the chains will not let them turn their heads. At some distance higher up is the light of a fire burning behind them; and between the prisoners and the fire is a track with a parapet built along it, like the screen at a puppet-show, which hides the performers while they show their puppets over the top.

I see, said he.

Now behind this parapet imagine persons carrying along various artificial objects, including figures of men and animals in wood or stone or other materials, which project above the parapet. Naturally, some of these persons will be talking, others silent. . . . Prisoners so confined would have seen nothing of themselves or of one another, except the shadows thrown by the fire-light on the wall of the Cave facing them, would they? . . . [And] if they could talk to one another, would they not suppose that their words referred only to those passing shadows which they saw?

Necessarily.

And suppose their prison had an echo from the wall facing them? When one of the people crossing behind them spoke, they could only suppose that the sound came from the shadow passing before their eyes.

No doubt.

In every way, then, such prisoners would recognize as reality nothing but the shadows of those artificial objects.

Inevitably.

Now . . . suppose one of them set free and forced suddenly to stand up, turn his head, and walk with eyes lifted to the light; all these movements would be painful, and he would be too dazzled to make out the objects whose shadows he had been used to see. . . . And if he were forced to look at the fire-light itself, would not his eyes ache, so that he would try to escape and turn back to the things which he could see distinctly, convinced that they really were clearer than these other objects now being shown to him?

Yes.

And suppose someone were to drag him away forcibly up the steep and rugged ascent and not let him go until he had hauled him out into the sunlight, would he not suffer pain and vexation at such treatment, and, when he had come out into the light, find his eyes so full of its radiance that he could not see a single one of the things that he was now told were real?

Certainly he would not see them all at once.

He would need, then, to grow accustomed before he could see things in that upper world. . . . Last of all, he would be able to look at the Sun and contemplate its nature. . . .

No doubt.

And now he would begin to draw the conclusion that it is the Sun that produces the seasons and the course of the year and controls everything in the visible world, and moreover is in a way the cause of all that he and his companions used to see.

Clearly he would come at last to that conclusion.

Then if he called to mind his fellow prisoners and what passed for wisdom in his former dwelling-place, he would surely think himself happy in the change and be sorry for them. . . . Would our released prisoner . . . not . . . endure anything rather than go back to his old beliefs and live in the old way?

Yes, he would prefer any fate to such a life.

Now imagine what would happen if he went down again to take his former seat in the Cave. Coming suddenly out of the sunlight, his eyes would be filled with darkness. He might be required once more to deliver his opinion on those shadows, in competition with the prisoners who had never been released, while his eyesight was still dim and unsteady; and it might take some time to become used to the darkness. They would laugh at him and say that he had gone up only to come back with his sight ruined; it was worth no one's while even to attempt the ascent. If they could lay hands on the man who was trying to set them free and lead them up, they would kill him.

Yes, they would.

Every feature in this parable, my dear Glaucon, is meant to fit our earlier analysis. The prison dwelling corresponds to the region revealed to us through the sense of sight, and the fire-light within it to the power of the Sun. The ascent to see the things in the upper world you may take as standing for the upward journey of the soul into the region of the intelligible. . . . In the world of knowledge, the last thing to be perceived and only with great difficulty is the essential Form of Goodness. Once it is perceived, the conclusion must follow that, for all things, this is the cause of whatever is right and good; in the visible world it gives birth to light and to the lord of light, while it is itself sovereign in the intelligible world and the parent of intelligence and truth. Without having had a vision of this Form no one can act with wisdom, either in his own life or in matters of state.

So far as I can understand, I share your belief. . . .

If this is true, then, we must conclude that education is not what it is said to be by some, who profess to put knowledge into a soul which does not possess it, as if they could put sight into blind eyes. On the contrary, our own account signifies that the soul of every man does possess the power of learning the truth and the organ to see it with; and that, just as one might have to turn the whole body round in order that the eye should see light instead of darkness, so the entire soul must be turned away from this changing world, until its eye can bear to contemplate reality and that supreme splendour which we have called the Good. Hence there may well be an art whose aim would be ιo effect this very thing . . . to ensure that, instead of looking in the wrong direction, [the soul] is turned the way it ought to be.[h]

Thus, according to Plato, any man who is fortunate enough and well endowed enough to extricate himself from the cave of ignorance sees the sun; the world the sun illumines is one, and it is beautiful, and it is good. That is to say, being and value coincide. The more being anything has—the higher it stands in the hierarchy of forms—the more knowable it is and the more beautiful and the better it is. Though the journey is slow and arduous, it is worth undertaking. Not only is our intellectual curiosity satisfied by ascertaining the absolute truth about things, but what we thus come to know proves to be supremely good. Those who have not seen this world that is illumined by the sun cannot possibly know "it as it really is." They can only be sure that there is "some such reality which it concerns us to see."[i]

Meanwhile, the cave dwellers are happy in their ignorance, which they do not recognize to be ignorance, and in their prejudices, which they do not know to be prejudices. They can, it is true, develop a crude empirical science, predicting the sequences of shadows (as the garage mechanic can discover by trial and error how to stop a certain squeak, without knowing why the squeak has occurred or why tightening this nut or bolt "cures" it). Such an empirical science may be useful, but it is not *knowledge*, for it is about shadows, or imitations, of real objects. Its objects, in other words, are at two removes from the truth, just as the fire that casts the shadows in the cave is only the imitation of that greater fire, the sun, which in its turn illumines the real objects of the real world.

Whether one can make the ascent out of the cave of ignorance depends in the last analysis on oneself, on one's native capacities. A teacher can only turn a student's head in the right direction, toward the mouth of the cave. True education is thus the opposite of indoctrination. It is not a process of pouring assorted facts into a student's head as rapidly as possible; it is a process of pointing. If the student is not blind, he will see the light when it is called to his attention. Seeing—even faintly as he must at first—the beautiful and good, he will strive towards it.

Finally, the man who makes the ascent into the real world realizes that, despite the joys of a free life in the sunlight, he must return to the cave and try to help his fellows. This he does though he also knows they will hate him for his pains and kill him if they can, even as they killed Socrates. Why make this sterile sacrifice? Because, in the first place, it may not be sterile. Some few of the cave men may listen and look and so be enabled to rise to that happier, sunlit life outside the cave; for every murdered Socrates in one generation there may be a Plato in the next. And because, in the second place, as Plato held, man is a social animal. He is a part, an organ, in a larger organism. The best life for him, therefore, is not one of individual communion with the good and true (like that of some Christian saint); it is rather one of association with his fellows, even if this requires him to live with them in a cave. Here is one of the most central of Plato's concepts—and one in which he is most typically Greek. Man, being a social and political creature, has moral and political responsibilities, the problem of being a good man is inseparable from the problem of being a good citizen.

### THE WAY OF ASCENT

Alongside of the passages from the *Republic* that have been given, it may be well to put one from the *Symposium* that brings out a few more important points in connection with the way of ascent and the vision of reality from the summit.[13]

"And now I shall . . . proceed with the discourse upon Love which I heard one day from a Mantinean woman named Diotima. . . . The readiest way, I think, will be to give my description that form of question and answer which the stranger woman used for hers that day. For I [said that] Love was a great god, and was of beautiful things; and she refuted me . . . showing that by my account that god was neither beautiful nor good.

" 'How do you mean, Diotima?' said I; 'is Love then ugly and bad?'

" 'Peace, for shame!' she replied: . . . 'when you find yourself admitting that he is not good nor beautiful, do not therefore suppose he must be ugly and bad, but something betwixt the two.'

" 'And what of the notion,' I asked, 'to which every one agrees, that he is a great god?' . . .

" 'How then can he be a god, if he is devoid of things beautiful and good?'

" 'By no means, it appears. . . . What then,' I asked, 'can Love be? . . .'

" 'A great spirit, Socrates: for the whole of the spiritual is between divine and mortal.'

" 'Possessing what power?' I asked.

" 'Interpreting and transporting human things to the gods and divine things to men . . . : being midway between, it makes each to supplement the other, so that the whole is combined in one. . . . God with man does not mingle: but the spiritual is the means of all society and converse of men with gods and of gods with men, whether waking or asleep. . . . Many and multifarious are these spirits, and one of them is Love.'

" 'From what father and mother sprung?' I asked.

" 'That is rather a long story,' she replied; 'but still, I will tell it you. When Aphrodite was born, the gods made a great feast, and among the company was Resource the son of Cunning. And when they had banqueted there came Poverty abegging, as well she might in an hour of good cheer, and hung about the door. Now Resource, grown tipsy with nectar—for wine as yet there was none—went into the garden of Zeus, and there, overcome with heaviness, slept. Then Poverty, being of herself so resourceless, devised the scheme of having a child by Resource, and lying down by his side she conceived Love. Hence it is that Love from the beginning has been attendant and minister to Aphrodite, since he was begotten on the day of her birth. . . . Now, as the son of Resource and Poverty, Love is in a peculiar case. First, he is ever poor, and far from tender or beautiful as most suppose him: rather is he hard and parched, shoeless and homeless; . . . true to his mother's nature, he ever dwells with want. But he takes after his father in scheming for all that is beautiful and good; for he is brave, strenuous and high-strung, a famous

13 It will be recalled (see p. 110) that each guest at Agathon's dinner party contracted to make a speech in praise of love. The following is Socrates' speech, which he pretended, with characteristic modesty, to have heard from "a Mantinean woman named Diotima."

hunter, always weaving some stratagem; desirous and competent of wisdom, throughout life ensuing the truth; a master of jugglery, witchcraft, and artful speech. By birth neither immortal nor mortal, . . . he stands midway betwixt wisdom and ignorance. The position is this: no gods ensue wisdom or desire to be made wise; such they are already. . . . Neither do the ignorant ensue wisdom, nor desire to be made wise: . . . the man who does not feel himself defective has no desire for that whereof he feels no defect.' . . .

"Upon this I observed: 'Very well then, madam, you are right; but if Love is such as you describe him, of what use is he to mankind?'

" 'That is the next question, Socrates,' she replied, 'on which I will try to enlighten you. While Love is of such nature and origin as I have related, he is also set on beautiful things, as you say. Now, suppose some one were to ask us: . . . What is the love of the lover of beautiful things?'

" 'That they may be his,' I replied.

" 'But your answer craves a further query,' she said, 'such as this: What will he have who gets beautiful things?' . . .

" 'He will be happy.'

" 'Yes,' she said, . . . 'and we have no more need to ask for what end a man wishes to be happy, when such is his wish: the answer seems to be ultimate.'

" 'Quite true,' I said.

" 'Now do you suppose this wish or this love to be common to all mankind, and that every one always wishes to have good things? Or what do you say?'

" 'Even so,' I said; 'it is common to all.' . . .

" 'Then we may state unreservedly that men love the good?'

" 'Yes,' I said.

" 'Well now, must we not extend it to this, that they love the good to be theirs?'

" 'We must.'

" 'And do they love it to be not merely theirs but theirs always?'

" 'Include that also.'

" 'Briefly then,' said she, 'love loves the good to be one's own for ever.'

" 'That is the very truth,' I said.

" 'Now if love is always for this,' she proceeded, . . . 'we needs must yearn for immortality no less than for good, since love loves good to be one's own for ever. And hence it necessarily follows that love is of immortality. . . .

" 'The mortal nature ever seeks, as best it can, to be immortal. In one way only can it succeed, and that is by generation; since so it can always leave behind it a new creature in place of the old. It is only for a while that each live thing can be described as alive and the same, as a man is said to be the same person from childhood until he is advanced in years: yet though he is called the same he does not at any time possess the same properties; he is continually becoming a new person, and there are things also which he loses, as appears by his hair, his flesh, his bones, and his blood and body altogether. And observe that not only in his body but in his soul besides we find none of his manners or habits, his opinions, desires, pleasures, pains or fears, ever abiding the same in his particular self; some things grow in him, while others perish. . . . Every mortal thing is preserved in this way; not by keeping it exactly the same for ever, like the divine, but by replacing what goes off or is antiquated with something fresh, in the semblance of the original. Through this device, Socrates, a mortal thing partakes of immortality, both in its body and in all other respects; by no other means can it be done. So do not wonder if everything naturally values its own offshoot; since all are beset by this eagerness and this love with a view to immortality. . . .

" 'Now those who are teeming in body betake them . . . to women, and . . . by getting children they acquire an immortality. . . . But pregnancy of soul—for there are persons,' she declared, 'who in their souls still more than in their bodies conceive those things which are proper for soul to conceive and bring forth; and what are those things? Prudence, and virtue in general; and of these the begetters are all the poets and those craftsmen who are styled *inventors*. Now by far the highest and fairest part of prudence is that which concerns the regulation of cities and habitations; it is called sobriety and justice. . . . Every one would choose to have got children such as these rather than the human sort. . . . Only look,' she said, 'at the fine children whom Lycurgus left behind him in Lacedaemon. . . .[14]

" 'Into these love-matters even you, Socrates, might haply be initiated; but I doubt if you could approach the rites and revelations to which these, for the properly instructed, are merely the avenue. . . . He who would proceed rightly in this business must not merely begin from his youth to encounter beautiful bodies. In the first place, indeed, if his conductor guides him aright, he must be in love with one particular body, and engender beautiful converse therein; but next he must remark how the beauty attached to this or that body is cognate to that which is attached to any other, and that if he means to ensue beauty in form, it is gross folly not to regard as one and the same the beauty belonging to all; and so, having grasped this truth, he must make himself a lover of all beautiful bodies, and slacken the stress of his feeling for one by contemning it and counting it a trifle. But his next advance will be to set a higher value on the beauty of souls than on that of the body, so that . . . finally he may be constrained to contemplate the beautiful as appearing in our observances and our laws, and to behold it all bound together in kinship and so estimate the body's beauty as a slight affair. From observances he should be led on to the branches of knowledge . . . ; until with the strength and increase there acquired he descries a certain single knowledge connected with a beauty which has yet to be told.

" 'This, Socrates, is the final object of all those previous toils. First of all, it is ever-existent and neither comes to be nor perishes, neither waxes nor wanes; next, it is not beautiful in part and in part ugly, nor is it such at such a time and other at another, nor in one respect beautiful and in another ugly, nor so affected by position as to seem beautiful to some and ugly to others. . . . In the state of life above all others, my dear Socrates,' said the Mantinean woman, 'a man finds it truly worth while to live, as he contemplates essential beauty. . . . He, above all men, is immortal.'

"This, Phaedrus and you others, is what Diotima told me, and I am per-

14 [See pp. 41–43—AUTHOR.]

suaded of it; in which persuasion I pursue my neighbours, to persuade them in turn that towards this acquisition the best helper that our human nature can hope to find is Love. . . ."ʲ

The language here is quite different from the language of the *Republic*. In the divided line and in the myth of the cave we hear of dialectic and of truth; we hear little of love and of beauty. The *Republic* tends to emphasize the cognitive side of the view from the top, that is, the satisfaction of our drive to understand the world and to learn what it really is. The *Symposium* emphasizes the esthetic side of the same experience. But these are not two (or three) separate drives with distinct satisfactions. For Plato (as, many centuries later, for Keats), beauty is truth and truth is beauty—and both are good.

Aside from this, the *Symposium* emphasizes (what is also brought out in the myth of the cave) that man is a social being: If one reaches the top it is only because of an opportunity for association with some initiate who has been willing to descend again into the cave.

The way of ascent is, as we have seen, by close association with some great-souled man. But love, which begins at the level of physical attraction, can be transmuted by gradual stages. What was originally an attraction to a face or a figure can pass into admiration for the character of the individual who possesses these happy attributes, and then can become in turn love for a group, or a college, or a cause—the underprivileged, world peace, or the rights of man—and even these can be absorbed in something higher, the love of the beautiful and good.

This notion of cooperative advance toward goodness and truth is also contained in the concept of dialectic as the method by which we progress from the lower forms of level C to the higher forms of level D. For dialectic, about which Plato said almost nothing in detail, is presumably only a very advanced type of the process of question and answer—of offering an hypothesis, hearing it criticized, and revising it—that constantly goes on in all Plato's dialogues. And underlying this method of dialogue, or dialectic, is the assumption that the persons conducting the dialogue are men of good will, not showing off or trying to get the best of opponents, but helping each other get nearer the truth.

One final point is brought out in the *Symposium*. The way of ascent is a process: One moves by stages, from one level to another, from one compartment of learning to another on which the former turns out to depend. But the view from the top is a vision: At the end there are no stages, no compartments. The whole is not experienced as a collection of neatly connected parts; it is a true whole—unified, harmonious, and complete.

## PROOF OF THE THEORY OF FORMS

Up to now we have been considering simply what Plato meant by "forms" and what role they have in his philosophical system. This long discussion can be summarized by saying that by "forms" Plato meant eternal and unchanging entities, which are encountered not in perception but in thought. They constitute that public world that the Sophists had denied and that functions at once as the object of the sciences—physical, social, and moral—and the objective criteria against which our judgments in these inquiries are evaluated. As the objects of thought, the forms justify thought in looking for objects. Without the forms there would be nothing, in Plato's view, to look for, and every individual would remain forever isolated in the cave of his own subjective states.

But *are* there forms? Do forms such as Plato described actually exist? Though the dialogues tend to assume their existence (this was natural since Plato was probably writing chiefly for friends and students), it is clear that the question of proof was much discussed in the Academy and that a variety of arguments were worked out. In general these proofs seem to have involved a challenge to find in the changing world of sense perception anything adequate to be an object of knowledge. Thus, anyone who doubts the existence of forms might be asked, "Do you allow that there is a knowledge of triangles?" If the doubter admits this, the argument might proceed, "Well, what is the triangle about which you admit there is knowledge? Not this or that particular drawn triangle, for none of these sense objects has exactly the qualities in question. They are not really triangles. Hence, if you admit that there really is such an object as a triangle and that we have knowledge of it, you have to admit there are nonempirical, nonsensible things. These objects are the forms." This type of argument appears in the *Phaedo* in connection with the notion of equality.[15]

> "Now how about such things as this, Simmias? Do we think there is such a thing as absolute justice, or not?"
> "We certainly think there is."
> "And absolute beauty and goodness."
> "Of course."
> "Well, did you ever see anything of that kind with your eyes?"
> "Certainly not," said [Simmias]. . . .
> "Now see," said [Socrates], "if this is true. We say there is such a thing as equality. I do not mean one piece of wood equal to another, or one stone to another, or anything of that sort, but something beyond that—equality in the abstract. Shall we say there is such a thing, or not?"
> "We shall say that there is," said Simmias, "most decidedly."
> "And do we know what it is?"
> "Certainly," said he.
> "Whence did we derive the knowledge of it? Is it not from the things we

---

15 This is the discussion that took place on the day of Socrates' death (see p. 117). The proofs of the forms are introduced in the course of an argument for the immortality of the soul, a subject which not unnaturally interested Socrates as he awaited his executioner. The speakers are Socrates and his friend Simmias.

were just speaking of? . . . Do not equal stones and pieces of wood, though they remain the same, sometimes appear to us equal in one respect and unequal in another?"

"Certainly."

"Well, then, did absolute equals ever appear to you unequal or equality inequality?"

"No, Socrates, never."

"Then," said [Socrates], "those equals are not the same as equality in the abstract."

"Not at all, I should say, Socrates."

"But from those equals," said he, "which are not the same as abstract equality, you have nevertheless conceived and acquired knowledge of it?" . . .

"Whenever the sight of one thing brings you a perception of another, whether they be like or unlike, that must necessarily be recollection."

"Surely."

"Now then," said [Socrates], "do the equal pieces of wood . . . seem to us to be equal as abstract equality is equal, or do they somehow fall short of being like abstract equality?"

"They fall very far short of it," said [Simmias].

"Do we agree, then, that when anyone on seeing a thing thinks, 'This thing that I see aims at being like some other thing that exists, but falls short and is unable to be like that thing, but is inferior to it,' he who thinks thus must of necessity have previous knowledge of the thing which he says the other resembles but falls short of?"

"We must." . . .

"Then we must have had knowledge of equality before the time when we first saw equal things and thought, 'All these things are aiming to be like equality but fall short.'"

"That is true."

"And we agree, also, that . . . it is through the senses that we must learn that all sensible objects strive after absolute equality and fall short of it. Is that our view?"

"Yes."

"Then before we began to see or hear or use the other senses we must somewhere have gained a knowledge of abstract or absolute equality. . . ."

"That follows necessarily from what we have said before, Socrates."

"And we saw and heard and had the other senses as soon as we were born?"

"Certainly."

"But, we say, we must have acquired a knowledge of equality before we had these senses?"

"Yes."

"Then it appears that we must have acquired it before we were born."

"It does."

"Now if we had acquired that knowledge before we were born, and . . . lost it at birth, but afterwards by the use of our senses regained the knowledge which we had previously possessed, would not the process which we call learning really be recovering knowledge which is our own? And should we be right in calling this recollection?"

"Assuredly." . . .

"Then, Simmias, the souls existed previously, before they were in human form, apart from bodies, and they had intelligence. . . . Is this the state of the case? If, as we are always saying, the beautiful exists, and the good, and every essence of that kind, and if we . . . compare our sensations with these, is it not a necessary inference that just as these abstractions exist, so our souls existed before we were born?" . . .

"Socrates, it seems to me that there is absolutely the same certainty, and our argument comes to the excellent conclusion that our souls existed before we were born, and that the essence of which you speak likewise exists."[k]

In the last few exchanges in this passage, Socrates and Simmias have moved from a proof of the existence of forms to a proof of the transmigration of the soul, by arguing that our knowledge of forms can be accounted for only on the assumption that we existed before we were born into this world. With this step we are not now concerned. The argument for the existence of forms ends at the point at which Simmias admits that our knowledge of abstract or absolute equality cannot have been acquired through the senses.

This argument is certainly not without force. It would be hard to deny that we know what equality is—how otherwise could we know that any two sticks are unequal? To observe *that*, we must apply the criterion of equality and find them wanting. And since it is agreed that sticks are never absolutely equal, our knowledge of this criterion cannot have been derived from sensory experience. Thus the empirical fact, which no one would deny, that we judge the sticks to be unequal proves both that we have a knowledge of equality and that this equality cannot be physical.

The argument may be generalized as follows: (1) Either we know something (that is, at least one thing) or we know nothing. (2) Suppose you opt for the second alternative. Either you claim to know that the second alternative is true or you do not make this claim. If you don't claim to know that the second alternative is true, we throw out your reply as worthless. If you do claim to know that the second alternative is true, you have contradicted yourself. For by your own account there is now at least one thing that you claim to know, namely, that you know nothing. Hence (3) the first alternative is true: There is at least one thing that is known. Therefore, (4) knowledge is possible. It follows that (5) forms exist, for only forms have the characteristics—immutability, eternity—requisite for knowledge.

This is the line of argument used in the *Timaeus*, in which Plato merely points out that if there is knowledge (as distinct from opinion) there must be forms (as distinct from sense objects).

> If intelligence and true belief are two different kinds, then forms that we cannot perceive but only think of, certainly exist in themselves. . . . Now we must affirm that they are two different things, for they are distinct in origin and unlike in nature: the one is produced in us by instruction, the other by persuasion; the one can always give a true account of itself, the other can give none; the one cannot be shaken by persuasion whereas the other can be won over; the true belief, we must allow, is shared by all mankind, intelligence only by the gods and a small number of men.[1]

Thus the logical form of Plato's argument is simple and straightforward. It is a challenge to account for the possibility of knowledge in any way other than on the assumption of forms. But no proof of this type ever establishes conclusively the proposition it is intended to maintain; it always rests on the inability of the critic to find an alternative explanation. This is weak, since (1) even if the critic himself cannot find an alternative, there may be one, and (2) he may find it. This, indeed, is exactly what happened in mathematics. Mathematics has always been the most plausible region in which to assert the existence of forms, both because mathematical knowledge is certain and because it is not about physical objects (not about the drawn or incised triangles). If mathematics is about something, there must be a nonphysical object, a form, for it to be about—thus the argument runs. But nowadays many people account for the certainty of mathematics very differently. Mathematics is certain, they say, not because it is about a nonphysical, as distinct from a physical, object but because it is not about objects at all. Mathematical certainty, in this view, results from the fact that the propositions of mathematics are all tautologies. When we affirm that parallel lines never meet, we are not asserting an eternal truth about the universe, but defining how we propose to use the word "parallel," just as when we say, "All cats are felines," we are merely stating how we are going to use the word "cat."

Whether this view of mathematics is correct is an extremely difficult matter—in fact, as we shall subsequently see, it is one of the great partings of the way in philosophy. And it is clearly impossible at this stage of our inquiry to settle the question of whether it is necessary to assume the existence of forms. But this need not prevent our accepting the forms provisionally as a working hypothesis—though this is not how Plato would have wanted us to have to proceed, for the forms were supposed to save us from the need of thinking hypothetically. Let us, then, proceed to study the way in which Plato applied this conception to physics, ethics, politics, and the other special sciences.

# CHAPTER 5

# Plato: The Special Sciences

## Physics

Although philosophy before Plato and Socrates had been chiefly concerned with physics, only one of Plato's dialogues, the *Timaeus,* is concerned to any great degree with natural science. In the first place, in view of the cultural malaise into which Greece had fallen, Plato felt it more important to know the truth about morals and politics than to discover the nature of the physical world. In the second place, he seems to have believed it impossible to achieve in the latter field more than what he called a "likely story."

Doubtless he was discouraged, as everyone else was, by the repeated failures of the scientists—of Anaximander and Anaximenes, Empedocles and Anaxagoras, Leucippus and Democritus—to reach agreement about the structure of the physical world. In the *Phaedo,* Plato says that as a young man Socrates had had "a prodigious desire to know that department of philosophy which is called the investigation of nature; to know the causes of things and why a thing is and is created or destroyed . . . ." But the more he studied the more disappointed he became, for "one man sets the earth within a cosmic whirling, and steadies it by the heaven; another gives the air as a support to the earth," and so on.[a] One and all they described only "conditions," rather than giving "causes."

Recognition that science had not yet achieved the truth about the physical world might, of course, have been accompanied by optimism about its eventual success. But Plato did not believe that physics *could* reach the truth. There are two reasons for his doubt, both of which follow from the theory of forms. The first is related to his relegation of change to the sphere of appearance. The aim of physics, as we understand it today and as it was understood by the Greeks, is to give an account of process. But from Plato's point of view, knowledge is solely of the eternal and unchanging. It follows that if physics is about the physical world, it is not knowledge; if it is knowledge, it is not about the physical world.

This is the thesis of the *Timaeus.* Just as the physical triangle drawn on the blackboard is only an imitation of the intelligible form "triangle," so the physical world itself—the object of physics—is but a changing "likeness" of an eternal form. No account of the physical world, therefore, can be more than a "likely story."[b]

Further, Plato believed that physics asks the wrong sort of question. It asks, "What are the 'conditions' under which such and such a change occurs?"—and it believes itself to answer satisfactorily when it gives an exhaustive account of these conditions. Plato not only denied that such an exact account is possible, but he held that the important question is not about the conditions under which the change occurs but about the "causes" of the change, or (as we might say) the reasons why the change occurs.

In the *Phaedo* Plato gives a vivid example of the difference between "condition" and "reason." Socrates is sitting in prison waiting for the death sentence to be carried out. If you were to ask a physicist, he says in this dialogue, why I sit here, he would give you an account in terms of muscles and bones. He would "show that I sit here because my body is made up of bones and muscles; and the bones, as he would say, are hard and have joints which divide them, and the muscles are elastic . . . and as the bones are lifted at their joints by the contraction or relaxation of the muscles, I am able to bend my limbs, and this is why I am sitting here in a curved posture," and so on.

But this description of the physiological conditions entirely neglects

> . . . to mention the true cause, which is, that the Athenians have thought it better to condemn me, and accordingly I have thought it better and more right to remain here and undergo my sentence. . . . There is surely a strange confusion of causes and conditions in all this. It may be said, indeed, that without bones and muscles and the other parts of the body I cannot execute

my purposes. But to say . . . that I do as I do because of them, and not from the choice of the best, is a very careless and idle mode of speaking.[c]

The distinction Plato is insisting on in the *Phaedo* is between a *teleological explanation* of why things happen and a *mechanistic description* of how they happen. But, though it may seem reasonable to talk about why Socrates sat in prison instead of fleeing to Megara, it does not seem as sensible (at least today) to talk about why rocks fall or planets gravitate. This is because we do not think of mind as being the cause of events in the physical world. In this respect we are much nearer the Atomists than Plato. Like the Atomists we think of the universe as indifferent to purpose, that is, as nonteleological. Whereas Plato held that the gravitation of bodies can, and should, be explained by showing that it is best for them to gravitate, we think of "gravity" simply as the term that names a mathematically precise description of how bodies behave under certain conditions.

Plato appears to have held that there is a mind at work in the universe, as there was a mind at work in Socrates' body. But whether he thought this world mind to be *like* Socrates' is debatable. It is clear, however, that, to the extent that he did think such a mind exists and that its purposes affect the behavior of the physical world, he must have thought physics subordinate to theology. Consideration of this question will be postponed, therefore, until we consider Plato's religion. For the present we shall concentrate on his account of the "conditions," remembering that even about the conditions we can, according to him, give only a "likely story."

### NATURE OF THE PHYSICAL WORLD

Let us begin with the objects of ordinary perception. When I look at Old Dobbin and see that he is brown, I believe that the brown color is "out there" where I perceive it to be. Both Democritus and the Sophists denied this, and Plato agreed with them. Colors, Plato thought, are not "self-existent." The brown that I experience is really a motion passing between my eye and the object. It is therefore peculiar to me. Do we think, Socrates asks in the *Theaetetus*, that "every color appears to a dog or any other creature just such as it appears to you?"[d] What we call "Dobbin" (and so, of course, what we call "eye") is a complex set of motions. The experience of color arises when the motions we call eye meet an "appropriate" motion out there. As regards colors and other sense qualities, then, Protagoras was correct. Every man (and every dog) is the measure for himself, because the motions that constitute his sense organs differ from those that constitute the sense organs of every other individual. In this Heraclitean flux we cannot say that Dobbin *is* brown; we can only say, "Dobbin appears brown to me now."

But Protagoras was correct only with regard to sense perception. Reason can ascertain what Dobbin "really" is, as distinct from what he appears to be. What is it, then, that operates on my sense organs and causes me to see, smell, and hear those sense experiences that, loosely speaking, I call Dobbin? The Atomists' answer was "matter"—either the qualitatively neutral atoms of Democritus or some qualitatively determinate stuff. In Plato's view this answer was inadequate. Matter, as the Atomists used this concept, explains nothing because it is itself unintelligible. It is only a brute fact, an unintelligible given, or—in the language of the *Republic*—only an hypothesis. Accordingly, in the *Timaeus* Plato attempted to sketch more general and fundamental concepts that would elucidate matter.

> We must consider in itself the nature of fire and water, air and earth. . . . For to this day no one has explained their generation, but we speak as if men knew what fire and each of the others is, positing them as original principles, elements (as it were, letters) of the universe; whereas one who has ever so little intelligence should not rank them in this analogy even so low as syllables.[e]

When Plato said he would explain the "generation" of earth, air, fire, and water, he was not talking about a process in time, in which something not earth or air or fire or water becomes these stuffs. He was not looking for a more ultimate material stuff that develops into them; he was making a logical analysis of them. If, for instance, we say that the square can be "reduced to" the right-angle isosceles triangle:

we do not mean that every square has actually been made by putting together (in time) two such triangles, but that the concept "square" may be analyzed as a construction based on (derived from) a simpler figure. (The triangle is "simpler" than the square because it has three sides instead of four.)

In this sense of analysis, let us now consider Plato's analysis of the Empedoclean stuffs—earth, air, fire, and water—into their simpler constituents. Plato distinguished here as always, between a form and the sensible thing that is its "image." Just as he distinguished between the form "horse" and Dobbin, he distinguished between the form "fire" and *its* sensible image. Of course we now know, from what has been said about his theory of sense perception, that the sensible image of the form "fire" is not hot, flickering, and reddish orange. Nor is the sensible image of the form "water" fluid, cold, and transparent. These sensory qualities, like those we experience in connection with Dobbin, exist only for sense organs like ours. These qualities are (in the language of the myth of the cave) the images of the sensible images, shadows cast by statues of men.

What, then, is the sensible image of the form "fire"—and of the forms of the other basic entities of which Plato believed the material universe to be constituted? This is equivalent to asking, "In what medium are these forms reflected?" For everything sensible is an imitation, or shadow, of some form—the reflection of that form in some medium. For instance, in the language of the divided line, the lowest levels of the line are "reflections in water and in polished surfaces." But this is only a metaphor. Leaving metaphor apart, what is the medium in which the four basic forms of nature are reflected? Plato's answer in the *Timaeus* is "space." Space is the "Receptacle of Becoming." "It is everlasting, not admitting destruction; providing a situation for all things that come into being, but itself apprehended without the senses by a sort of bastard reasoning, and hardly an object of belief."[f]

This is admittedly obscure. Even Plato would have admitted that it is obscure; indeed, he would have maintained that it *has* to be obscure. For space is and remains unintelligible—forever resistant to rational analysis. That this is the case follows from the theory of forms itself. For only forms are intelligible through and through; whatever cannot be analyzed into, or reduced to, form is, ultimately, unintelligible. Now, if we start with some complex physical object (for example, Dobbin), we can analyze it into its intelligible form ("horse") and the sensible image of that form (the spatiotemporal object that most of us take to be Dobbin but that is only the reflection of the form). And this physical entity is composed of flesh and blood. That is, it can be further analyzed into the form "flesh" and its sensible image and into the form "blood" and its sensible image. Both these forms, being forms, are intelligible; their sensible images can be (eventually) analyzed into the form "earth" and its sensible image, into the form "fire" and its sensible image, and into the other basic elements and their sensible images. But eventually this process of analysis must end in something sheerly unintelligible—unless, that is, we were to reach a point in our analysis at which nothing remained except some intelligible form. But, though Plato almost certainly would have liked to think that the nature of the universe is such as to make this a possibility, the theory of forms committed him to holding that there must be a medium, a "something," in which the forms are reflected. We can analyze complex media into forms and their corresponding media. But sooner or later we arrive at an ultimate medium that resists analysis precisely because it is medium, not form.

Plato's name for this ultimate, irreducible medium was "space." One can quarrel if one likes with his terminology, though it is not difficult to see why he chose the term: Ever since Parmenides' day, it had seemed that, though space is something (not "nothing"), it is the barest possible sort of existent that could be. But let us not quibble about terminology. The important point is that Plato was forced to hold that there is something in the universe, call it what you like, that is just brute factuality and so wholly inexplicable. One can say about it only that it "is" and that it "must be." This was Plato's way of admitting into his beautiful, rational universe that space-time realm of facts and events that empiricists, pragmatists, and positivists take to be the whole of reality. Only mystics deny this factualistic world any reality at all, but there is a basic temperamental difference between those who welcome this world and those who, like Plato, admit its existence only grudgingly.

Be that as it may, let us proceed with Plato's physical theory. The basic stuffs of the physical world are, then, the sensible images of the four forms "earth," "air," "fire," and "water." And each of these sensible images is the reflection in space of its corresponding form. That is, each is one of the possible (and elementary) configurations of space. Specifically, earth is the cube (for earth is the most immobile stuff and the cube is the figure with the most stable base); fire is the pyramid; water is the icosahedron; air, the octahedron. It is important to distinguish in each case between the pure form (which is wholly intelligible and which is the object of mathematical inquiry) and the sensible image (which, being the form's projection, or reflection, into space, is not wholly intelligible and which is the object of the physicist's inquiry). It is also important to distinguish between these sensible images and the atomic particles of Democritus. The sensible images are not material, as are the particles; they are spatial. That is, the form "fire" is not reflected in a material pyramid but in a spatial one. Matter, which was the Atomists' starting point, is constituted by various combinations of these more ultimate, sheerly spatial elements. In this way Plato reduced, even if he did not succeed in eradicating, the brute factuality in the universe.

Given these four basic elements, Plato could plausibly maintain that the various physical processes that are studied in physics (evaporation of water into air, condensation of air into water, and so on) are analyzable into, and can eventually be formulated in terms of, the various relationships that these basic geometric shapes are capable of. For instance, the icosahedron (water) can be "broken up" ("analyzed") into so many pyramids (fire), and so on. Thus, underlying each particular sense object and its mutations will be a series of geometrical transformations capable, theoretically, of precise mathematical formulation. Corresponding to Dobbin and his various features, as they exist for sense perception, are the motions of many thousands of tiny cubes, pyramids, icosahedra, and octahedra, undergoing various transformations in accordance with the various theorems formulated in geometry. What we *perceive* as a complicated brown sense object, neighing, pawing the ground, and galloping, is *understood* as the transpositions of certain elementary geometric shapes.

We say "elementary" geometric shapes, but Plato did not believe analysis has to stop at the four solids already enumerated. As a matter of fact, he "reduced" them to two triangles: the half-equilateral and the half-square. Thus the cube is analyzed into a series of squares (planes) and the square itself into the right-angle isosceles. Are these two elementary triangles "ultimates"? Plato hinted that they in their turn might be analyzed into "remoter principles"—into lines and, eventually, numbers.[1] Thus Plato reverted to an extreme Pythagoreanism. Things *are* numbers, in the sense that, ultimately, the ordinary world of sense perception reduces to geometry, and geometry in its turn reduces to arithmetic.

Why, then, is physics only a "likely story"? This is because physics cannot be reduced completely to mathematics. Physics is not about the various mathematical forms (for example, "pyramid") but about their sensible images, and these images are the reflections of the forms in space. But space exists independently, in its own right. It is an element of brute fact, the presence of which mind must acknowledge, but which mind cannot render intelligible. The case of motion is similar. So far it has been spoken of simply as "motion." But, though some motions are regular and so have an affinity, as it were, to the human intellect (for example, the motions of the planets), other motions are irregular and are produced, according to Plato, by the "Errant Cause." Being irregular and hence incomprehensible to the human mind, these motions have to be classified, along with space, as brute fact. Because the space in which the forms are reflected and the irregular motions that occur there resist the efforts of mind to comprehend them, physics must remain, from Plato's point of view, only a "likely story."

## Ethics

Though we have considered physics first, it was far from being Plato's chief interest. Indeed, for him physics, compared with ethics and politics, was only a side issue. Since he was convinced that the Sophistic attack on moderation and the other traditional virtues had been one of the main causes of the Athenian debacle, he was chiefly concerned, not with a knowledge of the physical world, but with a knowledge of values.

To meet Sophistic scepticism about the possibility of such knowledge he had to show that values are objective facts about the universe and that knowledge of them is possible. Logically, therefore, Plato should have tried to prove the existence of ethical forms, as he had proved, at least to his own satisfaction, the existence of mathematical forms. But unfortunately he seems to have assumed that his proof of the existence of mathematical forms validated the existence of forms in ethics and politics. This is far from being the case. It is certainly logically possible that there are mathematical forms but no ethical forms. This would mean, from Plato's point of view, that, whereas mathematical knowledge

---

1 F. M. Cornford's *Plato's Cosmology* (Harcourt, Brace & World, New York, 1937) has generally been followed in this account of the *Timaeus*. See p. 212 of that work.

is possible, ethics is a merely subjective business in which every man is the measure of right and wrong for himself.

As we have seen, Plato's proof of mathematical forms proceeds by asserting that there is objective mathematical knowledge and then arguing that such knowledge would be impossible unless there were (mathematical) forms. Of course, as we have also seen, this argument is inconclusive unless objective mathematical knowledge is impossible on any other hypothesis, and about this there is a difference of opinion. But most people would at least accept the first part of Plato's contention, namely, that there is mathematical knowledge. An attempt to validate ethical forms through the same line of reasoning would, however, at once encounter doubts about whether there is objective ethical knowledge. Even those who most strongly affirm the existence of such knowledge would have to admit that it is much less certain than the existence of mathematical knowledge. Hence, whereas disagreement with Plato about mathematical forms would turn primarily on whether mathematical knowledge does or does not depend on knowledge of forms, there is not merely a question of whether ethical knowledge is possible without knowledge of forms but also a question of whether there *is* ethical knowledge.

Plato would possibly have replied along the following lines: (1) The belief that objective knowledge in ethics is impossible is extremely paradoxical.[2] For instance, if we deny the possibility of ethical knowledge, we cannot say that Jesus was a better man than Hitler; in fact, we cannot say that anybody ever acts wrongly or makes an ethical mistake. (2) This position is indeed so paradoxical that nobody would adopt it unless he were driven to do so by an absolutely conclusive argument. (3) Further, the position is socially and politically deleterious and so should be rejected if at all possible. (4) The fact that mathematical knowledge is possible shows that there are at least *some* forms. (5) The existence of mathematical forms demonstrates that the existence of ethical forms is not impossible. (6) This provides a *prima facie* case for claiming that there are ethical forms. Since the consequences of denying their existence are so serious, the burden of the proof lies not on the man who affirms them but on the man who rejects them.

This proof is certainly far from invulnerable, and Plato did not in fact argue in this manner. But the discussions in the dialogues often proceed in a way that suggests he believed something like this. At any rate, many of the dialogues are concerned with the discovery of various ethical forms. Just as the mathematician makes use of the drawn triangle and the botanist makes use of the actual primrose, so the ethical philosopher makes use of the actual ethical judgments of ordinary men. Somehow these judgments participate in the various ethical forms, just as Old Dobbin, Traveller, Bucephalus, and all the other actual horses participate in the form "horse." Hence a

---

2 See p. 68–72.

proper analysis of actual ethical judgments ought, Plato reasoned, to reveal explicitly the character of the various forms these judgments participate in.

## ANALYSIS OF THE FORM "COURAGE"

In the *Laches,* an early dialogue, Plato gives an analysis of the plain man's use of the term "courage," in an attempt to clarify what courage "really" is, that is, to define with precision the nature of the form "courage."

SOCRATES. Tell me, if you can, what is courage.

LACHES.[3] Indeed, Socrates, I see no difficulty in answering; he is a man of courage who does not run away, but remains at his post and fights against the enemy; there can be no mistake about that.

SOCRATES. Very good, Laches; and yet I fear that I did not express myself clearly; and therefore you have answered not the question which I intended to ask, but another.

LACHES. What do you mean, Socrates?

SOCRATES. I will endeavour to explain; you would call a man courageous who remains at his post, and fights with the enemy?

LACHES. Certainly I should.

SOCRATES. And so should I; but what would you say of another man, who fights flying, instead of remaining?

LACHES. How flying?

SOCRATES. Why, as the Scythians are said to fight, flying as well as pursuing. . . .

LACHES. Yes, Socrates; . . . but the heavy-armed soldier fights, as I say, remaining in his rank.

SOCRATES. And yet, Laches, you must except the Lacedaemonians at Plataea, who, when they came upon the light shields of the Persians, are said not to have been willing to stand and fight, and to have fled; but when the ranks of the Persians were broken, they turned upon them like cavalry, and won the battle of Plataea.

LACHES. That is true.

SOCRATES. That was my meaning when I said that I was to blame in having put my question badly. . . . For I meant to ask you not only about the courage of the heavy-armed soldiers, but about the courage of cavalry and every other style of soldier; and not only who are courageous in war, but who are courageous in perils by sea, and who in disease, or in poverty, or again in politics. . . . I was asking about courage and cowardice in general. And I will . . . once more ask, What is that common quality, which is the same in all these cases, and which is called courage? Do you now understand what I mean?

LACHES. Not over-well.

SOCRATES. I mean this: As I might ask what is that quality which is called

---

3 [Laches was a distinguished Athenian general during the Peloponnesian War—AUTHOR.]

quickness, and which is found in running, in playing the lyre, in speaking, in learning, and in many other similar actions, or rather which we possess in nearly every action that is worth mentioning of arms, legs, mouth, voice, mind;—would you not apply the term quickness to all of them?

LACHES. Quite true.

SOCRATES. And suppose I were to be asked by someone: What is that common quality, Socrates, which, in all these activities, you call quickness? I should say the quality which accomplishes much in a little time—whether in running, speaking, or in any other sort of action.

LACHES. You would be quite correct.

SOCRATES. And now, Laches, do you try and tell me in like manner, What is that common quality which is called courage, and which includes all the various uses of the term . . . to which I was just now referring?

LACHES. I should say that courage is a sort of endurance of the soul, if I am to speak of the universal nature which pervades them all.

SOCRATES. But . . . I cannot say that every kind of endurance is, in my opinion, to be deemed courage. Hear my reason: I am sure, Laches, that you would consider courage to be a very noble quality.

LACHES. Most noble, certainly. . . .

SOCRATES. But what would you say of a foolish endurance? Is not that, on the other hand, to be regarded as evil and hurtful? . . . Then you would not admit that sort of endurance to be courage—for it is not noble, but courage is noble?

LACHES. You are right.

SOCRATES. Then, according to you, only the wise endurance is courage?

LACHES. It seems so.

SOCRATES. But as to the epithet "wise,"—wise in what? In all things small as well as great? For example, if a man shows the quality of endurance in spending his money wisely, knowing that by spending he will acquire more in the end, do you call him courageous?

LACHES. Assuredly not. . . .

SOCRATES. Again, take the case of one who endures in war, and is willing to fight, and wisely calculates and knows that others will help him, and that there will be fewer and inferior men against him than there are with him; and suppose that he has also advantages in position;—would you say of such a one who endures with all this wisdom and preparation, that he or some man in the opposing army who is in the opposite circumstances to these and yet endures and remains at his post, is the braver?

LACHES. I should say that the latter, Socrates, was the braver.

SOCRATES. But, surely, this is a foolish endurance in comparison with the other?

LACHES. That is true. . . .

SOCRATES. But foolish boldness and endurance appeared before to be base and hurtful to us.

LACHES. Quite true.

SOCRATES. Whereas courage was acknowledged to be a noble quality.

LACHES. True.

SOCRATES. And now on the contrary we are saying that the foolish endurance, which was before held in dishonour, is courage.

LACHES. So we are.

SOCRATES. And are we right in saying so?

LACHES. Indeed, Socrates, I am sure that we are not right. . . . I fancy that I do know the nature of courage; but, somehow or other, she has slipped away from me, and I cannot get hold of her and tell her nature.[g]

There are a number of things to note about this passage. First, as regards Socrates' method: He proceeds by refuting each of Laches' definitions with a "counterexample." Thus when Laches says, "Courage is so-and-so," Socrates replies, "No, it cannot be so-and-so, because we also call such-and-such courageous and such-and-such is different from so-and-so." Laches is thereupon forced to give a second definition of courage, which includes not only so-and-so but also such-and-such. But, as this new definition is criticized by means of another counterexample, a third and still more general definition is called for. Socrates uses this method, not because he wants to confuse Laches and force him to conclude that "there is no such thing as courage," but because, believing that courage is real, he thinks that all courageous acts must share a common quality, or property, however much they may differ in other respects. Unless we find the property that is identical in *all* such acts, we do not know what courage really is. This common quality is, of course, in Plato's view, the form "courage," and all the particular acts that Socrates and Laches are discussing are courageous because they participate—more or less fully—in this form. Since the form is the common property of all these otherwise diverse acts, we cannot be sure we have found it unless we have considered *all* the various kinds of acts called courageous. If we consider only some of these acts, we shall doubtless find the property (or form) common to all of *them,* but this is not necessarily the property (or form) common to the whole class of courageous acts. This is why Socrates keeps introducing counterexamples—to force Laches to consider all the varieties of acts that participate in the form.

This Socratic method rests on a number of metaphysical assumptions. One of these is that there are two kinds of knowledge. Thus Laches is a general, and a good one. He is a brave, well-trained, and successful soldier who therefore knows, in some sense, what courage is. Yet, in another sense, he is very confused about what courage is. Both these attitudes are expressed in Laches' puzzled remark at the conclusion of the passage given.

We may call these two kinds of knowledge—the kind of knowledge Laches has about courage and the kind of knowledge he lacks—(1) experiential knowledge and (2) formal knowledge. The former consists of certain attitudes and techniques picked up, for the most part unconsciously, in the course of normal everyday experience—beginning with what we absorb, as we say, as children at our mother's knee and being added to as we go on through life. This is the kind of knowledge an ingenious but uneducated mechanic has of a car. In Platonic language, experiential knowledge is acquaintance with the particulars in which the forms participate but not knowledge of the forms themselves.[4]

The formal kind of knowledge, on the other hand, is knowledge of the forms. Since this kind of knowledge has already been discussed, let us pass on now to consider the relationship between these two kinds of knowledge, which Plato intended the conversation between Laches and Socrates to bring out.

Formal knowledge develops out of experiential knowledge, because the experiential facts (the acts of courage, in this case) are rooted in the form (in this case, "courage"). In coming to know, we pass habitually from particulars to general propositions about particulars; but this is possible precisely because the particulars participate in, that is, imitate, reflect,[5] the form. Thus, in the order of reality forms come first; in the order of knowledge particulars come first.

It is easy to see what Plato meant by holding that in the order of knowledge particulars come first. We have opinions about particulars before we know forms. But what did he mean by saying that in the order of reality forms come first? This is a metaphysical assertion. Forms are first because they are more real than the particulars that imitate them. Just as the sun causes and sustains the objects it illumines, so objects gain whatever lesser reality they possess from the forms in which they participate. But this is an assertion of *value*. Knowledge of the forms is "better" than knowledge of particulars. Why? Well, in Laches' case the reasons are obvious. Though Laches is courageous at the level of experiential knowledge, and though this kind of courage works pretty well in simple, uncomplicated situations, such as standing in the face of the enemy, experiential knowledge may fail in more complicated cases. In other words, the line between courage and cowardice in the sphere of military affairs is often so sharply drawn that the correct thing to do is obvious. But most decisions in life do not involve such clear-cut blacks and whites. A good example of this is the difficulty many German officers had in deciding whether their duty to obey a superior officer applied to Hitler even after they were convinced that he was leading their country to its destruction.

Another reason for the superiority of formal knowledge is its greater permanence and stability. This kind of knowledge, being knowledge of reality, is not easily shaken. But a man who, like Laches, lives at the level of experiential knowledge is easily confused, becomes disillusioned about the possibility of any knowledge at all, and is easy game for the Sophists.

The relation between Laches' experiential knowledge and the formal knowledge that—if he possessed it—would make his conduct more consistent

4 Plato would have said that what we have called experiential knowledge is "mere" opinion, not knowledge at all.

5 See pp. 124–26.

and his beliefs more stable is precisely the relationship Plato held to exist between the old traditional, customary morality of the Greek community and the enlightened theory of ethics that he taught. Like Laches in his present condition, the Greek community was a prey to Sophistic scepticism. This was so because the community consisted of individuals like Laches whose values had been formed uncritically and unconsciously at the level of experiential knowledge. And just as the true enlightenment of Laches would result from a critical refinement of his existing beliefs, and would reinforce these beliefs by making him understand their *real* meaning, so Plato did not wish to substitute a brand new morality for the old one scorned by the Sophists. On the contrary, he wanted to rehabilitate it by showing its real basis, which neither its adherents nor its critics understood. Plato's sense of continuity with the past, his combination of conservatism and criticism, of traditionalism and enlightenment, is one of the most marked characteristics of his thought—and one of the great strengths of his position.

## THE DISTINCTION BETWEEN PLEASURE AND THE GOOD

So far in our study, Plato has not said what he takes the good life to be. Though he has implied that courage is a component of it, he has not yet defined courage; he has merely shown that Laches is badly confused. This negative stage was essential, Plato believed. Before a man will bother to try to discover the real truth about anything, he must be convinced that he is ignorant of it. Accordingly, many of Plato's dialogues end, like the *Laches*, in a confession of bewilderment. There is another sort of preliminary that Plato believed to be necessary before the positive theory could be developed. This is the refutation of false views. Whereas Plato's Laches is a good man who both knows and does not know what courage is, the Sophists were bad men who deliberately put forward false, and bad, views. It was essential, therefore, not merely to show them to be confused, but to show them to be mistaken. And the central mistake they made, according to Plato, was to confuse pleasure with the good. In contrast to Thrasymachus and Callicles, who held that to live well is simply to get as much pleasure as possible, Plato maintained: "There is such a thing as good, and . . . there is such a thing as pleasure, and . . . pleasure is not the same as good, and . . . of each of them there is a certain pursuit and process of acquisition, one the quest for pleasure, the other the quest for good. . . ."[h]

It was fairly easy for Plato to show that pleasure is not the *sole* good. In the *Gorgias*, for instance, Socrates points out to Callicles that scratching an itching place on the body is pleasant; if pleasure were our exclusive concern, a life passed in itching and scratching would be the supreme happiness. Even Callicles is obliged to admit that this is absurd. It follows that pleasures vary qualitatively and hence that there is some criterion for choice other than mere quantity of pleasure.

Also in the *Gorgias*, Plato gives a second and less convincing (because it is itself rather sophistical) argument that runs as follows: Good and bad are opposites; opposites cannot exist together at the same time in the same object; pleasure and pain do, however, exist in the same object at the same time. Pleasure therefore cannot be good nor pain evil.

> SOCRATES. You will admit, I suppose, that good and evil fortune are opposed to each other? . . . And if they are opposed to each other, then, like health and disease, they exclude one another; a man cannot have them both, or get rid of them both, at the same time? . . . Go back now to our former admissions.—Did you say that to hunger, I mean the mere state of hunger, was . . . painful? . . . And thirst . . . [and, generally], all wants or desires are painful? . . . And you would admit that to drink, when you are thirsty, is pleasant?
>
> CALLICLES. Yes.
>
> SOCRATES. And in the sentence which you have just uttered, the word "thirsty" implies pain? . . . and the word "drinking" is expressive of pleasure, and of the satisfaction of the want? . . . Do you see the inference:—that pleasure and pain are simultaneous, when you say that being thirsty, you drink? For are they not simultaneous, and do they not affect at the same time the same part, whether of the soul or the body? . . . You say also that no man could have good and evil fortune at the same time?
>
> CALLICLES. Yes, I do.
>
> SOCRATES. But you admitted that when in pain a man might also have pleasure. . . . Then pleasure is not the same as good fortune, or pain the same as evil fortune, and therefore the good is not the same as the pleasant.[i]

Because he felt so strongly that the extreme position taken by the Sophists was mistaken, and because he believed it all too easy to drift into a life of sheer pleasure-seeking, Plato often wrote as if all pleasure were positively bad. He wrote, rather too dramatically, about how the bodily passions torment us. In the *Republic*, for instance, the aged Cephalus praises old age on the grounds that, as one grows old, "the passions relax their hold" and one reaches a "great sense of calm and freedom." To escape from love is to escape from a furious master. Trying to satisfy the lusts of the flesh is as hopeless as trying to fill leaky and unsound casks: "But the more you pour in, the greater the efflux. . . ."[j]

But wholesale condemnations overstate the case. To insist that pleasure is not the sole good and that some types of pleasure-seeking are self-destructive is not to say that pleasure is not *a* good. And, indeed, Plato sometimes saw that the primary question about pleasure is not whether it is a good at all but how good a good it is. This question, he also saw, cannot be answered without distinguishing among different kinds of pleasures, and this, in its turn, presupposes a psychological analysis of the nature of pleasure.

On the subject of the nature of pleasure (as distinguished from the moral evaluation of it) Plato made some insightful observations. Pleasure and pain, he held, are feelings—specifically, the feelings that accompany a change to or from a state of equilibrium. Hunger is a depletion of the body; as such, it is painful. Eating enough to bring the body back to normal is therefore pleasant. If the body and mind are in a normal state, a sudden noise or light, or anything that upsets this normal state, is experienced as painful; a return to the normal state is experienced as pleasant. Changes from or to equilibrium are, of course, going on constantly in the living body, but most of them are so gradual as to be imperceptible. Only a change violent or sudden enough to reach the level of consciousness is experienced as pleasant or, as the case may be, painful. As a matter of fact, in Plato's view, this neutral state of equilibrium would be the best state of all for man, but it is possible only for the gods, who lead a blessed life above both joy and sorrow. Using this as a basis, and taking man as he is, Plato distinguished between (1) "necessary" pleasures, which seem to be connected with the functioning of the human body and to involve bringing it back to equilibrium, and (2) "harmless" pleasures, by which Plato seems to have meant what we would call the purely esthetic pleasures of sounds, tones, smells, and the like.

So much is straightforward. Unfortunately, at this point Plato's argument becomes muddled because of his belief that most men are egoistic hedonists. He reasoned that if you want them to be good, you must convince them that being good (being just, courageous, temperate, and so on) will in fact produce the pleasantest life. In the *Laws*, for instance, after describing "excessive love of self" as the "greatest of all evils" and asserting that a man ought to be interested only in "what is just, whether the just act be his own or that of another," Plato sadly remarks that such ideals of conduct apply to gods, not to men. "But of human things we have not as yet spoken, and we must. . . . Pleasures and pains and desires are a part of human nature, and on them every mortal being must of necessity hang and depend with the most eager interest. And, therefore, we must praise the noblest life as [the one] having a greater amount of pleasure." [k]

Consequently, he set himself to try to prove that the pleasures of temperance exceed the pains and that the pains of intemperance exceed the pleasures. The same is true, he held, for courage and the "rational life" and their opposites.

This manner of arguing confuses the issue. What Plato really wanted to maintain was that the just and courageous life, for instance, is *better* than the life of pleasure-seeking, not that it produces more pleasure. This he saw clearly enough in the *Republic*, in which he argues that justice is desirable for its own sake, not as a second-best thing (that is, to avoid some greater pain). In this dialogue he distinguishes between three classes of goods: (1) things good for their consequences only (for example, an appendectomy, bad in itself but useful in forestalling greater pain); (2) things good for their own sake only (the "harmless" pleasures of tones, colors, and so forth, which bring nothing in their train); (3) things good both for their own sake and for their consequences.

The Sophists, who held that pleasure is the sole good and who evaluated conduct simply on the basis of how efficient a producer of pleasure it was, put justice in the first group, along with a visit to the dentist and a dose of castor oil. Plato held that justice belongs in the third group because man's true good is not pleasure but something he called *eudaimonia*. What, then, is *eudaimonia*— or happiness, as this term is usually translated? Since Plato held that justice leads to happiness, not to pleasure, an analysis of his concept of justice, the main topic of the *Republic*, will throw light on the nature of *eudaimonia*.

### ANALYSIS OF THE FORM "JUSTICE"

The dialogue begins in the customary fashion (as in the *Laches*, with respect to courage) with a study of actual judgments about justice. Plato's intention was to show that though the form is reflected in the plain man's judgment, the judger does not know it, or at least does not know all that it implies. Just as I can judge that "Old Dobbin is a horse" or that "this is a carburetor" without knowing all that "horse" means for a zoologist or all that "carburetor" means to a trained mechanic, so Polemarchus, a well-brought-up young friend of Socrates', talks about "justice" with only the vaguest notion of what it means. When Socrates presses him for a definition, Polemarchus innocently declares that "justice is giving a man his due." Socrates finds it easy to show Polemarchus, just as he had showed Laches, that what seemed obvious (after all, he had read the definition in a book, so it *must* be true!) is anything but simple. However, after a long and careful analysis, it turns out that Polemarchus was correct—justice, in a sense, is giving every man his due. Polemarchus "spoke better than he knew"; that is, his original judgment participated in the form "justice."

Though this analysis is too long to follow in detail, the conclusion can be given fairly straightforwardly: Justice, whether in the individual man or in the individual state, is an attunement, or harmony, in which each element has its "due"—that is, does what it can do best. Thus justice is a kind of division of labor. Each element in the nature of the just man gets its due expression, gets to perform what it is best fitted to do. As a result, the life of the just man is healthy, happy, and strong.

> The just man does not allow the several elements in his soul to usurp one another's functions; he is indeed one who sets his house in order, by self-mastery and discipline coming to be at peace with himself, and bringing into tune those three parts, like the terms in the proportion of a musical scale, the highest and lowest notes and the mean between them, with all the intermediate intervals. Only when he has linked these parts together in well-tempered harmony and has made himself one man instead of many, will he be ready to go about whatever he may have to do, whether it be making money and satisfying bodily wants, or business transactions, or the affairs of state. . . .
>
> That is perfectly true, Socrates. . . .
> So be it. . . . Next, I suppose, we have to consider injustice.
> Evidently.

This must surely be a sort of civil strife among the three elements, whereby they usurp and encroach upon one another's functions. . . . Such turmoil and aberration we shall, I think, identify with injustice, intemperance, cowardice, ignorance, and in a world with all wickedness.

Exactly. . . .

So now it only remains to consider which is the more profitable course: to do right and live honourably and be just, whether or not anyone knows what manner of man you are, or to do wrong and be unjust, provided that you can escape the chastisement which might make you a better man.

But really, Socrates, it seems to me ridiculous to ask that question now that the nature of justice and injustice has been brought to light. People think that all the luxury and wealth and power in the world cannot make life worth living when the bodily constitution is going to rack and ruin; and are we to believe that, when the very principle whereby we live is deranged and corrupted, life will be worth living so long as a man can do as he will, and wills to do anything rather than to free himself from vice and wrongdoing and to win justice and virtue?

Yes, . . . it is a ridiculous question.[1]

## ORGANISM AND FUNCTION

The analysis of the form "justice" has led us to the concepts of organism and function. That happiness, not pleasure, is the goal of man follows from the fact that man is an organism whose varied functions must be brought into balance and harmony. These are not merely private opinions; they are, according to Plato, objective facts about human nature. The Sophists mistook the nature of the good either because they did not understand these facts or because they deliberately ignored them.

Since an organism's happiness is a product of that organism's activity, Plato began by analyzing the organic nature of man, with a view to showing what activities require expression and how they may be effectively interrelated. Thus the details of his moral theory are rooted in psychology and sociology. Nothing could show more strikingly the difference between the characteristic Greek mind and the characteristic Christian mind. Since getting into the right relation with God is the sum of happiness for Christians, a Christian philosopher like St. Augustine, asking what the good life is, depended on theology for the details of his answer. But Plato thought chiefly in terms of man's relation to his fellows and to his physical, that is, this-worldly, environment.

His views on this subject seem to have been much influenced by a medical analogy. When the body is well, its parts are in an harmonious attunement: heart pumping blood at the right rate (neither too fast nor too slow), liver secreting bile, lungs inhaling and exhaling air, intestines passing along waste products, and so on. Health, which is the *good* state of the body, is simply that state of affairs in which all the organs are cooperating fruitfully in their common life. Since the organs are all causally interdependent, the ill-functioning of any one of them affects the operation of the others. Hence the physician who seeks to bring the entire body back to a proper attunement must understand the interrelations of the organs.

> Eminent physicians say to a patient who comes to them with bad eyes, that they cannot undertake to cure his eyes by themselves, but that if his eyes are to be cured, his head must be treated too; and then again they say that to think of curing the head alone, and not the rest of the body also, is the height of folly. And arguing in this way they apply their régime to the whole body, and try to treat and heal the whole and the part together. . . . [These] physicians are quite right as far as they go, [but those others are even wiser who hold] that as you ought not to attempt to cure the eyes without the head, or the head without the body, so neither ought you to attempt to cure the body without the soul; and this . . . is the reason why the cure of many diseases is unknown to the physicians of Hellas, because they disregard the whole, which ought to be studied also; for the part can never be well unless the whole is well. ᵐ

The Sophists erred in the first place, then, through failing to grasp the simple physiological fact that the body is an organic whole. Their claim that the good is the greatest number of titillations, that is, units of pleasurable sensation, is incompatible with the nature of the bodily organism. They erred in the second place in thinking that the body is all that has to be considered, for it is only an organ of a larger whole, the self.

The term Plato used here is *psyche,* which is usually translated "soul." But "soul" has theological overtones that are foreign to Plato's view. His psyche is natural, not supernatural. Hence "self" is a safer translation. What, then, is the self? And in what sense is it an organism? These questions are tackled in a discussion between Socrates and Glaucon in the *Republic:*

> Here, then, we have stumbled upon another little problem: Does the soul contain . . . three elements or not? . . .
> [That] we have [different kinds of experience is] a fact which is easily recognized. But here the difficulty begins. Are we using the same part of ourselves in all these three experiences, or a different part in each? Do we gain knowledge with one part, feel anger with another, and with yet a third desire the pleasures of food, sex, and so on? Or is the whole soul at work in every impulse and in all these forms of behaviour? The difficulty is to answer that question satisfactorily.
> I quite agree.
> Let us approach the problem whether these elements are distinct or identical in this way. It is clear that the same thing cannot act in two opposite ways or be in two opposite states at the same time, with respect to the same part of itself, and in relation to the same object. So if we find such contradictory actions or states among the elements concerned, we shall know that more than one must have been involved.

Very well. . . .

Now, would you class such things as assent and dissent, striving after something and refusing it, attraction and repulsion, as pairs of opposite actions or states of mind—no matter which?

Yes, they are opposites. . . .

We conclude, then, that the soul of a thirsty man, just in so far as he is thirsty, has no other wish than to drink. That is the object of its craving, and towards that it is impelled.

That is clear.

Now if there is ever something which at the same time pulls it the opposite way, that something must be an element in the soul other than the one which is thirsting and driving it like a beast to drink; in accordance with our principle that the same thing cannot behave in two opposite ways at the same time and towards the same object with the same part of itself. . . .

Exactly.

Now, is it sometimes true that people are thirsty and yet unwilling to drink?

Yes, often.

What, then, can one say of them, if not that their soul contains something which urges them to drink and something which holds them back, and that this latter is a distinct thing and overpowers the other?

I agree.

And is it not true that the intervention of this inhibiting principle in such cases always has its origin in reflection; whereas the impulses driving and dragging the soul are engendered by external influences and abnormal conditions?

Evidently.

We shall have good reason, then, to assert that they are two distinct principles. We may call that part of the soul whereby it reflects, rational; and the other, with which it feels hunger and thirst and is distracted by sexual passion and all the other desires, we will call irrational appetite, associated with pleasure in the replenishment of certain wants.

Yes, there is good ground for that view.

Let us take it, then, that we have now distinguished two elements in the soul. What of that passionate element which makes us feel angry and indignant? Is that a third, or identical in nature with one of those two?

It might perhaps be identified with appetite.

I am more inclined to put my faith in a story I once heard about Leontius, son of Aglaion. On his way up from the Piraeus outside the north wall, he noticed the bodies of some criminals lying on the ground, with the executioner standing by them. He wanted to go and look at them, but at the same time he was disgusted and tried to turn away. He struggled for some time and covered his eyes, but at last the desire was too much for him. Opening his eyes wide, he ran up to the bodies and cried, 'There you are, curse you; feast yourselves on this lovely sight!'

Yes, I have heard that story too.

The point of it surely is that anger is sometimes in conflict with appetite, as if they were two distinct principles.[n]

This probably sounds strange and archaic. What Plato meant was simply that, although there are a large number of specific drives (or urges) that animate men, these can all be grouped into three main categories. Leaving for a moment the question of what these categories are, we see that Plato's basic thesis is simple: Since each of these three "parts," or "faculties," has motions proper to it, the good life (happiness) occurs only when all these several motions, instead of conflicting, harmonize. The good man, like the physician, orders the parts of an organism. But whereas the physician orders the parts of the body for the sake of its health, the good man organizes the parts of his *psyche* for the sake of his happiness.

So much for Plato's theory of the "tripartite psyche" in general. What, specifically, are the three types of psychological drives that must be harmonized in the interest of the whole man? The lowest group of drives (it will be necessary to ask shortly what Plato meant by terming it "lowest") are what he called the appetites. These are, of course, our old friends, the various bodily needs, each of which is closely connected with some physiological function. The highest group of drives Plato called "reason." If it seems odd to call reason a drive, it may be called "curiosity"—the urge to understand, to make sense of, a puzzling situation. Sometimes people work crossword puzzles in the hope of winning a prize or for the sake of the prestige involved (which would be being moved by appetite), but usually they struggle with the puzzles just because they want to solve them. Such people at such times are moved by what Plato called reason. Plato would doubtless have put crossword-puzzle solving at the bottom of the list of those activities to which we are moved by reason. A better example from his point of view would be solving mathematical theorems or, better still, thinking about what we would now call "metaphysics." These are better because, being more difficult puzzles, they exercise our reason more, and because (in a sense hereinafter to be explored) the objects on which they are employed are "higher."

The third type of urge, between appetite and reason on his qualitative scale, Plato called "spirit." He was thinking of what we might call passions or emotions, which are clearly different, he thought, from both appetite and reason. Men are sometimes moved to act by anger, for instance; and anger, Plato thought, is somehow irrational, though it is not merely the expression of a physiological need as are, for instance, hunger and the sexual "appetites."

Without stopping to ask whether this psychological analysis is sound (we can certainly accept, at least provisionally, his main thesis that man is a complex of drives and that the good life lies in the proper interrelations of these activities), let us go on to see how in Plato's view these three types of activity should be interrelated.

Plato did not treat this question (which would be central in any modern psychology) in as great detail as we could wish, for he was not interested in psychology per se but merely in its bearing on ethics. In fact, we will do well to turn, for our answer to this question, to Plato's account of the state. For the state, according to Plato, is an organism with organs corresponding exactly to those of the individual. In the state, therefore, we will find reproduced on a larger scale—"in letters writ large"—the kinds of interrelations that do, and that ideally ought to, exist between the member elements of an individual organism.

## PARALLEL BETWEEN INDIVIDUAL AND STATE

Plato analyzed the state, as he did the individual, into three types of activity, or function. First, no matter how simple or complex any particular state may be, it always has a governing or directing body, whether king and council, parliament, or congress. Second, all states have a producing class, whether (as in primitive communities) this consists simply of tillers of the soil and tenders of sheep, or whether (in communities like the Athens of Plato's day) it consists of agriculturists, industrial workers, merchants, transport workers, bankers, and all the other components of a complex society. It will be noted that in the producing class Plato included not only the actual producers, the laborers, but also those who exchange, transport, and otherwise make possible the utilization of this production. Third, Plato held that, in every state, between the governing class and the producing class there is a group responsible for maintaining the state against "internal and external enemies." In the case of advanced states, this class includes police, militia, national guard, army, navy, and so on. These "guards," as we may describe the whole class, stand between the other two classes because they partake of the character of both. Like the producers, the members of this class have no authority; like the administrators, they are unproductive. But in well-run states the guards are more closely affiliated with the administrators than with the producers. They are, indeed, the agents of the executive, backing up and giving force to its orders.

It should be obvious that the producing class in the state corresponds to appetite in the individual, that the governing class corresponds to reason, and that the guards correspond to spirit. Now what is the virtue, Plato asked, of each of these classes? This question may sound odd to us, for the word "virtue" has acquired through the centuries (especially from Christian thought) a good deal of color that it did not have in classical times. To inquire today whether someone, especially a woman, is "moral" or "virtuous" is to ask whether she is sexually chaste. For Plato, however, to ask about the virtue of anything was simply to ask what it could do best. It was therefore not a moral question (in *our* sense of "moral") but a practical question, in the field of what today would be psychology or biology, or even physics.[6]

This follows directly from the conception of organism. The parts of an organism are not discrete and complete in themselves, as are the bricks in a wall. They are *organs:* Each has a particular (and sometimes highly specialized) role to play in the whole. In a brick wall, each part is of the same size, weight,

---

6 Of course, Plato, thinking of "morals" in a broader sense, would have called this a moral, or ethical, inquiry.

strength, and texture as all the other parts, so that any one part may be indifferently substituted for any other. A stone wall is more of an organism than a brick wall because its parts are selected with an eye to size, texture, and so on—that is, in terms of their relation to the whole. (Actually, even in a brick wall the parts are not completely undifferentiated, as anyone who has seen a skilled mason choose bricks for a particular section of wall will know.) A watch is still more obviously an organism. Each spring and each wheel has a characteristic shape, weight, and size, determined by the role it plays—by the function it has—in the whole mechanism. Here, substituting one part indifferently for another is impossible. An animal body consists of even more elaborately articulated parts, or organs, each of which contributes to the life of the whole in a way that cannot be duplicated by any other part. It would be quite intelligible from Plato's point of view to ask about any organ of the body, "What is its virtue?" This means simply, "What is its function?" Thus, the virtue of the heart is to pump blood, the liver is being virtuous when it is secreting bile, and so on. That this is an entirely sensible way to speak will be clear if we remember that when an organ is correctly performing its function it is contributing to the fruitful and successful life of the organism of which it is a part. If this is not to be good and virtuous, what is to be good and to be virtuous?

Since the state is an organism, it seemed reasonable to Plato to inquire into the virtues of the different social classes of which the state is composed and which are therefore—on analogy with the animal body—its organs. To ask what the virtues of the three classes are is simply to ask what each should be contributing to the life of the whole state.

It seems clear, when the matter is put in this way, that (1) the function of the members of the producing class is to furnish themselves and the nonproductive classes with the necessities of life—food, clothing, shelter—and with the luxuries, too, though Plato would have preferred for men to content themselves with the simple life.[7] But if *everybody* is to be provided for adequately, it is clear that some of the producers will have to put up with having less than they might want. In a land of plenty (which Greece was not), this requirement may not seem important. But we have only to think of the underdeveloped countries today, with their problems of increasing population and stagnant production rates, to see what Plato had in mind here. In fact, Plato's thesis is applicable to the United States, where great poverty exists side by side with great wealth. If the state is to be strong and healthy, Plato thought, some of the food, some of the wealth, must be given up by those who have it for the sake of those who lack it.[8] Thus, to summarize, what is required of the producing class, whether

7 Plato's feeling about luxury in the state exactly corresponded to his feeling about pleasure in the individual. We would be far better off (individuals and states) if we dispensed altogether with pleasures and luxuries. Since we do not, we must be on the alert lest we become too intent on pleasure-seeking and lest the state in which we live becomes too luxurious.

8 Plato was not a radical equalitarian, of course. He did not think that everybody should have exactly equal amounts of food or of money, but simply that too great disparities are unsound.

it consists of laborers or capitalists, is moderation, or, as Plato called it, "temperance"—the readiness to restrict one's own consumption for the sake of achieving some sort of balance in the state as a whole. This is indeed *the* virtue of this class; if the producers are intemperate, the state cannot possibly be healthy, any more than a body can be entirely healthy if the heart falters.

(2) The guards, who constitute the second class, have to defend the state against its enemies. To perform this function efficiently they must be courageous. Courage, then, is the virtue of this class.

(3) So we come to the governors, who make decisions at the highest level of policy—who determine whether there will be peace or war, whether or not the militia will be called out to put down a riot, what the tax structure will be, what educational policy will be, and so on. Surely, to perform this function, to make correct decisions, they must have knowledge. This is their virtue: to know the forms, for instance, to know enough about economics to be able to decide what the best policy would be in regard to taxation, retirement of public debt, price control, governmental spending, and so on.

A state in which the rulers reach wise decisions, in which these decisions are executed with loyalty and courage by the soldiers and police, and in which the rest of the population exercises a decent restraint in its pursuit of material well-being will be a strong state, and its citizens will be happy. We can describe this state as "just," for every organ is performing its function and labor is efficiently divided. Thus, in a very real sense, Polemarchus was correct when he said that justice is a matter of everyone's getting his "due"—not in the strict legal sense, but in the larger sense that each plays that role for which his nature fits him. Polemarchus, of course, did not understand this; he merely quoted authority—and, at that, the authority of a poet! This fact symbolizes one of the most profound of Plato's beliefs. There is a wisdom in the people that poets express (often without understanding it) in the language of myth and metaphor. Philosophical analysis is a way of extracting this meaning and rendering it precise. Once again, we remind ourselves that we only reach the abstract, intelligible form via the concrete and often rather muddled image.

Since the three classes in the state exactly correspond to the three parts of the self, we are now in a position to see better how Plato understood these parts and what he took to be their respective virtues. Every individual has a "producer" part that keeps him alive and active, a rational part that is intended to guide and direct the energy produced by the body, and a spirited part that is intended to help keep the body in order. As the individual self's functions correspond to those of the state, so do its virtues. A man is virtuous when he is temperate[9] in the satisfaction of his various "physical" appetites, when he lives the life of

9 Here again the meaning has narrowed through the years. Today temperance often means (as it meant to the W.C.T.U.) total abstinence. For Plato it meant balanced restraint in the interest of the whole man—in the case of alcohol, neither complete license ending in hangover nor complete asceticism cutting off drinking altogether.

reason, and when his spirited element supports and backs up the dictates of reason—when he gets angry at the right things, when he stands in the face of the enemy because reason tells him to, even though his body wants to "get the hell out of there," and so on.

And such a man is not only virtuous; he is happy. Why? Because (in the same sense that the "virtuous" state is strong and successful) being virtuous means being an efficient, healthy, and successful organism, and this *is* being happy.

### THE LIFE OF REASON

A word must be added about what has just been called "living the life of reason." This may sound both pompous and vague. What Plato meant is that reason has a dual role: It is both means and end. Thinking is an end in the same way[10] that sleeping is an end—both are natural functions of the human organism, and in both, therefore, the human organism finds natural and proper satisfaction. Thought is also (and this is not true of sleep!) the instrument with which we decide how to portion our time and our energies—so much to this aspect of life, so much to that. Since every appetite demands unlimited satisfaction, life would be wretched unless thought allotted to each its proper share, and unless spirit enforced thought's decisions.

But it is not only the appetites that have to be disciplined by thought; thought must discipline itself. Insofar as one is rational, one enjoys thinking (solving puzzles, working mathematical theorems, reflecting on metaphysics). But these activities can get out of hand and usurp a disproportionate amount of time and energy. The man who, thinking too precisely on the event, fails to act decisively on appropriate occasions, the man who lives too exclusively the life of the mind, contradicts the Platonic conception of all-round development. Just as one man may be a slave to drink, another may be a pedant—a slave to thought. Both are bad because they are only partially living, because they are expressing only part of their multisided human nature. Hence in both cases thought must operate as a regulative agency controlling the complex life of the individual. The analogy with the state is complete. The governors of the state must also govern themselves: Legislators may not exempt themselves from the laws they make. The symbol for all this in the myth of the cave (to which readers of Plato must return again and again) is the fact that even though the great man finds the outer world beautiful and good and longs to live there in contemplation of the sun, he turns back into the cave to do what he can for his unenlightened fellows.

Someone may say at this point, "This is all very well, but I don't *like* to think. What *I* like to do is to make money, go out with blondes, and dance all night. Why shouldn't I do these things if they make me happy?" How could Plato have replied? To begin with, Plato's account of human nature is based

---

10 Of course for Plato it is a "higher" end. See pp. 130–32.

on his theory of forms. He believed himself to be analyzing the form "man," the form "justice," the form "happiness." Put in modern language, this amounts to saying that Plato was making a psychological analysis of human nature, on the basis of which he claimed to be able to say that a certain kind of behavior, which he called "justice," is better than another ("injustice"), since it promotes the general health and happiness of the organism. His position is therefore analogous to that of the watchmaker who, on the basis of his knowledge of how watches operate, claims that clean watches run better (are more just, more virtuous) than dirty ones.

But is Plato's psychological analysis of human nature correct? Is his account of the form "man" adequate? It seems clear that people who suffer from hangovers should not drink to excess and that people who have a tendency toward indigestion should not overeat. But one hardly needs to be a philosopher to discover this. How is Plato's theory to deal with the man with a cast-iron stomach who prefers lobster to lyrics, boogie-woogie to Bach, and sitting in the sun to differential equations? We may agree that such a man is not living a well-rounded life, but are we justified in telling him that he is less happy than the man who lives a well-rounded life?

We could say, of course, that the man who prefers boogie-woogie to Bach simply doesn't understand Bach. This line of argument is not without force. Bach is difficult; where the untrained ear hears only noise, the musically educated ear hears "exquisite harmonies." Hence it is not surprising that a great many people prefer boogie-woogie. If, however, they were to study music, they might find that an increased musical appreciation repaid them for their trouble. But suppose that, after devoting some time to Bach, the man who prefers boogie-woogie says, "Well, I still don't see anything in classical music." We might be tempted to reply, "If you don't, then so much the worse for you."

This retort discourteous is, of course, not conclusive, and Plato would not have wanted to rest his case merely on the possibility of cultivating one's taste. He wanted to maintain that the nature of man *really* is what he described it to be and that the man who doesn't find it so is mistaken, not merely deficient in taste. Here we must distinguish. When Plato said, "The virtue of man is such-and-such," he did not, of course, mean to claim that this description is true of every particular man. The nature he was analyzing is the form "man"; and a form, as we know, is never more than partially exemplified in any particular. The form "triangle" has angles equal to two right angles even if no drawn triangle has ever had *exactly* this property; so the fact that particular men lack some of the properties attributed to the form "man" does not disprove Plato's analysis. On the contrary it is only what we would expect. This amounts to saying, to put the matter in a slightly different way, that no particular man has ever been *all* that man might be.

That there are differences between individual men in respect to the degree to which they participate in the form "man" was, indeed, a major contention of Plato's. These differences, he held, cannot be removed by training and education. The man who prefers boogie-woogie may participate so feebly in the form "man" as to be incapable of enjoying Bach. To try to educate him up to it would be a waste of both our time and his. We would do better to leave him to extract what enjoyment he can from boogie-woogie. But on the other hand, if he has a native musical capacity that needs only to be cultivated to make him a sensitive musician, it would be tragic to leave him in boogie-woogie. Let us, therefore, devise a "musical-sensitivity" test that will indicate his native musical capacity and so show whether he is worth educating.

There will be, then, many men for whom the life of the mind is a dead tomb, and for whom "getting and spending" is the best thing in life. It is well that this is the case, for we need producers in the state, and where are they to be found but among those whose greatest happiness lies in bodily activity—in producing? The only hope of having a good state lies in finding a large number of men in whom appetite, not reason, is primary. These men, according to Plato, will be happy to the extent that they are fulfilling their function; they would be unhappy if they tried to be, or we tried to make them be, mathematicians or logicians. But though they are happy, they are not as happy as they would be if they could understand calculus.

The same applies to the spirited element. There are men for whom an eight-hour day, a newspaper before the fire, a radio, and an occasional movie would be utter boredom; likewise, mathematics and abstract thought do not appeal to them. These men—the strong, silent type—want a life of action. In searching them out from behind their desks and their books and making them soldiers, we do them and ourselves a service. We give them that to do which, being an expression of their nature, brings them happiness, and which is also necessary to the well-being of the state.

Finally we are left with those few in whom reason is primary, who really have a capacity for abstract thought—those who, for instance, are able to take a chaotic jumble of conflicting reports and reduce them to order, who are able to take an overlapping, bureaucratic department with conflicting lines of authority and reduce it to system, who are able to see through to the heart of a problem and then act decisively. Let us make these men the leaders of our government.

## ESTIMATE OF PLATO'S VIEW

The existence of a good state thus depends (as we might say today) on the fact that men differ widely in their capacities, or (as Plato would have said) on the fact that the degree of participation in the form "man" differs from person to person, and the more complete the degree of participation, the fewer the number of individuals at that level. It follows that the fact of individual differences, of wide variation in temperament, taste, and disposition, does not in itself invalidate Plato's psychological analysis or the ethical theory based upon it.

But Plato wanted to maintain much more than this. He was not content merely to say that the producer and the mathematician are both happy, though in different ways; he also wanted to say that the mathematician's happiness is "better" and "higher" and "more real." He wanted to say not only that the swing fan and the Bach enthusiast are both happy—each in his own way, listening to the music he likes best—but that, since Bach's music is "better" than boogie-woogie, the man who enjoys it is himself better and happier.

The argument rests on a number of metaphysical considerations connected with the theory of forms, and it may be summarized as follows: (1) Being and goodness are exactly parallel: The more real anything is, the better it is. (2) Things participate in their forms to different degrees; that is, they are more or less adequate exemplifications of their forms. (3) Those things that participate in their forms more fully are more real, and therefore better, than things that participate less fully. (4) Individual men differ in the degree to which they participate in the form "man." (5) Men in whom reason is the primary drive participate more fully in the form "man" than do men in whom appetite or emotion is the primary drive. (6) Therefore the former are better than the latter, and better on an absolute and objective scale. In a word, the qualitatively different happinesses of producers and rulers are evaluated on a metaphysical scale of degree of participation in the form "man."

Whether this argument is persuasive obviously depends on whether one accepts Plato's basic metaphysical position. Here, again, the theory of forms is central to his philosophy. To some it will appear that Plato was merely inventing an elaborate rationale to justify what he believed on other, and less imposing, grounds. Thus it might be argued that, because Plato disliked change, he was disposed to attribute more value to the permanent, that is, to whatever approximated more nearly his eternal and unchanging forms. It is also hard to avoid the suspicion that Plato was moved by his own prejudices and those of the class into which he was born, a class that scorned manual labor and trade as "vulgar" and found its own satisfaction primarily in intellectual pursuits.

However this may be, was it really necessary for Plato to maintain that some of the qualitatively different happinesses are objectively better than others? The main case against the Sophists had already been won. Plato's just man is certainly happier than Thrasymachus' unjust man, and stronger and better, and so is his just state. This follows upon the acceptance of the notion of organism. If an individual is an organism, then it is necessary to look at his life as a whole and to judge the various special activities that make up his life in terms of the contributions they make to it. If any particular activity gets badly out of line, the life of the organism falters; if this goes on long enough, the organism dies. To say this is to say that "injustice" (in Thrasymachus' sense) is bad, for injustice is precisely that narrow and particularistic life that, intent on its own local good, fails to see itself as a part of a larger whole. And the same argument applies, *mutatis mutandis*, to the state, in that it too is an organism.

Badness, or injustice, then, is doing anything that is disruptive of the life of the whole organism of which one is a part, and, though justice therefore calls for self-discipline in the interest of the larger life, this self-discipline is not self-sacrifice. The organ that disciplines itself for the sake of the whole is at the same time promoting its own long-run interests. Since it is an organ, anything that hurts the organism sooner or later hurts it. Hence the conflict is not between self and other; it is between self's immediate transitory interest and self's permanent, long-run interests. The real strength of Plato's argument is that it accepts the underlying egoism of Thrasymachus' position. Plato did not argue that Thrasymachus was wrong in wanting to be happy; he argued that, because Thrasymachus did not understand that man is an organism, what he advocated, rather than promoting happiness, is self-defeating.

Though this is an effective reply to the Sophists, it is largely irrelevant from the point of view of any ethic that, like Christianity, emphasizes duty instead of interest. The Christian claims that doing one's duty (obeying God's commands) is the good; this, the Christian recognizes, often conflicts not only with the individual's short-range, but also with his long-range, interest. Hence some modern critics of Plato, influenced by this ascetic Christian tradition, have maintained that Plato's ethical theory is founded on a mistake: If he wanted to hold that men should act justly, he should have shown that it is their duty to do so, not that it will make them happy.

This is another major parting of the ways in philosophy, which we cannot hope to resolve here. But as far as happiness is concerned, if it consists in living fruitfully and efficiently, it would seem to follow that there are as many qualitatively different happinesses as there are different kinds of men. In this case, the great question would not be whether we are at the top or at the bottom, but whether—wherever we stand—we are living at the maximum level of integration (harmony of functions) of which we are capable.

## Political Theory

So far we have considered Plato's view of the state only as it throws light on his ethical theory. But political theory is not merely an adjunct to ethical theory; indeed, for Plato it was almost the other way around, since he believed that the good life is possible only in the good state. Here again Plato is poles apart from the Christian tradition, which, in emphasizing the individual's effort to get into a right relationship with God, has tended to stress solitariness and to regard what sociologists call "interpersonal relations" as a dangerous distraction. Plato, in contrast, held that only in and through these relations can the individual achieve his good.

In the first place, he reasoned, man is a social animal. Just as he has natural desires for sleep, food, drink, and so on, he has a natural desire to associate with his fellows and to live in communities. Communal life is therefore a "good." And, in the second place, all the other human goods depend for any really adequate satisfaction on communal life. What kind of life would we lead if we had to supply our own food, clothing, and shelter? It would be a miserable life indeed. Nor is it only our need for physical goods whose fulfillment depends on cooperation with other men. Even thinking is more fruitful if we have the stimulation and criticism of fellow thinkers.

That this is true is no accident; it follows from the nature of organisms. Sever the foot from the body of which it is an organ, and it is a *foot* no longer. It can be preserved in alcohol as a laboratory specimen, but it cannot *do* any of the things feet do. An individual man, who is only an organ of a larger organism, the state, is no more complete and no more really himself in isolation than is the severed foot. In fact, using Plato's favorite sort of simile, the mathematical, we can set forth a ratio: Toe is to foot as foot is to leg as leg is to man as man is to state.

If, then, the good life for an individual is possible only in a community, the study of ethics passes over into, and is supplemented by, the study of politics, the art of communal living. The art of politics includes the art of ruling, for wherever numbers of men live and work together some sort of central direction is required. The question is what sort of rule is best, that is, what sort of rule will assure that each individual citizen leads a virtuous and happy life because all his drives are functioning efficiently? Plato's answer is that the rule of the many by the few is best. But not just any few who, because of birth or wealth, are in a position to exercise authority. It should be the rule by those few who are wise and good. This follows from the fact of differential participation in the form "man." If all men participated equally, and in high degree, in this form, reason would be the primary drive in all of us. Since reason is the instrument of self-discipline, every man would then govern himself in the interest of that organic life of which he saw himself to be a part. We would all be virtuous spontaneously, without the "encouragement" of police or laws. But, as we have seen, Plato held that most men are not sufficiently rational. Most of us, being incapable of knowing the good, are incapable of being virtuous of our own accord. This is why he believed that the many must be ruled by those few who are capable of knowing the good. In the ordinary affairs of life, everybody, as Plato pointed out, takes the advice of the wise few rather than the advice of the ignorant many. If I am ill, I go to the best specialist I can find; I don't stand on the street corner consulting casual passers-by. Paradoxically, it is only in the most serious affairs of all—in politics—that we seem to prefer the advice of the ignorant many:

> When we [Athenians] are met together in the assembly, and the matter in hand relates to building, the builders are summoned as advisers; when the question is one of ship-building, then the ship-wrights. . . . But when the question is an affair of state, then everybody is free to have a say— carpenter, tinker, cobbler, merchant, sea captain; rich and poor, high and low—anyone who likes gets up, and no one reproaches him, as in the former case, with not having learned, . . . and yet giving advice. . . .°

## PLATO'S CRITICISM OF DEMOCRACY

In a democracy the people choose their leaders, not because of their superior knowledge, but on all sorts of irrelevant grounds—a humble background, a mellifluous voice, a leonine mane. This is the basic reason for Plato's castigation of democracy. The art of ruling, which ought to be the art of determining what is best, becomes in a democracy the art of flattery, the art of appealing to the passions of the masses. This is why the Sophists were so much sought after by ambitious men. They taught rhetoric, which, as Gorgias says in the dialogue of the same name, "persuades the judges in the courts, the senators in the council, and the citizens in the assembly. [It is] that which gives to men freedom in their own persons, and to individuals the power of ruling over others in their several states."ᴾ

Rhetoric, that is to say, operates at the level of opinion and induces belief by emotive means, rather than operating at the level of knowledge, where the truth is discovered by an analysis of the forms. As Socrates replies to Gorgias, rhetoric is a pseudo-art, like cookery.

> In my opinion . . . the whole of which rhetoric is a part is a practical habit which has nothing of art in it but comes to a bold and astute mind with a natural talent for dealing with men: this practice I sum up under the word "flattery"; and it appears to me to have many other parts, one of which is cookery. . . . Cookery assumes the semblance of medicine, and pretends to know what food is the best for the body; and if the physician and the cook had to enter into a competition in which the children were the judges, or men who had no more sense than children, to decide which of them best understands the goodness or badness of food, the physician would be starved to death. A flattery I deem this to be . . . because it aims at pleasure without any thought of the best. An art I do not call it, but only a sort of practical skill, because it cannot give any account of the nature of the things it offers to the person to whom it offers them, and so cannot explain the reason why each is offered. And I do not call any irrational activity an art. . . .

Even the much admired Pericles was no better than a flatterer and a pastry-cook. He may have supposed himself to be acting in the best interests of the people, but actually he corrupted them. Still, Pericles was doubtless not as bad as most politicians. At least he and the men of his generation were not bunglers like Cleon. They were competent men, able to satisfy the people's wishes.

> But as to transforming those desires and not allowing them to have their way, and using the powers . . . they had . . . in the improvement of their fellow-citizens . . . I do not see that in these respects they were a whit superior to our present statesmen, although I do admit that they were more clever at providing ships and walls and docks, and all that. . . . You praise the men who feasted the citizens and satisfied their desires. People say that they have made the city great, not seeing that the swollen and ulcerated condition of the State is to be attributed to these elder statesmen; for they have filled

the city full of harbours and docks and walls and revenues and all that . . ., and have left no room for justice and temperance.

In other words, Plato's verdict on Pericles' policy was: He made the city "great" in the vulgar sense of the word; he made it rich and famous, and since these are values that appeal to the vulgar, his fellow citizens held him in great esteem. But he also destroyed the ancient probity and sense of public service. By paying citizens for performing tasks that were their duty as Athenians, he destroyed their moral fiber, rendering them unfit for the great struggle into which his policy finally plunged them.

Yet in Plato's view the real villain was not Pericles. For in a democracy there is no way to rule except by flattery, and there is no place for the good man or for the real politician—no place, that is, for the political scientist whose program is based on knowledge of the good rather than on what appeals to the electorate.

> I think that I am the only or almost the only Athenian living who seeks the true art of politics; and the only practising politician. . . . I look to what is best and not to what is most pleasant, having no mind to use those arts and graces [of rhetoric] which you recommend. . . . I shall be tried just as a physician would be tried in a court of little boys at the indictment of the cook. [The cook would rise in court and say,] "My boys, many evil things has this man done to you . . . cutting and burning and starving and suffocating you . . . he gives you the bitterest potions, and compels you to hunger and thirst. How unlike the variety of meats and sweets on which I feasted you!" What do you suppose that the physician would be able to reply? . . . He could only say, "All these evil things, my boys, I did for your health," and then would there not be a deafening clamour from a jury like that? How they would cry out!

## A PLANNED SOCIETY

It is essential, then, to get political power out of the hands of the many and into the hands of the wise few. But how is this transition, which would amount to a revolution, to be accomplished? Plato did not say, except to speak vaguely about the possibility of kings somehow becoming philosophers or, alternatively, of philosophers becoming kings. Presumably he regarded the problem of the actual transfer of power as a matter of practical politics that did not concern him, as a theorist. What he *did* concentrate on was the kind of regime the wise few would institute, if they ever had the opportunity.

The basic assumptions underlying Plato's description of the ideal regime are twofold: First, the many, being incurably ignorant, are incapable of disciplining themselves. Second, the wise, because they are wise, can and will provide external discipline as a substitute for the internal restraints that the many lack. In Plato's view, the parallel between the role of the rational class in the community and the role of reason in the individual is exact. Reason in the individual is an activity that disciplines itself and all the other activities of that individual in the interests of the whole self. In the state the rational class legislates for itself and for the other classes in the interest of the community as a whole. Thus, though it is correct to speak (as Plato did) of temperance as "the" virtue of the producing class, it is not a self-induced virtue. The producers love getting and spending too much not to go to excess if left to their own devices. Left alone, the rich get richer at the expense of the poor; extremes of wealth and poverty appear, civil dissension breaks out, and the state destroys itself in what, since Marx, we have come to call the "class struggle." Temperance, then, is the virtue of the producers in the sense that without moderation in profits the economy of the state becomes unhealthy. But the producers cannot achieve temperance for themselves. It has to be achieved for them by governmental regulation.

They may not like this regulation; they may regard it as an intrusion on their private rights. Its justification is that, whether they appreciate it or not, it is best for them. The task of the rulers is to find those who are temperamentally fitted to be producers and to make producers of them; then, and then only, will they be virtuous and will the state as a whole be just. The same, of course, applies to the other classes.

Thus, according to Plato, the art of ruling is concerned with two main problems: a problem of selection and a problem of control. First, it is necessary to ascertain what the special capabilities of the various citizens are, and especially to separate out the potential rulers from those who are fit merely to be producers. Second, since the ordinary citizen cannot be expected to do voluntarily all those things that are best for him, it is necessary to assure obedience. Plato was quite prepared to sanction the use of force when needed, but he thought it inefficient in the long run. Propaganda is a far better instrument of control.

The chief instrument of propaganda is the education that the rulers provide for the masses. Though they should be taught the trade—farming, banking, or whatever—for which their native capabilities fit them, most of their education should be directed toward indoctrinating them to accept the guidance of their betters. It is necessary to speak to them in language to which their emotional, sentimental, or practical natures can respond. It is pointless, for instance, to try to *explain* to them the organic nature of the state and the corresponding need of each individual to subordinate his immediate interests to the whole, for they cannot grasp such abstract concepts. But loyalty and patriotism are attitudes of mind easily inculcated, and they serve the same functional purpose of producing social cohesion, obedience, and so on. Flag-waving, patriotic music, and tales about heroic forefathers must therefore occupy a large part of the school curriculum. Whether these tales are true or untrue is quite beside the point, provided they inspire the children to behavior that is best for the state.

And, if on the one hand we must see to it that certain things are taught, we must be equally careful to see that other things are not taught. Since the whole basis of this education is an appeal to emotion rather than to intellect, it is important both that bad emotions (fear, for instance, or greed) are not stirred and that good emotions are not associated with the wrong sorts of objects (loyalty to one's family or class, for instance, instead of loyalty to the rulers, as the symbol for the state as a whole). Thus in Plato's state the Ministry of Propaganda and its complement, the Ministry of Censorship, are of the first importance.[11]

> Our first business will be to supervise the making of fables and legends, rejecting all which are unsatisfactory . . . . Most of the stories now in use must be discarded. . . .
>
> Which kind are you thinking of, and what fault do you find in them? . . .
>
> Even if [Homer's and Hesiod's] tales were true, I should not have supposed they should be lightly told to thoughtless young people. . . .
>
> I agree; such stories are not fit to be repeated.
>
> Nor yet any tales of warfare and intrigues and battles of gods against gods, which are equally untrue. If our future Guardians are to think it a disgrace to quarrel lightly with one another, we shall not . . . tell them of all the feuds of gods and heroes with their kith and kin. . . .
>
> Yes, that is reasonable. . . .
>
> Both poets and prose-writers [are also] guilty of the most serious misstatements about human life, making out that wrongdoers are often happy and just men miserable; that injustice pays, if not detected; and that my being just is to another man's advantage, but a loss to myself. We shall have to prohibit such poems and tales and tell them to compose others in the contrary sense. Don't you think so?
>
> I am sure of it. . . .
>
> There remains the question of . . . music. . . . We [do] not want dirges and laments. Which are the modes that express sorrow? Tell me; you are musical.
>
> Modes like the Mixed Lydian and Hyperlydian.
>
> Then we may discard those; men, and even women of good standing, will have no use for them.
>
> Certainly.
>
> Again, drunkenness, effeminacy, and inactivity are most unsuitable in Guardians. Which are the modes expressing softness and the ones used at drinking-parties?
>
> There are the Ionian and certain Lydian modes which are called "slack."
>
> You will not use them in the training of your warriors?
>
> Certainly not. You seem to have the Dorian and the Phrygian left.
>
> I am not an expert in the modes, I said; but leave me . . . the two which will best express the accents of courage in the face of stern necessity and misfortune, and of temperance in prosperity won by peaceful pursuits. . . .
>
> Then we must not only compel our poets, on pain of expulsion, to make their poetry the express image of noble character; we must also supervise

---

11 In the first part of this passage Socrates is talking with Adeimantus, one of Plato's elder brothers; in the latter part, with Glaucon. This passage should be compared with the contemporary account of educational practices in Sparta (see pp. 41–43).

> craftsmen of every kind and forbid them to leave the stamp of baseness, licence, meanness, unseemliness, on painting and sculpture, or building, or any other work of their hands; and anyone who cannot obey shall not practise his art in our commonwealth.q

Plato believed that heredity plays a large part in determining both one's bent and one's abilities. In general, therefore, the children of producers will be producers—the children of bankers and doctors and day laborers will grow up to be, respectively, bankers, doctors, and day laborers. Similarly, soldiers will generally have soldier sons, and bureaucrats, bureaucrats. But a farm laborer may just possibly have a son capable of being a banker, or even capable of rising altogether out of the producer class to become a soldier or a ruler. If so, he should be given the opportunity to develop these talents. Similarly, the son of one of the rulers may not have the intelligence and moral stamina that rulers need; if so, he should be reduced to the level for which his nature fits him. Thus, though Plato's concept of the primacy of heredity makes for a static society in which children tend to follow the trades of their fathers, it is a mistake to accuse him of recommending a caste system. Ability, in the Platonic state, can always find its own level.

When it has been said that producers need to be taught their trade, plus such myths as will inculcate obedience and patriotism, about all that needs to be said about this class has been said. In general, Plato believed that in the ideal state producers would lead much the same sort of life—home, family, children, fireside, amusements—that men of this type led in his own day, with the important exception that instead of being haphazard, the general pattern of life would be regulated by the government.

But in the life of the ruling classes Plato proposed radical innovations. This is where the problem of selection comes in. All children will be observed and it will be ascertained whether they have the native capacity that fits them for a *real* education—whether, that is, after a long and arduous training in mathematics, they can reach a knowledge of the forms. Those who show they have sufficient ability to warrant selection as prospective rulers will be taken from their families and placed in a public nursery. If they are eventually to rule the whole state, their first loyalty must be to that state, not to some smaller unit within it. From the very start they must learn to think of all their contemporaries as brothers and sisters, and of the state itself as their mother.[12]

> Let us consider how they should live and be housed. First, none of them must possess any private property beyond the barest necessaries. Next, no one is to have any dwelling or store-house that is not open for all to enter at will. Their food, in the quantities required by men of temperance and courage who are in training for war, they will receive from the other citizens

---

12 The speakers are Socrates and Plato's two brothers, Glaucon and Adeimantus.

as the wages of their guardianship . . . ; and they will have meals in common and all live together like soldiers in a camp. . . . They alone of all the citizens are forbidden to touch and handle silver or gold. . . .

The question under what conditions people born and educated as we have described should possess wives and children, and how they should treat them, can be rightly settled only by keeping to the course on which we started them at the outset. We undertook to put these men in the position of watch-dogs guarding a flock. Suppose we follow up the analogy and imagine them bred and reared in the same sort of way. . . .

Which do we think right for watchdogs: should the females guard the flock and hunt with the males and take a share in all they do, or should they be kept within doors as fit for no more than bearing and feeding their puppies, while all the hard work of looking after the flock is left to the males?

They are expected to take their full share, except that we treat them as not quite so strong.

Can you employ any creature for the same work as another, if you do not give them both the same upbringing and education?

No.

Then, if we are to set women to the same tasks as men, we must teach them the same things. . . . There is no occupation concerned with the management of social affairs which belongs either to woman or to man, as such. Natural gifts are to be found here and there in both creatures alike; and every occupation is open to both, so far as their natures are concerned, though woman is for all purposes the weaker.

Certainly. . . .

We come round, then, to our former position, that there is nothing contrary to nature in giving our Guardians' wives the same training for mind and body. . . . Rather, the contrary practice which now prevails turns out to be unnatural.

So it appears. . . .

It is for [the Rulers], who have already selected the men, to select for association with them women who are so far as possible of the same natural capacity. . . . How are we to get the best results? You must tell me, Glaucon, because I see you keep sporting dogs and a great many game birds at your house. . . . Do you breed from all indiscriminately? Are you not careful to breed from the best so far as you can?

Yes.

And from those in their prime, rather than the very young or the very old?

Yes. . . .

Dear me, said I; we shall need consummate skill in our Rulers, if it is also true of the human race. [For] it seems they will have to give their subjects a considerable dose of imposition and deception for their good. . . . If we are to keep our flock at the highest pitch of excellence, there should be as many unions of the best of both sexes, and as few of the inferior, as possible, and that only the offspring of the better unions should be kept. And again, no one but the Rulers must know how all this is being effected; otherwise our herd of Guardians may become rebellious.

Quite true. . . .

I think they will have to invent some ingenious system of drawing lots, so that, at each pairing off, the inferior candidate may blame his luck rather than the Rulers.

Yes, certainly. . . .

As soon as children are born, they will be taken in charge by officers appointed for the purpose. . . . The children of the better parents they will carry to the crèche to be reared in the care of nurses living apart in a certain quarter of the city. Those of the inferior parents and any children of the rest that are born defective will be hidden away, in some appropriate manner that must be kept secret.

They must be, if the breed of our Guardians is to be kept pure. . . .

This, then, Glaucon, is the manner in which the Guardians of your commonwealth are to hold their wives and children in common. Must we not next find arguments to establish that it is . . . the best plan? . . . Does not the worst evil for a state arise from anything that tends to render it asunder and destroy its unity, while nothing does it more good than whatever tends to bind it together and make it one?

That is true. . . .

And . . . disunion comes about when the words "mine" and "not mine," "another's" and "not another's" are not applied to the same things throughout the community. The best ordered state will be the one in which the largest number of persons use these terms in the same sense, and which accordingly most nearly resembles a single person. When one of us hurts his finger, the whole extent of those bodily connexions which are gathered up in the soul and unified by its ruling element is made aware and it all shares as a whole in the pain of the suffering part; hence we say that the man has a pain in his finger. The same thing is true of the pain or pleasure felt when any other part of the person suffers or is relieved.

Yes; I agree that the best organized community comes nearest to that condition.

And so it will recognize as a part of itself the individual citizen to whom good or evil happens, and will share as a whole in his joy or sorrow.[r]


### PRACTICALITY AND DESIRABILITY OF PLATO'S SCHEME

When we recall the divisive class struggles that the Peloponnesian War brought to cities like Corcyra, it is easy to see why Plato prized unity so highly. But, though we can understand his insistence on unity, we still have to ask whether his scheme is practicable and whether, if practicable, it is desirable. Many people will say that what Plato demanded in the way of self-sacrifice and discipline is more than can be expected of the average man. But of course Plato intended *most* citizens to grow up in a family, to marry, to have children, to acquire property. The life of ascetic discipline was to be limited to the few who were fitted for it by temperament and who had been trained from birth in preparation for it. The Society of Jesus is a good example of a special group of the kind Plato proposed. The Jesuits are an elite whose members are carefully selected and subsequently given rigorous training; indeed, the Jesuits lead a far more ascetic life than that envisaged by Plato. There is, then, nothing impossible in the notion of there being men prepared to give their whole lives willingly to some great enterprise of which they feel themselves to be a part.

But will the rulers, leading the life described, be "happy"? On one occasion, in reply to this objection, Plato said that it does not matter whether the rulers are happy; what matters is the happiness of the state as a whole. In a way, of course, this is true. But in his concern to point up his argument against the Sophists, namely, that the genuine ruler is not out for what he can get, Plato overstated the case. It is not that the rulers will be willing to sacrifice their happiness; rather, they will find their happiness in something beyond the immediate satisfaction of their own bodies. And this satisfaction, qualitatively different from that of the producers, who find *their* satisfaction in getting and spending, is (Plato believed) superior to that of the producers. The man who is born with the capacity for ruling and who is trained to be a ruler will find his happiness in shouldering responsibilities and in making difficult decisions for the state. He will be willing to return to the cave and will no more yearn after the life of the producer, with its glass-of-beer, slippers-before-the-fire, drowsing-while-the-children-play satisfactions, than will the producers yearn after the ascetic life of the rulers. No class will envy any other, but each will seek its "proper" happiness.

Thus Plato's scheme is not as impractical as has sometimes been supposed. But is it desirable? Placing supreme power in the hands of a specially trained elite would be desirable only if (1) there were irreducible differences in men's intellectual capacities; if (2) these differences could be discovered early in life; if (3) there is a truth about politics that can be infallibly known, namely, what is good for all; and if (4) the elite, knowing what is good for all, would act on its knowledge.

As regards (1), we say "irreducible" differences for the following reason: If the great differences that obviously now exist could be removed over a period of time by gradually improving man's environment, it might be sensible to overlook present differences and put political power in the hands of all. This is the kind of presupposition on which our own form of government operates. Letting everyone vote (putting the political power in the hands of all) may not be the way to get the best decisions *now*, but we believe it is worth the risk of all sorts of mistakes (which might not be made if voting were confined to the experts), because sharing in the responsibilities of power teaches men how to perform their political duties more intelligently. Hence it is not enough, in support of Plato's conclusion, to point to actual differences in intelligence among men; the question is whether these differences are irremovable.

As regards (2), even if government by experts were desirable, everything would still depend on being able to determine who the experts are. While much has been achieved in this field by psychologists, it can hardly be claimed that tests have been made precise enough to warrant our basing political power on them.

As for (3), if political science is like mathematics—if there are forms in politics like the triangles, cubes, and pyramids studied by the mathematician—it would be plausible to argue that political decisions should be left to the political scientists, as mathematics is left to the mathematicians. But if the truth about politics is complex and if men's judgments in this field are influenced by their biases, it may be better to adopt the policy finally agreed upon by many individuals, who represent different interests and points of view, than to rely on the judgment of a single individual or a small group, however able.

Finally, considering (4), let us suppose the other difficulties surmounted. Let us suppose that most men have been shown to be incorrigibly ignorant, that adequate intelligence tests are available, and that the truth in politics is as readily ascertainable as the truth in mathematics. Even so, rule by a Platonic elite would be desirable only if Plato were correct in maintaining that his rulers will act as rationally as they think. That they will do so, Plato firmly believed. Virtue is knowledge, he held; if we really know what is good we will do it. "Knowledge is a noble and commanding thing, which cannot be overcome, and will not allow a man, if he only knows the difference of good and evil to do anything which is contrary to knowledge." Of course, Plato was aware "that the majority of the world are of another mind; and that men are commonly supposed to know the things which are best, and not to do them when they might. And most persons whom I have asked the reason of this have said that when men act contrary to knowledge they are overcome by pain, or pleasure, or some [other] affection."

In this passage the phrase "overcome by pleasure" is ambiguous. Being so overcome turns out, at least according to Plato's analysis, to mean choosing a lesser pleasure instead of a greater. How can this be? Plato's answer is that, just as small objects near at hand look bigger than larger ones at a distance, so a small satisfaction that is imminent seems better than a greater satisfaction that will not be fulfilled for some time. Hence a bad choice is a mistake in judgment regarding size, and its proper corrective is knowledge, especially a knowledge of measurement, by which we accurately weigh the sizes of satisfactions against one another.

> Do not the same magnitudes appear larger to your sight when near, and smaller when at a distance? . . . And the same holds of thickness and number; also sounds which are in themselves equal are greater when near, and lesser when at a distance. . . . Now suppose happiness consisted in doing or choosing the greater, and in not doing or in avoiding the less, what would have been the saving principle of human life? Would not the art of measuring have been the saving principle; or would the power of appearance? Is not the latter that deceiving force which makes us wander up and down and take the things at one time of which we repent at another, both in our actions and in our choice of things great and small? But the art of measurement would have done away with the effect of appearances, and, showing the truth,

would have taught the soul at last to find rest in the truth, and would thus
have saved our life. . . . Men err in their choice . . . of good and evil from
defect of knowledge; and not only from defect of knowledge in general, but
of that particular knowledge which you have already admitted to be the
science of measurement. . . .

No man voluntarily pursues evil, or that which he thinks to be evil. To
prefer evil to good is not in human nature; and when a man is compelled
to choose one of two evils, no one will choose the greater when he may have
the less.[s]

Doubtless many of the bad choices people make are mistakes of calculation;
doubtless one of the causes of miscalculation is the perspectival distortion that
Plato cited. When a man on a diet eats a rich dessert despite knowing how many
calories it contains, we can probably explain his choice in this way: The small,
near-at-hand satisfaction of eating the dessert looks larger than the much greater
but more remote satisfaction of avoiding a heart attack. But is *all* wrongdoing
merely a matter of making an error in judgment? What about the Christian
conception of a bad, or perverted, will that desires, and deliberately chooses,
what it knows to be wrong? And what about Freud's conception of the id? From
his point of view, the superego—Plato's reason—is a pretty fragile instrument
of control. And what Plato called rationality, Freud would have reduced to
rationalization, that is, finding a respectable-sounding explanation for what we
are going to do anyway for other, and less respectable, reasons.

There does seem to be a certain amount of empirical evidence to support
the more pessimistic view of human nature that both St. Paul and Freud held.
It is pretty hard, for instance, to account for the wholesale extermination of Jews
during World War II by saying it was merely an error of judgment. But here
again, in the question of whether virtue is knowledge, we reach a parting of
the ways in philosophy, about which there will be fundamental differences of
opinion.

It is safe to say, however, that, whatever is true of mankind in general, rulers
are exposed to special temptations. The more we insist, along with Plato, on
the division of labor and on the specialization of function on which division of
labor rests, the more danger there is that the ruling class will confuse its class
interests with the good of the whole community of which, according to Plato,
it is only one organ. Any bureaucracy is a case in point. There is always a danger
that the bureaucrats will lose touch with the people they are supposed to serve
and come to lead a kind of private life of their own. Every organization is
constantly exposed to this virus. And the smaller the administrative group—the
more isolated the rulers, the more protected they are from criticism or from
the threat of recall—the greater the danger of infection.

The exercise of great power seems to act as a dissolving acid on the moral
virtues, as can be seen by the lives of many men (for example, Napoleon) who,
beginning with noble motives, have ended as tyrants. Hence, even if we could

accept as a general rule Plato's thesis that virtue is knowledge, we would still be loath to see *too* much power in any one man's hands, however great his knowledge might be.

But Plato was not a totalitarian *in intent*, even if, as we may suspect, this is where a state founded on Platonic principles would end *in fact*. It is true that in its externals the Platonic state is close to that of George Orwell's *1984*. There is a Ministry of Propaganda, indoctrinating the public with useful fictions; a Ministry of Censorship, rigidly suppressing dangerous thoughts; the same military flavor; the same powerful police, the same discipline, the same denial of a domain of private rights; the same omnipresent state; the same ruling and self-perpetuating clique. The only difference—but a basic one—is in the character of the ruling elite. The rulers of Plato's state know the truth and act in accordance with it for the good of all. The rulers of Orwell's state are Thrasymacheans, not Platonists; they have taken over Thrasymachus' nihilism, cynicism, and egoism and applied modern techniques of advertising and political control to accomplish results that Thrasymachus did not dream of, but that he certainly would have applauded. In Plato's state, the rulers lie to the people for the good of the people; in the Orwellian state, the rulers lie to the people for the good of the rulers. In Plato's state there is a tension of opposing economic, social, and political forces in the producing class, but this is held in check and in balance by the rulers, whose passionless knowledge has put them outside the struggle for power; in the Orwellian state the struggle for power infects the whole state and becomes more bitter, cruel, and savage in the more intelligent classes, for reason is not regarded as an instrument of self-discipline but as a tool for satisfying the passions. It is true that we have grounds for fearing that even Plato's rulers might be corrupted by power, but it would be unfair to assume, because of this doubt, that Plato was advocating a totalitarian state. At a theoretical level, at the level of what has been called intent, Plato was poles apart from the totalitarians.

This comment is relevant because, after all, Plato was writing a book on political theory, not a handbook on political practice. If we could have proved to Plato that his theory leads in practice to bad results, that is, to tyranny, he certainly would have modified the theory; hence we cannot say that Plato advocated tyranny. As a matter of fact, Plato had his own doubts about the workability of his theory. In the *Republic* Socrates hedges when asked the kind of question we have been raising: Will it work satisfactorily? Doubtless Plato himself was of two minds about it. Since, if it would work, it was a fine theory, he wanted very much to believe it would work. At the same time, he knew enough about human nature to fear it might not.[13] This is a very human, though not at all a comfortable, position to be in, and it is in the light of this attitude

---

13 This conclusion is supported by the tone of the *Laws*, a work written when Plato was an old man and was apparently still more aware of the difficulty of getting human nature to conform to the fine figure of some rational scheme.

of mind that we should read his discussion of the four types of degenerate states.[14]

## FOUR DEVIATIONS FROM THE IDEAL GOVERNMENT

We shall start with the constitution dominated by motives of ambition—it has no name in common use that I know of; let us call it timarchy or timocracy. . . . Let us try to explain how the government of the best might give place to a timocracy. Is it not a simple fact that in any form of government revolution always starts from the outbreak of internal dissension in the ruling class? The constitution cannot be upset so long as that class is of one mind, however small it may be.

That is true.

Then how, Glaucon, will trouble begin in our commonwealth? . . . Hard as it may be for a state so framed to be shaken, yet, since all that comes into being must decay, even a fabric like this will not endure for ever, but will suffer dissolution. . . . The rulers . . . , wise as they are, will not be able, by observation and reckoning, to hit upon the times propitious or otherwise for birth; some day the moment will slip by and they will beget children out of due season [who] will not be well-endowed or fortunate. The best of these may be appointed by the elder generation; but when they succeed to their fathers' authority as Guardians, being unworthy, they will begin to neglect us and to think too lightly first of the cultivation of the mind, and then of bodily training, so that your young men will come to be worse educated. Then . . . they agree to distribute land and houses for private ownership; they enslave their own people who formerly lived as free men under their guardianship and gave them maintenance; and, holding them as serfs and menials, devote themselves to war and to keeping these subjects under watch and ward.

I agree: that is how the transition begins.

And this form of government will be midway between the rule of the best and oligarchy,[15] will it not?

Yes.

Such being the transition, . . . it will resemble each of these in some respects and have some features of its own. . . . It will be like the earlier constitution in several ways. Authority will be respected; the fighting class will abstain from any form of business, farming, or handicrafts; they will keep up their common meals and give their time to physical training and martial exercises.

Yes.

On the other hand, it . . . will be afraid to admit intellectuals to office. . . . It will prefer simpler characters with plenty of spirit. . . .

Yes.

---

14 The speakers are Socrates, Glaucon, and Adeimantus. Socrates refers to himself occasionally in the first person because he is relating his conversation with Plato's brothers to a third party.
15 [The discussion of oligarchy follows immediately—AUTHOR.]

At the same time, men of this kind will resemble the ruling class of an oligarchy in . . . hav[ing] private homes where they can hoard their treasure in secret and live ensconced in a nest of their own, lavishing their riches on their women or whom they please. . . .

The society you describe is certainly a mixture of good and evil.

Yes, it is a mixture; but, thanks to the predominance of the spirited part of our nature, it has one most conspicuous feature: ambition and the passion to excel. . . .

The next type of constitution will be oligarchy.

What sort of régime do you mean?

The one which is based on a property qualification, where the rich are in power and the poor man cannot hold office.

I see.

We must start, then, by describing the transition from timocracy to oligarchy. No one could fail to see how that happens. The downfall of timocracy is due to the flow of gold into those private stores we spoke of. . . . Then, . . . the more they value money and the less they care for virtue. Virtue and wealth are balanced against one another in the scales; as the rich rise in social esteem, the virtuous sink. These changes of valuation, moreover, are always reflected in practice. . . . They fix by statute the qualification for privilege in an oligarchy . . . ; no one may hold office whose property falls below the prescribed sum. This measure is carried through by armed force, unless they have already set up their constitution by terrorism. That, then, is how an oligarchy comes to be established.

Yes, said Adeimantus; but what are [its] defects?

In the first place, I replied, the principle on which it limits privilege. How would it be, if the captain of a ship were appointed on a property qualification, and a poor man could never get a command, though he might know much more about seamanship?

The voyage would be likely to end in disaster. . . .

Is it any less serious that such a state must lose its unity and become two, one of the poor, the other of the rich, living together and always plotting against each other?

Quite as serious.

Another thing to its discredit is that they may well be unable to carry on a war. Either they must call out the common people or not. If they do, they will have more to fear from the armed multitude than from the enemy; and if they do not, in the day of battle these oligarchs will find themselves only too literally a government of the few. Also, their avarice will make them unwilling to pay war-taxes. . . . Such, then, is the character of a state ruled by an oligarchy. It has all these evils and perhaps more.

If the aim of life in an oligarchy is to become as rich as possible, that insatiable craving would bring about the transition to democracy. In this way: since the power of the ruling class is due to its wealth, they will not want to have laws restraining prodigal young men from ruining themselves by extravagance. . . . This neglect to curb riotous living sometimes reduces to poverty men of a not ungenerous nature. They settle down in idleness, some of them burdened with debt, some disfranchised, some both at once; and these drones are armed and can sting. Hating the men who have acquired their property and conspiring against them and the rest of society, they long for a revolution. . . . As for [the oligarchs] themselves, luxurious indolence of body and mind makes [them] too lazy and effeminate to resist pleasure or to endure pain. . . . This state, then, is in the same precarious condition as a person so unhealthy that the least shock from outside will upset the balance or, even without that, internal disorder will break out. . . .

Quite true.

And when the poor win, the result is a democracy. They kill some of the opposite party, banish others, and grant the rest an equal share in civil rights and government, officials being usually appointed by lot.

Yes, that is how a democracy comes to be established. . . .

Now what is the character of this new régime? . . . First of all, they are free. Liberty and free speech are rife everywhere; anyone is allowed to do what he likes. . . . You are not obliged to be in authority, however competent you may be, or to submit to authority, if you do not like it. . . . A wonderfully pleasant life, surely, for the moment.

For the moment, no doubt. . . .

With a magnificent indifference to the sort of life a man has led before he enters politics, [a democracy] will promote to honour anyone who merely calls himself the people's friend.

Magnificent indeed.

These then, and such as these, are the features of a democracy, an agreeable form of anarchy with plenty of variety and an equality of a peculiar kind for equals and unequals alike. . . .

How does despotism arise? That it comes out of democracy is fairly clear. Does the change take place in the same sort of way as the change from oligarchy to democracy? Oligarchy was established by men with a certain aim in life: the good they sought was wealth, and it was the insatiable appetite for money-making to the neglect of everything else that proved its undoing. Is democracy likewise ruined by greed for what it conceives to be the supreme good?

What good do you mean?

Liberty. In a democratic country you will be told that liberty is its noblest possession, which makes it the only fit place for a free spirit to live in. . . . Perhaps the insatiable desire for this good to the neglect of everything else may transform a democracy and lead to a demand for despotism. A democratic state may fall under the influence of unprincipled leaders, ready to minister to its thirst for liberty with too deep draughts of this heady wine. . . . The citizens become so sensitive that they resent the slightest application of control as intolerable tyranny, and in their resolve to have no master they end by disregarding even the law, written or unwritten. [Their] leaders [distribute] to the people what they have taken from the well-to-do, always provided they can keep the lion's share for themselves. The plundered rich are driven to defend themselves in debate before the Assembly. . . . Then follow impeachments and trials, in which each party arraigns the other.

Quite so.

And the people always put forward a single champion of their interests, whom they nurse to greatness. . . . Then comes the notorious device of all who have reached this stage in the despot's career, the request for a bodyguard to keep the people's champion safe for them. The request is granted, because the people, in their alarm on his account, have no fear for themselves.

Quite true. . . .

In the early days he has a smile and a greeting for everyone he meets; disclaims any absolute power . . . ; sets about the relief of debtors and the distribution of land to the people and to his supporters; and assumes a mild and gracious air towards everybody. But soon . . . he begins stirring up one war after another, in order that the people may feel their need of a leader. . . . This course will lead to his being hated by his countrymen more and more. . . . If the despot is to maintain his rule, he . . . will need to keep a sharp eye open for anyone who is courageous or high-minded or intelligent or rich; it is his happy fate to be at war with all such, whether he likes it or not, and to lay his plans against them until he has purged the commonwealth.

A fine sort of purgation!

Yes, the exact opposite of the medical procedure, which removes the worst elements in the bodily condition and leaves the best.

There seems to be no choice, if he is to hold his power. . . .

No doubt he will spend any treasure there may be in the temples, so long as it will last, as well as the property of his victims, thus lightening the war-taxes imposed on the people.

And when that source fails?

Clearly he will support himself, with his boon-companions, minions, and mistresses, from his parent's estate.

I understand: the despot and his comrades will be maintained by the common people which gave him birth.

Inevitably.

But how if the people resent this and say it is not right for the father to support his grown-up son—it ought to be the other way about . . . ?

Then, to be sure, the people will learn what sort of a creature it has bred and nursed to greatness in its bosom, until now the child is too strong for the parent to drive out.

Do you mean that the despot will dare to lay violent hands on this father of his and beat him if he resists?

Yes, when once he has disarmed him.

So the despot is a parricide. . . . That freedom which knew no bounds must now put on the livery of the most harsh and bitter servitude, where the slave has become the master.[t]

This account of the process by which the best state degenerates into the worst has been criticized on the ground that states do not always go through just the sequence Plato described. A military oligarchy is sometimes succeeded by a tyranny; democracy has followed tyranny as often as tyranny has followed democracy. But Plato probably did not mean to be taken literally here. It is likely that he was far less interested in describing the stages of an alleged historical process than in making an analysis of certain types of deviation—tyranny, oligarchy, democracy, and so on—from the ideal state.

We have, then, an account of certain abiding tendencies, present to a greater or lesser degree in all actual states. *Every* actual state, for example, the Soviet Union, has certain oligarchical characteristics—the power of the Central Committee and its Presidium; certain military characteristics—the influence generals exert on policy decisions; certain democratic characteristics—universal suffrage; certain tyrannical characteristics—secret police. Insofar as some one of these sets of characteristics is primary, we may, loosely speaking, call the state in question by the name of this type. Thus we call Switzerland a democracy and Czarist Russia a tyranny. But in calling a state by the name of its primary type we must not forget (1) that no actual state possesses all the characteristics of any one type and (2) that every actual state possesses characteristics of several types. All this follows from the theory of forms. Every complex object participates primarily in some one form, by virtue of which it gets its name. But, being a physical thing, its participation in any form is only partial. And just because its whole nature is not absorbed in this form, it always participates in other forms to a greater or lesser degree.

This is perhaps the nearest Plato came to answering our question about the desirability and practicability of his political theory. Because man is a natural creature and the state is a natural institution, we cannot expect this political theory to "work" perfectly. No *theory* ever works perfectly in the physical world, precisely because the physical world, being physical, falls short of, and only partially participates in, those forms whose essences and interrelations are reflected in the theory. Hence it is no criticism of his theory, Plato would have said, to complain that it does not translate satisfactorily into political actualities. This is no fault of the theory but simply the way the world is. No actual state can ever be ideal; no actual ruler, being a mere man, will ever behave as man should behave.

Even in the *best* of possible actual worlds, then, the organic nature of man and society will not be completely realized. Rulers, however well educated, will never entirely free themselves from the mistake of identifying their own selfish interests with those of the whole, will never achieve a completely balanced division of labor. But, Plato would have concluded, the state he sketched, in which the wise rule and the ignorant obey, though not fully realizable in this world, is the ideal at which we should aim.

This reply is only partially satisfactory. Why must there be such a radical distinction between theory and actuality? What worth has a theory that is too elegant and logically perfect to have predictive value in real-life circumstances? In setting up an impossibly high theoretical ideal, Plato doomed himself to disappointment. Hence his thought is tinged with sadness. In any theory that, like Plato's, creates an inseparable chasm between the ideal and the actual, there is an inevitable pessimism arising from foreordained failure. Some major differences between Platonism and Christianity have already been pointed out; by contrast, this characteristic of Plato's thought gives it an affinity with Christianity. Christianity, too, sets itself an impossibly high goal (though a different one from Plato's) in the presence of which man's best efforts are always doomed to defeat. It is this affinity that has made Platonism a recurrent influence on Christian thought.

## Theory of Art

To ascertain the truth about ethics and politics was, for obvious reasons, Plato's primary concern. But ethics and politics do not, of course, exhaust the field of values. There are also, for instance, religious values and esthetic values. We must examine Plato's views on these subjects.

Turning first to Plato's esthetic theory, we can see that here, too, Plato's point of view was determined by the theory of forms. There is, as we might expect, a form "beauty," which is wholly beautiful. Physical objects, whether natural objects such as women's faces and sunsets or art objects such as paintings, are beautiful only insofar as they partake of the form. Physical objects may be more or less beautiful, but none is wholly beautiful, just as different physical horses partake to a greater or lesser degree of the form "horse," though none is wholly "horse." It follows that, just as looking at Dobbin and Bucephalus will give us only very inadequate information about "horse," so looking at physical objects, no matter how beautiful they are, will at best give us only an inadequate hint of real beauty. Indeed, people who enjoy the beauties of tones and colors usually miss the immaterial, intelligible beauty altogether. Thus, paradoxically enough, the enjoyment of what most people call "art," or beautiful objects, is for Plato a distraction.

If it is "beauty" that makes things beautiful, what, then, is "beauty" itself—that is, what is the form? It is not easy to say, but it appears that Plato felt that *order* anywhere in the universe is esthetic—the order, for instance, of the motions of the planets. Plato would presumably have agreed with those mathematicians who speak of one proof of a theorem as being "more elegant" than another. Since both prove the theorem, preference for the more elegant may have an esthetic basis.

We can now see both why physical objects are beautiful and why they are never as beautiful as the form in which they participate. To the degree that any physical object possesses order, it is beautiful—the starry heavens, for instance. But since no physical object is ever as well ordered as it might be, or as well ordered as are, say, the theorems of Euclidean geometry, it follows that physical objects are not as adequate a source of esthetic enjoyment as is the study of mathematics. It follows, too, that natural physical objects are much more beautiful than art objects. Dobbin, for instance, is more beautiful than a painting of Dobbin; for, though Dobbin himself is far away from the form "beauty," the painting (being only an imitation of Dobbin) is at two removes from it. The artist, then, is a liar and a deceiver—a kind of flatterer,[16] like the cook and the rhetorician, who by tickling men's fancy palms off inadequate imitations on an unsuspecting public. The paintings that we prize as works of art are but shadows of shadows.

This criticism comes of Plato's taking art as primarily cognitive. If art is supposed to give us information about horses or giraffes, the zoologist is a much better artist than the painter. But though Plato emphasized the cognitive *intent* of art much more than we would today, he was also aware of what we may call its emotive and conative aspects. He thought of the artist as a kind of magician whose rites and incantations release powerful and undisciplined emotions otherwise kept in check. All the arts, but particularly music and poetry, have great influence in molding character. It is no wonder that Plato, taking this view of the nature of art, insisted on rigid censorship of artists' activities, or that he judged artists harshly. When he thought of the cognitive intent of art, he found the artist a poor failure; when he thought of its emotive powers, he found the artist a social menace.

That this evaluation of art is inadequate is shown by Plato's own life and work. If we knew nothing else about Plato, we would be tempted to say his criticisms of art were the reflection of his own lack of esthetic sensitivity. No one, we might say, who knew anything about beauty could write about it in this fashion. But Plato was actually a consummate artist (as the dialogues amply prove), and in his writings he repeatedly employed an art form (the myth) to convey his meaning.

Plato's use of myths, as a matter of fact, throws light on how he understood the cognitive aspect of art, and furnishes, at the same time, a correction of the theory as it is formally stated. When Plato came to a particularly difficult and abstruse point in his argument, he often resorted to use of a myth to convey his meaning. When, for instance, in the *Republic*, Socrates is asked what he means by the Form of the Good, he replies that to describe "the actual nature of the Good . . . would be too great an effort"; that the Good is "like" the sun; and that he will have to answer in terms of this "offspring," not of the "parent" itself.

On Plato's part, this was neither a confession of personal failure nor a recognition of the inability of his readers to follow abstract discourse. The myths of Plato are not like the parables of Jesus, nor were Glaucon and Adeimantus simple fisherfolk in Palestine. According to Plato, the need for a myth is rooted in the

16 "Poetry is a sort of rhetoric . . . which is addressed to a crowd of men, women, and children, freemen and slaves. And this is not much to our taste, for . . . it [has] the nature of flattery" —*Gorgias* (Jowett), 502.

nature of the subjects discussed and in a fundamental limitation of verbal communication. Mathematics is a first-rate language for communicating about mathematical forms, and its study is a necessary preliminary for philosophical discourse. But both languages, the abstract language of mathematics and the technical prose of philosophy, are inadequate for communicating about the highest and most important forms—about the meaning and the value of life, for instance.

But what method of communication is there except the symbols employed by the mathematician and the words (written or spoken) employed by the trained dialectician? If these techniques are inadequate, must we admit that any communication about such high matters is impossible? Is the only possibility a mystic but incommunicable trance, in which we feel that we know, but we cannot utter, what we mean?

Plato thought not. Meanings can be communicated without words, by a kind of intellectual osmosis. In fact, this is the way all the really important things in life are communicated—not formally via lectures or books, but gradually over a long period of time. If the teacher knows the truth and the pupil has the potentiality for acquiring this knowledge, and if they live in close and sympathetic relationship, over the years the former's knowledge will be transferred to the latter in a way that neither of them clearly understands.

"Writing," Plato says in the *Phaedrus*, "has one grave fault in common with painting, for the creations of the painter have the attitude of life, and yet if you ask them a question they preserve a solemn silence." But there is another kind of word with far greater power than the written word. This is "the living word of knowledge which has a soul." These words are like the seeds a gardener plants. The good gardener sows them in fitting soil, tends them carefully, and patiently awaits their slow fruition. So the philosopher, ". . . finding a congenial soul, by the help of science sows and plants therein words which are able to defend themselves and him who planted them, and are not unfruitful, but have in them a seed which others brought up in different soils render immortal, making the possessors of it happy to the utmost extent of human happiness."[17,u]

Because this method of communication requires close personal contact over a long period of time, Plato used myth as a short cut, or substitute. Though a myth is a verbal communication, it uses the concrete, imagistic words of the artist, not the abstract prose of the dialectician. The meaning it communicates must not be taken literally (for it is a myth, not a history), and it cannot be translated into ordinary abstract prose. If it could be translated—if its meaning could be stated in such terms—there would be no need to employ a myth in the first place. A myth in fact is a work of art, and like every work of art it is unique. It is the condensation, as it were, of a complex meaning into a concrete object—a pattern of tones or pigment, a piece of marble, an arrangement of words.

17 See pp. 119–20.

In this sense, art is cognitive, though it is not cognitive in exactly the same way as are dialectic and the other sciences. An analogy will show the differences. Consider a soldier's experience of being under fire.[18] The civilian reading his newspaper, even the staff officer at headquarters, knows nothing, really, about what it means to be under fire.

On the other hand, the man who is pinned down by an enemy barrage often does not know what is happening to the rest of his unit. Still less does he know anything about how the battle as a whole is going. He is too overwhelmed by the immediacy of his experience—too submerged in its urgency—to understand it or to see beyond it. The survivor can seldom tell us at all adequately what happened to him; so much happened that his consciousness of it, like a fuse blown out by too much current on the wire, failed to record what occurred. From this point of view, the staff officer (or even the newspaper reader) knows much more about what happened than the survivor. The staff officer, sitting over his maps and his dispatches at headquarters, sees the event in its bearing on the course of the war. Was this attack merely a feint, or was it the beginning of a major offensive in this area? And so on. In this sense, no one is better informed than the staff officer, and no one more ignorant than the survivor.

It seems, then, that we are dealing with two quite different kinds of knowledge: direct experience, which is a confrontation with the event itself, in all its vividness and uniqueness (no attack is just like any other), and conceptual knowledge, which is about the relations of this experience to other experiences.[19] Now art stands halfway between these two kinds of knowledge, partaking of some of the characteristics of each. Art is immediate, vivid, and concrete like direct experience, but it also has the objectivity, perspective, and generality that direct experience lacks and that are characteristic of conceptual knowledge. The artist seems to be the sort of person who can live through an experience and not be so absorbed in it that he fails to observe and remember it; his fuse is not blown out by the urgency of immediate experience. Hence he is able to recall his experience and describe it in terms that evoke similar feelings, even in those who have never had such an experience. Tolstoy's account in *War and Peace* of young Rostoff's feelings as he takes part in his first cavalry charge presumably owes something to the fact that Tolstoy himself had lived through a similar experience as a young man in the Crimean War. His description is very different from the account of the charge that might be given by a military historian; the latter does not make one *feel* like a participant. It is also different from direct experience, because most participants in a cavalry charge feel too much to be able to feel anything very clearly. Art is thus in a way a substitute for direct experience, just as myth is a substitute for master and pupil leading a long life together.

18  See pp. 133–34.
19  See p. 158.

## Religion

Plato's conception of the function of myth is relevant to his view of religion, for, since religion is concerned with very high and important matters, his discussion of it was usually in terms of myth. This adds to the difficulty of understanding his view. Let us begin therefore by examining some passages in which Plato attempted to give a nonmythical account of the divine nature.

Such an account, following the usage established in the Middle Ages, may be called a natural theology—"theology" because it is concerned with god, "natural" because our knowledge is arrived at by means of a human power (reason) instead of a supernatural power (faith or intuition). In the *Republic*, for instance, Plato argues that certain properties of god can be inferred, or discovered by the use of reason. Thus (1) since god is good and since no good thing is hurtful, god is not the author of hurtful things. Again, (2) god "is not the author of all things, . . . and not of most things that occur to men. For few are the goods of human life, and many are the evils, and . . . of the evils the causes are to be sought elsewhere." However, (3) since the wicked are benefited by receiving punishment, we can infer that god is the author of the punishments they suffer. (4) God is unchangeable. This follows from the fact that he is good; in a good thing any change would be for the worse. For the same reason, (5) god does not lie or make false representations of himself, for there is no conceivable purpose that could move such a being to lie or misrepresent himself.ᵛ

### THE SELF-MOVING MOVER

These brief proofs are greatly expanded in Plato's last work, the *Laws*. The argument here begins with the enumeration of eight types of motion: (1) circular motion around a fixed center; (2) locomotion (gliding or rolling); (3) combination; (4) separation; (5) increase; (6) decrease; (7) becoming; (8) perishing. Plato then points out that this list omits the two most important types of motion, namely, "that motion which is always able to move other things, but unable to move itself; and that motion which always is able to move both itself and other things. . . ." Though Plato treats these as if they were on the same footing with the eight types already enumerated, the first eight are designations of empirically observable differences in the ways things move, whereas the last two are alternative accounts of the causes of motion. The point is that, if we want to avoid an infinite regress of causes of causes of causes . . . , we must sooner or later admit the existence of a self-caused motion—of a motion, that is, "which always is able to move both itself and other things." The argument then proceeds:

> ATHENIAN. Further, let us question and answer ourselves thus:—Supposing that the Whole of things were to unite and stand still, . . . which of the motions mentioned would necessarily arise in it first? That motion, of course, which is self-moving; for it will never be shifted beforehand by another thing, since no

shifting force exists in things beforehand. Therefore we shall assert that inasmuch as the self-moving motion is the starting-point of all motions and the first to arise in things at rest and to exist in things in motion, it is of necessity the most ancient and potent change of all. . . . Now . . . if we should see that this motion had arisen in a thing of earth or water or fire, whether separate or in combination, what condition should we say exists in such a thing?

CLINIAS. What you ask me is, whether we are to speak of a thing as "alive" when it moves itself?

ATHENIAN. Yes.

CLINIAS. It is alive, to be sure. . . .

ATHENIAN. What is the definition of that object which has for its name "soul"? Can we give it any other definition than . . . "the motion able to move itself"?

CLINIAS. Do you assert that "self-movement" is the definition of that very same substance which has "soul" as the name we universally apply to it?

ATHENIAN. That is what I assert. . . .ʷ

The argument, then, is (1) there must be a first cause of movement; (2) this first cause is a self-mover; (3) "soul" is the name given to self-movers;[20] therefore (4) soul is "more ancient" than those natural processes like evaporation, contraction, and expansion that the natural scientists erroneously asserted to be the primary causes of things. But to say that soul is the primary cause means, Plato thought, to say that there is purpose in the universe.

ATHENIAN. We recollect, of course, that we previously agreed that if soul could be shown to be older than body, then the things of soul also will be older than those of body.

CLINIAS. Certainly we do.

ATHENIAN. Moods and dispositions and wishes and calculations and true opinions and considerations and memories will be prior to bodily length, breadth, depth and strength, if soul is prior to body.

CLINIAS. Necessarily.

ATHENIAN. Must we then necessarily agree, in the next place, that soul is the cause of things good and bad, fair and foul, just and unjust, and all the opposites, if we are to assume it to be the cause of all things?

CLINIAS. Of course we must.

ATHENIAN. And as soul thus controls and indwells in all things everywhere that are moved, must we not necessarily affirm that it controls Heaven also?

CLINIAS. Yes.

ATHENIAN. One soul, is it, or several? I will answer for you—"several." Anyway, let us assume not less than two—the beneficent soul and that which is capable of effecting results of the opposite kind.

CLINIAS. You are perfectly right.

20 "Psyche" might be a better translation. Because of our Judeo-Christian heritage "soul" has connotations for us that it would be misleading to read into Plato's account.

ATHENIAN. Very well, then. . . . Which kind of soul, then, shall we say is in control of Heaven and earth and the whole circle? That which is wise and full of goodness, or that which has neither quality?

After some further discussion Clinias and the Athenian conclude that, as motions become more irregular, they become "more akin" to "absolute unreason," whereas the more regular a motion is, the more akin it is to reason. The motion most akin to the "motion of reason" is a regular, uniform, circular motion around a center. This is just the motion of the planets. It follows that they are moved by very good and very rational souls.

ATHENIAN. So now there is no longer any difficulty in stating expressly that, . . . concerning all the stars and the moon, and concerning the years and months and all seasons, [no] other account [can] be given than this . . . namely, that, inasmuch as it has been shown that they are all caused by one or more souls, which are good also with all goodness, we shall declare these souls to be gods . . . ?

## GODS EXIST

We can now take it as established that gods exist. The next step is to show that they are providential—that "they pay regard to human affairs." That they do is implied by the fact that the gods are good:

ATHENIAN. Come now, do we say that prudence and the possession of reason are parts of goodness, and the opposites of these of badness?
CLINIAS. We do say so. . . .
ATHENIAN. Well, then, shall we reckon neglect, idleness and indolence as goodness of soul? . . .
CLINIAS. How could we? . . .
ATHENIAN. That God has such a character we must certainly deny. . . . When a person whose duty it is especially to act and care for some object has a mind that cares for great things, but neglects small things, [it is] either because he thinks that neglect of the small things makes no difference to the whole, or else, owing to laziness and indolence, he neglects them, though he thinks they do make a difference. Or is there any other way in which neglect occurs? For when it is impossible to care for all things, it will not in that case be neglect of great things or small when a person—be he god or common man—fails to care for things which he lacks the power and capacity to care for.
CLINIAS. Of course not.
ATHENIAN. Now [we have] agreed that the gods are good, yea, exceeding good.
CLINIAS. Most certainly.
ATHENIAN. . . . Is it not impossible to allow that they do anything at all in a lazy and indolent way? For certainly amongst us mortals idleness is the child of cowardice, and laziness of idleness and indolence.

CLINIAS. Very true.

ATHENIAN. None, then, of the gods is neglectful owing to idleness and laziness. . . . Shall we then assume that . . . the gods are ignorant, and that it is through ignorance that they are neglectful when they ought to be showing care,—or that they know indeed what is needful, yet act as the worst of men are said to do, who, though they know that other things are better to do than what they are doing, yet do them not, owing to their being somehow defeated by pleasures or pains?

CLINIAS. Impossible. . . .

ATHENIAN. Let us never suppose that God is inferior to mortal craftsmen who, the better they are, the more accurately and perfectly do they execute their proper tasks, small and great, by one single art,—or that God, who is most wise, and both willing and able to care, cares not at all for the small things which are the easier to care for—like one who shirks the labour because he is idle and cowardly,—but only for the great. . . . And now, as I think, we have argued quite sufficiently with him who loves to censure the gods for neglect.

On the other hand, we must not suppose that the gods are *especially* interested in man and his affairs. Their concern for man is the same as their concern for any other part of the universe—not for that part's well-being as an isolated entity, but for its well-being *as a part*.

ATHENIAN. Let us persuade the young man by our discourse that all things are ordered systematically by Him who cares for the World-all with a view to the preservation and excellence of the Whole, whereof also each part, so far as it can, does and suffers what is proper to it. . . . All partial generation is for the sake of the Whole, in order that for the life of the World-all blissful existence may be secured,—it not being generated for thy sake, but thou for its sake. . . . May we now say that we have fully proved our three propositions,—namely, that the gods exist, and that they are careful, and that they are wholly incapable of being seduced to transgress justice?

CLINIAS. Certainly we may.

This is probably as much as Plato thought could be proved about the divine nature. But Plato was not only a rationalist; he was also a mystic who held that the highest truths transcend rational formulation. Let us therefore turn to the *Timaeus*, in which his views are put in mythical terms. Here we must follow the rule that a myth is to be taken seriously but not literally. It is true, but true in its own terms, not as translated into abstract prose.

## CREATOR AND COSMOS

One important point brought out in the *Timaeus* is that god is a creator. Another is that what god creates is a cosmos.

> Let us state for what reason becoming and this universe were framed by
> him who framed them. He was good; and in the good no jealousy in any
> matter can ever arise. So, being without jealousy, he desired that all things
> should come as near as possible to being like himself. . . . Taking thought,
> therefore, he found that among things which are by nature visible, no work
> that is without intelligence will ever be better than one that has intelligence.
> . . . In virtue of this reasoning, when he framed the universe, he fashioned
> it [as] a living creature with soul and reason. . . . What was the living creature
> in whose likeness he framed the world? We must not suppose that it was
> any creature that ranks only as a species; for no copy of that which is
> incomplete can ever be good. Let us rather say that the world is like, above
> all things, to that Living Creature of which all other living creatures, sever-
> ally, and in their families, are parts. . . .ˣ

This passage is difficult. It seems clear, however, that Plato did not mean
that creation was a process in time—that there was a time when all was chaos
and then there came a time when this chaos was ordered by the act of a god.
Nor did he mean that god "desires" or "thinks" in the sense that men do, nor,
again, that he has purposes or intentions as men do.

On the contrary, what he meant to assert was that the universe is a purposive
whole. Before Plato, scientific and philosophic thought had conceived natural
processes to be indifferent to purpose. True, Anaxagoras had talked of "mind"
as the cause of motion, but he had merely introduced mind as the initiator of
a circular, whirling motion. Once begun, he had held, the sequence of natural
events occurs mechanically. This doctrine was formulated explicitly by the
Atomists. The existence of a human mind that asks questions, puzzles about the
meaning of the universe, and reads purposes into it is sheer accident. The mind
with its particular propensities exists only because such-and-such a combination
of atoms happens to have occurred. Eventually "blows from without" will destroy
this combination; when this happens the mind and its questionings (and the
meanings) will disappear. All that will be left is a rain of atoms falling through
infinite empty space.

This is the view Plato intended to deny when he described the universe as
a "living creature." If we make the mistake of taking myth literally, this will
sound absurd. But in *mythical* language, to say that the universe is living means
that it has intelligence and is capable of spontaneous motion. And to say that
it is intelligent means, basically, that its behavior is *ordered*. What reason and
intelligence do for man is to bring the chaos of conflicting desires and passions
into order. This, we have seen, is the fundamental idea in Plato's ethics and
politics. An unintelligent man flits from one thing to another; there is no stability,
no order, to his behavior. An intelligent man, on the other hand, is precisely
one whose behavior (even seen merely from the outside) has a systematic structure.

Thus to say that the universe is a living creature and intelligent means that
*its* behavior is ordered, that (just as with the intelligent man) things do not happen

hit-or-miss, but "for the best." And to say that its motion is spontaneous (another point involved in calling the universe a living creature) means (in opposition to the Atomists, who held motion to be the result of atoms falling and pushing one another) that motion originates from within. Here, again, the analogy of the intelligent man is helpful. What an unintelligent man does is the product of what happens to him, of the environmental stimuli that reach his body, rather than the product of his intent. An intelligent man initiates his own conduct to a greater degree than the unintelligent man; he molds his environment to his own terms, rather than being formed by it. This indeed is precisely what gives order to the intelligent man's behavior. Thus, order and spontaneity come together as different aspects of the same phenomenon.

Plato held, then, that the universe is well ordered. He also held that it is ordered "for the best." By this he meant that its order satisfies not merely our intellectual curiosity but also our moral demands. Atomism, he believed, could never do this. To the extent that it satisfied our curiosity by disclosing the nature of the universe to our intellects, it was bound to defeat our moral natures by making us and our efforts, our hopes and our fears, insignificant. On the contrary, Plato held that the universe must be such that, insofar as we can know it, it satisfies our whole nature. The world the cave dweller finally sees in the light of the sun is beautiful and good.

But this goes beyond the somewhat meager results Plato thought he could achieve in natural theology. It is what we would call an act of faith, or, as he would have said, it is a truth to be talked about only in myth.

If this account of Plato's religion is correct, it will be seen that, unlike the Christians, he was much less interested in god the creator than in god's creature, the universe. Indeed, it seems that Plato's theology served two main functions, neither of which was to give information about the deity and his nature. The first was to suggest, by the attributes of god that were enumerated, certain characteristics of the world that Plato believed significant; the second was to remind us of the limitations of our own finite understandings. Thus in the *Timaeus* Plato warns us against taking his god too literally: "The maker and father of this universe it is a hard task to find, and having found him it would be impossible to declare him to all mankind." [y]

## PLATO'S RELIGION COMPARED WITH CHRISTIANITY

There are, however, some obvious similarities between Plato's theology and Christian theology. Like the Christian God, Plato's is good; he is a creator; what he creates is a universe oriented and ordained in terms of human destiny. Because of these similarities, and for other reasons as well,[21] Platonism had a marked

---

21 Among these reasons is the historical accident that only the *Timaeus*, of all Plato's dialogues, was known in the Middle Ages. Since, moreover, the Christians naïvely took the myth of the *Timaeus* literally, Plato seemed to them much closer to their own view than in point of fact he was.

influence on Christianity. Much of the thought of the early Middle Ages was Platonic in the sense that many of the Church fathers formulated their specifically Christian insights into a philosophy whose basic concepts were borrowed from Plato. On the other hand, Plato's god is not really an object of worship; his god is good, but hardly a loving father. And he is not omnipotent, for in the myth he works upon an independently existing material, or (in simpler language) he is limited by those elements of disorder that prevent physics from ever being more than a "likely story."

This latter point is especially important.[22] In the myth of the *Timaeus* the creator uses a perfect model—the form "Living Creature"; the universe he produces is an imitation, or reflection, of the model. As such, it suffers from all the inadequacies that, as we have seen, sensible particulars always suffer from. The model—the form—is real, immutable, intelligible through and through; the copy is unstable ("always becoming"), unreal, and unintelligible.

> We must . . . make this distinction: what is that which is real and has no becoming, and what is that which is always becoming and is never real? That which is apprehensible by thought with a rational account is the thing that is always and unchangeably real; whereas that which is the object of belief together with unreasoning sensation is the thing that becomes and passes away, but never has real being. . . . An account is of the same order as the things which it sets forth—an account of that which is abiding and stable and discoverable by the aid of reason will itself be abiding and unchangeable . . . ; while an account of what is made in the image of that other, but is only a likeness, will itself be but likely. . . .[z]

It seems, then, that what god has created—the world that the ordinary man thinks of as being real, the world of changing, growing, living things—is not real at all. It is but an inadequate imitation of the real but changeless realm of forms. The form "Living Creature," for example, is not itself living, not a creature (not created), and not in motion, just as the form "triangle" is not a plane figure and does not have three angles. About the relation between actual living creatures and the form "Living Creature," and about the relation between physical triangles and the form "triangle," Plato was able to give only a metaphor: The former participate in (or are "reflections," or "imitations," of) the latter.

Here then, in Plato's theory of religion, we come to the same basic question that we reached in his physics, ethics, and politics. This is the problem of the relation between the ideal and the actual, between theory and practice, between a world of perfectly intelligible forms and a completely separate world of brute fact.

---

22 See pp. 149–52. Compare also the passage already cited (p. 196) from the *Republic* in which Plato says that god does not make all things.

# Criticism of the Theory of Forms

It is now time to examine the problems created by the apartness of the forms, and this takes us back once more to Plato's theory of knowledge. This should not be surprising, for, as has been said at the beginning, his claim that the forms are the objects of knowledge is the foundation on which his special studies in physics, politics, ethics, religion, and art rest. Hence any difficulty in his theory of knowledge inevitably undermines his accounts of these special fields.

We know why Plato separated form from spatiotemporal things: He hoped thereby to resolve the contradiction between the theories of Parmenides and Heraclitus. The doctrine of two worlds did indeed give Plato a formal solution of this dilemma, but since he could not give a meaningful account of the way the sense world participates in the forms and gains some degree of reality from them, his whole spatiotemporal world seems mere appearance. Unfortunately, as Plato admits in the *Timaeus*, the "copies of the eternal things [are] impressions taken from them in a . . . manner that is hard to express. . . ."[a]

## PLATO'S OWN CRITICISM: THE *PARMENIDES*

But the problem is far worse than that; the relation between eternal things and their changing spatiotemporal copies is not merely "hard to express." In the *Parmenides* Plato himself suggests that the notion of participation is intrinsically confused. At least, objections are raised in this dialogue that Socrates is much embarrassed to find he cannot answer.[23]

> Have you yourself [asked Parmenides] drawn this distinction you speak of and separated apart on the one side Forms themselves and on the other the things that share in them? Do you believe that there is such a thing as Likeness itself apart from the likeness that we possess, and so on with Unity and Plurality . . . ?
> Certainly I do, said Socrates.
> And also in cases like these, asked Parmenides: is there, for example, a Form of Rightness or of Beauty or of Goodness, and of all such things?
> Yes.
> And again, a Form of Man, apart from ourselves and all other men like us—a Form of Man as something by itself? Or a Form of Fire or of Water?
> I have often been puzzled about those things, Parmenides. . . .
> Are you also puzzled, Socrates, about cases that might be thought absurd, such as hair or mud or dirt or any other trivial and undignified objects? Are

---

23 The attack on the theory of forms is put in the mouth of Parmenides, although the historical Parmenides of course knew nothing of the theory. The discussion between him and Socrates is supposed by Plato to have occurred "many years ago," when Parmenides was a venerable old man and Socrates was very young.

you doubtful whether or not to assert that each of these has a separate Form distinct from things like those we handle?

Not at all, said Socrates; in these cases, the things are just the things we see; it would surely be too absurd to suppose that they have a Form. All the same, I have sometimes been troubled by a doubt whether what is true in one case may not be true in all. Then, when I have reached that point, I am driven to retreat, for fear of tumbling into a bottomless pit of nonsense. Anyhow, I get back to the things which we were just now speaking of as having Forms, and occupy my time with thinking about them.

That, replied Parmenides, is because you are still young, Socrates, and philosophy has not yet taken hold of you so firmly as I believe it will some day. You will not despise any of these objects then. . . . However that may be, tell me this. You say you hold that there exist certain Forms, of which these other things come to partake and so to be called after their names: by coming to partake of Likeness or Largeness or Beauty or Justice, they become like or large or beautiful or just?

Certainly, said Socrates.

Then each thing that partakes receives as its share either the Form as a whole or a part of it? Or can there be any other way of partaking besides this?

No, how could there be?

Do you hold, then, that the Form as a whole, a single thing, is in each of the many, or how?

Why should it not be in each, Parmenides?

If so, a Form which is one and the same will be at the same time, as a whole, in a number of things which are separate, and consequently will be separate from itself.

No, it would not, replied Socrates, if it were like one and the same day, which is in many places at the same time and nevertheless is not separate from itself. . . .

You might as well spread a sail over a number of people and then say that the one sail as a whole was over them all. . . . Then would the sail as a whole be over each man, or only a part over one, another part over another?

Only a part.

In that case, Socrates, the Forms themselves must be divisible into parts, and the things which have a share in them will have a part for their share. Only a part of any given Form, and no longer the whole of it, will be in each thing. . . . Are you, then, prepared to assert that we shall find the single Form actually being divided? Will it still be one?

Certainly not.

No, for consider this. Suppose it is Largeness itself that you are going to divide into parts, and that each of the many large things is to be large by virtue of a part of Largeness which is smaller than Largeness itself. Will not that seem unreasonable?

It will indeed. . . .

Well then, Socrates, how are the other things going to partake of your Forms, if they can partake of them neither in part nor as wholes?

Really, said Socrates, it seems no easy matter to determine in any way.

. . . The best I can make of the matter is this: that these Forms are as it were patterns fixed in the nature of things; the other things are made in their image and are likenesses; and this participation they have come to have in the Forms is nothing but their being made in their image.

Well, if a thing is made in the image of the Form, can that Form fail to be like the image of it, in so far as the image was made in its likeness? If a thing is like, must it not be like something that is like it?

It must.

And must not the thing which is like share with the thing that is like it in one and the same thing (character)?

Yes.

And will not that in which the like things share, so as to be alike, be just the Form itself that you spoke of?

Certainly.

If so, nothing can be like the Form, nor can the Form be like anything. Otherwise a second Form will always make its appearance over and above the first Form; and if that second Form is like anything, yet a third; and there will be no end to this emergence of fresh Forms, if the Form is to be like the thing that partakes of it. . . . It follows that the other things do not partake of Forms by being like them; we must look for some other means by which they partake. . . . You see then, Socrates, said Parmenides, what great difficulties there are in asserting their existence as Forms just by themselves?

I do indeed. . . .

The worst difficulty will be this, though there are plenty more. Suppose someone should say that the Forms, if they are such as we are saying they must be, cannot even be known. One could not convince him that he was mistaken in that objection, unless he chanced to be a man of wide experience and natural ability, and were willing to follow one through a long and remote train of argument. . . .

Why so, Parmenides?

Because, Socrates, I imagine that you or anyone else who asserts that each of them has a real being "just by itself," would admit, to begin with, that no such real being exists in our world.

True; for how could it then be just by itself?

Very good, said Parmenides. And further, those Forms which are what they are with reference to one another, have their being in such references among themselves, not with reference to those likenesses (or whatever we are to call them) in our world, which we possess and so come to be called by their several names. And, on the other hand, these things in our world which bear the same names as the Forms are related among themselves, not to the Forms; and all the names of that sort that they bear have reference to one another, not to the Forms.

How do you mean? asked Socrates.

Suppose, for instance, one of us is master or slave of another; he is not, of course, the slave of Master itself, the essential Master, nor, if he is a master, is he master of Slave itself, the essential Slave, but, being a man, is master or slave of another man: whereas Mastership itself is what it is (mastership) of Slavery itself, and Slavery itself is slavery to Mastership itself. The significance of things in our world is not with reference to things in that other world, nor have these their significance with reference to us; but, as I say, the things in that world are what they are with reference to one another and towards one another; and so likewise are the things in our world. You see what I mean?

Certainly I do.

And similarly Knowledge itself, the essence of Knowledge, will be knowledge of that Reality itself, the essentially real. . . . Whereas the knowledge in our world will be knowledge of the reality in our world; and it will follow again that each branch of knowledge in our world must be knowledge of some department of things that exist in our world.

Necessarily.

But, as you admit, we do not possess the Forms themselves, nor can they exist in our world.

No.

And presumably the Forms, just as they are in themselves, are known by the Form of Knowledge itself.

Yes.

The Form which we do not possess.

True.

Then, none of the Forms is known by us, since we have no part in Knowledge itself.

Apparently not.

So Beauty itself or Goodness itself and all the things we take as Forms in themselves, are unknowable to us. . . .

But on the other hand, Parmenides continued, if, in view of all these difficulties and others like them, a man refuses to admit that Forms of things exist or to distinguish a definite Form in every case, he will have nothing on which to fix his thought, so long as he will not allow that each thing has a character which is always the same; and in so doing he will completely destroy the significance of all discourse. But of that consequence I think you are only too well aware.

True.

What are you going to do about philosophy, then? Where will you turn while the answers to these questions remain unknown?

I can see no way out at the present moment.

That is because you are undertaking to define "Beautiful," "Just," "Good," and other particular Forms, too soon, before you have had a preliminary training. . . . You must make an effort and submit yourself, while you are still young, to a severer training in what the world calls idle talk and condemns as useless. Otherwise, the truth will escape you.[b]

## COMMENT ON THE *PARMENIDES*

Why did Plato attack his own theory so severely? Some scholars have concluded that the theory simply cannot have been his: He portrayed Socrates as a young man, they believe, in order to indicate that we should attribute the theory to the historical Socrates, not to Plato himself. This interpretation of the *Parmenides* does not seem plausible, for (1) in dialogues that were almost certainly written later Plato gives every indication of continuing to assume the theory of forms, and, (2) in any case it would have been odd of Plato to devote so much attention in the early dialogues to views that depend on a theory he believed to be hopelessly confused.

It seems more reasonable to suppose that the references to Socrates as "too young" and to philosophy as requiring a long training were Plato's way of pointing out that the pursuit of truth is endless. No man can grasp it completely; the most we can hope is to be moving in the right direction.

Plato must have been persuaded that he was moving in the right direction in continuing to affirm the existence of forms, despite all the objections raised in the *Parmenides*. Critics who are puzzled by the fact that Plato was willing to formulate criticisms that he did not know how to meet overlook Plato's intellectual honesty. They also miss the point of his preference for dialogue. In the *Parmenides* Plato is treating himself in just the way that, in the *Republic*, his Socrates treats Glaucon and Adeimantus. He believed that the truth, insofar as men can attain it, emerges in the thrust and counterthrust of argument conducted jointly by truth-seekers. If the full truth about the forms did not emerge in the joint enterprise called the *Parmenides*, even if it did not emerge in any of Plato's dialogues, he probably saw his whole career as a contribution to an on-going dialogue reaching into the far distant future.

But, whatever the correct interpretation of what one critic has called the "enigma" of the *Parmenides*, we must now (1) review and appraise the criticisms of the forms that occur in that dialogue and (2) note the modifications Plato subsequently introduced into the theory in an effort to meet these criticisms.

The first question raised by Parmenides is whether there are forms for such things as mud and dirt. At first sight it might be supposed that there must be, for if we can know mud and dirt, must there not be the forms "mud" and "dirt" to be the objects of our knowledge? But, granted that whatever we *know* about mud is some form or other, it does not follow that the object we know is the form "mud." On the assumptions of Plato's physics, at least as they have been interpreted here, what we call mud is a composite of earth, air, fire, and water in certain proportions. There are forms of these elements, of course; they and the mathematical formula of their combination can be known. And that is all that can be known about mud. Mud itself remains at best a "likely story." Thus Platonism can survive with a very limited number of forms. It is not necessary to assume a separate form for each physical object, nor for man-made objects, like beds or chairs—though Plato certainly seems on occasion to have done so.

It would seem, then, that Plato's Socrates need not have felt embarrassment at Parmenides' challenge. But perhaps Parmenides' question had a different point. It should be noted that mud and dirt are given as examples of "trivial and undignified" objects, and that Socrates confesses he prefers to spend his time in thinking about such high-class forms as "beauty," "rightness," and "goodness." There is little doubt that the Academy did chiefly concern itself with such forms; there is a constant tendency in Platonism to assume that what is more valuable is necessarily more real. Perhaps Parmenides' prediction that when Socrates is older he will cease to despise the trivial and the undignified is a warning against the equation of reality with value. If so, the historical Plato would have done well to attend more closely to the words of this fictitious Parmenides.

The next question raised by Parmenides concerns participation. In the *Republic* only a metaphor is given in explanation of this concept—participation is like the relation of a physical thing to its shadow. But unfortunately the metaphor breaks down at just the point at which it is supposed to help us. The relation between shadow and physical object is clear—or at least not particularly puzzling. This is because both the physical object and the shadow are physical, that is, in space and time, and hence the relation between them is definable in spatiotemporal terms. But how can our understanding of this spatiotemporal relation throw any light (as Plato attempted to make it do in his metaphor) on the nature of a relation that cannot be spatiotemporal, since one of the terms in the relation (the form) is by definition nonspatial and nontemporal?

Presumably attempts were made in the Academy to get beyond metaphor and to formulate the relationship precisely. In this dialogue Parmenides subjects these attempted solutions to merciless criticism. How can many particular objects—Dobbin, Bucephalus, and Traveller—participate in the same form "horse"? Is the form divided up, like a cake cut into pieces and shared by greedy children at a party? Clearly not. Is the form wholly in each of the particulars? Again, clearly not. It seems that the old problem of the one and the many, which the theory of forms was intended to solve, breaks out again, this time most embarrassingly in the theory itself.

Again, whatever else it may mean to say that Bucephalus participates in the form "horse," it at least means that Bucephalus resembles "horse." But what is meant by "resemblance"? When we say that Dobbin and Bucephalus resemble each other, all we mean, and according to Plato all we *can* mean, is that they share (have in common) the property "horseness." Well, then, if Dobbin resembles the form "horse," there must be another form, "horse$_2$," that Dobbin and the first form, "horse$_1$," share. But then, if Dobbin and horse$_1$ both resemble horse$_2$, all three must share another form, horse$_3$—and so on ad infinitum. Thus to assert that the participation of physical things in forms amounts to resemblance involves Plato in an absurdity.

The upshot of all Parmenides' criticism is that, on the original theory, forms and sense objects are too separate; ideal and actual are separated by an unbridgeable chasm. We have already seen how this separation, or transcendence, which has been called apartness, infected Plato's political and ethical theory and his theology. What the *Parmenides* points out is that transcendence creates equally grave problems with regard to his theory of knowledge. Here Plato faced a dilemma. On the one hand, if the forms are not apart, they are not (Plato thought) true objects, and if there are no form-objects, there is nothing to have knowledge *of*. On the other hand, if they are apart, they are unknowable.

Some people might say that the solution of this dilemma is to give up the forms. Instead, Plato tried in later dialogues to bridge the chasm between the intelligible world and the sensible world. The instrument he chose for this purpose was soul, or psyche. So far we have seen that psyche is immortal and supremely valuable. It is also a self-mover, and it consists of three basic types of drives. One of these—reason—is the instrument by means of which we comprehend the forms. Now we have to examine what may be called the metaphysical role of soul.

## SOUL MEDIATES TRANSCENDENCE

Assuming as a basic principle the old dictum that "like knows like," it was clear to Plato that psyche must be like the forms. Like the forms, psyche is immortal and eternal; like them it has a kind of unchanging identity. But psyche is also a self-mover, and because it moves it is like the Heraclitean flux Plato conceived the sense world to be. Moreover, if one part of the soul knows the forms, another part perceives sense objects. Hence, on the like-knows-like principle, one part of the psyche must be like the sense world. Finally, the emotions and the passions that have their seat in the lower parts of the psyche clearly have an affinity with the lower sense world, just as mind, the highest part of the psyche, has an affinity with the higher and more real world. For these reasons, psyche seemed well suited to serve as a link between the sensible and the intelligible worlds, to redeem the former from utter unreality and to mediate the splendid but awful purity and isolation of the latter.

This conception is discussed in several of the later dialogues. A representative (and characteristically puzzling) passage occurs in the *Sophist,* in which Plato criticizes two rival theories, both of which he held to be mistaken. The first is the view of the "materialists." There is nothing puzzling about their view or about why Plato opposed it. But the second Plato describes as the view of the "friends of forms." Some modern critics hold Plato could not have been criticizing his own position; they think that he was perhaps seeking to correct some of his pupils who had branched out on their own. There is, however, no discernible difference between the position ascribed to the "friends of the forms" and the doctrine of the *Republic* and the *Phaedo,* and it seems more reasonable to conclude that in the *Sophist,* as in the *Parmenides,* Plato is criticizing his own earlier view. But, unlike the criticism in the *Parmenides,* that in the *Sophist* is followed by what seems to be an attempt to modify the original theory.[24]

24 In this dialogue Socrates plays a very minor role. The principal speakers are "an Eleatic stranger" and Theaetetus.

STRANGER. Let us turn, then, to the . . . friends of Forms. . . . You shall act as their spokesman.

THEAETETUS. I will.

STRANGER. We understand that you make a distinction between "Becoming" and "Real being" and speak of them as separate. Is that so?

THEAETETUS. Yes.

STRANGER. And you say that we have intercourse with Becoming by means of the body through sense, whereas we have intercourse with Real being by means of the soul through reflection. And Real being, you say, is always in the same unchanging state, whereas Becoming is variable.

THEAETETUS. We do.

STRANGER. Admirable. But now what are we to take you as meaning by this expression "intercourse" which you apply to both? Don't you mean . . . the experiencing an effect or the production of one, arising, as the result of some power, from things that encounter one another? Perhaps, Theaetetus, you may not be able to catch their answer to this, but I, who am familiar with them, may be more successful.

THEAETETUS. What have they to say, then? . . .

STRANGER. They reply that a power of acting and being acted upon belongs to Becoming, but neither of these powers is compatible with Real being.

THEAETETUS. And there is something in that answer?

STRANGER. Something to which we must reply by a request for more enlightenment. Do they acknowledge further that the soul knows and Real being is known?

THEAETETUS. Certainly they agree to that.

STRANGER. Well, do you agree that knowing or being known is an action, or is it experiencing an effect, or both? Or is one of them experiencing an effect, the other an action? Or does neither of them come under either of these heads at all?

THEAETETUS. Evidently neither; otherwise our friends would be contradicting what they said earlier.

STRANGER. I see what you mean. They would have to say this: If knowing is to be acting on something, it follows that what is known must be acted upon by it; and so, on this showing, Reality when it is being known by the act of knowledge must, in so far as it is known, be changed owing to being so acted upon; and that, we say, cannot happen to the changeless.

THEAETETUS. Exactly.

STRANGER. But tell me, in heaven's name: are we really to be so easily convinced that change, life, soul, understanding have no place in that which is perfectly real—that it has neither life nor thought, but stands immutable in solemn aloofness, devoid of intelligence?

THEAETETUS. That, sir, would be a strange doctrine to accept.

STRANGER. But can we say it has intelligence without having life?

THEAETETUS. Surely not.

STRANGER. But if we say it contains both, can we deny that it has soul in which they reside?

THEAETETUS. How else could it possess them?

STRANGER. But then, if it has intelligence, life, and soul, can we say that a living thing remains at rest in complete changelessness?

THEAETETUS. All that seems to me unreasonable.

STRANGER. In that case we must admit that what changes and change itself are real things.

THEAETETUS. Certainly. . . .

STRANGER. . . . Only one course is open to the philosopher who values knowledge and the rest above all else. He must refuse to accept from the champions either of the One or of the many Forms the doctrine that all Reality is changeless; and he must turn a deaf ear to the other party who represent Reality as everywhere changing. Like a child begging for "both," he must declare that Reality or the sum of things is both at once—all that is unchangeable and all that is in change.

THEAETETUS. Perfectly true.

STRANGER. Well then, does it not look now as if we had fairly caught reality within the compass of our description?

THEAETETUS. Certainly it does.

STRANGER. And yet—oh dear, Theaetetus, what if I say after all that I think it is just at this point that we shall come to see how baffling this question of reality is?

THEAETETUS. How so? Why do you say that?

STRANGER. My good friend, don't you see that now we are wholly in the dark about it, though we fancy we are talking good sense?

THEAETETUS. I certainly thought so, and I don't at all understand how we can be deceived about our condition.

STRANGER. Then consider these last conclusions of our more carefully. . . . When you speak of Movement and Rest, these are things completely opposed to one another, aren't they?

THEAETETUS. Of course.

STRANGER. At the same time you say of both and of each severally, that they are real?

THEAETETUS. I do.

STRANGER. And when you admit that they are real, do you mean that either or both are in movement?

THEAETETUS. Certainly not.

STRANGER. Then, perhaps, by saying both are real you mean they are both at rest?

THEAETETUS. No, how could I?

STRANGER. So, then, you conceive of reality (realness) as a third thing over and above these two; and when you speak of both as being real, you mean that you are taking both movement and rest together as embraced by reality and fixing your attention on their common association with reality?

THEAETETUS. It does seem as if we discerned reality as a third thing, when we say that movement and rest are real.

STRANGER. So reality is not motion and rest "both at once," but something distinct from them.

THEAETETUS. Apparently.

STRANGER. In virtue of its own nature, then, reality is neither at rest nor in movement.

THEAETETUS. I suppose so.

STRANGER. If so, where is the mind to turn for help if one wants to reach any clear and certain conclusion about reality?

THEAETETUS. Where indeed?

STRANGER. It seems hard to find help in any quarter. If a thing is not in movement, how can it not be at rest? Or how can what is not in any way at rest fail to be in movement? Yet reality is now revealed to us as outside both alternatives. Is that possible?

THEAETETUS. As impossible as anything could be.[c]

## DIFFICULTIES WITH PLATO'S VIEW

In Plato's later and revised view, then, the realm of forms is not the only reality. Besides forms, there are souls and the motions they initiate, and the Receptacle of Becoming out of which sensible things are fashioned. There is no doubt that such a view is an improvement on Plato's earlier position, according to which change is contradictory and unintelligible. Doubtless Plato had never gone as far as Parmenides in holding change to be sheerly an illusion. But he *had* said it is unreal and mere appearance, and it is not easy to find a significant difference between these two modes of expression.

On the other hand, Plato did not work out his later view in detail (and it is difficult to see how he could have done so without more drastic modification of the theory of forms than he was willing or able to make). For instance, the way in which psyche initiates motion in accordance with the "best"—whether at the human level or at the world-soul level—is far from clear. Again (as Plato himself admits in the *Timaeus*) it is "very puzzling . . . very hard to apprehend" how the Receptacle, which is "invisible and characterless, all-receiving, partak[es] of the intelligible. . . ."[d] And finally, the attempt to make psyche bridge the chasm between the two worlds only creates a corresponding duality in psyche itself. The part of psyche that contemplates eternal forms and the part that initiates life and movement in the sense world are really as far apart as the sense world and the intelligible world themselves.

Now all these objections and difficulties turn on taking forms as entities. If, for instance, the form were not, somehow, another thing or object (nonphysical, of course), the infinite-regress argument of the *Parmenides* would not hold and "apartness" would not be a problem. But how, Plato might have asked, is a form to be an object of knowledge without being an object? This is the problem to which, as we shall see in the next chapter, Aristotle applied himself. His revision of the theory of forms certainly did not say the last word on the nature of knowledge or on the problems of change and appearance, but it did meet most of the objections to Plato's formulation that have been discussed.

Thus, if philosophy be a continuing dialogue from one generation to another, Plato was right not to abandon the theory of forms. He could have had a neater view either by sticking to his original theory of forms and abandoning change or by throwing out the forms. But one of Plato's great strengths, and one of the sources of his perennial appeal, was his ability to see all sides of a question. He was an idealist who gave his allegiance to a vision of perfection, but he was also fully aware that men are men and that the good life for man is this side of the forms (the world outside is beautiful and good, but we must descend again into the cave). He was a rationalist who held that knowledge at its best transcends conceptual means of communication. He believed that there is a kind of knowledge that is absolutely valid, but he denied that it is possible to have knowledge of this kind about the changing world of sense experience. It is true that Plato kept all these insights in suspension without managing to bring them into systematic order. But the point is he *did* keep them in view, and in the theory of forms he provided the framework on which Aristotle was to work out a more unified world view.

# CHAPTER 6

# Aristotle: Metaphysics, Natural Science, Logic

## Life

In 384 B.C., when Plato was forty-three years old and when Socrates had been dead for fifteen years, Aristotle was born in Stagira in Thrace, where his father was physician to the king of Macedonia. When Aristotle was about seventeen he was sent to Athens, as any bright young provincial might have been, to complete his education at Plato's Academy, already a distinguished institution. He arrived about the time when Plato was engaged in his political experiments in Sicily, and he remained in the Academy (not the whole time as a student, of course) for almost twenty years.

During this period he must have written some of the many dialogues of which only a few fragments survive today. From these fragments it appears (as one might expect) that Aristotle's early thought was very much influenced by Plato. Not only are the dialogues stylistically Platonic, but the views expressed in them—the account of the soul in the *Eudemus,* for instance—are characteristically Platonic and are at variance with the theories subsequently developed by Aristotle. It is important to emphasize this Platonic period in Aristotle's development because some writers have seen him as the opponent of Platonism. But though Aristotle rejected the apartness of the forms, he was fundamentally and acknowledgedly a Platonist, and his work can be understood only as an effort to reformulate the insights of Plato. His primary interest, like Plato's, was to reaffirm the existence of a public and knowable reality and to answer the question, "What is the good life for man?" Like Plato again, he found that answer, not in radically new doctrines, but in a reinterpretation and reformulation of the traditional beliefs of the Greeks. He and Plato together gave these beliefs a new vitality by grounding them in a comprehensive metaphysics—by showing that the traditional ethical and political values were rooted in the nature and structure of the universe as they conceived of it.

How, except on the basis of the closest sympathy, could Aristotle's long association with the Academy be explained? As a matter of fact he departed only after Plato's death (347 B.C.), when Plato's own tendency to emphasize mathematics and mathematical knowledge was carried to an extreme by his successor as head of the institution. After leaving the Academy, Aristotle spent some years in travel, then in 343 or 342 B.C. he became tutor to the young Alexander, son of King Philip of Macedonia.

It is not easy to assess the influence Alexander and Aristotle—two of the greatest geniuses the Western world has produced—exercised on each other. In any event, their connection lasted no more than two or three years. Whether or not in conscious reaction to Aristotle, Alexander eventually developed a policy that certainly ran counter to Aristotle's views. Aristotle, for instance, held that the largest organization in which political values could be realized is the city-state; Alexander founded a world empire in which the old city-state civilization was drowned. Again, Aristotle, believing in the native superiority of Greeks over barbarians, would have opposed Alexander's attempt to base his empire on a racial merging of Westerners and Orientals.

Nevertheless, Alexander seems not to have forgotten his old teacher. There is a pleasant story, which may have a basis in fact, that his armies were instructed to collect and ship back to Aristotle any rare flora and fauna they discovered in their expeditions into the remote corners of the world.

By 335 B.C. Aristotle was back in Athens, where he set up his own school, the Lyceum. It was during his years there, presumably, that he composed most of his extant works. As we know them today these are treatises on separate subjects—logic, physics, biology, ethics, meteorology, and so on. They are often repetitious, sometimes break off abruptly, and seem to have been hastily put together from previously existing materials. Perhaps the most reasonable explanation for this is that each of the various treatises consists of notes written by

Aristotle for his lectures. These notes, sometimes sketchy, sometimes worked out carefully, were presumably collected, for the most part after Aristotle's death. As a result, all his writings on a given subject—say, political science—extending across a long period of years, in the course of which his views naturally underwent development, were lumped together in a single treatise, in this case labeled *Politics*.

For twelve years—until Alexander's death in 323 B.C.—Aristotle directed the course of studies at the Lyceum. Alexander's death, however, released a strong tide of anti-Macedonian feeling, pent up during the period of Macedonian hegemony in Greece. Aristotle thereupon withdrew from Athens to the protection of a nearby Macedonian garrison. There he died the next year, not having purchased much time by his discretion.[1]

Aristotle's will has been preserved; it reveals an attractive nature, full of careful thought for his family, affection for his friends, generosity to his slaves, and a touching sentiment for his long-dead wife, beside whom he asked to be buried.

## Aristotle's Aim

Aristotle's aim was identical with that of Plato and with that of all their philosophical predecessors. He wanted to discover what is real. Thales and the other Milesians, and later the Atomists, had undertaken to find this in the material universe. Matter—variously defined as "water," "air," "boundless," "seeds," "atoms"—had been asserted by the thinkers of this school to be the only real. But in the course of the century or so after Thales, the failure of this materialistic answer had been demonstrated. The materialists were unable to give an adequate account of the nature of man as a moral and religious creature. Value is not material, and in the exclusively material world of these thinkers there was, therefore, no place for value.

Plato had sought to locate reality in an immaterial world of forms. But like the materialists' answer, this was too exclusive; like their answer, it oversimplified, though in an exactly opposite direction. Because he had affirmed that the forms are apart from things, Plato had been unable to relate values to the world of sense perception.

From Aristotle's point of view, this, too, was inadequate. He wanted to establish a theory of reality that would allow both values and sense objects to

---

1 It is reported that Aristotle explained his departure by saying he did not want "the Athenians to sin twice against philosophy." He felt his exile keenly but adopted a philosophical attitude toward the insults heaped upon him by his enemies during his absence. He wrote to his friend Antipater, Alexander's regent in Greece: "About the voting at Delphi and their depriving me of my honors my feeling is that I am sorry but not extremely sorry"—quoted in W. Jaeger, *Aristotle* (Clarendon Press, Oxford, 1934), p. 320, n. 2.

be real. Moreover, he saw that a satisfactory account of reality must resolve the problem of change. This problem has been with us from the start, for though change is one of the most obvious facts of experience, it is also seemingly irrational. Every philosopher from Thales' day on had wrestled with this problem in vain. The best the Atomists could do was to reduce all qualitative change to motion, that is, change of place. As for Plato, originally he had virtually denied the fact of change, affirming with Parmenides that the real and the knowable must be unchangeable. Subsequently he had relaxed this position and allowed a motion that was supposedly initiated by psyche. But neither his procedure nor that of the Atomists was satisfactory, and as long as the problem of change defied the best efforts of human reason, a doubt existed about the power of reason.

Any adequate metaphysics, Aristotle saw, must show that reality really changes, as it appears to do, and thus rehabilitate reason as a valid instrument for obtaining knowledge. Further, it must vindicate our intuition of man as a moral creature, a focus of values. This was the great dual undertaking to which Aristotle set himself.

## The Nature of Reality

Before Aristotle's conception of reality is examined, some preliminaries must be dealt with. First there is a matter of terminology. We shall find Aristotle using Platonic-sounding expressions—for instance, the term "form." This can properly be taken as a sign of Aristotle's Platonic inheritance, but we must not suppose that identical words have identical meanings for different writers. Plato tended to equate form with reality; Aristotle denied that form is coextensive with the real. Let us begin our discussion of Aristotle's philosophy by comparing his notion of form with Plato's. This will lead us naturally to his conception of reality, which, as we shall see, was designed to solve the problem of change and the other questions on which the Platonic theory of forms had broken. Then we can turn from metaphysics and theory of knowledge to the special sciences—physics, ethics, politics. Throughout the whole discussion it will be interesting to see how the modifications Aristotle made in Plato's theory of forms in order to solve the problem of change are reflected in corresponding changes and shifts of emphasis in Aristotle's treatment of the special sciences.

The root of all the differences between Plato and Aristotle, one may be tempted to say, lies in Aristotle's struggle to correct Plato's theory of knowledge. This is true, but it is only a part of the truth. Aristotle's reformulation of the theory of forms was the result, in part, of a purely intellectual struggle to solve the epistemological problem; but it was also rooted in a temperamental difference. Like the Gilbert and Sullivan Englishman who is born either a Liberal or a Conservative, it has been remarked that everyone is born either a Platonist or an Aristotelian. Plato and Aristotle, that is, represent two different attitudes toward the world. Plato was a perfectionist whose inclination, even in discussing the problems of practical politics, was always toward a utopian solution that was impractical precisely because the perfect is never realized in this world. Where Plato was otherworldly and idealistic, Aristotle was practical and empirical.

Plato's bias toward mathematics was symptomatic of his general point of view; the mathematical triangle is not found in this world. It is an ideal object transcending the imperfections of physical triangles. For Aristotle, in contrast, biology was the leading and, as it were, model science. Just as it is natural in discussing Plato's views to draw examples from the field of mathematics, so it is natural in any discussion of Aristotle's views to take examples from biology. In mathematics we are dealing with perfect but lifeless entities; in biology, with imperfect but living ones. This difference corresponds exactly to the difference between Plato's and Aristotle's conceptions of the forms and (still more fundamentally) to the difference between their basic emotional and temperamental preferences. In politics, for instance, Plato thought constantly in terms of an absolutely ideal state and shrugged off the question of whether such a state is "possible" with a characteristically perfectionist reply; "It is laid up as a pattern in heaven. . . . But whether such a city exists or even will exist in fact, is no matter. . . ." Aristotle, on the other hand, began his study of politics by a careful survey of more than one hundred actual states. What sort of state would be best under such-and-such actual conditions? What kind of constitution should a small state have? What sort should a wealthy state have? These questions, rather than questions about the nature of the absolutely ideal state, are the ones that interested Aristotle.

Whether one prefers Plato's philosophy or Aristotle's depends in large measure on one's own basic temperamental bias. To some, Plato may seem too visionary and impractical; these people will probably prefer Aristotle as a cool, level-headed realist. Those who are moved by Plato's "lofty idealism" will probably feel that Aristotle by comparison is pedestrian and uninspiring. To the present author it seems reasonable to say (at the risk of revealing his own temperamental bias!) that Aristotle's position is sounder than Plato's. He shared with Plato that nisus beyond the actual that is the mark of idealism everywhere, that uplifts and transports us. But he never forgot, as Plato tended to forget, that the nisus is from one actual to another. Aristotle, unlike Plato, believed every "higher" is eventually, somewhere, a here and now; the world is through and through one world; all ideals are somewhere embodied and all embodiments are in some respect ideals achieved. To put this another way, it might be said that Aristotle was more a Platonist than Plato was an Aristotelian.

### ARISTOTLE'S REVISION OF PLATO'S FORMS

How then—given these differences in Aristotle's temperament as well as the greater emphasis he put on change—did Aristotle's theory of forms differ from

Plato's? Plato thought of the forms as separate entities in which the individual particulars of this world obscurely participate; Aristotle held them to be embedded in the particulars. It has already been argued that Plato's tendency to hypostatize the forms, that is, to treat them as independently existing *things*, had serious consequences in every department of his thought. If what we know is form and if form is separate from the space-time world, it follows that we cannot know the space-time world. If only form is truly real and form is separate from the things we experience in sense perception, those things are not truly real. Further—so it seemed to Aristotle—separation leads to otherworldliness, to a chasm between the actual and the ideal. It means that discussion of what *is* can never amount to more than a "likely story," and knowledge of what *ought to be* has little or no relevance to pressing moral, political, and social problems.

Hence Aristotle was led to deny Plato's dualism, to reject his separation of the universe into two worlds. For Aristotle, there was but one world, the world of actual things. Form is simply one aspect of this world, distinguishable in thought (as we may in thought distinguish color and shape) but not distinguished in fact (we never find shapes that are uncolored or colors that have no shape). According to Aristotle, taking the forms as separate entities results from confusing intellectual analysis and ontological status. It is as if, because we can think of color abstracted ("separated") from shape, we were to suppose there exists somewhere, in absolute purity and perfection, color by itself.

What then is reality in Aristotle's view? Not Plato's forms, for they are, according to Aristotle, mere abstractions—not illusions, of course, but certainly not the whole of reality. Reality for Aristotle consists of that from which the forms are abstractions, and this is individual things—particular men, plants, rocks, and animals—Socrates, Plato, Dobbin, Bucephalus. These particulars Aristotle called "substances," and his analysis of reality was in terms of individual substances. But what *is* an individual substance?

Every particular thing, taken as it is at any given time, has two aspects. In the first place, it has properties it shares with other particulars. Socrates has properties he shares with Plato (for that matter also with Dobbin and Bucephalus); Dobbin has properties he shares with Bucephalus. We may call this aspect of an individual substance its "whatness," because these are the properties we normally think of when we are asked what the substance is. In reply to the question, "What is Socrates?" we say that he is a man, a rational animal, a living thing, and so on, until we have enumerated all the properties that Socrates shares with other things and that define his whatness. It is clear that we can know any object only insofar as it has such common properties. About an absolutely unique object, which had no properties in common with other objects, it would be impossible to communicate. About it we could not answer the question, "What is it?"

But enumerating the common properties of a thing never gets at the thing's individuality—at that about it which makes it *this* horse or *this* man. For the common properties are *common;* they are characteristics this object shares, or might share, with other objects. Enumerate as many properties of Socrates as you like: his pug nose, his shambling gait, his midwife mother, his conviction by the Athenian court, his death by hemlock, and so on. Each of these is a property that other individuals have had. So, too, the totality of them might theoretically describe another individual. Hence we may say that Socrates (and every other individual substance) has a "thisness" as well as a whatness. Every individual is a member of a class, but it is also *this* particular member of its class.

### FORM AND MATTER

The terms Aristotle used in making this distinction between whatness and thisness are "form" and "matter." In the most elementary sense, matter is the physical "stuff" out of which something is made; form is the physical shape that the thing has. For instance, a brick is made of clay—that is its matter; it has a characteristic shape—that is its form. Normally we would not talk about a lump of clay as being a "thing," but we do not hesitate to call a brick, made of that clay, a thing. We hesitate to call the lump of clay a thing because it does not seem to us to have a characteristic shape; on the contrary, it is "just a lump." The brick, however, is a thing precisely because it does have a specific shape. This illustrates Aristotle's point that a thing (an individual substance) is *formed* matter (or, in the case of the brick, "shaped" matter).

But shape and stuff are only very rudimentary instances of form and matter. In something as simple as a brick, form (whatness) may be virtually exhausted by physical form, or shape. But Socrates' shape is obviously a very minor aspect of his whatness. The difference between a form like "brick" and a form like "man" can be seen if we consider the way we answer when someone points to a certain object and asks, "What is this?" If the object pointed to happens to be a piece of baked clay of an oblong rectangular shape, the correct answer to the question is, "This is a brick." Why? Because the questioner is inquiring about the "whatness" of the object pointed to. The "what" of the question asks the name of the class to which the object belongs, and this is determined by the property (oblong, rectangular shape) that this object shares with numerous other objects. But the "this" of the question (as indicated by pointing) refers to this particular bit of clay. Shape of such-and-such a character is something this brick shares with many others; what distinguishes it from all those other bricks is its being made of this particular bit of clay.

But suppose the object pointed to happens to be a certain pug-nosed, shambling-gaited, Athenian son of a midwife. In this case we might answer the question, "What is this?" in all sorts of ways. "This is a pug-nosed man," "This is an Athenian citizen," "This is the son of a midwife," "This is a philosopher," "This is the teacher of Plato," "This is Socrates"—all are possible answers. Hence we may reply with another question: "What do you mean, 'what is that?' " This is a request for a specification of the "whatness" of the object pointed to, and it reflects our awareness of the richness and complexity of that object's whatness (that is, its form).

Now consider the brick again: It has a characteristic shape, and it has been said that this is its form. But why does it have this shape? Because, since it is used as an element in constructing walls, it is handy for it to be a unit with flat sides on which other units can be firmly placed. The brick has the shape that it has because of the use to which it is put.

Speaking generally, each thing has the form that it has because of the purpose, or function, that it serves. The form of a knife differs from the form of a spoon because the former is used for cutting and the latter for ladling. The form of a private house differs from the form of an office building because its function is different. In these examples it should be noted that we have passed from the simple notion of form as merely the physical shape of an object to the notion of form as the overall plan of an object. In a word, function determines form in the sense of giving an object the characteristic structure that it has. To say this is to say that a thing's function gives it unity, makes it the sort of whole it is. Indeed, it is a *whole*, instead of being merely a collection of discrete elements, only because the elements are organized into a specific arrangement that serves some purpose. This is easier to see in the case of man-made objects than in the case of natural objects, in which no conscious purpose is at work. But it is not too far-fetched in the case of an organism. What is the form of the hand or some other organ? Not, certainly, merely its shape, but the arrangement of parts that enables it to do certain things. The uses to which the body (or the hand) can be put give unity to the body, just as physical shape (which in its turn gives unity to the undifferentiated mass of clay) makes the brick one particular thing. This obviously expands the notion of form.

A similar expansion occurs in the concept of matter. If form comes to mean the purpose, or use, anything serves, matter comes to mean the possibility of serving a purpose, the possibility of being of use. Matter is simply that aspect of a thing that opens opportunities for further development. For instance, it has been noted that clay is the matter of the brick. It is the brick's matter both in the literal sense that it is the material out of which the brick is made and (as we now see) in the more extended sense that it is the opportunity, given this form, for there to be bricks. Similarly, the bricks are the matter of a wall, that is, the existence of bricks creates the possibility of there being walls.

Thus every particular thing is, as it were, on a mountain path looking two ways: downward toward something (for example, clay) in comparison with which it is an end—a more articulated structure, and upward toward something (for example, a wall) for whose further articulation it is the necessary condition. The world presents itself, then, not as a collection of utterly separate and discrete things, but as an ordered hierarchy of individuals related to one another in such a way that each individual is at the same time the fulfillment of the purpose inherent in some other individual and the basis for a further development beyond itself.

To summarize, every individual thing has two aspects, matter and form, and either without the other is an abstraction and unreal. Every individual thing has properties that make it *what* it is, properties that it shares with other things (whatness); every individual thing is just this particular thing and not another thing (thisness).

So far we have been considering an individual substance at any particular given time. But substances develop through time (that is, they grow), and in order to think effectively of a substance as it endures, yet changes, we must reinterpret matter and form as potentiality and actuality. Any given particular growing thing (say, an acorn), thought of as existing at some particular moment, can be analyzed in the way that has been described into material and formal elements. The formal elements are those it shares with other acorns; the material elements are those (for example, occupancy of this particular bit of space) that makes it *this* acorn. But an acorn grows to be an oak tree. In this sense, the oak is the form of the acorn. It is the purpose, as it were, that the acorn serves (just as the wall is the purpose that the bricks serve). It is that which, by giving unity and direction to the acorn's development, makes what we call growth, a process. Similarly, just as the bricks are the basis for the possibility of a wall, so the acorn is the potentiality of there being an oak tree, and the oak tree is the actuality of this potentiality. The acorn is the basis that makes an oak tree possible; the oak is the purpose, or end, toward which the acorn grows.

It has already been said that Aristotle conceived of the universe as a hierarchy of individuals related to each other as matter to form. It must now be added that he conceived each of these individuals to be itself a life in which these relations are repeated. Each individual is a process of development in which what is not yet becomes completely itself. What we call life (or growth, or development) is a coming-to-be. A form, at the outset existing only potentially, operates upon matter, shaping and molding it as a sculptor models his clay, and eventually becomes its fully articulated self, just as the esthetic form is finally realized under the sculptor's hands. The sculptor's purpose is outside the clay, in his mind; moreover, this purpose is at least partially conscious. In a natural object the purpose is the form working unconsciously to shape the inert matter.[2] Form can therefore be conceived of as a kind of driving force working its way to fulfillment. "Entelechy" is the term Aristotle used to describe this property of form, and what we call "growth" is nothing but the visible result of form at work.

## CHANGE

This brings us to the problem of change. Change, it will be recalled, is a puzzle because it seems to involve a contradiction. If we say that A changes

---

2 It remains to be asked what, exactly, an "unconscious purpose" is. See pp. 233–35 and 266.

to B, we seem to be saying that A is both itself and not itself. It must be A, for we say, "A changes"; it cannot be A, because we say it is B. If water is water, it is not ice; if it is ice, it is not water. None of Aristotle's predecessors, including Plato, had wrestled with this paradox successfully. Plato had had to confess that according to his theory, though change "participates" in some mysterious way in the unchanging forms, it is only appearance.

Aristotle's analysis of reality in terms of form and matter made it possible for the first time to come to grips with change. The individual A turns out on analysis to be a complex; it is a substance, a formed matter. During its change into B some part of A endures unchanged and some part of A alters. What endures is A's matter; what changes is its form. Consider a piece of clay being worked on by a sculptor. Throughout his successive manipulations the clay endures; what changes are the forms (that is, the shapes) through which the sculptor advances to the final, esthetically satisfactory object that is the end of his activity.

We may generalize by saying that in any change from A to B one identical material factor loses one form, A, and acquires another, B. In the simplest case (for example, when dough is cut into stars, circles, and squares for baking) one form (shape) is lost and another acquired without any internal transformation of the matter. Here matter equals physical material, form equals physical shape, and change is simply the substitution of one physical shape for another. In more complicated kinds of changes the principle is the same. When the acorn becomes (changes into) the oak tree, more is involved than a substitution of one physical shape for another. To begin with, a whole succession of physical shapes replace one another according to a well-defined scheme. But in addition there is an articulation of structure, in which each successive stage appears as the actualization of the form that was potentially present in an earlier stage and becomes in turn the matter of a later stage. In spite of these complexities, the analysis is identical. The change that we speak of loosely as acorn-becoming-oak is a succession of smaller changes, in each of which matter loses and gains form. Instead of the simple alteration of form (physical shape) that occurs when a cooky-cutter is used to shape dough, a succession of immensely complicated forms (including physical shape) follow one another in a systematic way. Indeed, we can now draw a distinction between "change" and "development." Development, or growth, is change in which a succession of steps follow a pattern toward an end.

This concept of a thing as formed matter also resolves the old puzzle over the one and the many. In the successive changes by which an acorn gets to be an oak we certainly have a "many," a plurality. But we feel this many to be also one; otherwise we would not say the acorn becomes an oak. What is the one that we feel to be uniting this diversity? Surely it is the fact of development, of movement toward an end. What unites all the various stages is simply that they *are* stages. The purpose (whatever it is) unifies all the steps that are the means to its fulfillment.

### ARISTOTLE'S FOUR CAUSES

From this it follows that one of the ways of understanding anything is to relate it to the subsequent stages in the series of which it is a member. In a game of chess, for instance, a move made by an expert may seem incomprehensible to a tyro; but the move that appears irrelevant at the time it is made turns out to be only too comprehensible when it leads to a mate. The move is a means to an end—winning the game. Understanding the end, therefore, throws light on the means. Since the thing's end is its form, Aristotle could say with Plato that the form of anything throws light on its nature. Plato understood this to mean that knowledge of the transcendent form illumines the changing, unreal particular; Aristotle understood it to mean simply that knowing the purpose, or function, of a thing in the total economy of nature is indispensable to understanding that thing.

But a thing's function, or purpose, is only one part of its nature. Although the function (which Aristotle called the "final cause") is in his view the prime concern of the scientist, an adequate scientific understanding of anything must include an account of three other aspects, which he called the "material cause," the "formal cause," and the "efficient cause." Thus, besides knowing the purpose[3] of a piece of sculpture (to decorate a building, to win fame or money for the artist, or whatever), we must know what material (wood, bronze, marble) it is made of. For, since a sculptor cannot achieve identical effects with all materials, we cannot fully know the piece unless we know its material. Third, we must identify the esthetic *form* of the particular sculpture (a human figure, a centaur, a Pallas Athene, or whatever), for knowledge of this, too, throws light on the nature of the work.[4] Finally, we must know the *efficient* cause of the sculpture, the sculptor who fashioned it.

These four factors are usually referred to as the "four Aristotelian causes," but only one of them, the efficient cause, would be called a cause today. This linguistic difference points up sharply the contrast between Aristotle's conception of scientific knowledge and our own. Aristotle believed that in order to understand any individual thing we must know four aspects of it, each of which operates to determine its nature. We must know (1) the material of which it is composed (the material cause); (2) the motion or action that began it (the efficient cause); (3) the function or purpose for which it exists (the final cause); and (4) the form it actualizes and by which it fulfills its purpose (the formal cause).

---

3 Ignorance of this factor is often a problem for the archeologist. We discover a fragment of a marble head. Was its purpose portraiture or religious ceremonial? Was it an architectural embellishment or a free-standing figure? If we knew the answers to these questions, we might be able to date the figure or to identify the artist.

4 The archeologist is also handicapped if he is unable to tell from the fragment what the full esthetic form is. Is this the head of a man? a woman? a centaur? As long as he is ignorant of this he lacks full knowledge of the piece.

This fourfold analysis works pretty well with regard to man-made objects, like houses or pieces of sculpture. Here there is an efficient cause, or agent, outside the object; here, because there is a conscious purpose, form and end are relatively distinct.[5] But the analysis becomes very strained when it is extended to natural objects and events—for instance, growing plants and falling rocks. What are the final causes of a rock's fall or of a plant's growth? We have either to admit that there are none or to invent them—we say that the rock falls because it is seeking the center of the earth, that the plant grows because it is seeking the upper air. On the other hand, we can certainly specify the material of the plant and the rock. We can also specify the form, or pattern, of the plant's growth (for example, its direction and rate) and of the rock's fall. But what are the efficient causes of growth and of fall? It may be tempting to say that life is the cause of the growth of plants and that gravity is the cause of the fall of rocks, for this would preserve the Aristotelian scheme. But life is not (though Aristotle constantly wrote as if it were) a kind of power, or entelechy, in living things; gravity is not an external agent that causes rocks to fall, as the sculptor is an external agent that causes stone to acquire such-and-such a shape. On the contrary, when a body behaves in a certain way we say that it is alive; when it accelerates at such-and-such a rate we say that it is gravitating. Thus "life" and "gravity" do not designate causes of behavior; they are terms designating two different patterns of behavior, that is, they are formal, not efficient, causes. We can indeed, if we like, say that an earlier stage in the patterned sequence of events is the cause of a later stage, but then the efficient cause is simply one aspect, or phase, of the formal cause. The fundamental idea is that of regularity of pattern. Accordingly, if we eliminate final causes altogether and if we combine efficient and formal causes, we are left with our two original concepts, matter and form.

The fourfold causal analysis thus simply repeats the form-matter analysis from the point of view of theory of knowledge. Because reality is analyzable into formal and material aspects, it follows that we know reality when we know these aspects. If we recall that every object faces two ways, upward toward its fulfillment and downward toward the basis on which it rests,[6] we will see that explanation consists in making this upward and downward reference. Until we locate the individual substance (person, event, or object) in this double relation, we cannot understand it. The extent to which we manage to trace these two strands that connect the individual with the rest of the world is exactly the extent to which we fathom its own individual nature.

Take some particular person at any particular moment in his life—say, Hitler at the moment he became chancellor of Germany. Obviously we cannot under-

---

5 It is necessary to say "relatively" distinct, because even here form and end tend to fuse. Suppose the sculptor's purpose were not to make money but simply to produce this particular esthetically satisfying form.

6 See p. 221.

stand him as he was at that moment in 1933, nor why he did the things he then did, unless we know the "matter" from which the Hitler of 1933 grew—the unhappy child, the frustrated artist, the social failure, the defeated veteran. Nor can we know the Hitler of 1933 unless we know where he was going, what he wanted, what he became. These things were hidden from us in 1933, and only as they were gradually revealed to us in the course of time did we come gradually to understand the Hitler of that earlier year. Thus a present event is always explained in the light of both the process that leads up to it and the process that extends beyond it. This is what Aristotle meant when he said that we understand things only in terms of their causes. If we want to use the term "cause," we can say that everything has a material and a formal cause—the cause out of which it has come and that into which it is going. But this is only a way of saying that to understand any "life," that is, any process through time, we must see how and why the later stages develop out of the earlier stages.

So far "understanding Hitler better" has been spoken of. But when do we understand him *best?* Obviously, when we have made a complete analysis of his material and formal "causes." But this is impossible, for, as we have seen, the universe is a single interlocking hierarchy of matter and form. As we go back into Hitler's past, we see that his childhood was conditioned by and grew out of the social and cultural milieu in which his family lived, and there is no end, clearly, to this process of going back. As we go forward into the future there is no end to the consequences of Hitler's acts. Hence, just because Hitler (or any other individual) is but one link in the interlocking hierarchy that is the universe, eventually a knowledge of the whole universe is relevant to our knowledge of Hitler, just as our knowledge of Hitler is relevant to our knowledge of the universe—a knowledge that consists in the same way of interlocking and correlative "formed matters."

This, of course, is Aristotle's reformulation of Plato's Form of the Good. And the reformulation is characteristic. Aristotle agreed with Plato that the universe is a relational structure and that every element in it can be known only by transcending that element, by seeing it in relation to other elements (and eventually to all of them) in the universe. But whereas Plato's acceptance of the transcendental character of knowledge led him to a separate world of forms and eventually to the Form of the Good, mysterious and incommunicable, Aristotle never passed beyond this world to a supersensible realm of forms. For him, knowledge of an individual particular requires transcendence of this individual, but the supplement that is required is merely knowledge of other individual particulars.

Plato and Aristotle agreed that knowledge of the isolated particular is not knowledge at all. They agreed that complete knowledge is impossible. Yet there was a radical difference between them. The knowledge Plato thirsted for is abstract, general, static—knowledge from which all particularity has been purged. For Aristotle complete knowledge would have been the same *sort* of knowledge we now have, that is, knowledge of the multiple interrelatedness of particulars—of "formed matters."

So far we have been considering the nature of reality in general, that is, characteristics that are true of the real everywhere. It is time now to turn to Aristotle's account of the physical world and to see how he applied the principles that have been discussed to the study of nature.

## Natural Science

What is nature? What is the subject matter of natural science? According to Aristotle, nature is the *sensible*. It consists in those substances of which men become aware by perception. In this way we distinguish natural substances from other, nonsensible substances (for instance, god), which we know in other ways.

But nature is not identical with the sensible world. Stones, plants, and animals are natural, but beds and houses (though sensible) are not. Natural objects have within themselves an innate impulse to change. Rocks "naturally" fall (that is, change place); fire naturally rises; men and animals naturally move about, seek the companionship of their fellows, flee danger, pursue the good, Such natural objects, which have a spontaneous power of movement, must be distinguished from artifacts, which lack this spontaneous power and require an outside agent to move them. Trees grow of themselves; therefore they are natural objects. Houses grow, but only as a result of the acts of carpenters and masons. Houses therefore are artifacts. It might be objected that houses and beds fall, if they are left unsupported, just as naturally as do rocks. But it is not *qua* houses or beds that they fall; it is *qua* some natural material (wood, for instance) that they fall. *Qua* artifacts, therefore, they do not have a natural movement. Nature may thus be defined as the totality of sensible objects capable of spontaneous change.

Aristotle formulated these and other distinctions at the beginning of Book II of the *Physics*.

> Of things that exist, some exist by nature, some from other causes.
> "By nature" the animals and their parts exist, and the plants and the simple bodies (earth, fire, air, water). . . .
> All the things mentioned present a feature in which they differ from things which are *not* constituted by nature. Each of them has *within itself* a principle of motion and of stationariness (in respect of place, or of growth and decrease, or by way of alteration). On the other hand, a bed and a coat and anything else of that sort, *qua* receiving these designations—i.e. in so far as they are products of art—have no innate impulse to change. But in so far as they happen to be composed of stone or of earth or of a mixture of the two, they *do* have such an impulse, and just to that extent—which seems to indicate that *nature is a source or cause of being moved and of being at rest in that*

*to which it belongs primarily,* in virtue of itself and not in virtue of a concomitant attribute.

I say "not in virtue of a concomitant attribute," because (for instance) a man who is a doctor might cure himself. Nevertheless it is not in so far as he is a patient that he possesses the art of medicine: it merely has happened that the same man is doctor and patient—and that is why these attributes are not always found together. So it is with all other artificial products. None of them has in itself the source of its own production. . . .

*What* nature is, then, . . . has been stated. *That* nature exists, it would be absurd to try to prove; for it is obvious that there are many things of this kind, and to prove what is obvious by what is not is the mark of a man who is unable to distinguish what is self-evident from what is not.[b]

Natural science, then, is concerned with the changes of natural objects, and every change is the fulfillment (the coming to actuality) of some potentiality Whenever an object A that is potentially B becomes B, there is change. Change is the process by which A's potentiality to be B is realized. For instance, a cold dish is potentially hot. If it becomes hot this is (1) *qualitative* change. Other types of changes are (2) *quantitative*, in which something increases or decreases in amount, and (3) *locomotive*, in which something changes place. These are the kinds of changes that occur in, or to, substances. Finally, there is (4) *substantival* change, in which substances themselves come into being or pass out of being. The best example of this change is the process by which parents procreate offspring—new individual members of their species.

### MOTION IS ETERNAL

Was there ever a time when there was no change? Will there be such a time in the future? Aristotle dealt very effectively with arguments that deny the eternity of motion. Conceive a time, he said, at which there is no change. Then conceive the beginning of the first change. Why does it begin at this time? Something must have hindered it from beginning earlier (otherwise it would have begun earlier), and this, whatever it is, must have changed, otherwise it would still be a hindrance. Therefore a change occurred before our hypothetical first change.

It remains to consider the following question. Was there ever a becoming of motion before which it had no being, and is it perishing again so as to leave nothing in motion? Or are we to say that it never had any becoming and it is not perishing, but always was and always will be? Is it in fact an immortal never-failing property of things that are, a sort of life as it were to all naturally constituted things? . . .

Let us take our start from what we have already laid down in our course on Physics. Motion, we say, is the fulfilment of the movable in so far as it is movable. Each kind of motion, therefore, necessarily involves the presence of the things that are capable of that motion. . . . Moreover, these things also must either have a beginning before which they had no being, or they must be eternal. Now if there was a becoming of every movable thing, it follows that before the motion in question another change or motion must have taken place in which that which was capable of being moved or of causing motion had its becoming. . . . For if we are to say that . . . there is a time when there is a first movent and a first moved, and another time when there is no such thing but only something that is at rest, then this thing that is at rest must previously have been in process of change: for there must have been some cause of its rest, rest being the privation of motion. Therefore, before this first change there will be a previous change.[c]

There was, then, no initial impetus that started the whole process of natural change at some particular point in time. Every change that occurs is caused by some antecedent change, and this by another, and so on. For nothing moves until something (either a part of itself, in the case of a complex object, or some other object) occasions its change. So we can trace movement back from one mover to another—A's movement is caused by B's, B's by C's, and so on.

And yet, Aristotle thought, there must eventually be a mover who is himself unmoved, who transmits motion but who is moved by no anterior, external movement:

The following considerations will make it clear that there must necessarily be some . . . thing, which, while it has the capacity of moving something else, is itself unmoved and exempt from all change. . . . Suppose it possible that some principles that are unmoved but capable of imparting motion at one time are and at another time are not. Even so, this cannot be true of *all* such principles, since there must clearly be something that *causes* things that move themselves at one time to be and at another not to be. For . . . the fact that some things become and others perish, and that this is so continuously, cannot be caused by any one of those things that, though they are unmoved, do not always exist: nor again can it be caused by any of those which move certain particular things, while others move other things. The eternity and continuity of the process cannot be caused either by any one of them singly or by the sum of them, because this causal relation must be eternal and necessary, whereas the sum of these movements is infinite and they do not all exist together. It is clear, then, that though there may be countless instances of the perishing of some principles that are unmoved but impart motion, and though many things that move themselves perish and are succeeded by others that come into being, and though one thing that is unmoved moves one thing while another moves another, nevertheless there is something that comprehends them all, and that as something apart from each one of them, and this it is that is the cause of the fact that some things are and others are not and of the continuous process of change: and this causes the motion of the other movents, while they are the causes of the motion of other things. Motion, then, being eternal, the first movent, if there is but one, will be eternal also: if there are more than one, there will be a plurality of such eternal movents. We ought, however, to suppose that there is one rather than many, and a finite rather than an infinite number. When the consequences of either assumption are the same, we should always assume that things are finite rather than infinite in number, since in things constituted by nature that which is finite and that which is better ought, if possible, to be present rather than the reverse: and here it is sufficient to assume only one movent, the first of unmoved things, which being eternal will be the principle of motion to everything else. . . .

But evidently there *is* a first principle, and the causes of things are neither an infinite series nor infinitely various in kind. For neither can one thing proceed from another, as from matter, *ad infinitum* (e.g. flesh from earth, earth from air, air from fire, and so on without stopping), nor can the sources of movement form an endless series (man for instance being acted on by air, air by the sun, the sun by Strife, and so on without limit). Similarly the final causes cannot go on *ad infinitum,*—walking being for the sake of health, this for the sake of happiness, happiness for the sake of something else, and so one thing always for the sake of another: . . . If there is no first there is no cause at all.[d]

## THE UNMOVED MOVER

An eternal motion, Aristotle held, must have an eternal cause. But what kind of movement does this unmoved mover cause? The original motion must be change of place, for all the other types of motions involve change of place. Quantitative change (increase or decrease in amount) obviously involves change of place. So does qualitative change, for "the fact that a thing is altered requires that there should be something that alters it, something, e.g. that makes the potentially hot into the actually hot: so it is plain that the movent does not maintain a uniform relation to it but is at one time nearer to and at another farther from that which is altered: and we cannot have this without loco-motion."[e]

Hence an eternal mover will cause an eternal locomotion. Further, this eternal locomotion must be circular, for all other possibilities are excluded. Locomotion is either in a straight line or circular (or a combination of the two). But infinite motion in a straight line would have to be either (1) along an infinite line or (2) backward and forward along a finite line. But (1) is ruled out because there is (Aristotle thought) no actual infinite, and (2) is ruled out because such a motion is composite. Therefore, the motion originated by the unmoved mover must be circular.

Other arguments demonstrate that the unmoved mover must be immaterial and "unmixed"—in fact, something rather like the "mind" that Anaxagoras had supposed to be the originator of the whirling of his seeds.

The next question is, "How does the unmoved mover cause the eternal circular motion that is the basis of all the complex motions of natural objects every-where?" Aristotle's answer was that every good thing is desired insofar as it is known; as a perfect and eternal being the unmoved mover is peculiarly an object of desire and of love. The universe turns in emulation of his goodness; its regular circular motion is the nearest approximation to his perfection that a sensible object can achieve.

"There is something which moves without being moved, being eternal, substance, and actuality. And the object of desire and the object of thought move in this way; they move without being moved."[f] Since the unmoved mover has no body to restrict his activity, he is, as Aristotle says in this passage, pure and complete actuality. But what is the nature of his activity? Obviously, it can be nothing that depends on body. This rules out sensation and desire. (Desire is ruled out anyway, because to desire something is to lack something, and the unmoved mover, being complete actuality, lacks nothing.) In fact, the unmoved mover's activity can only be thinking, and his thought obviously must be the best thought. From these considerations certain characteristics both of the nature of his thought and of its object can be inferred.

Much of man's thought is discursive; it moves from point to point, laboriously, until it reaches a conclusion. The kind of thought that goes into the writing (and reading) of a book like this one is of the discursive type. Occasionally, however, we simply "see" a connection, all at once, without any process of proof. We express this by saying, for instance, that such-and-such a thing suddenly "dawns on us." Now, all the unmoved mover's thought must be of this latter type. When he thinks (and he always thinks), he understands at once, wholly and completely; he does not have to "reason things out" step by step.

And what is the object of his thought? Clearly it can be only himself. This follows because the unmoved mover knows only the best, and the best is the unmoved mover. His knowledge, then, is immediate and complete self-consciousness.

Aristotle called his unmoved mover "god." It was natural for him, therefore, to call this part of his physics "theology," for theology is literally the *logos* (account) of god (*theos*). But there are virtually no religious overtones in Aristotle's theology. Hence it is misleading to modern ears to talk about Aristotle's theology. It is better to use the neutral expression, "Aristotle's account of his unmoved mover."

Thus there is, in Aristotle's view, no divine providence, which is so important an aspect of the Judeo-Christian view of the world. His god does not look out for, care about, and provide for man. He did not create the universe, for it is eternal, and he is utterly indifferent to it. It is true that he causes its motion, but only as a beautiful picture might cause a man to purchase it. God is the object of desire for the lesser intelligences, but he is unconscious of their admiration and would be indifferent to them if he were aware of them.

In Aristotle's view god is a metaphysical necessity—the system requires an unmoved mover, a completely actual and fully realized form, but he is not an object of worship. Aristotle did not experience the Christian's love of a heavenly father, nor the Orphic's need for union with a mysterious, infinite power. Aristotle's god is transcendent and remote, and his attitude toward this god, at least as revealed in the *Metaphysics* and other works of his maturity,[7] was emotionally neutral.

> We assume the gods to be above all other beings blessed and happy; but what sort of actions must we assign to them? Acts of justice? Will not the gods seem absurd if they make contracts and return deposits, and so on? Acts of a brave man, then, confronting dangers and running risks because it is noble to do so? Or liberal acts? To whom will they give? It will be strange if they are really to have money or anything of the kind. And what would their temperate acts be? Is not such praise tasteless, since they have no bad appetites? If we were to run through them all, the circumstances of action would be found trivial and unworthy of gods. Still, every one supposes that they *live* and therefore that they are active; we cannot suppose them to sleep like Endymion. Now if you take away from a living being action, and still more production, what is left but contemplation? Therefore the activity of God, which surpasses all others in blessedness, must be contemplative; and of human activities, therefore, that which is most akin to this must be most of the nature of happiness.[8]

This discussion of the nature of Aristotle's god has led us aside from Aristotle's physics.[8] Let us leave the unmoved mover and turn back to the world that is moved by love of him.

## ASTRONOMY AND PHYSICS

Aristotle conceived of the universe as a set of concentric spheres, with the earth stationary at the center. Outermost is the sphere of the fixed stars. Within are the spheres of the various planets, with that of the moon innermost and nearest the earth. An eternal and absolutely regular motion is imparted to (or better, inspired in) the outer sphere by the unmoved mover, and this motion is passed successively to each of the inner spheres. Between the spheres bearing the planets Aristotle was obliged to introduce others (fifty-five in all) to help account for the observed relative motions of the planets. Besides the motion transmitted to each sphere by that of the outer sphere that it touches, each sphere has its own original motion, imparted to it by its own incorporeal agent, or intelligence. To this extent there are, besides god, no less than fifty-five lesser unmoved movers.[9] The motion of any planet (say, the sun) is compounded of (1) the original motion inspired in the sphere of the fixed stars by their love of

---

7 Jaeger (*Aristotle*, pp. 159 ff.) finds a deep religious feeling in Aristotle's early writings, but only fragments of them remain in the form of quotations by much later writers.
8 It is characteristic of the difference between Aristotle's view and Christianity that, whereas for the latter physics is simply one aspect of God's creativity, for Aristotle theology was but a part of physics.
9 This has naturally raised the question of whether Aristotle was a monotheist or a polytheist.

god, (2) the original motions of the other spheres, and (3) the original motion of this planet's own sphere.

So much perhaps will suffice to summarize Aristotle's astronomy. As regards sublunary things (that is, those below the sphere of *luna*, the moon), Aristotle first considered the four elements and the locomotions proper to them, then the various spatial movements of these elements, by which the qualitative and quantitative changes of ordinary natural objects are produced.

Aristotle thought that each of the four elements—fire, air, water, earth—has its own natural place and that each has a natural motion by which it seeks that place. The place of fire, for instance, is next under the sphere of the moon. The natural movement of fire is therefore upward, away from the earth and toward the sphere of fire.

The "things" of this sublunary world—plants, animals, and inanimate objects— are mixtures made up of the four elements in various combinations. Earth, air, fire, and water are the "matter"[10] of plants, animals, and inanimate objects. These four elements are the "material causes" of physical things, or (as we would say) they are the basic physical factors that analysis of physical objects reveals. The "formal cause" of any particular thing is simply that structure into which its material factor is organized. It is the "formula" that expresses the ratio of the different elements entering into this particular compound.


## Biology—Psychology

### ARISTOTLE'S EMPIRICISM

In Aristotle's biology, what has been called his temperamental difference from Plato is evident from the start. Aristotle mentioned close to five hundred animals. Although in some cases he relied for information on travelers' or old wives' tales, much of his work was based on close observation of actual animals, and many of his conclusions were verified in later times. Indeed, some of his discoveries were not "rediscovered" until modern times.

This interest in empirical fact was certainly not absolutely new in Greek thought—witness Thales, Anaximander, and Empedocles. But certainly the dominant tendency of earlier thinkers had been toward rationalism. Philosophers and scientists had been more interested in logical consistency than in facts. Having accepted some initially plausible hypothesis, they were content to deduce

---

10 The four elements are matter, but only in relation to the higher structures they subserve. As distinct elements they naturally already contain formal factors, and below them is the "pure matter" that these formal factors order. This pure matter is not a separate entity, like the Receptacle in Plato's *Timaeus;* it is simply the bare possibility of being something. For a discussion of this difficult concept, see J. H. Randall, *Aristotle* (Columbia University Press, 1960), pp. 212–14.

its consequences, leaping overhastily to the conclusion that what is logically consistent must be true, instead of asking themselves whether logical consistency is a sufficient, as well as a necessary, condition of truth. Thus Aristotle's method was a healthy corrective to the overrationalism of his philosophical predecessors, including Plato.

In the *History of Animals,* a vast compendium of information about the anatomy and behavior of all sorts of animals, including man, there is ample evidence of Aristotle's empirical interest and of the effort he made to ascertain the facts. Here, for instance, is his account of the development of the embryo chicken.

> Generation from the egg proceeds in an identical manner with all birds, but the full periods from conception to birth differ. . . . With the common hen after three days and three nights there is the first indication of the embryo; with larger birds the interval being longer, with smaller birds shorter. Meanwhile the yolk comes into being, rising towards the sharp end, where the primal element of the egg is situated, and where the egg gets hatched; and the heart appears, like a speck of blood, in the white of the egg. This point beats and moves as though endowed with life, and from it two vein-ducts with blood in them trend in a convoluted course . . . ; and a membrane carrying bloody fibres now envelops the yolk, leading off from the vein-ducts. A little afterwards the body is differentiated, at first very small and white. The head is clearly distinguished, and in it the eyes, swollen out to a great extent. . . . It is only by degrees that they diminish in size and collapse. At the outset the under portion of the body appears insignificant in comparison with the upper portion. . . . The life-element of the chick is in the white of the egg, and the nutriment comes through the navel-string out of the yolk.[h]

And so on for several pages. Aristotle drew his information about animal development and behavior from all sorts of sources—from herdsmen and animal breeders, from fishermen and farmers, from direct observation. Alexander's armies may have sent him specimens.[11] It is difficult, of course, to draw a firm line between experiment and observation. Did Empedocles, for instance, merely happen to observe what occurs when the end of a tube is submerged in water and seize on this as support for his theory about the plenum?[12] Or was the tube a device to test the theory? Probably the former. On the other hand, the Pythagoreans must have experimented to discover the ratios of their tuned lyre.[13] Was Aristotle experimenting when he observed the embryo chicken? This question cannot be answered by a simple "yes" or "no," for this is a borderline case in which we cannot be sure what Aristotle's intent was. Yet there *is* a difference in principle

11 See p. 215.
12 See p. 26.
13 See pp. 35–36.

between (1) recognizing the interest and importance of some fact when one chances to see it and (2) deliberately planning a situation that will test some hypothesis.

The Greek neglect of experiment is one of the chief points that distinguish their method from that of modern science. Perhaps "neglect" is too strong a word, for it may suggest they left something undone that they might easily have done. Experiment is connected with an appreciation of the complexity of nature, with a recognition of the necessity of deciding between alternatives. And the Greeks had no reason at the outset of the development of science to believe nature to be as complex as we now know it to be. Though their conviction that nature is a simply organized cosmos may have made them too facile, it had its fortunate aspect. Had they been aware of how complex the order really is they might have been too discouraged even to begin investigating it.

Whether or not Aristotle actually "experimented," he did make a notable beginning. Just as he laid the basis for his political theory by collecting and studying all available constitutions, so in biology he began by recording everything he could discover about such natural processes as reproduction, nutrition and growth, local movement, and so on. Thus his psychological theories were based on empirical evidence about nutrition and growth, local motion and sensation, perception, and thought.

Aristotle's interpretation of these phenomena naturally involved his fundamental concepts, matter and form. At each level of life there is, he held, a certain structure, or organized pattern, that yields the activity in question, and each of these structures is the basis for the next successively higher structure. His term for these structures was "soul" (*psyche*); hence his work on this subject was called psychology—the study of soul. Aristotle used this term in a much wider sense than we do today. Psyche is simply the form of a living object, and psychology is in effect the study of the formal factor in living objects.

Thus it is clear that Aristotle had a firm grasp of the fact, which modern students have had to rediscover, that all human activity (or any animal activity) is rooted in, and develops out of, the activity of lower organisms. But Aristotle also knew that it is necessary to explain human behavior (or any behavior), not only in terms of the lower structures from which it has developed, but also in terms of the higher structures toward which it is unfolding. To this day this second part of Aristotle's doctrine has not been as successfully relearned as the first.

## PSYCHOLOGY: ITS METHOD AND SCOPE

> Let us now . . . endeavour . . . to give a precise answer to the question, What is soul? i.e. to formulate the most general possible definition of it. . . .
>
> Among substances are by general consent reckoned bodies and especially natural bodies; for they are the principles of all other bodies. Of natural bodies some have life in them, others not; by life we mean self-nutrition and growth

(with its correlative decay). It follows that every natural body which has life in it is a substance in the sense of a composite.

But since it is also a *body* of such and such a kind, viz. having life, the *body* cannot be soul; the body is the subject or matter, not what is attributed to it. Hence the soul must be a substance in the sense of the form of a natural body having life potentially within it. But substance is actuality, and thus soul is the actuality of a body as above characterized. Now the word actuality has two senses corresponding respectively to the possession of knowledge and the actual exercise of knowledge. It is obvious that the soul is actuality in the first sense, viz. that of knowledge as possessed, for both sleeping and waking presuppose the existence of soul, and of these waking corresponds to actual knowing, sleeping to knowledge possessed but not employed, and, in the history of the individual, knowledge comes before its employment or exercise.

That is why the soul is the first grade of actuality of a natural body having life potentially in it. The body so described is a body which is organized. The parts of plants in spite of their extreme simplicity are "organs"; e.g. the leaf serves to shelter the pericarp, the pericarp to shelter the fruit, while the roots of plants are analogous to the mouth of animals, both serving for the absorption of food. If, then, we have to give a general formula applicable to all kinds of soul, we must describe it as the first grade of actuality of a natural organized body. That is why we can wholly dismiss as unnecessary the question whether the soul and the body are one: it is as meaningless as to ask whether the wax and the shape given to it by the stamp are one, or generally the matter of a thing and that of which it is the matter. . . .

We have now given an answer to the question, What is soul?—an answer which applies to it in its full extent. . . .

We resume our inquiry from a fresh starting-point by calling attention to the fact that what has soul in it differs from what has not in that the former displays life. Now this word has more than one sense, and provided any one alone of these is found in a thing we say that thing is living. Living, that is, may mean thinking or perception or local movement and rest, or movement in the sense of nutrition, decay and growth. . . .

Of the psychic powers above enumerated some kinds of living things, as we have said, possess all, some less than all, others only one. Those we have mentioned are the nutritive, the appetitive, the sensory, the locomotive, and the power of thinking. Plants have none but the first, the nutritive, while another order of living things has this *plus* the sensory. If any order of living things has the sensory, it must also have the appetitive; for appetite is the genus of which desire, passion, and wish are the species; now all animals have one sense at least, viz. touch, and whatever has a sense has the capacity for pleasure and pain and therefore has pleasant and painful objects present to it, and wherever these are present, there is desire, for desire is just appetition of what is pleasant. . . . Certain kinds of animals possess in addition the power of locomotion, and still another order of animate beings, i.e. man and possibly another order like man or superior to him, the power of thinking, i.e. mind. It is now evident that a single definition can be given of soul only in the same sense as one can be given of figure. For, as in that case there is no figure distinguishable and apart from triangle, &c., so here there is no soul apart from the forms of soul just enumerated. . . .

It is evident that the way to give the most adequate definition of soul is to seek in the case of *each* of its forms for the most appropriate definition. . . .

It follows that first of all we must treat of nutrition and reproduction, for the nutritive soul is found along with all the others and is the most primitive and widely distributed power of soul, being indeed that one in virtue of which all are said to have life. The acts in which it manifests itself are reproduction and the use of food—reproduction, I say, because for any living thing that has reached its normal development and which is unmutilated, and whose mode of generation is not spontaneous, the most natural act is the production of another like itself, an animal producing an animal, a plant a plant, in order that, as far as its nature allows, it may partake in the eternal and divine. That is the goal towards which all things strive, that for the sake of which they do whatsoever their nature renders possible. . . . Since then no living thing is able to partake in what is eternal and divine by uninterrupted continuance (for nothing perishable can for ever remain one and the same), it tries to achieve that end in the only way possible to it, and success is possible in varying degrees; so it remains not indeed as the self-same individual but continues its existence in something *like* itself—not numerically but specifically one. . . .

Let us now speak of sensation in the widest sense. Sensation depends, as we have said, on a process of movement or affection from without, for it is held to be some sort of change of quality. . . .

In dealing with each of the senses we shall have first to speak of the objects which are perceptible by each. The term "object of sense" covers . . . two kinds, of which . . . one (a) consists of what is perceptible by a single sense, the other (b) of what is perceptible by any and all of the senses. I call by the name of special object of this or that sense that which cannot be perceived by any other sense than that one and in respect of which no error is possible; in this sense colour is the special object of sight, sound of hearing, flavour of taste. Touch, indeed, discriminates more than one set of different qualities. Each sense has one kind of object which it discerns, and never errs in reporting that what is before it is colour or sound (though it may err as to what it is that is coloured or where that is, or what it is that is sounding or where that is). Such objects are what we propose to call the special objects of this or that sense.

"Common sensibles" are movement, rest, number, figure, magnitude; these are not peculiar to any one sense, but are common to all. There are at any rate certain kinds of movement which are perceptible both by touch and by sight. . . .

The following results applying to any and every sense may now be formulated.

(A) By a "sense" is meant what has the power of receiving into itself the sensible forms of things without the matter. This must be conceived of as taking place in the way in which a piece of wax takes on the impress of a signet-ring without the iron or gold; we say that what produces the impression is a signet of bronze or gold, but its particular metallic constitution makes no difference: in a similar way the sense is affected by what is coloured or flavoured or sounding, but it is indifferent what in each case the *substance* is; what alone matters is what *quality* it has, i.e. in what *ratio* its constituents are combined.

(B) By "an organ of sense" is meant that in which ultimately such a power is seated. . . .

If the movement set up by an object is too strong for the organ, the equipoise of contrary qualities in the organ, which just *is* its sensory power, is disturbed; it is precisely as concord and tone are destroyed by too violently twanging the strings of a lyre. This explains also why plants cannot perceive, in spite of their having a portion of soul in them and obviously being affected by tangible objects themselves. . . . The explanation is that they have no mean of contrary qualities, and so no principle in them capable of taking on the forms of sensible objects without their matter; in the case of plants the affection is an affection by form-and-matter together.[i]

## THE NUTRITIVE PSYCHE

Aristotle's psychology thus begins with what he called the nutritive soul—that form, or structure, that appears in, and is the fulfillment of, the most rudimentary of living objects. But the nutritive soul is also the base on which the more fully developed and articulated souls of complex organisms rest. This is what Aristotle meant when he said: "The sentient faculty [and all the other higher faculties] never exists without the nutritive; but the nutritive may exist without the sentient, as in the case of plants."[j]

The immediate function of the nutritive psyche is to maintain the ratio of the various organs of the body. As the body consumes food (adds to its quantity), something must control this addition so that the process of growth is in accordance with the "plan" of this body. The food can no more do this itself than a rudder by itself can steer a ship. In both cases form is required: The rudder requires a hand to steer it; the food requires a nutritive soul to "guide" the qualitative changes by which it is transformed into body. The food taken into the body becomes flesh; therefore, before it was eaten, it was potentially flesh. The nutritive soul, then, makes the potential actual. In this process heat operates as the "efficient cause." Just as the heat of the sun causes the changes of seasons, so in the body the heat of the heart boils the food taken into the stomach and transforms it into blood. The blood then oozes through the body. In this process the blood is transformed again, this time by cold, into flesh and other solid parts.

So much for the immediate function of nutrition—to keep the body alive, to enable it to grow. Its long-range function is the perpetuation of the species. Since, as Aristotle pointed out, we tend to name things after the function they serve, we might also call the nutritive soul the reproductive soul.

## THE SENSITIVE PSYCHE

The sensitive soul is the type of form that exists at the animal level. Here there is a more developed structure that includes sense organs, for instance, the eye and the ear.

What happens in my eye when I see something—say, my desk? Clearly the sense organ is modified in the same general way that the body is modified by taking on food, but with this difference: In nutrition the matter itself is taken into the body and transformed into blood and eventually into flesh, whereas in sensation it is not the matter of the desk but only its form that enters the eye. When I eat a steak, the steak enters my body. But when I perceive my desk, it does not enter my eye; what enters is its "sensible form." So, when I impress a seal on wax, it is not the matter of the seal (the metal) that enters the wax, but its sensible form. (To say that it is the *sensible* form means only that it is the kind of form that is sensible.)

Now, before I see a red object, my eye is potentially red. When I see a red object, this potentiality is made actual. The eye is potentially red (and yellow and green) just as a cold plate is potentially hot. Of course, not every form is capable of being actualized in every medium. Each sense organ has, in fact, a certain range of potentiality, and it is only within this range that it is capable of experiencing sensations. Sounds lying beyond the ear's range cannot be heard, colors lying beyond the eye's range cannot be seen, and so on.

But not only the sense experience is brought to actuality in perception; so also is the object perceived. Until it is actually perceived it is only perceivable, that is, potentially an object of perception. Thus perception is a dual actualization—an actualization of the object as an object of perception and an actualization of the sense organ as a percipient. In perception, then, a form is actualized in two different media—"out there" in the object and "in here" in the sense organ. We perceive truly just because, and insofar as, the same form is both here in the sense organ and out there in the object.

This, it must be allowed, leaves much to be explained. First, for instance, the change in the sense organ may be the basis of the perception, but it is not itself perception. Perception seems also to involve something that we may for the present call "consciousness." This was recognized implicitly by Aristotle, but he did not know how to deal with it.

> The problem might be raised: Can what cannot smell be said to be affected by smells or what cannot see by colours, and so on? It might be . . . argued that what cannot smell cannot be affected by smells and further that what can smell can be affected by it only in so far as it has in it the power to smell (similarly with the proper objects of all the other senses). Indeed that this *is* so is made quite evident as follows. Light or darkness, sounds and smells leave *bodies* quite unaffected; what does affect bodies is not these but the bodies which are their vehicles, e.g. what splits the trunk of a tree is

> not the sound of the thunder but the air which accompanies thunder. Yes, but . . . is not the true account this, that all bodies *are* capable of being affected by smells and sounds, but that some on being acted upon, having no boundaries of their own, disintegrate, as in the instance of air, which does become odorous, showing that *some* effect is produced on it by what is odorous? But smelling is more than such an affection by what is odorous—*what* more? Is not the answer that, while the air owing to the momentary duration of the action upon it of what is odorous does itself become perceptible to the sense of smell, smelling is an *observing* of the result produced?[k]

For Aristotle to insist, as he does here, on the difference between (1) physiological change and (2) perception—that is, for him to insist on the difference between the way air is affected by odor and the way the nose is—amounts to admitting the inadequacy of his attempt to account for perception in purely physiological terms.

Second, is the sensation we experience a copy of the object that causes it? As plain men we take it for granted that the world "out there" is what our sense organs report it to be. But is this assumption justified? Atomism, for example, held that it is not. Atomism distinguished radically between the world as it really is—atoms in a void—and the world as it appears to sense organs like ours—shoes, ships, sealing wax, cabbages, and kings. Aristotle, however, is usually taken as a realist, that is, as holding that we perceive the world as it is. But how can we know that the red out there in the object is like the red in here in me? The matter is admittedly different, Aristotle would have said, but the form is the same, and this validates perception. But *is* the form the same? How did Aristotle know that the sensible form of the object enters the eye unchanged?

This question becomes even more acute when we turn from sensation (for example, of colors and sounds) to cognition.

### THE RATIONAL PSYCHE

> Thinking both speculative and practical is regarded as akin to a form of perceiving; for in the one as well as the other the soul discriminates and is cognizant of something which *is* . . . [but] perceiving and practical thinking are not identical . . . for the former is universal in the animal world, the latter is found in only a small division of it. Further, speculative thinking is also distinct from perceiving—I mean that in which we find rightness and wrongness—rightness in prudence, knowledge, true opinion, wrongness in their opposites; for perception of the special objects of sense is always free from error, and is found in all animals, while it is possible to think falsely as well as truly, and thought is found only where there is discourse of reason as well as sensibility. . . .
>
> Turning now to the part of the soul with which the soul knows and thinks (whether this is separable from the others in definition only, or spatially as well) we have to inquire (1) what differentiates this part, and (2) how thinking can take place.

If thinking is like perceiving . . . the thinking part of the soul must . . . be . . . capable of receiving the form of an object; that is, must be potentially identical in character with its object without being the object. Mind must be related to what is thinkable, as sense is to what is sensible.

Therefore, since everything is a possible object of thought, mind . . . must be pure from all admixture; for the co-presence of what is alien to its nature is a hindrance and a block: it follows that it too, like the sensitive part, can have no nature of its own, other than that of having a certain capacity. Thus that in the soul which is called mind (by mind I mean that whereby the soul thinks and judges) is, before it thinks, not actually any real thing. For this reason it cannot reasonably be regarded as blended with the body: if so, it would acquire some quality, e.g. warmth or cold, or even have an organ like the sensitive faculty: as it is, it has none. It was a good idea to call the soul "the place of forms," though (1) this description holds only of the intellective soul, and (2) even this is the forms only potentially, not actually. . . .

Mind is in a sense potentially whatever is thinkable, though actually it is nothing until it has thought. What it thinks must be in it just as characters may be said to be on a writing-tablet on which as yet nothing actually stands written: this is exactly what happens with mind. . . .

The thinking then of the simple objects of thought is found in those cases where falsehood is impossible: where the alternative of true or false applies, there we always find a putting together of objects of thought in a quasi-unity. As Empedocles said that "where heads of many a creature sprouted without necks" they afterwards by Love's power were combined, so here too objects of thought which were given separate are combined, e.g. "incommensurate" and "diagonal": if the combination be of objects past or future the combination of thought includes in its content the date. For falsehood always involves a synthesis; for even if you assert that what is white is not white you have included not-white in a synthesis. It is possible also to call all these cases division as well as combination. However that may be, there is not only the true or false assertion that Cleon is white but also the true or false assertion that he *was* or *will be* white. In each and every case that which unifies is mind. . . .

The so-called abstract objects the mind thinks just as, if one had thought of the snub-nosed not as snub-nosed but as hollow, one would have thought of an actuality without the flesh in which it is embodied: it is thus that the mind when it is thinking the objects of Mathematics thinks as separate elements which do not exist separate. In every case the mind which is actively thinking is the objects which it thinks. . . .

Knowledge and sensation are divided to correspond with the realities, potential knowledge and sensation answering to potentialities, actual knowledge and sensation to actualities. Within the soul the faculties of knowledge and sensation are *potentially* these objects, the one what is knowable, the other what is sensible. They must be either the things themselves or their forms. The former alternative is of course impossible: it is not the stone which is present in the soul but its form.

It follows that the soul is analogous to the hand; for as the hand is a tool of tools, so the mind is the form of forms and sense the form of sensible things.

Since according to common agreement there is nothing outside and separate in existence from sensible spatial magnitudes, the objects of thought are in the sensible forms, viz. both the abstract objects and all the states and affections of sensible things. Hence (1) no one can learn or understand anything in the absence of sense, and (2) when the mind is actively aware of anything it is necessarily aware of it along with an image; for images are like sensuous contents except in that they contain no matter. . . .[1]

Just as the nutritive soul occurs in isolation from the sensitive soul (for example, in plants) but also occurs in combination with it (in animals), so the sensitive soul occurs both in isolation from, and in combination with, the rational soul. And just as, again, the functions of the nutritive soul are mediated by association with a higher form (reproduction is more complicated in animals than in plants), so the functions of the sensitive soul are mediated by association with the rational soul. In other words, human sensation is more complex than animal sensation precisely because every human activity, even those "shared" with animals and plants, is modified by the fact that man is a rational creature capable of thought. Aristotle's may indeed be a "faculty" psychology, but not in the sense that the psyche is a simple collection of discrete faculties. The psyche is a group of powers mutually conditioned by the relations in which they stand to one another.

Even in animals there are signs of a rudimentary intelligence. A dog, we say, "knows" his name and "recognizes" his master. What makes this possible, according to Aristotle, is that successive sensible experiences may be "remembered," that is, may fuse to make a new kind of experience that is richer in meaning than any single sense experience could possibly be. When the dog sees his master he sees more than just a man who happens to be out there in front of him. He sees *his* master—the man who on other occasions has fed, trained, punished, and praised him. The totality of what this experience means to him is, then, far larger than what is contained in this single perception. Even at the level of the sensitive soul, perception transcends the sensible form of what is present here and now.

At the human level of experience this process of transcendence expands. When I see my desk I see not only *my* desk (as the dog sees his master), but a *desk*, that is, a member of the class "table-frame-or-case-with-a-sloping-or-flat-top-for-the-use-of-readers-or-writers." When a dog looks at this object he presumably has much the same sensory experience that I have, that is, he experiences the same sensible forms. He may even "combine" the present experience with re-membered experiences. But he does not know that he sees a *desk*.

Yet, though the dog does not rise to the full and articulate experience of the universal "desk," he is on the way to it because, like me, he is capable of remembering and fusing together past experiences.

Out of this remembering and fusing there emerges, at the human level, knowledge of what Aristotle called the intelligible form, or the universal—the generic character shared by all members of a class. Hence true thought goes beyond mere remembering, beyond the dog's recognition of his master.

With the activity of thought we reach the level of the rational psyche. The intelligible form is not, of course, a separate entity. To suppose it to be such would be to fall into the fallacy of Platonism. The form is embedded in the particulars and does not exist apart from them. Nevertheless, it is capable of impressing itself on the human mind so that the mind comes to know it. The expression "impressing itself on the mind" is used advisedly. The intelligible form was supposed by Aristotle to stand in the same relation to the mind as that in which the sensible form stands to the sense organ or the seal stands to the wax. When the seal is impressed on the wax, the form (not the matter) of the seal is transferred; the same form is present in two media. Just as the wax is the potentiality for various impressions, so the mind is the potentiality for various intelligible forms, or universals. When the mind thinks, it takes on the intelligible form of the object out there and becomes identical with it. Not identical with the object, of course (any more than the wax becomes identical with the seal), but identical with the object's intelligible form.

In thought, then, mind and its object are supposedly identical, but thought occurs only (here is another radical departure from Platonism) in the presence, and as a result of a succession, of sense experiences. Just as the movement of my hand is the efficient cause of the wax's taking the impression of the seal, so sense experience (present and recollected) of desks is the efficient cause of my thought of the intelligible form "desk." Thus, whereas for Plato the best thought was freed from sense experience altogether, for Aristotle it remained rooted in sense experience.

This should throw some light on Aristotle's remark that thought is the form of forms, just as the hand is the tool of tools. A seal is a tool fashioned by man; it is used by an instrument of a higher order, the hand. So the sensible form is utilized by a cognitive faculty of a higher order, the mind. Thought works upon, and utilizes for higher cognitive ends, the sensible forms, just as the hand works upon, and uses for further practical ends, the tools of its own fashioning. The relation between sensible form and intelligible form is another example of the relation between matter and form. Sense data are the matter out of which universals are constructed; universals are their end.

So much for the general nature of thought and its relation to sensation. We must now note that, according to Aristotle, thought can be divided into two main kinds, depending on its object. If its object is an unanalyzable whole, it is (like simple sense perception) infallible. If its object is the result of a prior synthesis, it is fallible.[14] We must, therefore, try to discover rules that will enable us to distinguish true from false thinking.

---

14 If I simply perceive a white color patch, my perception is infallible; if I judge that this white patch is a handkerchief, I may well be mistaken. It may be a piece of paper.

## Logic

This reference to truth and falsity presents us with the question, "How is good thinking to be distinguished from bad?" Since logic is the science that makes this distinction, let us now briefly turn to Aristotle's logic.

Aristotle was the inventor of formal logic in the sense that he was the first person to draw up precise rules for distinguishing valid from invalid thinking. Suppose I know that all Greeks are mortal and that Aristotle is a Greek. It follows that Aristotle is mortal. What makes this conclusion true? Why would the conclusion that Aristotle is a man not follow from these premises? Of course there *are* premises from which the latter conclusion could be drawn—for instance, "All Greeks are men" and "Aristotle is a Greek." But even though it is true that Aristotle is a man, this proposition does not *follow* from the facts that he is a Greek and that all Greeks are mortal.

Thus, as Aristotle saw, we must distinguish between *truth* and *validity*. Truth is a characteristic of individual propositions: An individual proposition is true if it correctly classifies things and false if it does not. Thus "Aristotle is a Greek" is true, and "Aristotle is a Turk" is false. Validity is *not* a characteristic of individual propositions. It is the logical relation between premises, whether they are true or false, and the conclusion that follows from these premises. Thus, although the proposition "Aristotle is a man" is true, it follows validly from some premises but not from others.

The two chief questions Aristotle set himself to answer in his study of logic were: (1) When we have two true propositions, what are the rules of inference by which a conclusion can be drawn? (2) How can we know that the premises we start with are true? Since the bulk of Aristotle's logic is concerned with the first of these two questions, we shall start with it.

Aristotle called an arrangement of propositions in which a conclusion follows from two premises *syllogism*. A syllogism, to be precise, is a "discourse in which, certain things being stated, something other than what is stated follows of necessity from their being so. I mean by the last phrase that they produce the consequence, and by this, that no further term is required from without to make the consequence necessary."ᵐ

Aristotle's problem was to find the rules for valid syllogism, that is, the conditions under which the third proposition follows or does not follow. Here are a few examples of syllogism, some valid and some invalid:

1. All men are mortal
   All Greeks are Europeans
   _____
   All Greeks are mortal

2. All Greeks are philosophers        All M is P
   All Athenians are Greeks           All S is M
   _____           _____
   All Athenians are philosophers    All S is P

3. No mortals are angels                 No M is P
   All men are mortal                     All S is M
   ─────────────────────                  ─────────
   No men are angels                      No S is P

4. All Athenians are Greeks              All M is P
   Some men are Athenians                 Some S is M
   ─────────────────────                  ──────────
   Some men are Greeks                    Some S is P

5. No Athenians are Spartans             No M is P
   No Englishmen are Athenians            No S is M
   ─────────────────────────
   No Englishmen are Spartans

## ANALYSIS OF FIRST ARGUMENT

Obviously the third proposition in the first example is true, but the question is, "Does it follow from the first two propositions in this arrangement?" In order to ascertain whether it does, let us draw a diagram in which circles represent the class relationships asserted in the various propositions. Thus if we think of every mortal thing as falling within one circle,

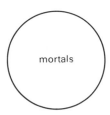

we can represent proposition 1 as follows:

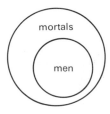

Similarly, using another circle for the term "Europeans," proposition 2 gives

Finally, proposition 3 can be represented by

It will be seen that propositions 1 and 2, when taken together, do not yield proposition 3. The "Greek" circle is inside the "European" circle (by proposition 2); we want it to be inside the "mortal" circle (for this is what the conclusion claims). But on the basis of the information given in the premises (and this is what we must confine ourselves to, since we want to know whether or not the conclusion follows from them), there is no relation between the "mortal" circle and the "European" circle. Hence, as it stands, this syllogism is invalid. Proposition 3 does not follow from propositions 1 and 2.

It is easy to see, however, what would make the argument valid. It has been said that the "Greek" circle is inside the "European" circle and that we want it to be inside the "mortal" circle. Hence, if we had a way of bringing "European" under "men," we would have the desired conclusion, for the "European" circle would take the "Greek" circle with it. Thus,

This arrangement of class relations is asserted in the following two syllogisms:

| | |
|---|---|
| Premise 1 of original argument | All men are mortal |
| New premise | All Europeans are men |
| New conclusion and premise of second syllogism | All Europeans are mortal |
| Premise 2 of original argument | All Greeks are Europeans |
| Conclusion of original syllogism | All Greeks are mortal |

The trouble with the first syllogism was that it contained no way of connecting the subject and the predicate of the conclusion, no evidence on the basis of which we would be warranted in asserting that predicate of that subject. What we did in the two new syllogisms was to supply this link by showing that the "men" circle contains the "European" circle and is contained by the "mortal" circle. We can say in fact that every syllogism must contain, besides the subject and predicate terms of the conclusion, a third term that enables us to pass from subject to predicate, that supplies the *evidence* for the conclusion. The first argument failed, then, because it lacked this evidential link. And it lacked this link because it contained four terms (mortals, men, Europeans, Greeks) instead of three terms. Two syllogisms were required to bring these four terms into a valid argument.

Sometimes an argument looks as if it has only three terms but is invalid because one of the terms is used equivocally. Suppose, for instance, we were to say:

> All Greeks are mortal
> Aristotle's logic is Greek to me

Obviously no conclusion can be drawn. Though we have only three terms (Greek, mortal, Aristotle's logic), one of them (Greek) is used equivocally and there is no bridge. Aristotle called this "the fallacy of four terms." We can, then, put down as our first rule that a syllogism must have three and only three terms. And we can note that, strictly speaking, we should not say (as has been said above), "Syllogism 1 is invalid"; rather, we should say, "Arrangement 1 is not a syllogism."

### ANALYSIS OF SECOND ARGUMENT

Let us now examine argument 2 (which *is* a syllogism in that it contains only three terms) and see whether this arrangement is such that the premises furnish evidence for the conclusion. In other words, is "Greeks" an adequate bridge between "Athenians" and "philosophers"? We must not worry about whether the premises are true. It is merely a question of whether, from the premises stated, the conclusion follows. According to proposition 1:

According to proposition 2:

Taken together the two premises may be represented as follows:

Since the diagram for the two premises includes what is asserted in proposition 3 (All Athenians are philosophers), the conclusion follows and the syllogism is valid. It will be seen that this is just the arrangement of class relationships we ended with when argument 1 was corrected.

This yields the so-called *dictum de omni*: Whatever is asserted of a whole class must be asserted of every subclass within it. Thus, whatever is asserted of men (for example, that they are mortal) must also be asserted of the subclass, European men. Similarly, whatever is asserted of Greeks (for example, that they are philosophers) must also be asserted of Athenians, a subclass of Greeks.

Note, too, that this argument, or arrangement of propositions, has a certain pattern. Let us call the subject of the conclusion "S," the predicate of the conclusion "P," and the bridge term (or "middle") "M." Accordingly, this syllogism has the following pattern:

> All M is P
> All S is M
> ―――――――
> All S is P

It follows that when the arrangement of terms is such that (1) the subject of the conclusion (S) is the subject of the second premise, (2) the predicate of the conclusion (P) is the predicate of the first premise, and (3) the bridge term (M) is the subject of the first premise and the predicate of the second premise, then the conclusion is valid. In other words, merely from inspecting the pattern, without taking account of the "sense" of the propositions, we can tell automatically whether the syllogism is valid. For instance, the following set of propositions

> All higgledy-pigs are gobbledy-gooks
> All mubbley-moos are higgledy-pigs
> ───────────────────────────────
> All mubbley-moos are gobbledy-gooks

is a valid syllogism.

### ANALYSIS OF THIRD ARGUMENT

Corresponding to the *dictum de omni* is the *dictum de nullo:* Whatever is denied of a whole class must also be denied of each of its subclasses. This is illustrated by syllogism 3.

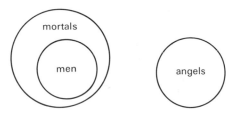

If the class of men is included in the class of mortals, and the class of mortals is excluded from the class of angels, then the class of men is also excluded from the class of angels. As can easily be seen, the conclusion of the syllogism follows from the premises. This syllogism is therefore valid.

### ANALYSIS OF FOURTH ARGUMENT

In syllogism 4, proposition 1, "All Athenians are Greeks," gives

Proposition 2, "Some men are Athenians," gives

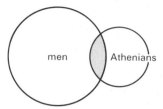

Here again we have to distinguish between what, on other grounds, we know, or think we know, and what the premise states. We may believe that *all* Athenians are men and want to diagram accordingly:

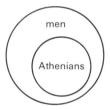

But the premise merely says that *some* men are Athenians, leaving open the possibility of there being men who are not Athenians (and Athenians who are not men). Hence the "men" circle and the "Athenian" circle must merely overlap as first diagrammed.

Now, putting propositions 1 and 2 together, we get

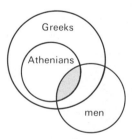

Since this is what proposition 3 asserts, the conclusion follows and the syllogism is valid.

### ANALYSIS OF FIFTH ARGUMENT

As for syllogism 5, we can represent proposition 1, "No Athenians are Spartans," as follows:

Proposition 2, "No Englishmen are Athenians," gives

Thus the syllogism gives us only three separate classes, with no information on the relations that may or may not exist between Englishmen and Spartans. No conclusion of any kind follows from these propositions, and the syllogism as stated is therefore invalid.

Since the syllogism is invalid not because of the particular terms that appear in it but because of its form, or pattern, we can formulate another rule to the following effect: Any syllogism that contains two negative premises will be invalid.

This syllogism can be used to illustrate the distinction already drawn between truth and validity. Proposition 3, "No Englishmen are Spartans," may or may not be true; syllogism tells us nothing about this. It tells us only whether the relation between the premises and the conclusion is valid. However, to assert the *truth* of the conclusion we must know not only that the argument is valid but also that the premises are true. This brings us to Aristotle's second main question, "How do we know whether the premises are true?"

### INTUITIVE TRUTHS

Each premise, of course, can be taken as the conclusion of an antecedent syllogism and other premises can be found from which (in accordance with the rules of logic) it may be validly drawn. If these antecedent premises are true, then the original premises (and *their* conclusion) will be true. But how do we know the antecedent premises are true? Though we can carry the process of syllogizing back as far as we like, syllogism, which is only correct deduction from premises, must be supplemented by some other intellectual operation. This Aristotle called "intuitive reason" (*nous*). It is the faculty, we may say, that knows without proof. That there are some things that are known without proof seemed clear to Aristotle. Otherwise we should have a hopeless regress of proofs of proofs of proofs, without ever being able to reach certainty. There must be, then, a starting point to syllogistic deduction—a point that is certain without proof.

Perhaps the simplest examples of intuitively known truths are the "law of identity," the "law of contradiction," and the "law of excluded middle."[15] These, however, we reason *with*, not *from*. Examples of truths we reason from are the axioms of Euclidean geometry, which Aristotle regarded as certain, but unproved, starting points. Whereas an ordinary proposition (All Greeks are mortal) requires a connecting link to mediate and unite subject and predicate (for example, the middle, "men"), axioms are propositions that require no such link, since subject and predicate are in themselves seen to be necessarily related—"The whole is greater than the part." As soon as we understand the meaning of the terms, we grasp the necessary truth of the assertion. No proof—no connecting middle—is required; instead, this unproved proposition serves as the basis for the proof of other propositions. Truths known self-evidently in this way exist, Aristotle thought, in every science.

If this be the nature of the first principles of science, how does intuitive reason grasp them? In a way analogous to that we have already found operating in the case of ordinary universals, that is, through perception. Yet, because these are the highest and most general of universals, it cannot be simple sense perception.

> Scientific knowledge through demonstration is impossible unless a man knows the primary immediate premises. But there are questions which might be raised in respect of the apprehension of these immediate premises: one might not only ask whether it is of the same kind as the apprehension of the conclusions, but also whether there is or is not scientific knowledge of both; or scientific knowledge of the latter, and of the former a different kind of knowledge; and, further, whether the developed states of knowledge are not innate but come to be in us, or are innate but at first unnoticed. Now it is strange if we possess them from birth; for it means that we possess apprehensions more accurate than demonstration and fail to notice them. If on the other hand we acquire them and do not previously possess them, how could we apprehend and learn without a basis of pre-existent knowledge? . . . So it emerges that neither can we possess them from birth, nor can they come to be in us if we are without knowledge of them to the extent of having no such developed state at all. Therefore we must possess a capacity of some sort, but not such as to rank higher in accuracy than these developed states. And this at least is an obvious characteristic of all animals, for they possess a congenital discriminative capacity which is called sense-perception. But though sense-perception is innate in all animals, in some the sense-impression comes to persist, in others it does not. So animals in which this persistence does not come to be have either no knowledge at all outside the act of perceiving, or no knowledge of objects of which no impression persists; animals in which it does come into being have perception and can continue

---

15 *Law of identity:* A is A; *law of contradiction:* A cannot both be B and not be B; *law of excluded middle:* A either is or is not B.

to retain the sense-impression in the soul: and when such persistence is frequently repeated a further distinction at once arises between those which out of the persistence of such sense-impressions develop a power of systematizing them and those which do not. So out of sense-perception comes to be what we call memory, and out of frequently repeated memories of the same thing develops experience; for a number of memories constitute a single experience. From experience again—i.e. from the universal now stabilized in its entirety within the soul, the one beside the many which is a single identity within them all—originate the skill of the craftsman and the knowledge of the man of science, skill in the sphere of coming to be and science in the sphere of being.

We conclude that these states of knowledge are neither innate in a determinate form, nor developed from other higher states of knowledge, but from sense-perception. It is like a rout in battle stopped by first one man making a stand and then another, until the original formation has been restored. The soul is so constituted as to be capable of this process. . . .

Thus it is clear that we must get to know the primary premisses by induction; for the method by which even sense-perception implants the universal is inductive. Now of the thinking states by which we grasp truth, some are unfailingly true, others admit of error—opinion, for instance, and calculation, whereas scientific knowing and intuition are always true: further, no other kind of thought except intuition is more accurate than scientific knowledge, whereas primary premisses are more knowable than demonstrations, and all scientific knowledge is discursive. From these considerations it follows that there will be no scientific knowledge of the primary premisses, and since except intuition nothing can be truer than scientific knowledge, it will be intuition that apprehends the primary premisses—a result which also follows from the fact that demonstration cannot be the originative source of demonstration, nor, consequently, scientific knowledge of scientific knowledge. If, therefore, it is the only other kind of true thinking except scientific knowing, intuition will be the originative source of scientific knowledge. And the originative source of science grasps the original basic premiss, while science as a whole is similarly related as originative source to the whole body of fact.[n]

The development of every science thus consists in a twofold movement of thought. First there is discovery. Study of the sense objects that lie within the sphere of the science leads us gradually to higher and higher universals. When the highest of all are reached, the process is reversed. Now comes exposition. Using the first principles thus discovered as a basis, we work out syllogisms that reveal the structural and logical relations holding between the various universals embedded in the particular objects that lie within the sphere of this science. This is Aristotle's version of that mysterious dialectic discussed by Plato in connection with the divided line. Comparison of these two accounts will throw a good deal of light on the differences, as well as the underlying similarities, of the two thinkers' philosophical positions.

### LIMITATIONS OF ARISTOTLE'S LOGIC

Aristotle's version, certainly, is not without difficulties—both with regard to the intuitive starting points and with regard to the syllogistic process that depends on them. As regards *nous*, it is far from clear that "the primary premises" it perceives have the character Aristotle attributed to them. For instance, "The whole is greater than the part" is certain, but only because it is a tautology. Or, to put this differently, there *is* a "bridge" after all: the meaning of the terms "whole," "greater," and "part." The word "part" means "less than whole." Hence the proposition is not making a necessary assertion about the nature of reality, as Aristotle supposed; it is merely reporting how, as a matter of fact, we happen to use the words "whole" and "part." If this is true of *all* Aristotle's allegedly self-evident primary premises, his vision of science as an absolutely necessary body of truths requires radical emendation. But it is hardly fair to blame Aristotle for not having seen this. Until Hume and Kant drew a firm distinction between analytic and synthetic propositions, almost all philosophers took for granted, with Aristotle, that a completely rational and deductive science of nature is possible.

Second, with regard to the process of deriving conclusions from premises, it can be said that Aristotle's fault was less one of commission than one of omission. He assumed that all propositions are of the subject-predicate form, that is, he assumed that whenever we judge we affirm (or deny) some property of a subject. We say S is (or has) P. That we do this in many judgments is clear, but it seems equally clear that many judgments do not have this "S is P" form. Suppose we reason as follows: A is larger than B. B is larger than C. Therefore A is larger than C. Everyone would agree that this argument is valid. It consists of three propositions—two premises and a conclusion. It also seems to have three and only three terms (A, B, C), and B seems to be the link between A and C. But is it a syllogism? No, for when we say, "A is larger than B," the verb "is" does not mean what it means when we say, "Socrates is a man." When we say, "A is larger than B," we do not mean that A belongs to the *class* "larger-than-B," but that A and B are related by the relation "is-larger-than." This difference is hidden by the fact that we use the same term, "is," in both judgments.

Thus Aristotle was mistaken in holding that the relation asserted in judgment is always attribution. Since many other relations are actually asserted, Aristotle's logical rules cover only a relatively small part of reasoning. Reasoning in mathematics, for instance, which is concerned with such relations as is-larger-than, is not covered satisfactorily by Aristotle's logic. However, to concentrate on the deficiencies in Aristotle's logic distorts the picture. Not only did Aristotle invent the science of logic, but much that he said on the subject is still valid—valid at least for some kinds of reasoning, though not (as he thought) for all.

# CHAPTER 7

# Aristotle: Ethics, Politics, Art

## Animal Drives and Practical Reason

So much for Aristotle's account of thought, the study of which has taken us from psychology to logic—from an investigation of thought's nature to an analysis of the criteria by which Aristotle believed we can determine both truth and validity. But man is not only a thinking animal; he is also a *behaving* animal. We must therefore reverse our steps and examine briefly the psychological bases of behavior as Aristotle saw them. When we have done so, we shall proceed, paralleling our study of thought, to the question of value—to the criteria by which behavior is to be evaluated. This will bring us to ethics and politics.

Although local movement is omnipresent on the earth, it is only with animals that we reach a level at which behavior, properly speaking, begins. According to Aristotle, just as there is a continuous process on the cognitive side from animal awareness to the highest levels of human intellection, so on the side of behavior there is a continuous process from animal appetite to the highest levels of ethical conduct.

## APPETITE

The soul of animals is characterized by two faculties, (a) the faculty of discrimination which is the work of thought and sense, and (b) the faculty of originating local movement. Sense and mind we have now sufficiently examined. Let us . . . ask what that is which originates local movement of the animal. . . .

That it is not the nutritive faculty is obvious; for this kind of movement is always for an end and is accompanied either by imagination or by appetite; for no animal moves except by compulsion unless it has an impulse towards or away from an object. Further, if it were the nutritive faculty, even plants would have been capable of originating such movement and would have possessed the organs necessary to carry it out. Similarly it cannot be the sensitive faculty either; for there are many animals which have sensibility but remain fast and immovable throughout their lives. . . .

Further, neither can the calculative faculty or what is called "mind" be the cause of such movement; for mind as speculative never thinks what is practicable, it never says anything about an object to be avoided or pursued, while this movement is always in something which is avoiding or pursuing an object. No, not even when it is aware of such an object does it at once enjoin pursuit or avoidance of it; e.g. the mind often thinks of something terrifying or pleasant without enjoining the emotion of fear. It is the heart that is moved (or in the case of a pleasant object some other part). Further, even when the mind does command and thought bids us pursue or avoid something, sometimes no movement is produced; we act in accordance with desire, as in the case of moral weakness. And, generally, we observe that the possessor of medical knowledge is not necessarily healing, which shows that something else is required to produce action in accordance with knowledge; the knowledge alone is not the cause. Lastly, appetite too is incompetent to account fully for movement; for those who successfully resist temptation have appetite and desire and yet follow mind and refuse to enact that for which they have appetite.

These two at all events appear to be sources of movement: appetite and mind (if one may venture to regard imagination as a kind of thinking; for many men follow their imaginations contrary to knowledge, and in all animals other than man there is no thinking or calcuation but only imagination).

Both of these then are capable of originating local movement, mind and appetite: (1) mind, that is, which calculates means to an end, i.e. mind practical (it differs from mind speculative in the character of its end); while (2) appetite is in every form of it relative to an end: for that which is the object of appetite is the stimulant of mind practical; and that which is last in the process of thinking is the beginning of the action. It follows that there is a justification for regarding these two as the sources of movement, i.e. appetite and practical thought; for the object of appetite starts a movement and as a result of that thought gives rise to movement, the object of appetite being to it a source of stimulation. So too when imagination originates movement, it necessarily involves appetite.

That which moves therefore is a single faculty and the faculty of appetite; for if there had been two sources of movement—mind and appetite—they would have produced movement in virtue of some common character. As it is mind is never found producing movement without appetite (for wish is a form of appetite; and when movement is produced according to calculation it is also according to wish), but appetite can originate movement contrary to calculation, for desire is a form of appetite. Now mind is always right, but appetite and imagination may be either right or wrong. That is why, though in any case it is the object of appetite which originates movement, this object may be either the real or the apparent good. . . .[a]

Objects are experienced by an animal, then, not simply as neutral things but also as good or bad, that is, as objects of pursuit or avoidance. Hence, intimately involved in an animal's perceptual awareness of an object is movement, either toward or away from it. Physiologically, what happens is this: The object (in this respect an unmoved mover) not only causes in the sense organ the change that we call seeing or hearing, but it also causes a change in the temperature of the heart. This change in turn effects changes in the adjacent parts of the body and thus, eventually, in the muscles that move our limbs. As Aristotle noted, even a small change at the center can produce considerable change at the circumference. The heart does not have to move very much in order to occasion large motions at the outer limits of the body.

This is the basic nature of all animal motion, regardless of how complex it may become. But, of course, as we advance from the lower to the higher animals, we find that behavior evolves into more articulate forms.

In the first place, the motion caused in the lower animals by a sense object is relatively stereotypic. The object has a kind of all-or-none effect: If the animal reacts at all, it is with a standardized response that occurs identically to fairly diverse stimuli. In higher forms the motion becomes more discriminatory and shows a finer adjustment to the specific nature of the object and its environment. This exactly parallels what happens in cognition, where in the higher species sensation shows a more sensitive adjustment to the nuances of the object perceived.

In the second place, for the lower animals the good is identical with pleasure, the bad with pain. For them there is no consideration other than a present satisfaction. This, of course, sometimes happens in man: "I want to drink, says appetite; this is drink, says sense, or imagination, or thought. Straightway I drink."[b] *Sometimes* I straightway drink, but not always.[1] Sometimes a thought intervenes, for instance, "This water is foul," or "This wine is poisoned," or—a still more complicated case—"Your need is greater than mine."

Human behavior is thus much more complicated than animal behavior. Man distinguishes between a real good and an apparent good, just as (cognitively) he distinguishes between what is true and what is false though it seems true. Pleasure, though good, is not identical with man's good. Again, since an animal cannot look beyond the pleasure (or pain) of the immediate situation, we would never call an animal incontinent. But a man may be incontinent because, being capable of looking beyond present pleasure, he is culpable if he fails to do so. The emergence of mind adds new dimensions to the kind of behavior an animal is capable of. By bringing us up to the level of true universals, in distinction from those merely rudimentary universals the sensitive soul is capable of, it enables us to look behind and before.

But Aristotle insisted that despite the great differences between human and animal behavior, these behaviors are basically alike. Indeed, one of the most striking features of his psychological theory is the way in which, within a single conceptual scheme, both the similarities and the differences can be described. Thus animal behavior (in distinction from the kinds of changes that occur in plants) is dependent on the existence in an animal of the sensitive soul, which perceives and remembers what it perceives. "An animal is capable of self-movement so far as it is appetitive, and it cannot be appetitive without images."[c] We have seen, when discussing cognition, that at the most elementary level past experiences are recalled and related to the present. These are the rudimentary universals that gradually, with growing cognitive power, develop (in man) into the full universals of scientific knowledge.

Appetition grows out of and depends on a similar power. Just as the dog recognizes the man (it is we who say and think "man," of course, not the dog) calling to him as the trainer-feeder-punisher of past experiences, so, when he is hungry, he turns up in the kitchen because (as Aristotle would have said) the image of food-in-kitchen from past experiences appears to him and moves him. Both in cognition and in behavior a present experience is mediated by other experiences not immediately present. To draw an artificially sharp distinction, in cognition the past is remembered; in behavior the future is anticipated (but anticipated, of course, only because of the remembered past). In man the dimensions of these memories and anticipations are greatly expanded, and with this expansion comes greater power but also greater complexity. And complexity makes problems. Whereas for an animal there is usually, in any given set of

---

1 This is a good example of the difference between pure cognition and desire. I might recognize this to be drink, but unless I *wanted* to I would not drink. An animal without desire (without, in this case, bodily needs) would never act, even if it were omniscient. On the other hand, desire alone will never lead to action. No matter how thirsty I am, I do not drink unless something (reason or sense) tells me, "This is drink." This is why Aristotle maintained that cognition and appetition are distinct faculties.

circumstances, only one thing to do, a man usually perceives alternatives. He must therefore choose. This means he must have criteria on which to base his choices. How is he to evaluate one of the perceived alternatives in comparison with another? How is he to estimate the value of present pleasure as compared with long-range interest? Because animals do not have to face these problems, they do not study ethics. But the intellect, which creates these problems by expanding the dimensions of human experience, provides us with the tools for solving them.

## Ethics

Ethics is the science of conduct (What are the criteria for the good life?) corresponding to logic (What are the criteria for correct thinking?). It differs from anthropology, which also studies the human value judgment, because it attempts to formulate norms for evaluating these judgments, whereas anthropology merely collects, describes, and generalizes about them. Anthropologists treat value judgments as neutrally as facts: Here are so-and-so many various value judgments; here are so-and-so many other products of human activity—pots, pans, houses, clothing. Into what classes do they fall? What genera can be observed? What are the definitions of these genera? The anthropologist deals with these problems exactly as the botanist deals with varieties of plants or the zoologist studies the species of animal life.

Ethics, of course, is based on anthropology—how could one proceed without empirical data? However, its purpose is not to classify the various objects that from time to time men have judged to be good, but to ascertain what the good *really* is. This goal, Aristotle allowed at the outset, can never be achieved with precision.

> Our discussion will be adequate if it has as much clearness as the subject-matter admits of, for precision is not to be sought for alike in all discussions, any more than in all the products of the crafts. Now fine and just actions, which political science investigates, admit of much variety and fluctuation of opinion, so that they may be thought to exist only by convention, and not by nature. And goods also give rise to a similar fluctuation because they bring harm to many people; for before now men have been undone by reason of their wealth, and others by reason of their courage. We must be content, then, in speaking of such subjects and with such premises to indicate the truth roughly and in outline, and in speaking about things which are only for the most part true and with premises of the same kind to reach conclusions that are no better. In the same spirit, therefore, should each type of statement be *received;* for it is the mark of an educated man to look for precision in each class of things just so far as the nature of the subject admits;

> it is evidently equally foolish to accept probable reasoning from a mathe-
> matician and to demand from a rhetorician scientific proofs. . . .[d]

Thus, to ask for precision in ethics is simply to reveal one's ignorance of the nature of science. An exact science is based, as we have seen, on principles whose truth is recognized in an intuitive act of intellect, and it consists in a set of syllogisms deduced from these principles. For Aristotle, geometry was the model science insofar as it consists in a set of theorems deduced from self-evident axioms.[2]

Ethics, in contrast, is based on opinions, on men's judgments about the good, not on self-evident and certain principles. Its conclusions, therefore, can never be definitive and certain.

This may make Aristotle sound rather like a Sophist. But Aristotle held that, in any particular set of circumstances in which a man faces alternatives, there is some act that is the right thing for that particular man to do in just those circumstances. So far he agreed with Plato: There is a truth-about-ethics. But unlike Plato, he thought we can never be sure that we have hit on the correct act.

Central to Aristotle's position here—and distinguishing him from Plato on the one hand and from the Sophists on the other—is the role he assigned to opinion. Plato, of course, had derogated opinion, and along with it anthropology. Opinion, in his view, should be replaced by knowledge. And knowledge is arrived at by means of dialectic. The Sophists, like Aristotle, had held that ethics is based on opinion, and they had inferred from this that ethical judgments are doomed to utter subjectivity and relativity. Aristotle thought he could show this inference to be invalid. The Sophists had supposed that, because one is dealing with opinions, one is somehow not dealing with reality. Plato had agreed. He differed from the Sophists only in holding that there is another and infinitely better authority—the Form of the Good.

But Aristotle pointed out that even in physics one deals with opinions—the opinions of other physicists. It is a poor scientist who ignores the work of his predecessors and attempts to start from scratch. True to this insight, Aristotle always began his own treatises on the special sciences with an analysis of the views of other scientists. Similarly, in ethics he rested not on the opinion of the vulgar multitude but on the opinion of the expert—the man who, like the scientist, has reflected on the facts of his field and who has had the background, the training, and the patience to discover at least some of the relations that hold there.

Every science, then, consists in the articulation of opinion and rests on the hope that the result will be an intellectual structure, a theory, that increasingly approximates reality. This is not a vain hope (as the Sophists had supposed) precisely because there is no absolute cleavage between the experience (or thought, or opinion) going on here in me and the objects out there that are

---

2 Aristotle failed to see that the reasoning in mathematics is not syllogistic. See p. 254.

independent of me. As we have seen, when I know or perceive the object out there, its form is realized here in me. Scepticism about the possibility of knowledge arises only if we first presuppose a radical cleavage between mind and its objects and then discover that, on this presupposition, knowledge is of our own state only, not of the object out there. Instead of accepting this consequence, we ought to conclude that our initial presupposition was false and that there is no radical cleavage. This is the whole basis of Aristotle's theory of knowledge, and it holds as much for the science of ethics as for the science of physics.

To summarize this rather involved discussion, ethics differs from physics and the other sciences, not in not being scientific (not in not being a body of knowledge about the real), but in not being precise.

And there is a second important difference between ethics and the other sciences. Physics is concerned simply with knowing the real, not with changing it. Though ethics is cognitive, it is also practical. It not only asks, "What is the good?" It also asks, "How can I be good?" The concern of ethics is not merely to evaluate men's judgments but also, having done so, to develop good habits, or, as we might say today, good "behavior patterns." Thus ethics is tied to psychology in several ways: (1) Ethics grows out of the need of choosing among the multiple courses of behavior that the human soul perceives as options at any given time. (2) The good, whatever it is, is the good *for* man and therefore can be ascertained only by discovering what man is. (3) The study of psychology is valuable in pedagogy and especially in the learning of good behavior and attitudes.

Aristotle began his chief treatise on ethics by relating this subject to his general metaphysical position. It follows from his version of the theory of forms that everything aims at some end; everything, that is to say, has a form that is that thing's purpose and fulfillment, the place where the thing can rest after having achieved whatever it had in it to become. This end, because it is the thing's fulfillment, is fairly called its "good." After all, the good for anything is what ultimately and truly satisfies that thing, and this final satisfaction can only be the thing's purpose, or end—the thing's form. Naturally, every activity has its own end (the activity of brushing one's teeth has for its end clean teeth), just as every substance has its own form. But just as every substance is also the matter out of which some higher substance develops, so every end is a means to a higher and more inclusive end (clean teeth are a means to good health). The higher and more inclusive the end, the better it is. All this, Aristotle thought, applies as much to simple as to complex things, as much to unconscious as to conscious fulfillment. But in his *Ethics* Aristotle was of course concerned primarily with man, for whom the end, whatever it is, is complex, and for whom it is achieved by deliberation and conscious planning.

It should be noted that Aristotle assumed what many people today would question, namely, that there is *one* ultimate end for man. It is no problem, Aristotle thought, to identify this final end verbally. Everyone agrees that it can be called "happiness." The only problem is to determine what happiness is. On this question there are many opinions. Aristotle began, characteristically, by examining some of the more plausible.

## THE GOOD

Every art and every inquiry, and similarly every action and pursuit, is thought to aim at some good; and for this reason the good has rightly been declared to be that at which all things aim. . . . Now, as there are many actions, arts, and sciences, their ends also are many; the end of the medical art is health, that of shipbuilding a vessel, that of strategy victory, that of economics wealth. But where such arts fall under a single capacity—as bridle-making and the other arts concerned with the equipment of horses fall under the art of riding, and this and every military action under strategy, in the same way other arts fall under yet others—in all of these the ends of the master arts are to be preferred to all the subordinate ends; for it is for the sake of the former that the latter are pursued. It makes no difference whether the activities themselves are the ends of the actions, or something else apart from the activities, as in the case of the sciences just mentioned.

If, then, there is some end of the things we do, which we desire for its own sake (everything else being desired for the sake of this), and if we do not choose everything for the sake of something else (for at that rate the process would go on to infinity, so that our desire would be empty and vain), clearly this must be the good and the chief good. Will not the knowledge of it, then, have a great influence on life? Shall we not, like archers who have a mark to aim at, be more likely to hit upon what is right? . . .

[Unfortunately, opinions differ about] what is the highest of all goods achievable by action. Verbally there is very general agreement; for both the general run of men and people of superior refinement say that it is happiness, and identify living well and doing well with being happy; but with regard to what happiness is they differ, and the many do not give the same account as the wise. For the former think it is some plain and obvious thing, like pleasure, wealth, or honour; they differ, however, from one another—and often even the same man identifies it with different things, with health when he is ill, with wealth when he is poor; but, conscious of their ignorance, they admire those who proclaim some great ideal that is above their comprehension. Now some thought that apart from these many goods there is another which is self-subsistent and causes the goodness of all these as well. To examine all the opinions that have been held were perhaps somewhat fruitless; enough to examine those that are most prevalent or that seem to be arguable. . . .

To judge from the lives that men lead, most men, and men of the most vulgar type, seem (not without some ground) to identify the good, or happiness, with pleasure; which is the reason why they love the life of enjoyment. . . . A consideration of the prominent types of life shows that people of superior refinement and of active disposition identify happiness with honour; for this is, roughly speaking, the end of the political life. But it seems too superficial to be what we are looking for, since it is thought to depend on

those who bestow honour rather than on him who receives it, but the good
we divine to be something proper to a man and not easily taken from him.
Further, men seem to pursue honour in order that they may be assured of
their goodness; at least it is by men of practical wisdom that they seek to
be honoured, and among those who know them, and on the ground of their
virtue; clearly, then, according to them, at any rate, virtue is better. . . .

But even this appears somewhat incomplete; for possession of virtue seems
actually compatible with being asleep, or with lifelong inactivity, and, further,
with the greatest sufferings and misfortunes; but a man who was living so
no one would call happy, unless he were maintaining a thesis at all costs.
. . . Third comes the contemplative life, which we shall consider later.[3]

The life of money-making is one undertaken under compulsion, and wealth
is evidently not the good we are seeking; for it is merely useful and for the
sake of something else. . . .

We had perhaps better consider the universal good[4] and discuss thoroughly
what is meant by it, although such an inquiry is made an uphill one by the
fact that the Forms have been introduced by friends of our own. Yet it would
perhaps be thought to be better, indeed to be our duty, for the sake of
maintaining the truth even to destroy what touches us closely, especially as
we are philosophers or lovers of wisdom; for while both are dear, piety
requires us to honour truth above our friends. . . .

And one might ask the question, what in the world they *mean* by "a thing
itself," if (as is the case) in "man himself" and in a particular man the account
of man is one and the same. . . .

Let us separate then things good in themselves from things useful, and
consider whether the former are called good by reference to a single Idea.
What sort of goods would one call good in themselves? Is it those that are
pursued even when isolated from others, such as intelligence, sight, and
certain pleasures and honours? Certainly, if we pursue these also for the sake
of something else, yet one would place them among things good in themselves.
Or is nothing other than the Idea of good good in itself? In that case the
Form will be empty. But if the things we have named are also things good
in themselves, the account of the good will have to appear as something
identical in them all, as that of whiteness is identical in snow and in white
lead. But of honour, wisdom, and pleasure, just in respect of their goodness,
the accounts are distinct and diverse. The good, therefore, is not some
common element answering to one Idea. . . .

Let us again return to the good we are seeking, and ask what it can be.
It seems different in different actions and arts; it is different in medicine,
in strategy, and in the other arts likewise. What then is the good of each?
Surely that for whose sake everything else is done. . . .

So the argument has by a different course reached the same point; but
we must try to state this even more clearly. Since there are evidently more
than one end, and we choose some of these (e.g. wealth, flutes, and in general

3 [See pp. 285–86—author.]
4 [Here Aristotle takes up, along with other views about the nature of the highest good, the
Platonic thesis that there is an abstract form "good"—author.]

instruments) for the sake of something else, clearly not all ends are final ends; but the chief good is evidently something final. Therefore, if there is only one final end, this will be what we are seeking, and if there are more than one, the most final of these will be what we are seeking. Now we call that which is in itself worthy of pursuit more final than that which is worthy of pursuit for the sake of something else, and that which is never desirable for the sake of something else more final than the things that are desirable both in themselves and for the sake of that other thing, and therefore we call final without qualification that which is always desirable in itself and never for the sake of something else.

Now such a thing happiness, above all else, is held to be; for this we choose always for itself and never for the sake of something else, but honour, pleasure, reason, and every virtue we choose indeed for themselves (for if nothing resulted from them we should still choose each of them), but we choose them also for the sake of happiness, judging that by means of them we shall be happy. Happiness, on the other hand, no one chooses for the sake of these, nor, in general, for anything other than itself. . . .

Happiness, then, is something final and self-sufficient, and is the end of action.

Presumably, however, to say that happiness is the chief good seems a platitude, and a clearer account of what it is is still desired: This might perhaps be given, if we could first ascertain the function of man. For just as for a flute-player, a sculptor, or any artist, and, in general, for all things that have a function or activity, the good and the "well" is thought to reside in the function, so it would seem to be for man, if he has a function. Have the carpenter, then, and the tanner certain functions or activities, and has man none? Is he born without a function? Or as eye, hand, foot, and in general each of the parts evidently has a function, may one lay it down that man similarly has a function apart from all these? What then can this be? Life seems to be common even to plants, but we are seeking what is peculiar to man. Let us exclude, therefore, the life of nutrition and growth. . . . And, as "life of the rational element" also has two meanings, we must state that life in the sense of activity is what we mean; for this seems to be the more proper sense of the term. Now if the function of man is an activity of soul which follows or implies a rational principle, and if we say "a so-and-so" and "a good so-and-so" have a function which is the same in kind, e.g. a lyre-player and a good lyre-player, and so without qualification in all cases, eminence in respect of goodness being added to the name of the function (for the function of a lyre-player is to play the lyre, and that of a good lyre-player is to do so well): if this is the case (and we state the function of man to be a certain kind of life, and this to be an activity or actions of the soul implying a rational principle, and the function of a good man to be the good and noble performance of these, and if any action is well performed when it is performed in accordance with the appropriate excel- lence: if this is the case), human good turns out to be activity of soul in accordance with virtue, and if there are more than one virtue, in accordance with the best and most complete.

But we must add "in a complete life." For one swallow does not make a summer, nor does one day; and so too one day, or a short time, does not make a man blessed and happy. . . .ᵉ

We have already seen that the term "virtue" had a much broader meaning for the Greeks than it has in the Christian tradition.[5] For Aristotle, as for Plato, anything was virtuous when it was performing its function, and happiness consisted in efficient and fruitful activity.

Aristotle proceeded, however, to give this old Greek insight new meaning by interpreting it in terms of his basic metaphysical concepts. What would otherwise have been simply an isolated and relatively insignificant insight about morality was deepened through being related to his thought about other aspects of the universe. And, conversely, the metaphysical concepts were enriched by being given added—in this instance, ethical—content. Without concrete, empirical application they might have been interesting and ingenious ideas, but they would have remained empty and abstract, and so useless. This is the value of *system*. Insofar as apparently diverse and isolated fields of knowledge can be interpreted, without distortion, in terms of a single conceptual scheme, these various fields gain significance from the interrelatedness thus revealed.

Measured from this point of view, Aristotle's achievement was very great. He defined a relatively few basic concepts—form, matter, actuality, potentiality—which he then used to interpret in a meaningful and unified way the phenomena of physics, psychology, ethics, and politics. His world was one harmonious system. By comparison, our modern intellectual world is a collection of disparate and independent areas of knowledge. For reasons that we shall have to go into later, we have yet to find concepts as pervasive and as unifying for the world of *our* experience as were Aristotle's for the world of *his* experience. Metaphysics, which ought to be the science of such unifying concepts, hardly exists today, and in many quarters the attempt to discover such concepts has been abandoned.

### HAPPINESS, FUNCTION, AND FORM

For Aristotle, then, applying the now familiar thesis that every individual thing is a composite of form and matter, anything is happy to the extent that it is performing the function—actualizing the form—for which it was designed by nature or by art. In his view, the problem of discovering how any particular kind of thing can be happy boils down, therefore, to the problem of discovering what function that kind of thing has. This is identical with the question, "What is that thing's form?" or "What is the end or purpose that is working itself out in this particular kind of substance?"

This is a cognitive inquiry: A thing's form is an objective fact about the world to be ascertained by scientific analysis. Hence (to adopt a modern formulation

5 See p. 167.

of an important distinction), for Aristotle ethics was cognitive, not emotive, in character. That is, an ethical judgment (for instance, "Murder is wrong") is a statement about facts (of course, it may not be a statement of fact, for it may be mistaken), not merely an expression of the speaker's attitude of approval or disapproval.

To ascertain the form (and so the good) of man-made objects is often easy. Take an ax, for example. Simple inspection shows that its purpose is to cut wood. And if, for any reason, we are doubtful about its purpose, we have only to inquire of its maker. But with regard to complex natural substances we need the expert assistance of the scientist in order to discover the universal embedded in the particular. Thus a problem for the botanist is to define those generic properties that distinguish the oak from other trees. An adequate definition would be an account of the form that Aristotle held to be in-dwelling in the acorn and working its way to fruition in the oak. Of course, acorns do not experience pleasure as they grow into oak trees. But the principle is the same in all substances, including animals and men. At every level in the hierarchy of substances, some form is capable of being realized by means of motions specific to that form (falling, rising, digesting, and so forth). To the extent that these motions actually occur and form is thereby realized, they are virtues specific to the particular substance in question. In a word, if the acorn were endowed with consciousness (with a rational, instead of a merely nutritive, soul), it would experience various states of feeling as it grew. Insofar as the conditions of its life and its environment enabled it to grow into an oak tree—insofar, in other words, as it fulfilled its purpose—it would be happy. Insofar as the conditions of life prevented or frustrated this fulfillment, it would experience unhappiness. The oak tree, however, is unconscious. And because it is unconscious, how it grows does not depend on plans or decisions that it makes. With consciousness (the sensitive soul) come feeling and awareness of feeling. With mind (the rational soul) comes the ability to make a plan and to act on it. Because at this level we know what our end is and have the capacity to organize our environment to promote this end, the study of ethics and politics at this level is not only possible but also worthwhile.

But with consciousness also come complexity and the multiplication of possibilities. Neither a plant nor an animal has choices. An animal's behavior issues directly in (that is, is felt as) pleasure or pain, depending on whether its present purpose is fulfilled. Pleasure, therefore, is at this level identical with the good. For man, however, as we saw in the discussion of the psychology of desire, there is always a distinction between the good and the pleasurable, between the good and the seemingly good. Since a man always has options, it follows that some of the paths open to him are better, others worse, and one of them best. He must try to choose wisely just because of the existence of such alternatives. Pleasure is the name we give to immediate, short-range satisfaction, which is all that is open to animals. Happiness is the name for that longer-range, more complete, more stable satisfaction that reason gives men the possibility of achieving, but whose achievement it at the same time makes more difficult by in order to become good, since otherwise our inquiry would have been of no use), we must examine the nature of actions, namely how we ought to do them; for these determine also the nature of the states of character that are produced. . . . Now, that we must act according to the right rule is a common principle and must be assumed—it will be discussed later, i.e. both what the right rule is, and how it is related to the other virtues. . . .

First, then, let us consider this, that it is the nature of such things to be destroyed by defect and excess, as we see in the case of strength and of health (for to gain light on things imperceptible we must use the evidence of sensible things); both excessive and defective exercise destroys the strength, and similarly drink or food which is above or below a certain amount destroys the health, while that which is proportionate both produces and increases and preserves it. So too is it, then, in the case of temperance and courage and the other virtues. . . .

Temperance and courage, then, are destroyed by excess and defect, and preserved by the mean.$^f$

Here again we see the power of system at work.[6] The notion that virtue is a mean is anything but a novelty—Aristotle merely took over the old Greek notion of *sophrosyne* (moderation), which we have encountered from the very start in Homer and the other poets. Indeed, how, Aristotle would have asked, could a sound ethical theory be completely new? Ethical theory always begins with the opinions of men. What Aristotle did was to give the opinions new significance by interpreting them in the light of his basic metaphysical ideas. This Plato had already done in terms of *his* conceptual scheme: In the *Republic*, for instance, moderation becomes justice, the all-inclusive virtue. In his turn, Aristotle proceeded to take the virtues accepted by the ordinary decent citizen of his day—courage, temperance, justice, pride, magnanimity—and show (1) that each is an activity of practical reason and (2) that each operates efficiently (virtuously) only when it is in a mean between excess and deficiency.

The following table gives the chief activities that Aristotle believed to fall under practical reason:

| ACTIVITY | VICE (*Excess*) | VIRTUE (*Mean*) | VICE (*Deficit*) |
|---|---|---|---|
| Facing death | Too much fear (i.e., Cowardice) | Right amount of fear (i.e., Courage) | Too little fear (i.e., Foolhardiness) |
| Bodily actions (eating, drinking, sex, etc.) | Profligacy | Temperance | No name for this state, but it may be called "insensitivity" |
| Giving money | Prodigality | Liberality | Illiberality |
| Large-scale giving | Vulgarity | Magnificence | Meanness |
| Claiming honors | Vanity | Pride | Humility |
| Social intercourse | Obsequiousness | Friendliness | Sulkiness |
| According honors | Injustice | Justice | Injustice |
| Retribution for wrongdoing | Injustice | Justice | Injustice |

6 See p. 235.

presenting men with alternatives undreamed of by the relatively simple sensitive soul. The possibility of more ignominious failure than any animal is capable of is the risk the rational soul must run for the possibility of much greater fulfillment.

## PRACTICAL REASON

We have then to ask, "What is man's end?" It is easy to reply, as Aristotle does at the end of the long passage just quoted, "It is life in accordance with a rational principle." But what, exactly, does this mean? Aristotle devoted the remainder of the *Ethics* to answering this question. He began, as we would expect after our study of his psychology, by distinguishing between (1) reason as a cognitive faculty and (2) reason as a practical faculty. There are in us two powers, one that understands the world and one that desires and acts in accordance with what is understood. For example, there is a faculty that desires drink and a faculty that says, "This is drink." That these are separate faculties seemed to Aristotle clear, since a man can know "This is drink" without drinking and can be thirsty without knowing how to satisfy his desire. Though they are connected, each of these faculties has its own special activities, its own special modes of fulfillment. Aristotle proceeded to examine first the faculty of practical reason and its end. What are the activities special to it and what is their virtue, that is, when and under what conditions are they operating at their best?

> By human virtue we mean not that of the body but that of the soul; and happiness also we call an activity of soul. But if this is so, clearly the student of politics must know somehow the facts about soul, as the man who is to heal the eyes or the body as a whole must know about the eyes or the body. . . .
>
> Some things are said about it, adequately enough, even in the discussions outside our school, and we must use these; e.g. that one element in the soul is irrational and one has a rational principle. . . .
>
> That the irrational element is in some sense persuaded by a rational principle is indicated also by the giving of advice and by all reproof and exhortation. And if this element also must be said to have a rational principle, that which has a rational principle (as well as that which has not) will be twofold, one subdivision having it in the strict sense and in itself, and the other having a tendency to obey as one does one's father.
>
> Virtue too is distinguished into kinds in accordance with this difference; for we say that some of the virtues are intellectual and others moral, philosophic wisdom and understanding and practical wisdom being intellectual, liberality and temperance moral. . . .
>
> Virtue, then, being of two kinds, intellectual and moral, intellectual virtue in the main owes both its birth and its growth to teaching (for which reason it requires experience and time), while moral virtue comes about as a result of habit. . . .
>
> Since, then, the present inquiry does not aim at theoretical knowledge like the others (for we are inquiring not in order to know what virtue is, but

Aristotle's analysis of all these virtues is too long to quote. It is possible, however, to get a fair idea of both his method and his general point of view by examining his accounts of courage and of pride. First, as for courage:

That it is a mean with regard to feelings of fear and confidence has already been made evident; and plainly the things we fear are terrible things, and these are, to speak without qualification, evils; for which reason people even define fear as expectation of evil. . . . Nor is a man a coward if he fears insult to his wife and children or envy or anything of the kind; nor brave if he is confident when he is about to be flogged. With what sort of terrible things, then, is the brave man concerned? Surely with the greatest; for no one is more likely than he to stand his ground against what is awe-inspiring. Now death is the most terrible of all things; for it is the end, and nothing is thought to be any longer either good or bad for the dead. But the brave man would not seem to be concerned even with death in *all* circumstances, e.g. at sea or in disease. In what circumstances, then? Surely in the noblest. Now such deaths are those in battle; for these take place in the greatest and noblest danger. And these are correspondingly honoured in city-states and at the courts of monarchs. Properly, then, he will be called brave who is fearless in face of a noble death, and of all emergencies that involve death; and the emergencies of war are in the highest degree of this kind. . . . Now the brave man is as dauntless as man may be. Therefore, while he will fear even the things that are not beyond human strength, he will face them as he ought and as the rule directs, for honour's sake; for this is the end of virtue. But it is possible to fear these more, or less, and again to fear things that are not terrible as if they were. Of the faults that are committed one consists in fearing what one should not, another in fearing as we should not, another in fearing when we should not, and so on; and so too with respect to the things that inspire confidence. The man, then, who faces and who fears the right things and from the right motive, in the right way and at the right time, and who feels confidence under the corresponding conditions, is brave; for the brave man feels and acts according to the merits of the case and in whatever way the rule directs. . . .

The coward, the rash man, and the brave man, then, are concerned with the same objects but are differently disposed towards them; for the first two exceed and fall short, while the third holds the middle, which is the right, position; and rash men are precipitate, and wish for dangers beforehand but draw back when they are in them, while brave men are keen in the moment of action, but quiet beforehand.

As we have said, then, courage is a mean with respect to things that inspire confidence or fear, in the circumstances that have been stated; and it chooses or endures things because it is noble to do so, or because it is base not to do so. But to die to escape from poverty or love or anything painful is not the mark of a brave man, but rather of a coward; for it is softness to fly from what is troublesome, and such a man endures death not because it is noble but to fly from evil.

Courage, then, is something of this sort, but the name is also applied to five other kinds. (1) First comes the courage of the citizen-soldier; for this is most like true courage. Citizen-soldiers seem to face dangers because of the penalties imposed by the laws and the reproaches they would otherwise incur, and because of the honours they win by such action; and therefore those peoples seem to be bravest among whom cowards are held in dishonour and brave men in honour. . . . This kind of courage is most like to that which we described earlier, because it is due to virtue; for it is due to shame and to desire of a noble object (i.e. honour) and avoidance of disgrace, which is ignoble. . . .

(2) Experience with regard to particular facts is also thought to be courage. . . . Professional soldiers exhibit it in the dangers of war; for there seem to be many empty alarms in war, of which these have had the most comprehensive experience; therefore they seem brave, because the others do not know the nature of the facts. Again, their experience makes them most capable in attack and in defence, since they can use their arms and have the kind that are likely to be best both for attack and for defence; therefore they fight like armed men against unarmed or like trained athletes against amateurs; for in such contests too it is not the bravest men that fight best, but those who are strongest and have their bodies in the best condition. Professional soldiers turn cowards, however, when the danger puts too great a strain on them and they are inferior in numbers and equipment; for they are the first to fly, while citizen-forces die at their posts. . . .

(3) Passion is also sometimes reckoned as courage; those who act from passion, like wild beasts rushing at those who have wounded them, are thought to be brave, because brave men also are passionate; for passion above all things is eager to rush on danger. . . .

Men, then, as well as beasts, suffer pain when they are angry, and are pleased when they exact their revenge; those who fight for these reasons, however, are pugnacious but not brave; for they do not act for honour's sake nor as the rule directs, but from strength of feeling; they have, however, something akin to courage.

(4) Nor are sanguine people brave; for they are confident in danger only because they have conquered often and against many foes. Yet they closely resemble brave men, because both are confident . . . (Drunken men also behave in this way; they become sanguine). . . .

(5) People who are ignorant of the danger also appear brave, and they are not far removed from those of a sanguine temper, but are inferior inasmuch as they have no self-reliance while these have. Hence also the sanguine hold their ground for a time; but those who have been deceived about the facts fly if they know or suspect that these are different from what they supposed. . . .[g]

[So much for courage. As for pride, it] seems even from its name to be concerned with great things; what sort of great things, is the first question we must try to answer. . . . Now the man is thought to be proud who thinks himself worthy of great things, being worthy of them; for he who does so beyond his deserts is a fool, but no virtuous man is foolish or silly. . . . He who is worthy of little and thinks himself worthy of little is temperate, but not proud; for pride implies greatness, as beauty implies a good-sized body, and little people may be neat and well-proportioned but cannot be beautiful.

On the other hand, he who thinks himself worthy of great things, being unworthy of them, is vain; though not every one who thinks himself worthy of more than he really is worthy of is vain. The man who thinks himself worthy of less than he is really worthy of is unduly humble, whether his deserts be great or moderate, or his deserts be small but his claims yet smaller. . . . The proud man, then, is an extreme in respect of the greatness of his claims, but a mean in respect of the rightness of them; for he claims what is in accordance with his merits, while the others go to excess or fall short.

If, then, he deserves and claims great things, and above all the greatest things, he will be concerned with one thing in particular. . . . And this is honour; that is surely the greatest of external goods. Honours and dishonours, therefore, are the objects with respect to which the proud man is as he should be. . . .

Pride, then, seems to be a sort of crown of the virtues; for it makes them greater, and it is not found without them. Therefore it is hard to be truly proud; for it is impossible without nobility and goodness of character. It is chiefly with honours and dishonours, then, that the proud man is concerned; and at honours that are great and conferred by good men he will be moderately pleased, thinking that he is coming by his own or even less than his own; for there can be no honour that is worthy of perfect virtue, yet he will at any rate accept it since they have nothing greater to bestow on him; but honour from casual people and on trifling grounds he will utterly despise, since it is not this that he deserves, and dishonour too, since in his case it cannot be just. . . . Hence proud men are thought to be disdainful. . . .

He does not run into trifling dangers, nor is he fond of danger, because he honours few things; but he will face great dangers, and when he is in danger he is unsparing of his life, knowing that there are conditions on which life is not worth having. And he is the sort of man to confer benefits, but he is ashamed of receiving them; for the one is the mark of a superior, the other of an inferior. . . .

Nor is he given to admiration; for nothing to him is great. Nor is he mindful of wrongs; for it is not the part of a proud man to have a long memory, especially for wrongs, but rather to overlook them. Nor is he a gossip; for he will speak neither about himself nor about another, since he cares not to be praised nor for others to be blamed; nor again is he given to praise; and for the same reason he is not an evil-speaker, even about his enemies, except from haughtiness. . . .

Further, a slow step is thought proper to the proud man, a deep voice, and a level utterance; for the man who takes few things seriously is not likely to be hurried, nor the man who thinks nothing great to be excited, while a shrill voice and a rapid gait are the results of hurry and excitement.

Such, then, is the proud man. . . .[h]

## ETHICAL IDEALS

Perhaps the first thing that strikes us about these analyses is the extent to which Aristotle's list of virtues is relative to the conditions of Greek society.

Living in an environment of city-state communities that were almost continuously at war with one another but that had no professional military class as we have today, Aristotle naturally thought of courage in terms of a man's conduct on the battlefield, and the conduct of the citizen-soldier rather than of the professional soldier. Again, Aristotle's prideful man, whom he took as a model of virtue and nobility, strikes most of us today as a stuffed shirt. Similarly, with regard to his concern with "large-scale giving," we are likely to feel that his "magnificence" is ostentation and so to rate this Aristotelian virtue as a vice. Aristotle's view simply reflects a culture that concentrated attention on the good life for the well-born and wealthy Athenian aristocrat.

This should not surprise us. In the first place, Aristotle himself insisted that ethics begins with opinion, and obviously his ethical theory had to deal with the opinions of Greeks of the fourth century B.C., not with those of twentieth-century Americans. In the second place, that ethical ideals vary with changing cultural patterns is hardly news today in view of the immense amount of information sociologists and anthropologists have accumulated on the subject of cultural relativism.

How would modern views on this subject have been received by Aristotle? Despite his willingness to start from opinion, there is some reason to believe that he would not have greeted the notion of cultural relativism with a glad cry. On this whole question Aristotle was rather ambivalent. Since he seems to have had no idea how much opinions actually vary, and since he was much too ready to identify "expert" opinion with what was in fact only the view of the social class with which he sympathized, he never faced the issue of relativity squarely. As a result, he tended to write as if he believed himself to be laying down ethical ideals for all societies for all time.

Nevertheless, Aristotle certainly would not have been as unsympathetic to the idea of cultural relativism as Plato would have been. Plato, holding to the thesis that separate ethical forms exist, would certainly have maintained that ethical values are what they are for all time, just as the interior angles of a triangle equal 180° everywhere for all eternity. Accordingly, in his view, to just the extent that ethical (or mathematical) judgments reflect cultural differences and deviate from these eternal norms, they are false. The whole problem for Plato was simply to find these norms and to measure existing institutions by them. To admit that such absolute norms do not exist would have seemed to him a complete surrender to the Sophists' contention that every man (and every culture) is his own measure.

Since Aristotle held that the forms are not separate but embedded in their particulars, he could take a much less extreme position. There is, he would have said, an ideal of what an oak tree ought to be, but what this ideal is, is only ascertainable by examining what acorns actually grow up to be. When we do examine how they grow and what they become, we find not a single, identical type, "oak," but a number of varieties. Each of these species is a fulfillment of the ideal oak, but each is a *different* fulfillment because of, among other factors, the different environment in which it has grown. To admit variation is, therefore, not necessarily to surrender to the Sophists. Though there is an ideal of what man has it in him to be, this ideal is not "separate" from the variety of fulfillments found in differing cultures. Just as different physical environments produce different trees that are, nevertheless, all oaks, so different cultural and physical environments produce different ethical ideals that are, nevertheless, all human.

Aristotle actually worked all this out in detail in his *Politics*, in which he contrasts the absolutely ideal state (on Plato's model) with various best-possible-under-such-and-such-conditions states, in each of which the good life has its own form of political organization, depending on the nature of the social and physical environment. Hence it was by no means necessary for him to set up an absolutely ideal set of ethical values. On the contrary, taking into account both his temperament and his general metaphysical position, there was every reason for him to adopt a similar position with regard to ethics and to view the variety of ethical systems as reflecting the different ways in which the form "man" fulfills itself in differing circumstances.

## THE DOCTRINE OF THE MEAN

This, indeed, is the central meaning of the doctrine of the mean. Aristotle did not advocate a fence-sitting, play-it-safe mediocrity, which the mean has sometimes been misinterpreted as signifying. His view was rather an attempt to mediate between a narrow, un-Greek repudiation of "nature" and the Sophistic insistence on nature as the primary and exclusive standard of conduct. A Christian ascetic, for example, believes that the "natural" appetites are always bad and that they should, if possible, be suppressed. A Thrasymachus or a Callicles, on the other hand, believes in the satisfaction of *every* appetite, anywhere, any time. Aristotle's view is that the "rightness" of the satisfaction depends on the milieu, as it were, of the desire—on the time, the place, the circumstances, the who-you-are, the who-he-is, and so on. There is a right amount of money for me to give this year to such-and-such a charity. What this amount is depends on my income this year, the number of dependents I have, the immediate needs of this particular organization (which vary, of course, from year to year), and so on. That there is no single ideal amount appropriate to give under all circumstances everyone would surely allow. Aristotle simply held this to be typical of all moral situations. What is right for a man to do *always* depends on his milieu, and this varies from individual to individual and from occasion to occasion.

Thus, whereas Plato held there is a "the" right thing to do, a "the" good to be realized, and whereas the Sophists held there is no objective right or good at all, Aristotle maintained there is a right-relative-to-me, a good-for-me-now-in-this-set-of-conditions. It is characteristic of the difference between Plato and Aristotle that Plato believed his universal, eternal good to be knowable by reason, whereas Aristotle held his individual, variable good to be knowable only in perception: "It is no easy task to find the middle, e.g. to find the middle of a circle. . . . So, too, any one can get angry—that is easy—or give or spend money; but to do this to the right person, to the right extent, at the right time, with the right motive, and in the right way, *that* is not for every one, nor is it easy. . . . Such things depend on particular facts, and the decision rests with perception."[i]

Hence, though the amount of money to give to charity is known only in perception, and though one may easily fail to perceive it, there is for each donor a right amount to give this year to his charity. If he gives more or less he has missed the mark. Since moral virtue is thus variable (even though objective), we can say no more about it universally than that it lies in a mean between extremes that err through either excess or deficiency.

So far only Aristotle's account of the nature of a morally good *act* has been discussed, but he emphasized equally the moral significance of motive—what may be called the internality of the moral act. There are, in fact, two sides to every moral situation—the change brought about in the state of affairs (for example, the transfer of money from my banking account to that of the Red Cross) and the reason this change is made. Most moral theorists have neglected one or the other of these factors; surely Aristotle was correct in insisting on both.

Let us return to Aristotle's account of courage.[7] After describing the external shape and character of a courageous act (standing in the face of the enemy), Aristotle made a careful analysis of the internal factors involved in "true" courage. On many occasions a man may face the enemy in a way that looks courageous but is not really so. For his act is not truly courageous unless what moves him to face the enemy is the thought that it is "noble to do so and base not to do so."

Aristotle listed five types of pseudo-courage, that is, five kinds of standing-in-the-face-of-the-enemy that qualify externally to be called courage but that lack the essential quality of truly courageous motivation. These five kinds of pseudo-courage (defined in terms of the actual motive operating to cause standing in the face of the enemy) are the pseudo-courage of (1) the citizen-soldier, (2) the professional soldier, (3) the man of a passionate nature, (4) the man of an optimistic nature, and (5) the ignorant man. A man of the first type shows pseudo-courage when he stands and faces the enemy because of what his friends back home will say or because he wants a medal or a laurel wreath—not bad motives at all, Aristotle held, but not as good as the motive of true courage. The second pseudo-courage is that of the professional soldier, who has had enough experience of warfare to know the situation is not as dangerous as it appears to be. But when it *is* dangerous, this type of man flees. Similarly, the choleric man holds his ground, but only because rage has driven fear temporarily from

---

7 See pp. 269–71.

his heart. When his anger subsides he too will run. And so on for the remaining two types listed by Aristotle: At each successive level there is an inferior motive—inferior because it results in less stable conduct. The courage of the citizen-soldier (since it has a noble object, honor) is most like true courage; most unlike true courage is the courage of ignorance, which stems from no habit of facing danger but merely from a failure to recognize that those "curious whistling noises are bullets."

The only completely stable behavior, however, is that which issues from a courageous motive. The desirable act (in this case, courage) may occasionally and, as it were, accidentally issue from some other attitude, but if we want to be able to count on people to perform courageous acts regularly, we must cultivate the correct attitude in them. This can be done if we realize the relation between conduct and pleasure. Most people who do base acts do them because they are pleasant; they shrink from noble ones because they are painful. What we must do, then, is to educate men, starting when they are children, to take pleasure in noble acts and to experience pain in doing bad ones.[8] Pleasure and pain are indeed the sole considerations for young children, as they are for animals. We must, therefore, build up a habit of courage (or truthfulness, or justice, or whatever behavior we regard as desirable) in the child by arranging situations in which it will be pleasant for him to act courageously and painful for him to act otherwise. In this way, over a period of time, a certain pattern of responses to situations will be built up that will issue in courageous acts even when the situation alters.[9] The man so educated will learn to find pleasure in being courageous, not merely in the kind word or the lollypop he received for being courageous as a child. "In educating the young we steer them by the rudders of pleasure and pain. . . ."

About such a man it will be said that "it is his nature" to be courageous. But to say that he is naturally courageous (that his externally courageous acts flow from an internally courageous attitude) does not mean that he was born with courage inside him waiting to be released. This, Aristotle thought, is nonsense. The "naturally" courageous man was born with what all men are born with, namely, a capacity of a certain kind, a potentiality to be courageous. His environment, his education in the broadest sense, was such that his capacity for courage was developed and was actualized. In a different environment courage might not have been actualized in the same soul.

There is thus a difference between potentiality in, say, the sensitive soul and in the rational soul. An acorn has only the potentiality of becoming an oak tree. The rational soul has the potentiality of developing in many different ways.

8  "For these things [feelings of pleasure and pain] extend right through life, with a weight and power of their own in respect both to virtue and to the happy life, since men choose what is pleasant and avoid what is painful . . ."—Nichomachean Ethics (Ross), 1172a23.

9  This is what Aristotle meant by saying that moral virtue is a "disposition to choose." Virtue is not just an act, but an act flowing from a disposition (or from an "attitude" or "state of character" or "habit of decision," as the Greek expression may be variously translated). See Nichomachean Ethics (Ross), 1106b36.

Moral virtue comes about as a result of habit. . . . None of the moral virtues arises in us by nature; for nothing that exists by nature can form a habit contrary to its nature. For instance the stone which by nature moves downward cannot be habituated to move upwards, not even if one tries to train it by throwing it up ten thousand times. . . . Neither by nature, then, nor contrary to nature do the virtues arise in us; rather are we adapted by nature to receive them, and are made perfect by habit. . . . The virtues we get by first exercising them, as also happens in the case of the arts as well. For the things we have to learn before we can do them, we learn by doing them, e.g. men become builders by building and lyre-players by playing the lyre; so too we become just by doing just acts, temperate by doing temperate acts, brave by doing brave acts. . . . If this were not so, there would have been no need of a teacher, but all men would have been born good or bad at their craft. . . . Thus in one word, states of character arise out of like activities. This is why the activities we exhibit must be of a certain kind; it is because the states of character correspond to the difference between these. It makes no small difference, then, whether we form habits of one kind or another from our very youth; it makes a very great difference, or rather *all* the difference.j

"Character" is the name Aristotle gave to the whole settled pattern, or structure, of a man's habits. What a man does in the long run reveals his character: A courageous man will, in the long run, act differently from a cowardly man. But Aristotle saw that on occasion a man may act in a way that runs counter to his character. For what a man does in any given set of circumstances is a product of his character plus these particular circumstances, and circumstances can result in acts that are "out of character." For instance, there are circumstances in which anybody—even the bravest of men—will run.

### RESPONSIBILITY

Considerations of this kind led Aristotle to examine the notion of responsibility. When is a man responsible for his actions? Primitive societies are not likely to make fine distinctions here: If A has killed B he must suffer the full consequences, even though his hand slipped and nothing was actually farther from his mind than the intention of killing B. What matters is simply that B died by A's hand. As Euthyphro said to Socrates, "the pollution is the same." But eventually people come to distinguish between the internal and the external aspects of morality. They are not content to know merely that it was A's hand that killed B. They ask (to phrase the question in Aristotle's terms) whether the killing of B flowed from A's character or whether it occurred only "incidentally." If, for instance, A's character is loving and kind, and if circumstances over which A had no control caused the knife to slip in his hand, A's killing of B was out of character. In this event most people would say that A was not responsible, or at least that he was much less responsible than if he had knowingly and deliberately killed B.

But what exactly do we mean by "circumstances over which A had no control," and what sorts of circumstances relieve a man of responsibility for his acts? Aristotle's way of getting at the answers to these questions was to draw a distinction between the voluntary and the involuntary. Accordingly, the question, "When is a man responsible for what he does?" becomes the question, "Under what circumstances is an act voluntary (that is, the issue of character) and under what circumstances is it involuntary (that is, not a part of the agent's moral nature, however much it may issue from his physical body)?"

> To distinguish the voluntary and the involuntary is presumably necessary for those who are studying the nature of virtue, and useful also for legislators with a view to the assigning both of honours and of punishments.
>
> Those things, then, are thought involuntary, which take place under compulsion or owing to ignorance; and that is compulsory of which the moving principle is outside, being a principle in which nothing is contributed by the person who is acting or is feeling the passion, e.g. if he were to be carried somewhere by a wind, or by men who had him in their power.
>
> But with regard to the things that are done from fear of greater evils or for some noble object (e.g. if a tyrant were to order one to do something base, having one's parents and children in his power, and if one did the action they were to be saved, but otherwise would be put to death), it may be debated whether such actions are involuntary or voluntary. . . . Such actions, then, are mixed. . . . The man acts voluntarily; for the principle that moves the instrumental parts of the body in such actions is in him, and the things of which the moving principle is in a man himself are in his power to do or not to do. Such actions, therefore, are voluntary, but in the abstract perhaps involuntary; for no one would choose any such act in itself.
>
> For such actions men are sometimes even praised, when they endure something base or painful in return for great and noble objects gained. . . . On some actions praise indeed is not bestowed, but pardon is, when one does what he ought not under pressure which overstrains human nature and which no one could withstand. But some acts, perhaps, we cannot be forced to do, but ought rather to face death after the most fearful sufferings. . . . It is difficult sometimes to determine what should be chosen at what cost, and what should be endured in return for what gain, and yet more difficult to abide by our decisions. . . .
>
> What sort of acts, then, should be called compulsory? We answer that without qualification actions are so when the cause is in the external circumstances and the agent contributes nothing. . . .
>
> But if some one were to say that pleasant and noble objects have a compelling power, forcing us from without, all acts would be for him compulsory; for it is for these objects that all men do everything they do. And those who act under compulsion and unwillingly act with pain, but those who do acts for their pleasantness and nobility do them with pleasure; it is absurd to make

external circumstances responsible, and not oneself, as being easily caught by such attractions, and to make oneself responsible for noble acts but the pleasant objects responsible for base acts. The compulsory, then, seems to be that whose moving principle is outside, the person compelled contributing nothing. . . .

Acting by reason of ignorance seems also to be different from acting *in* ignorance; for the man who is drunk or in a rage is thought to act as a result not of ignorance but of one of the causes mentioned, yet not knowingly but in ignorance.

Now every wicked man is ignorant of what he ought to do and what he ought to abstain from, and it is by reason of error of this kind that men become unjust and in general bad; but the term "involuntary" tends to be used not if a man is ignorant of what is to his advantage—for it is not mistaken purpose that causes involuntary action (it leads rather to wickedness), nor ignorance of the universal (for *that* men are *blamed*), but ignorance of particulars, i.e. of the circumstances of the action and the objects with which it is concerned. For it is on these that both pity and pardon depend, since the person who is ignorant of any of these acts involuntarily.

Perhaps it is just as well, therefore, to determine their nature and number. A man may be ignorant, then, of who he is, what he is doing, what or whom he is acting on, and sometimes also what (e.g. what instrument) he is doing it with, and to what end (e.g. he may think his act will conduce to some one's safety), and how he is doing it (e.g. whether gently or violently). Now of all of these no one could be ignorant unless he were mad, and evidently also he could not be ignorant of the agent; for how could he not know himself? But of what he is doing a man might be ignorant, as for instance people say "it slipped out of their mouths as they were speaking," or "they did not know it was a secret," as Aeschylus said of the mysteries, or a man might say he "let it go off when he merely wanted to show its working," as the man did with the catapult. Again, one might think one's son was an enemy, as Merope did, or that a pointed spear had a button on it, or that a stone was pumice-stone; or one might give a man a draught to save him, and really kill him; or one might want to touch a man, as people do in sparring, and really wound him. The ignorance may relate, then, to any of these things, i.e. of the circumstances of the action, and the man who was ignorant of any of these is thought to have acted involuntarily, and especially if he was ignorant on the most important points; and these are thought to be the circumstances of the action and its end. Further, the doing of an act that is called involuntary in virtue of ignorance of this sort must be painful and involve repentance.

Since that which is done under compulsion or by reason of ignorance is involuntary, the voluntary would seem to be that of which the moving principle is in the agent himself, he being aware of the particular circumstances of the action.[k]

An outline may assist in disentangling the rather complicated argument:

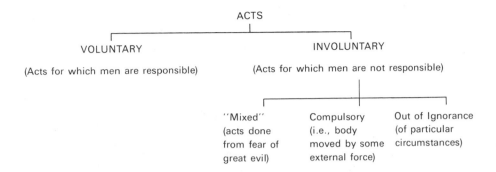

Aristotle's purpose was to ascertain under what conditions a man is not to be blamed (nor to feel ashamed) for doing wrong. These turn out to be as follows: (1) When the act is done under great pain or threat of pain. How great must the pain be to exempt us from blame? Aristotle's answer was characteristic: "It is difficult to make a generalization except to say that there are circumstances so painful that nobody could withstand them." (2) When the act is caused by some external circumstance to which the agent contributes nothing. (For instance, when I trip on an icy pavement and knock you down. So-called compulsions, like the "compelling" force of pleasure, are not compulsions at all, Aristotle held.) (3) When the act is done in ignorance. Here Aristotle was obliged to make further distinctions since "in ignorance" is a phrase of many meanings. For instance, here are two cases in which most people would assess responsibility very differently: (1) B is thirsty. A offers him a drink from a bottle labeled "Water," not knowing that C has filled the bottle with poison. (2) A is so enraged or so drunk that he is not aware that he has a knife in his hand when he strikes B. In both cases A is ignorant of some highly relevant circumstance: in the first case, that he has a bottle of poison in his hand; in the second, that he has a knife in his hand. Most people would say that the former kind of ignorance excuses A but that the latter does not. How can we formulate this difference that virtually everybody feels? According to Aristotle, the difference is this: In the former case A acts "by reason of ignorance"; in the latter case A acts "in ignorance by reason of rage or drunkenness." That is, though in both cases A is ignorant, in the latter case he has brought ignorance on himself; hence the reason for his act is not ignorance but whatever it was (rage or drink) that caused him to be ignorant. Thus we can say that when a man acts in ignorance but not by reason of ignorance he is responsible, and so culpable, for what he does.

Again, a man who is ignorant of the "major premise" is not excused, for *that* is something he ought to know (for example, since everyone ought to know that murder is wrong, a man cannot be excused for not knowing it). Excusable cases, therefore, are only those in which a man is ignorant of some particulars of the situation. Hence we may conclude that voluntary acts (those for which the agent may be blamed and of which he should feel ashamed) are (1) those that originate in the agent and (2) those about which the agent knows the relevant circumstances.

This analysis enabled Aristotle, when he later came to questions of law and justice, to draw further important distinctions.

> When [a man acts] involuntarily, he acts neither unjustly nor justly except in an incidental way; for he does things which happen to be just or unjust. Whether an act is or is not one of injustice (or of justice) is determined by its voluntariness or involuntariness; for when it is voluntary it is blamed, and at the same time is then an act of injustice; so that there will be things that are unjust but not yet acts of injustice, if voluntariness be not present as well. . . . But in the case of unjust and just acts alike the injustice or justice may be only incidental; for a man might return a deposit unwillingly and from fear, and then he must not be said either to do what is just or to act justly, except in an incidental way. Similarly the man who under compulsion and unwillingly fails to return the deposit must be said to act unjustly, and to do what is unjust, only incidentally. . . . There are three kinds of injury in transactions between man and man; those done in ignorance are *mistakes* when the person acted on, the act, the instrument, or the end that will be attained is other than the agent supposed; the agent thought either that he was not hitting any one or that he was not hitting with this missile or not hitting this person or to this end, but a result followed other than that which he thought likely (e.g. he threw not with intent to wound but only to prick), or the person hit or the missile was other than he supposed. Now when (1) the injury takes place contrary to reasonable expectation, it is a *misadventure*. When (2) it is not contrary to reasonable expectation, but does not imply vice, it is a *mistake* (for a man makes a mistake when the fault originates in him, but is the victim of accident when the origin lies outside him). When (3) he acts with knowledge but not after deliberation, it is an *act of injustice*—e.g. the acts due to anger or to other passions necessary or natural to man; for when men do such harmful and mistaken acts they act unjustly, and the acts are acts of injustice, but this does not imply that the doers are unjust or wicked; for the injury is not due to vice. But when (4) a man acts from choice, he is an *unjust man* and a vicious man.[1]

Aristotle's discussion of the involuntary presupposes a point of view very different from Plato's. Aristotle's class of "mixed" actions (those that are involuntary because of great pain or fear) could not have been allowed by Plato. Nor could Plato have admitted the phenomenon of incontinence, in which a man is "mastered" by some desire and knowingly (as we say) does what is wrong. For, following Socrates, Plato had held that virtue *is* knowledge, that no one knowingly does wrong. Though in the post-Freudian world of the twentieth century Aristotle looks like a rationalist who finds it hard to understand how anyone could deliberately choose the bad, his rationalism was much less extreme than Plato's. His study of the voluntary and the involuntary made it possible for him to give a more adequate account of the phenomenon of a "bad will" than Plato had been able to do.[10]

### INCONTINENCE

Now we may ask . . . how a man who judges rightly can behave incontinently. That he should behave so when he has knowledge, some say is impossible; for it would be strange—so Socrates thought—if when knowledge was in a man something else could master it and drag it about like a slave. For *Socrates* was entirely opposed to the view in question, holding that there is no such thing as incontinence; no one, he said, when he judges acts against what he judges best—people act so only by reason of ignorance. Now this view plainly contradicts the observed facts. . . .

Since we use the word "know" in two senses (for both the man who has knowledge but is not using it and he who is using it are said to know), it *will* make a difference whether, when a man does what he should not, he has the knowledge but is not exercising it, or *is* exercising it; for the latter seems strange, but not the former. . . .

Further, since there are two kinds of premisses, there is nothing to prevent a man's having both premisses and acting against his knowledge, provided that he is using only the universal premiss and not the particular; for it is particular acts that have to be done. And there are also two kinds of universal term; one is predicable of the agent, the other of the object; e.g. "dry food is good for every man," and "I am a man," or "such and such food is dry"; but whether "this food is such and such," of this the incontinent man either has not or is not exercising the knowledge. There will, then, be, firstly, an enormous difference between these manners of knowing, so that to know in one way when we act incontinently would not seem anything strange, while to know in the other way would be extraordinary.

And further . . . the possession of knowledge in another sense than those just named is something that happens to men; for within the case of having knowledge but not using it we see a difference of state, admitting of the possibility of having knowledge in a sense and yet not having it, as in the instance of a man asleep, mad, or drunk. But now this is just the condition of men under the influence of passions; for outbursts of anger and sexual appetites and some other such passions, it is evident, actually alter our bodily condition, and in some men even produce fits of madness. It is plain, then, that incontinent people must be said to be in a similar condition to men asleep, mad, or drunk. The fact that men use the language that flows from knowledge proves nothing; for even men under the influence of these passions utter scientific proofs and verses of Empedocles, and those who have just begun to learn a science can string together its phrases, but do not yet know it; for it has to become part of themselves, and that takes time; so that we

10 For Plato's views on this point, see p. 175.

> must suppose that the use of language by men in an incontinent state means no more than its utterance by actors on the stage.[m]

The phenomenon of incontinence thus grows out of the difference between the rational soul and the soul that is merely sensitive, and it illustrates once more how ethics, with the distinction it implies between pleasure and happiness, is the concern exclusively of the former. Animals, being moved solely by appetite, are never incontinent. Nor are superhuman creatures (the intelligences in the planets, or god, for instance), but for the exactly opposite reason—because, not having bodies, they are not moved by appetite at all. Incontinence, then, is a peculiarly human failing. Man has a body and so experiences appetites; he also has reason, which reveals to him alternatives undreamed of by animals.

With his account of incontinence Aristotle was reaffirming, and at the same time reinterpreting in terms of his own metaphysical scheme, the view Hesiod had affirmed centuries earlier: "To birds and to beasts Zeus, the son of Cronos, gave one law, that they should devour one another [that is, satisfy their appetites insofar as they are able], but to man he gave another law—a law of justice, which was for the best." Like Hesiod, Aristotle recognized that, since this higher law is not always respected by men, it is not a description of how they do behave but of how they ought to behave. But Hesiod (and many later philosophers)[11] had interpreted this higher law in theological and mystical terms as god's law. Hence he had held that men have an obligation to obey it as the voice of an authority higher than human. Aristotle, in contrast, interpreted it in purely natural terms: Given the nature of man, incontinence in the long run causes unhappiness. Thus the sanction for continence is not duty but self-interest.

Because reason gives man the capacity to look ahead, he is not confined, as an animal is, to the pursuit of short-range (bodily) satisfactions and the avoidance of short-range (bodily) pains. An animal eats whenever he is hungry (providing food is available); he does not know about, and so does not worry about, over-eating. But because man has developed the science of dietetics, long-range possibilities connected with eating appear to him. He still feels the hunger that the animal experiences, and he still desires to satisfy it, but against this desire another makes itself felt—the desire to avoid excess weight and its attendant discomforts and dangers some years hence. We call a man incontinent if he prefers a smaller (but intense) short-range satisfaction to a greater but more remote long-range satisfaction. Thus morality has a natural, not a supernatural, or transcendental, basis: It is grounded on the fact that man is a rational animal.

Other important consequences follow from the fact that man is a rational animal. Because he is an animal, he has a body with its own characteristic types of fulfillment. It needs food, exercise, and sleep. Because he is rational, a whole new range of fulfillments are open to him—the life of contemplation, for instance.

---

11 See pp. 7–8, 11, and 19.

Aristotle agreed with Plato that the activities of reason are not only qualitatively different from the satisfactions of appetite but also superior to them:

> Pleasures seem, too, to differ in kind. For things different in kind are, we think, completed by different things (we see this to be true both of natural objects and of things produced by art, e.g. animals, trees, a painting, a sculpture, a house, an implement); and, similarly, we think that activities differing in kind are completed by things differing in kind. Now the activities of thought differ from those of the senses, and both differ among themselves, in kind; so, therefore, do the pleasures that complete them. . . .
>
> Each animal is thought to have a proper pleasure, as it has a proper function; viz. that which corresponds to its activity. If we survey them species by species, too, this will be evident; horse, dog, and man have different pleasures, as Heraclitus says "asses would prefer sweepings to gold"; for food is pleasanter than gold to asses. So . . . the same things delight some people and pain others, and are painful and odious to some, and pleasant to and liked by others. This happens, too, in the case of sweet things; the same things do not seem sweet to a man in a fever and a healthy man—nor hot to a weak man and one in good condition. The same happens in other cases. But in all such matters that which appears to the good man is thought to be really so. If this is correct, as it seems to be, and virtue and the good man as such are the measure of each thing, those also will be pleasures which appear so to him, and those things pleasant which he enjoys. If the things he finds tiresome seem pleasant to some one, that is nothing surprising; for men may be ruined and spoilt in many ways; but the things are not pleasant, but only pleasant to these people and to people in this condition. Those which are admittedly disgraceful plainly should not be said to be pleasures, except to a perverted taste; but of those that are thought to be good what kind of pleasure or what pleasure should be said to be that proper to man? Is it not plain from the corresponding activities? The pleasures follow these. Whether, then, the perfect and supremely happy man has one or more activities, the pleasures that perfect these will be said in the strict sense to be pleasures proper to man, and the rest will be so in a secondary and fractional way, as are the activities.[n]

## THE INTELLECTUAL VIRTUES

This brings us to Aristotle's account of the intellectual virtues, for he held that intellect (reason in pursuit of truth) is, above all else, "proper to man." That is to say, so far only the virtues of practical reason (reason directing action) have been discussed, and we have found that these virtues all lie in a disposition to seek the mean in given circumstances. But man is also endowed with reason as a purely cognitive activity. Man not only acts and uses reason to choose among the alternatives open to him. He also thinks and uses reason simply to discover the truth about things.

There are, Aristotle thought, five levels at which "the soul possesses truth." These are the levels of scientific knowledge, art, practical wisdom, intuitive reason, and philosophic wisdom. Each, of course, has its own virtue.

(1) Enough has already been said in another connection about Aristotle's conception of scientific knowledge.[12] (2) As regards art, we need only remind ourselves that Aristotle was thinking not of "fine" art but of what we would call technology—engineering, for instance. This involves scientific knowledge because in it we apply the "laws" of physics to the problems of bridge-building or architecture. "Art," Aristotle held, "is a state concerned with making, involving a true course of reasoning."

(3) In contrast to science, which is concerned with fields in which we can start from absolutely certain axioms and deduce complete sets of syllogisms, practical wisdom is concerned with fields in which certainty cannot be achieved. Thus ethics is a subject of study for the practically wise man, not for the scientist in the strict sense. And the practically wise man studies ethics not only because the study makes him a better man (that is, not only for the sake of moral virtue), but also because he derives an intellectual satisfaction from coming to know such truths as this study discloses.

> Regarding *practical wisdom* we shall get at the truth by considering who are the persons we credit with it. Now it is thought to be the mark of a man of practical wisdom to be able to deliberate well about what is good and expedient for himself, not in some particular respect, e.g. about what sorts of thing conduce to health or to strength, but about what sorts of thing conduce to the good life in general. . . . Now no one deliberates about things that are invariable, nor about things that it is impossible for him to do. Therefore, since scientific knowledge involves demonstration, but there is no demonstration of things whose first principles are variable (for all such things might actually be otherwise), and since it is impossible to deliberate about things that are of necessity, practical wisdom cannot be scientific knowledge nor art; not science because that which can be done is capable of being otherwise, not art because action and making are different kinds of thing. The remaining alternative, then, is that it is a true and reasoned state of capacity to act with regard to the things that are good or bad for man. . . . It is for this reason that we think Pericles and men like him have practical wisdom, viz. because they can see what is good for themselves and what is good for men in general; we consider that those can do this who are good at managing households or states. . . .
>
> Practical wisdom, then, must be a reasoned and true state of capacity to act with regard to human goods.°

(4) Intuitive reason is the faculty by which we apprehend those necessary connections between subjects and their attributes that constitute the first principles of the sciences. Science is concerned with syllogistic deduction (demonstration)

12 See pp. 251–53.

from the axioms; it does not and cannot give the axioms themselves, for these cannot be ascertained by demonstration.

(5) The combination of intuitive reason, which gives the axioms in a flash of insight, and science, which demonstrates logically the valid implications of these insights, is philosophic wisdom.

> Scientific knowledge is judgement about things that are universal and necessary, and the conclusions of demonstration, and all scientific knowledge, follow from first principles (for scientific knowledge involves apprehension of a rational ground). This being so, the first principle from which what is scientifically known follows cannot be an object of scientific knowledge, of art, or of practical wisdom; for that which can be scientifically known can be demonstrated, and art and practical wisdom deal with things that are variable. . . . If, then, the states of mind by which we have truth and are never deceived about things invariable or even variable are scientific knowledge, practical wisdom, philosophic wisdom, and intuitive reason, and it cannot be any of the three (i.e. practical wisdom, scientific knowledge, or philosophic wisdom), the remaining alternative is that it is *intuitive reason* that grasps the first principles. . . .
>
> Therefore wisdom must plainly be the most finished of the forms of knowledge. It follows that the wise man must not only know what follows from the first principles, but must also possess truth about the first principles. Therefore wisdom must be intuitive reason combined with scientific knowledge—scientific knowledge of the highest objects which has received as it were its proper completion.[p]

### CONTEMPLATION IS PERFECT HAPPINESS

Happiness, then, is what we experience when we are living at our best and fullest, when we are functioning in accordance with our nature, when our end is realizing itself without impediment, when our form is being actualized. And since man's form is complex and his activities are many, the best and highest happiness for him will be experienced in connection with the best and highest activity, that is, the activity that most completely expresses and realizes man's nature as man. Who can doubt, Aristotle believed, that this activity is contemplation? Hence in contemplation—in the cognition of the supreme truths about the universe—lies the greatest happiness of which man is capable.

> If happiness is activity in accordance with virtue, it is reasonable that it should be in accordance with the highest virtue; and this will be that of the best thing in us. Whether it be reason or something else that is this element which is thought to be our natural ruler and guide and to take thought of things noble and divine, whether it be itself also divine or only the most divine element in us, the activity of this in accordance with its proper virtue will be perfect happiness. . . . This activity is contemplative. . . .

Firstly, this activity is the best (since not only is reason the best thing in us, but the objects of reason are the best of knowable objects); and, secondly, it is the most continuous, since we can contemplate truth more continuously than we can *do* anything. And we think happiness has pleasure mingled with it, but the activity of philosophic wisdom is admittedly the pleasantest of virtuous activities; at all events the pursuit of it is thought to offer pleasures marvellous for their purity and their enduringness, and it is to be expected that those who know will pass their time more pleasantly than those who inquire. And the self-sufficiency that is spoken of must belong most to the contemplative activity. . . . So if among virtuous actions political and military actions are distinguished by nobility and greatness . . . and are not desirable for their own sake, but the activity of reason, which is contemplative, seems both to be superior in serious worth and to aim at no end beyond itself, and to have its pleasure proper to itself (and this augments the activity), and the self-sufficiency, leisureliness, unweariedness (so far as this is possible for man), and all the other attributes ascribed to the supremely happy man are evidently those connected with this activity, it follows that this will be the complete happiness of man, if it be allowed a complete term of life. . . .

But such a life would be too high for man; for it is not in so far as he is man that he will live so, but in so far as something divine is present in him; and by so much as this is superior to our composite nature is its activity superior to that which is the exercise of the other kind of virtue. If reason is divine, then, in comparison with man, the life according to it is divine in comparison with human life. But we must not follow those who advise us, being men, to think of human things, and, being mortal, of mortal things, but must, so far as we can, make ourselves immortal, and strain every nerve to live in accordance with the best thing in us. . . . That which is proper to each thing is by nature best and most pleasant for each thing; for man, therefore, the life according to reason is best and pleasantest, since reason more than anything else *is* man. This life therefore is also the happiest.q

The life of contemplation, then, is the supreme good for man. Not all men, of course, aim at it. Indeed, most men are quite incapable of understanding it; they are excluded from participating in the highest happiness because they lack the native endowments—the higher ranges of intellect—whose exercise *is* happiness.

In describing the joys of contemplation, Aristotle, as can be seen, was carried away almost to the point of forgetting that man has a body. This line was, indeed, to be seized on by men of a different temperament living in a different age in order to give ethics a supernatural, instead of a natural, basis. But Aristotle himself characteristically returned to earth with a realistic and practical observation. He reminded us that in order to attain the highest good we need not only talent and the "divine" gift of intellectual capacity, but also leisure and serenity in which to develop and to exercise these natural endowments. Wealth, therefore, though not a *part* of happiness, is an essential condition of happiness.[13]

13 "No man can practice virtue who is living the life of a mechanic or labourer"—*Politics* (Jowett), 1278a20.

[Happiness] needs . . . external goods as well; for it is impossible, or not easy, to do noble acts without the proper equipment. In many actions we use friends and riches and political power as instruments; and there are some things the lack of which takes the lustre from happiness, as good birth, goodly children, beauty; for the man who is very ugly in appearance or ill-born or solitary and childless is not very likely to be happy, and perhaps a man would be still less likely if he had thoroughly bad children or friends or had lost good children or friends by death. . . . Happiness seems to need this sort of prosperity in addition. . . .[r]

### TRANSITION FROM ETHICS TO POLITICS

All this takes us beyond the individual to the community in which he lives—from ethics to politics. For no man, it is clear, is sufficient to himself. A man may be able to live, that is, to survive, in isolation and solitariness, but he cannot live well except in a community. This comes out clearly in Aristotle's account of friendship. He distinguished three types of friendships: (1) "friendships of utility," which are based upon the facts of economic interdependence (for example, partnerships for mutual advantage and division of labor); (2) friendships for pleasure, which are based upon social needs and desires (for example, the associations we may form with "ready-witted people" whom we love not because of their character but because of the pleasure we take in their company); (3) friendships between men who are good and alike in virtue.

Friendships of the third type are infrequent, for such men are rare. Such friendships require time and familiarity to mature, but once formed they are permanent, for "each gets from each in all respects the same as, or something like, what he gives." What each gets (and gives) is stimulus, encouragement, and example in the art of living well and being virtuous. None of the virtues is possible, obviously, unless one lives in some sort of a community. How can a man be just without other men to be just to? Or magnificent? Or courageous? But if he lives in a society of just and courageous men he is much more likely to develop these virtues, supposing of course that he has the capacity for them, than if he lives in a society of evil men. This is true even of contemplation, the most self-sufficient of the virtues. Though it is less difficult to contemplate in isolation than to be courageous or just, the most fruitful kind of contemplation is that shared by friends. "The philosopher, even when by himself can contemplate truth, [but] he can perhaps do so better if he has fellow-workers. . . ."[s]

## Political Theory

In the *Politics*, then, we have to consider in detail the conditions that make the good life possible. Since it can be realized only in a community, it is necessary to ask, "What sort of community, with what sort of constitution, laws, and organization, is the most hopeful environment for virtue?"

Aristotle agreed with Plato that the community must be small—a city-state—and that it must be governed by an elite whose leisure is made possible by a large slave class. But in the detailed working out of these basic principles he differed markedly from his teacher.

The *Politics* opens with the same emphasis on purpose (form, end, good) that we found at the start of the *Ethics:*

> Every state is a community of some kind, and every community is established with a view to some good; for mankind always act in order to obtain that which they think good. But, if all communities aim at some good, the state or political community, which is the highest of all, and which embraces all the rest, aims at good in greater degree than any other, and at the highest good.
>
> Some people think that the qualifications of a statesman, king, householder, and master are the same, and that they differ, not in kind, but only in the number of their subjects. For example, the ruler over a few is called a master; over more, the manager of a household; over a still larger number, a statesman or king, as if there were no difference between a great household and a small state. . . .
>
> But all this is a mistake; for governments differ in kind. . . . The family is the association established by nature for the supply of men's everyday wants. . . . When several families are united, and the association aims at something more than the supply of daily needs, the first society to be formed is the village. . . .
>
> When several villages are united in a single complete community, large enough to be nearly or quite self-sufficing, the state comes into existence, originating in the bare needs of life, and continuing in existence for the sake of a good life. And therefore, if the earlier forms of society are natural, so is the state, for it is the end of them, and the nature of a thing is its end. For what each thing is when fully developed, we call its nature, whether we are speaking of a man, a horse, or a family. Besides, the final cause and end of a thing is the best, and to be self-sufficing is the end and the best.
>
> Hence it is evident that the state is a creation of nature, and that man is by nature a political animal. And he who by nature and not by mere accident is without a state, is either a bad man or above humanity; he is like the "Tribeless, lawless, heartless one," whom Homer denounces. . . .
>
> Now, that man is more of a political animal than bees or any other gregarious animals is evident. Nature, as we often say, makes nothing in vain, and man is the only animal whom she has endowed with the gift of speech. And whereas mere voice is but an indication of pleasure or pain, and is therefore found in other animals . . . the power of speech is intended to set forth the expedient and the inexpedient, and therefore likewise the just and the unjust. And it is a characteristic of man that he alone has any sense of good and evil, of just and unjust, and the like, and the association of living beings who have this sense makes a family and a state. . . .

> The proof that the state is a creation of nature and prior to the individual
> is that the individual, when isolated, is not self-sufficing; and therefore he
> is like a part in relation to the whole.[t]

"Man is by nature a political animal," that is, his good as defined in the *Ethics* is possible only if he lives in a *polis*, a city-state. This was Aristotle's answer to the Sophists, who had maintained that every man is a self-sufficient individual who can realize his own good by his own efforts alone.

If men can live well only in a state, the next question is, "What, exactly, is a state and (since there are obviously many different kinds) which kind of state is best?" This way of putting the question invites a Platonic answer—an analysis of the ideal state. And indeed a part of the *Politics* (Books VII and VIII, which are presumably early essays written while Aristotle was still under Plato's influence) is devoted to just such an account. But in the main body of the *Politics* Aristotle shows concern with a more lowly but more practical question—not the nature of the best state as such, but the nature of the best state under such-and-such conditions. Political science, he held, has to consider not only

> . . . what government is best and of what sort it must be, to be most in
> accordance with our aspirations, if there were no external impediment, [but]
> also what kind of government is adapted to particular states. For the best
> is often unattainable, and therefore the true legislator and statesman ought
> to be acquainted, not only with (1) that which is best in the abstract, but
> also with (2) that which is best relatively to circumstances. We should be
> able further to say how a state may be constituted under any given conditions
> (3); both how it is originally formed and, when formed, how it may be longest
> preserved; the supposed state being so far from having the best constitution
> that it is unprovided even with the conditions necessary for the best; neither
> is it the best under the circumstances, but of an inferior type.
>
> He ought, moreover, to know (4) the form of government which is best
> suited to states in general; for political writers, although they have excellent
> ideas, are often unpractical. We should consider, not only what form of
> government is best, but also what is possible and what is easily attainable
> by all.[u]

## CLASSIFICATION OF STATES

In order to determine which is the best state under such-and-such conditions, we must make an exhaustive classification of all possible kinds of states, so as to be sure we do not fail to consider any type of government.[14] A state may be ruled by one, by few, or by many, and these rulers may rule either for their own private benefit or with a view to the common interest. This yields six types of states, as follows:

14 Actually, several different classifications are given in the *Politics*, but this seems to be the
   principal one.

| Number of Rulers | True | Perverted |
|---|---|---|
| One | Monarchy | Tyranny |
| Few | Aristocracy | Oligarchy |
| Many | Polity | Democracy |

Aristotle made a detailed analysis of each of these types.

(1) First, let us consider monarchy. On the basis of his knowledge of Greek history and constitutional practice, Aristotle distinguished five types of monarchies. Of these the one most likely to be approved, he thought, is an "absolute kingship," in which the monarch rules his subjects with the same sort of complete authority that an individual man exercises in the control of his family. Aristotle considered various arguments for and against this type of rule and concluded that only one kind of situation could justify an absolute monarchy.

> When a whole family, or some individual, happens to be so pre-eminent in virtue as to surpass all others, then it is just that they should be the royal family and supreme over all, or that this one citizen should be king of the whole nation.
>
> [Suppose there should be in some state] some one who is pre-eminent in virtue,—what is to be done with him? Mankind will not say that such an one is to be expelled and exiled; on the other hand, he ought not to be a subject—that would be as if mankind should claim to rule over Zeus, dividing his offices among them. The only alternative is that all should joyfully obey such a ruler, according to what seems to be the order of nature, and that men like him should be kings in their state for life.ᵛ

But such a situation occurs only rarely, if at all. Usually the liabilities of monarchy outweigh its advantages, for the rule of law is better than the arbitrary will of an individual, however disinterested he may be. Also, sounder decisions are made by a group than by a single individual, however wise he may be. And finally, kingship involves problems of succession. We cannot be certain that a wise king's son will be wise.

> The advocates of royalty maintain that the laws speak only in general terms, and cannot provide for circumstances; and that for any science to abide by written rules is absurd. . . . Yet surely the ruler cannot dispense with the general principle which exists in law; and that is a better ruler which is free from passion than that in which it is innate. Whereas the law is passionless, passion must ever sway the heart of man. Yes, it may be replied, but . . . when the law cannot determine a point at all, or not well, should the one best man or should all decide? According to our present practice assemblies meet, sit in judgement, deliberate, and decide, and their judgements all relate to individual cases. Now any member of the assembly, taken separately, is certainly inferior to the wise man. But the state is made up

of many individuals [and] a multitude is a better judge of many things than any individual.

Again, the many are more incorruptible than the few; they are like the greater quantity of water which is less easily corrupted than a little. The individual is liable to be overcome by anger or by some other passion, and then his judgement is necessarily perverted; but it is hardly to be supposed that a great number of persons would all get into a passion and go wrong at the same moment. . . .

Even supposing the principle to be maintained that kingly power is the best thing for states, how about the family of the king? Are his children to succeed him? If they are no better than anybody else, that will be mischievous. But, says the lover of royalty, the king, though he might, will not hand on his power to his children. That, however, is hardly to be expected, and is too much to ask of human nature.[w]

(2) If monarchy (in which the ruler is supposed to be disinterested) is bad, its perversion, tyranny, in which the ruler governs solely in his own interest, is far worse. Aristotle needed but a few words to dispose of this type: "Tyranny is just that arbitrary power of an individual which is responsible to no one, and governs all alike, whether equals or betters, with a view to its own advantage, not to that of its subjects, and therefore against their will. No freeman, if he can escape from it, will endure such a government."[x]

(3) Since the extant *Politics* contains little on the subject of aristocracy, it is difficult to reconstruct Aristotle's view on this type of state. Taken literally, an aristocracy is the government of the best (*aristos* = best). Naturally, the best government is that in which the best men, those who "have at heart the best interests of the state and of the citizens," rule. But this only reintroduces the notion of the ideal state, and the question of whether such a government is possible. Aristotle probably felt about aristocracy as he felt about kingship. If ever there were "some one who is pre-eminent in virtue," he ought to rule; if ever there were a few such men, all equally preeminent, they ought to rule. But to concern oneself overmuch with these possibilities or to devote much attention to them would be to fall into mere utopian idealism. Such paragons of virtue occur only rarely, if at all. A political realist like Aristotle would therefore not be disposed to devote much attention to "governments of the best."

(4) The perverted form of rule by few is oligarchy, in which the few rule in their own selfish interest, not in the interest of the state as a whole. For this type of government Aristotle recognized that his method of classification (by the number of rulers) is not altogether adequate. Suppose, for instance, that in a city with 1300 inhabitants, "1000 are rich and do not allow the remaining 300 who are poor . . . a share of the government." No one will say that this is not an oligarchy, even though "the many" rule. In a word, the essence of oligarchy is rule by the rich, but since the rich are usually few in number, we tend to think of oligarchy as the rule of the few. Accordingly, we may say that

"the form of government is . . . an oligarchy when the rich and the noble govern, they being at the same time few in number."

Aristotle distinguished four types of oligarchies:

> Of oligarchies, too, there are different kinds:—one where the property qualification for office is such that the poor, although they form the majority, have no share in the government, yet he who acquires a qualification may obtain a share. Another sort is when there is a qualification for office, but a high one, and the vacancies in the governing body are filled by co-optation. If the election is made out of all the qualified persons, a constitution of this kind inclines to an aristocracy, if out of a privileged class, to an oligarchy. Another sort of oligarchy is when the son succeeds the father. There is a fourth form, likewise hereditary, in which the magistrates are supreme and not the law. Among oligarchies this is what tyranny is among monarchies . . . and in fact this sort of oligarchy receives the name of a dynasty (or rule of powerful families). . . .
>
> Of oligarchies, one form is that in which the majority of the citizens have some property, but not very much; and this is the first form, which allows to any one who obtains the required amount the right of sharing in the government. The sharers in the government being a numerous body, it follows that the law must govern, and not individuals. . . . But if the men of property in the state are fewer than in the former case, and own more property, there arises a second form of oligarchy. For the stronger they are, the more power they claim, and having this object in view, they themselves select those of the other classes who are to be admitted to the government; but, not being as yet strong enough to rule without the law, they make the law represent their wishes. When this power is intensified by a further diminution of their numbers and increase of their property, there arises a third and further stage of oligarchy, in which the governing class keep the offices in their own hands, and the law ordains that the son shall succeed the father. When, again, the rulers have great wealth and numerous friends, this sort of family despotism approaches a monarchy; individuals rule and not the law. This is the fourth sort of oligarchy, and is analogous to the last sort of democracy.[y]

(5) Next we come to democracy (the "perverted" form of polity in Aristotle's classification), which Aristotle defined as that form of government in which "the free, who are also poor and the majority, govern." Aristotle's study of the history of Greek states had revealed an increasing tendency toward the rule of the many. "No other form of government," he thought, "appears to be any longer even easy to establish," let alone to maintain. Hence democracy, unlike aristocracy, received a detailed analysis:

> Of forms of democracy first comes that which is said to be based strictly on equality. In such a democracy the law says that it is just for the poor to have no more advantage than the rich; and that neither should be masters, but both equal. For if liberty and equality, as is thought by some, are chiefly

to be found in democracy, they will be best attained when all persons alike share in the government to the utmost. And since the people are the majority, and the opinion of the majority is decisive, such a government must necessarily be a democracy. Here then is one sort of democracy. There is another, in which the magistrates are elected according to a certain property qualification, but a low one; he who has the required amount of property has a share in the government, but he who loses his property loses his rights. Another kind is that in which all the citizens who are under no disqualification share in the government, but still the law is supreme. In another, everybody, if he be only a citizen, is admitted to the government, but the law is supreme as before. A fifth form of democracy, in other respects the same, is that in which, not the law, but the multitude, have the supreme power, and supersede the law by their decrees. This is a state of affairs brought about by the demagogues. For in democracies which are subject to the law the best citizens hold the first place, and there are no demagogues; but where the laws are not supreme, there demagogues spring up. For the people becomes a monarch, and is many in one; and the many have the power in their hands, not as individuals, but collectively. . . . This sort of democracy, which is now a monarch, and no longer under the control of law, seeks to exercise monarchical sway, and grows into a despot; the flatterer is held in honour; this sort of democracy being relatively to other democracies what tyranny is to other forms of monarchy. The spirit of both is the same, and they alike exercise a despotic rule over the better citizens. The decrees of the demos correspond to the edicts of the tyrant; and the demagogue is to the one what the flatterer is to the other. Both have great power;—the flatterer with the tyrant, the demagogue with democracies of the kind which we are describing. The demagogues make the decrees of the people override the laws, by referring all things to the popular assembly. And therefore they grow great, because the people have all things in their hands, and they hold in their hands the votes of the people, who are too ready to listen to them. Further, those who have any complaint to bring against the magistrates say, "let the people be judges"; the people are too happy to accept the invitation; and so the authority of every office is undermined. Such a democracy is fairly open to the objection that it is not a constitution at all; for where the laws have no authority, there is no constitution. The law ought to be supreme over all, and the magistracies should judge of particulars, and only this should be considered a constitution. . . .

These then are the different kinds of democracy.[z]

(6) Finally, there is polity. Aristotle's system of classification leads to a definition of polity as the "true" form of democracy, that is, rule by the many in the interests of the state as a whole. But here (as with oligarchy) Aristotle realized that to distinguish types of states by number of rulers is to oversimplify. It turns out that "Polity . . . may be described generally as a fusion of oligarchy and democracy." Thus polity, as readers of the *Ethics* will have anticipated, is a mean. It is that constitution in which a balance is achieved between the rule of the many and the rule of the few, between the rule of the rich and the rule

of the poor. It is, in fact, a state in which the balance of power is held by the middle class. Whatever may be true of a utopian state, this is the best constitution for most actual states. Unfortunately, few achieve it, since most tend to go to one or the other of the extremes—to become either oligarchies or democracies.

> We have now to inquire what is the best constitution for most states, and the best life for most men, neither assuming a standard of virtue which is above ordinary persons, nor an education which is exceptionally favoured by nature and circumstances, nor yet an ideal state which is an aspiration only, but having regard to the life in which the majority are able to share, and to the form of government which states in general can attain. . . .
> Now in all states there are three elements: one class is very rich, another very poor, and a third in a mean. It is admitted that moderation and the mean are best, and therefore it will clearly be best to possess the gifts of fortune in moderation; for in that condition of life men are most ready to follow rational principle. . . . The middle class is least likely to shrink from rule, or to be over-ambitious for it; both of which are injuries to the state. Again, those who have too much of the goods of fortune, strength, wealth, friends, and the like, are neither willing nor able to submit to authority. The evil begins at home; for when they are boys, by reason of the luxury in which they are brought up, they never learn, even at school, the habit of obedience. On the other hand, the very poor, who are in the opposite extreme, are too degraded. So that the one class cannot obey, and can only rule despotically; the other knows not how to command and must be ruled like slaves. Thus arises a city, not of freemen, but of masters and slaves, the one despising, the other envying; and nothing can be more fatal to friendship and 'good fellowship in states than this: for good fellowship springs from friendship; when men are at enmity with one another, they would rather not even share the same path. But a city ought to be composed, as far as possible, of equals and similars; and these are generally the middle classes. Wherefore the city which is composed of middle-class citizens is necessarily best constituted in respect of the elements of which we say the fabric of the state naturally consists. And this is the class of citizens which is most secure in a state, for they do not, like the poor, covet their neighbours' goods; nor do others covet theirs, as the poor covet the goods of the rich; and as they neither plot against others, nor are themselves plotted against, they pass through life safely. . . .
> Thus it is manifest that the best political community is formed by citizens of the middle class, and that those states are likely to be well-administered, in which the middle class is large, and stronger if possible than both the other classes, or at any rate than either singly; for the addition of the middle class turns the scale, and prevents either of the extremes from being dominant.[a]

To summarize, of the good forms of government, kingship is (ideally) best and aristocracy (ideally) next best, but for all practical purposes polity is the best and most effective state. As regards the perverted forms,

It is obvious which . . . is the worst, and which is the next in badness. That which is the perversion of the first and most divine is necessarily the worst. And just as a royal rule, if not a mere name, must exist by virtue of some great personal superiority in the king, so tyranny, which is the worst of governments, is necessarily the farthest removed from a well-constituted form; oligarchy is little better, for it is a long way from aristocracy, and democracy is the most tolerable of the three.[b]

### THE RULE OF LAW

So far we have been considering the question, "Where in the population ought the weight of political power lie?" Aristotle's answer was that "save in exceptional circumstances, it ought to lie in the middle class." But in this analysis, and especially in his discussion of the perverted forms, Aristotle constantly touched on a second question: "Ought men or the laws be supreme?"

If we recall the catastrophic mismanagement in Athens during the Peloponnesian War, it will be clear why this question seemed vital to Aristotle. During those years the vote of the people in the Assembly had been sovereign. There was no written constitution or body of law (hardly even a body of precedents) that could not be repudiated by a simple majority vote of those who happened to be present at any particular meeting. No one could know from day to day what his duties or privileges were. This Aristotle rightly regarded as chaotic. What he advocated, therefore, was a body of written laws detailed enough to cover most situations. When exceptional situations arose and the decisions of men were required, he proposed to trust the judgment of the many rather than of the few, and he believed that the constitution should be arranged in such a way that the preponderance of political power on such occasions would be in the hands of the middle class, who would, he thought, mediate between the rival demands of the rich and the poor.

> We will begin by inquiring whether it is more advantageous to be ruled by the best man or by the best laws. . . . The rule of the law . . . is preferable to that of any individual.
>
> Nothing [is so clear] as that laws, when good, should be supreme; and that the magistrate or magistrates should regulate those matters only on which the laws are unable to speak with precision owing to the difficulty of any general principle embracing all particulars.
>
> Even if it be better for certain individuals to govern, they should be made only guardians and ministers of the law. For magistrates there must be. . . . There may indeed be cases which the law seems unable to determine, but . . . the law trains officers for this express purpose, and appoints them to determine matters which are left undecided by it, to the best of their judgement. . . . Therefore he who bids the law rule may be deemed to bid God and Reason alone rule, but he who bids man rule adds an element of the beast; for desire is a wild beast, and passion perverts the minds of

rulers, even when they are the best of men. The law is reason unaffected by desire. . . .

As in other sciences, so in politics, it is impossible that all things should be precisely set down in writing; for enactments must be universal, but actions are concerned with particulars. Hence we infer that sometimes . . . laws may be changed; but . . . great caution would seem to be required. For the habit of lightly changing the laws is an evil, and, when the advantage is small, some errors both of law-givers and rulers had better be left; the citizen will not gain so much by making the change as he will lose by the habit of disobedience. . . . The law has no power to command obedience except that of habit, which can only be given by time, so that a readiness to change from old to new laws enfeebles the power of the law. . . .

[Since] matters of detail . . . cannot be included in legislation . . . the decision of such matters must be left to man. [The only question is whether there] should be many judges [or] only one. . . .

The many, of whom each individual is but an ordinary person, when they meet together may very likely be better than the few good, if regarded not individually but collectively, just as a feast to which many contribute is better than a dinner provided out of a single purse. For each individual among the many has a share of virtue and prudence, and when they meet together, they become in a manner one man, who has many feet, and hands, and senses; that is a figure of their mind and disposition. Hence the many are better judges than a single man of music and poetry; for some understand one part, and some another, and among them they understand the whole. . . . When they meet together their perceptions are quite good enough, and combined with the better class they are useful to the state (just as impure food when mixed with what is pure sometimes makes the entire mass more wholesome than a small quantity of the pure would be), but each individual, left to himself, forms an imperfect judgement. . . . If the people are not utterly degraded, although individually they may be worse judges than those who have special knowledge—as a body they are as good or better.[c]

Aristotle intended this, of course, as a reply to Plato's contention that sovereign power should be in the hands of a few experts, unlimited by any written or unwritten constitution. Their difference on this point goes back to their fundamental disagreement about the ontological status of the forms and the relation of forms to the spatiotemporal world. Not even Plato had believed that politics could be an exact science (after all, even physics is only a "likely story"). But, in Plato's view, imprecision enters only when we attempt to apply theory to practice; political *theory* can be as exact and as absolutely true as he believed geometry to be. Hence came all of Plato's emphasis on higher mathematics as the most appropriate education for rulers. If Plato were correct about this, there would be some reason for leaving politics in the hands of those who understand it, just as we leave bridge-building to engineers and medical treatment to doctors. And since the experts in any field are necessarily few, this would mean putting government in the hands of an elite. But if, as Aristotle held, forms are embedded in particulars and can be got at only through empirical study of the changing spatiotemporal world, political science is very different from mathematics. Though it does not follow that every man's opinion is just as good as every other man's, it does follow that every individual opinion must be checked by other individual opinions. This is especially true of a field in which personal prejudices and biases are likely to affect one's judgment. When a group of men have to reach a decision, their different prejudices are likely to cancel one another out. The decision on which they finally agree (provided, of course, that neither side resorts to force) is likely to be much better and fairer than that of an expert. After all, in making the decision the expert would only be putting *his* biases into effect. What we ought to aim at in government, then, is an equality of dissatisfactions and, correspondingly, an equality of advantages gained. This sort of compromise, or mean, between (say) what would especially favor the wealthy or the poor, labor or capital, farm or urban classes is much more likely to be achieved if the balance of power lies with the middle class, whose prejudices are themselves a mean between those of the upper and lower classes. So far, surely, there is much in Aristotle's view with which we can sympathize. No better defense of democratic parliamentary procedure has ever been written.

Similarly, we probably feel a great deal of sympathy with Aristotle's emphasis on the rule of law—more today, after seeing the operations of personal dictatorships and police states, than ever before. Yet it is manifestly impossible today to legislate in such a way as to take into account all the complicated circumstances that are bound to arise. Hence the tremendous growth of administrative agencies that make decisions and establish precedents in a great variety of fields—just those "experts" Aristotle wished to exclude.

The same observation may be made with regard to Aristotle's views on judicial practice. When, for instance, we try complicated tax or public utility cases before ordinary juries, we are following Aristotle's recommendation that the decision be left to the "many"; but this practice creates difficulties today that it could not have created in the Greek state of the fourth century B.C. As life has grown more complicated, the argument that the "many" can reach sound decisions has grown more and more strained.

Along with greater complexity has come another change pertinent to this discussion. Recent years have seen the application of statistical methods and other techniques to the fields of economics and sociology, and if politics is still far from being the exact science Plato dreamed of, it has certainly become more scientific than it was in Aristotle's day. Nobody today would deny that population trends, housing, sanitation, and money and banking—to name a few fields in which politics is concerned—are fields in which expert knowledge is (relatively speaking) possible and highly relevant to sound decision-making. Hence, even while recognizing the dangers pointed out by Aristotle, we have come more and more to depend on expert opinion—on "bureaucrats." The problem today is not whether to get on without them but how, while making use of them, to keep sovereignty in the hands of the "many."

And indeed we may suspect that Aristotle underestimated the extent to which, even in his own day, the decisions of men are constantly, if unobtrusively, substituted for the alleged rule of law. For instance, he seems to have been unaware of the fact that courts inevitably make new law through their interpretations of the statutes. Since in Aristotle's time there were no judges distinct from juries, it was doubtless easier then than it is today to overlook the role of judge-made law. But the truth is that, then as now, the notion of a constitutional state in which the laws rule was a Platonic ideal rather than an Aristotelian actuality.

Another point at which Aristotle allowed himself to be influenced by an unrealistic ideal was the matter of the size of the state. There were plenty of large states in Aristotle's time (Persia, for instance), and he was, of course, only too familiar with the great empire that was emerging as a result of Alexander's conquests. Hence his repeated affirmation that the good state must be small was surely deliberate.[15] He wanted all citizens to participate fully in government, and he saw no way to accomplish this if the state were large. Such techniques as representative government and initiative and recall would not have satisfied him, even if he had thought of them. These measures may indeed keep (ultimate) political power in the hands of the many and so protect us from the worst excesses of rule by men, but when Aristotle said that man is a political animal, he meant that man is an animal who can achieve his good only by full and active participation in government—by sitting on the magistracies, doing jury duty, taking up arms and fighting for his city, and so on. From this point of view representative government—the mere right, which many do not even avail themselves of, to vote for someone else to be a political animal—is an empty shell.

### ARISTOTLE'S VIEW OF CITIZENSHIP

For us the state is essentially an organization that protects us from enemies within and without, provides us with essential services, and otherwise leaves us to lead our private lives. In return for these services we pay our taxes and (occasionally) go to the polls. For Aristotle, the state existed not merely to maintain order and to make life possible, but to make the *good* life possible. Hence not every place called by the name is really a state. A state is not a mere society

> . . . having a common place, established for the prevention of mutual crime and for the sake of exchange. These are conditions without which a state cannot exist; but all of them together do not constitute a state, which is a com-

---

15 Babylon, Aristotle noted with distaste, was so large that the city had been captured for three days before some of the inhabitants became aware of the fact. Though enclosed with one wall, it was not a city but a nation. "Who could be the general of such a vast multitude, or who the herald, unless he had the voice of a Stentor?"—*Politics* (Jowett), 1276a29 and 1326b6.

munity of families and aggregations of families in well-being, for the sake of a perfect and self-sufficing life. Such a community can only be established among those who live in the same place and intermarry. Hence arise in cities family connexions, brotherhoods, common sacrifices, amusements which draw men together. But these are created by friendship. . . . The end of the state is the good life, and these are the means towards it. And the state is the union of families and villages in a perfect and self-sufficing life, by which we mean a happy and honourable life.

Our conclusion, then, is that political society exists for the sake of noble actions, and not of mere companionship.[d]

It follows that only those who can benefit from this life, who have within them the potentiality for the kind of development that the city-state environment makes possible, should be citizens. Aristotle believed that it is both wasteful and harmful to allow those incapable of this kind of development to become citizens, just as it would be silly to send a dog to college. And he thought that those who possessed the greatest potentialities should receive the greatest opportunities.

They who contribute most to such a society have a greater share in it than those who have the same or a greater freedom or nobility of birth but are inferior to them in political virtue; or than those who exceed them in wealth but are surpassed by them in virtue.

If life only were the object, slaves and brute animals might form a state, but they cannot, for they have no share in happiness or in a life of free choice. Nor does a state exist for the sake of alliance and security from injustice, nor yet for the sake of exchange and mutual intercourse. . . . A state exists for the sake of a good life, and not for the sake of life only. . . .[e]

Thus, like Plato, Aristotle coupled qualitative excellence and quantitative limitations. The same considerations that shaped the character of his political ideal restricted its range. He excluded from the good life mechanics and laborers (because they lack leisure to develop whatever talents they may possess) and slaves and women (because they lack the talents, whatever leisure they may possess).

At his best, however, Aristotle recognized that political capacity, not birth, wealth, or social status, ought to determine a man's place in the state. This created a serious difficulty for him, since in his day political capacity certainly did not determine the extent of a man's opportunity to share in offices.

## THE PROBLEM OF SLAVERY

The most obvious instance of this disparity is the institution of slavery, and it is highly instructive to see how Aristotle struggled to reconcile the existence of slavery with his moral principles. He was saved from having to face this dilemma in its cruelest form by his belief that men are naturally unequal and hence that slavery is not in itself unjust. But, unfortunately for his peace of mind, even if the institution of slavery were justified as a matter of general principle, it is still unjust in particular cases, that is, in Aristotle's terms, whenever an actual slave happens to be superior to his master in political capacity.

Let us then follow Aristotle's treatment of the problem of slavery, not only because of the intrinsic interest of the subject, but also because this analysis is a good example of one of the social functions of philosophical thinking. To begin with, when Aristotle maintained that slavery is natural he was not so much drawing a conclusion from empirical evidence as relying on his basic metaphysical position. Everywhere in the universe, he held, the relation of ruler and subject, means and end, occurs. The inferior everywhere exists for the sake of the superior to which it is a means. Since this, of course, is just another way of stating the relation of form and matter, it is still another example of the "power of system." But here we may feel that the conceptual scheme, instead of being used to interpret the empirical evidence, is being used to distort it—in the interest of a conclusion already reached on other grounds.

> Let us . . . speak of master and slave, looking to the needs of practical life and also seeking to attain some better theory of their relation than exists at present. For some are of opinion that . . . the rule of a master over slaves is contrary to nature, and that the distinction between slave and freeman exists by law only, and not by nature; and being an interference with nature is therefore unjust.
>
> Property is a part of the household, and the art of acquiring property is a part of the art of managing the household; for no man can live well, or indeed live at all, unless he be provided with necessaries. And as in the arts which have a definite sphere the workers must have their own proper instruments for the accomplishment of their work, so it is in the management of a household. Now instruments are of various sorts; some are living, others lifeless; in the rudder, the pilot of a ship has a lifeless, in the look-out man, a living instrument; for in the arts the servant is a kind of instrument. Thus, too, a possession is an instrument for maintaining life. And so, in the arrangement of the family, a slave is a living possession. . . .
>
> But is there any one thus intended by nature to be a slave, and for whom such a condition is expedient and right, or rather is not all slavery a violation of nature?
>
> There is no difficulty in answering this question, on grounds both of reason and of fact. For that some should rule and others be ruled is a thing not only necessary, but expedient; from the hour of their birth, some are marked out for subjection, others for rule.
>
> And there are many kinds both of rulers and subjects . . . ; for in all things which form a composite whole and which are made up of parts, whether continuous or discrete, a distinction between the ruling and the subject element

comes to light. Such a duality . . . originates in the constitution of the universe; even in things which have no life there is a ruling principle, as in a musical mode. But we . . . will restrict ourselves to the living creature, which, in the first place, consists of soul and body: and of these two, the one is by nature the ruler, and the other the subject. But then . . . it is clear that the rule of the soul over the body, and of the mind and the rational element over the passionate, is natural and expedient; whereas the equality of the two or the rule of the inferior is always hurtful. . . . The male is by nature superior, and the female inferior; and the one rules, and the other is ruled; this principal, of necessity, extends to all mankind. Where then there is such a difference . . . the lower sort are by nature slaves, and it is better for them as for all inferiors that they should be under the rule of a master. For he who can be, and therefore is, another's, and he who participates in rational principle enough to apprehend, but not to have, such a principle, is a slave by nature. . . . It is clear, then, that some men are by nature free, and others slaves, and that for these latter slavery is both expedient and right.[f]

Thus the argument is that at the human level of development, as at every level in the hierarchy of substance, there are those who are themselves incapable of full development but who are the necessary condition of the full development of others. A slave is an instrument (a "minister of action") who makes possible the leisure without which no man can live well. That the slave himself has no leisure Aristotle tried to justify by arguing that even with leisure he would be incapable of living well or being happy. He can *understand,* and this makes him an excellent instrument, more flexible than inanimate instruments. But he cannot *reason;* he lacks that cognitive power in whose exercise *real* happiness resides. Hence he would not be happy even if he were free, and we are morally justified in enslaving him.

Even if we allow for the sake of argument that natural inequalities exist—that some men are natural masters and others are natural slaves—Aristotle's conclusion does not follow. For some natural slaves are actual masters and (far worse from Aristotle's point of view) some natural masters are actual slaves. Aristotle was aware of this difficulty, but he did not know how to resolve it.

There is a slave or slavery by law as well as by nature. The law of which I speak is a sort of convention—the law by which whatever is taken in war is supposed to belong to the victors. But this right many jurists impeach. . . . : they detest the notion that, because one man has the power of doing violence and is superior in brute strength, another shall be his slave and subject. . . .

Others . . . think that as men and animals beget men and animals, so from good men a good man springs. But this is what nature, though she may intend it, cannot always accomplish.

We see then that . . . all are not either slaves by nature or freemen by nature, and also that there is in some cases a marked distinction between the two classes, rendering it expedient and right for the one to be slaves and the others to be masters: the one practising obedience, the others exercising the authority and lordship which nature intended them to have. The abuse of this authority is injurious to both; for the interests of part and whole, or body and soul, are the same, and the slave is a part of the master, a living but separated part of his bodily frame. Hence, where the relation of master and slave between them is natural they are friends and have a common interest, but where it rests merely on law and force the reverse is true.[g]

And there is an even greater difficulty with Aristotle's defense of slavery. What if there are no natural slaves in Aristotle's sense? What if it is the condition of a slave's life, not his innate potentialities or lack of them, that makes him a mere instrument? Aristotle's own emphasis elsewhere on the role of habit and his acute observations on the importance of early education should have made him cautious here. Nature, in his own view, is flexible; what limits anything's development is doubtless matter—not merely its own matter, that which makes it *this* individual, but also matter in the larger sense of the environment in which the individual lives and grows. No amount of environmental advantage will ever cause an acorn to grow into a pine tree (or a man to grow into a god). But environment can make the difference between whether the acorn becomes a noble oak or a stunted one. Obviously, it would be meaningless to offer the stunted oak as evidence that one was justified in having treated the acorn meanly and inadequately. Aristotle unfortunately left himself open to the criticism expressed by Rousseau centuries later:

> Aristotle held that men are not by nature equal, but that some are born for slavery and others for mastery. Aristotle was right; but he took the effect for the cause. Nothing is more certain than that every man born in slavery is born for slavery. Slaves lose everything in their chains, even the desire to be free of them. They come to love their servitude, just as the companions of Ulysses came to love their sottishness. If, then, there are now natural slaves, it is because formerly there were slaves against nature. Force made the first slaves; their baseness has kept them slaves.[h]

Even supposing that there are natural superiors and inferiors and that these get sorted out correctly in terms of opportunities for self-improvement, we are left with the question of whether it is right for superiors to treat inferiors merely as instruments. Aristotle seems to have assumed that because a means-end relationship holds both in physics and in ethics, the *same* things are means in both fields. This is equivalent to assuming that because the relation "greater than" holds both in geometry and in, say, art, the esthetic value of paintings is determined by their size. It is just as absurd to suppose that, because one thing is physically a means to another thing, it is also ethically subordinate to that thing.

Further, at least to people brought up in the Judeo-Christian tradition, it seems that Aristotle confused two different kinds of value. The value of intellectual or cultural excellence is different, we believe, from the value of personality. No one, in our view, is justified in excluding anyone else from such a basic right as liberty. Immanuel Kant, writing in the eighteenth century at about the time when our founding fathers were composing the Declaration of Independence, stated this point of view, so antithetical to Aristotle's, with great clarity. The fundamental moral principle, he said, is to treat all men as *persons*, as possessing a worth in themselves. "Treat humanity whether in thine own person or in that of any other in every case as an end withal, never as a means only." In contrast, Aristotle could think of equality only with regard to a relatively small elite. He saw no reason why this small group, endowed by nature with superior talents, should not treat the rest of humanity as a means only.

In criticizing this point of view it is only fair to remember that Aristotle's notions about slavery must have seemed to his contemporaries dangerously radical. His distinction between natural masters and actual masters was implicitly an attack on the whole institution of slavery; hence it was a great advance over the facile assumption of the average Greek that masters are masters and slaves are slaves. Thus a philosophical theory that is used at one time as an elaborate rationalization for prejudice can become, at a later time, the point around which new moral insights are condensed.

## MANUAL FOR ANTIREVOLUTIONISTS

In this discussion of the state we have seen that Aristotle was usually guided by a practical, rather than a utopian, ideal. It was characteristic that he should append to the *Politics* a little manual on revolutions and their causes.

> In considering how dissensions and political revolutions arise, we must first of all ascertain the beginnings and causes of them which affect constitutions generally. They may be said to be three in number; and we have now to give an outline of each. We want to know (1) what is the feeling? (2) what are the motives of those who make them? (3) whence arise political disturbances and quarrels? The universal and chief cause of revolutionary feeling [is] the desire of equality, when men think that they are equal to others who have more than themselves; or, again, the desire of inequality and superiority, when conceiving themselves to be superior they think that they have not more but the same or less than their inferiors; pretensions which may and may not be just. Inferiors revolt in order that they may be equal, and equals that they may be superior. Such is the state of mind which creates revolutions. The motives for making them are the desire of gain and honour, or the fear of dishonour and loss; the authors of them want to divert punishment or dishonour from themselves or their friends. . . . Other causes are insolence, fear, excessive predominance, contempt, disproportionate increase in some part of the state; causes of another sort are election intrigues, carelessness, neglect about trifles, dissimilarity of elements.

What share insolence and avarice have in creating revolutions, and how they work, is plain enough. When the magistrates are insolent and grasping they conspire against one another and also against the constitution from which they derive their power, making their gains either at the expense of individuals or of the public. . . .

Another cause of revolution is fear. Either men have committed wrong, and are afraid of punishment, or they are expecting to suffer wrong and are desirous of anticipating their enemy. Thus at Rhodes the notables conspired against the people through fear of the suits that were brought against them. Contempt is also a cause of insurrection and revolution; for example, in oligarchies—when those who have no share in the state are the majority, they revolt, because they think that they are the stronger. Or, again, in democracies, the rich despise the disorder and anarchy of the state; at Thebes, for example, where, after the battle of Oenophyta, the bad administration of the democracy led to its ruin. . . .

Another cause of revolution is difference of races which do not at once acquire a common spirit; for a state is not the growth of a day, any more than it grows out of a multitude brought together by accident. Hence the reception of strangers in colonies, either at the time of their foundation or afterwards, has generally produced revolution; for example, the Achaeans who joined the Troezenians in the foundation of Sybaris, becoming later the more numerous, expelled them. . . .

Revolutions are effected in two ways, by force and by fraud. Force may be applied either at the time of making the revolution or afterwards. Fraud, again, is of two kinds; for (1) sometimes the citizens are deceived into acquiescing in a change of government, and afterwards they are held in subjection against their will. . . . (2) In other cases the people are persuaded at first, and afterwards, by a repetition of the persuasion, their goodwill and allegiance are retained. . . .

Nothing affords a better insight into Aristotle's difference from Plato than comparing this discussion with the account of degenerate states in the *Republic*. Where Plato is fanciful and whimsical, abstract and ideal, Aristotle is matter-of-fact, detailed, rich in illustrative examples, and completely realistic. Setting aside what he thought desirable, Aristotle dispassionately discussed in turn the dangers for each type of state and how they can be avoided.

Revolutions in democracies are generally caused by the intemperance of demagogues, who either in their private capacity lay information against rich men until they compel them to combine (for a common danger unites even the bitterest enemies), or coming forward in public stir up the people against them. . . .

There are two patent causes of revolutions in oligarchies: (1) First, when the oligarchs oppress the people, for then anybody is good enough to be their champion, especially if he be himself a member of the oligarchy, as Lygdamis at Naxos, who afterwards came to be tyrant. But revolutions which commence outside the governing class may be further subdivided. Sometimes, when the government is very exclusive, the revolution is brought about by persons of the wealthy class who are excluded, as happened at Massalia and Istros and Heraclea, and other cities. . . .

(2) Of internal causes of revolutions in oligarchies one is the personal rivalry of the oligarchs, which leads them to play the demagogue. . . .

Oligarchy is liable to revolutions alike in war and in peace; in war because, not being able to trust the people, the oligarchs are compelled to hire mercenaries, and the general who is in command of them often ends in becoming a tyrant. . . .

We have next to consider what means there are of preserving constitutions in general, and in particular cases. . . .

There is nothing which should be more jealously maintained than the spirit of obedience to law, more especially in small matters; for transgression creeps in unperceived and at last ruins the state. . . .

In the first place, then, men should guard against the beginning of change. . . . Further, we note that oligarchies as well as aristocracies may last, not from any inherent stability in such forms of government, but because the rulers are on good terms both with the unenfranchised and with the governing classes, not maltreating any who are excluded from the government, but introducing into it the leading spirits among them. They should never wrong the ambitious in a matter of honour, or the common people in a matter of money; and they should treat one another and their fellow-citizens in a spirit of equality. . . .

Constitutions are preserved when their destroyers are at a distance, and sometimes also because they are near, for the fear of them makes the government keep in hand the constitution. Wherefore the ruler who has a care of the constitution should invent terrors, and bring distant dangers near, in order that the citizens may be on their guard, and, like sentinels in a night-watch, never relax their attention. He should endeavour too by help of the laws to control the contentions and quarrels of the notables, and to prevent those who have not hitherto taken part in them from catching the spirit of contention. . . .

It is a principle common to democracy, oligarchy, and every other form of government not to allow the disproportionate increase of any citizen. . . . Especially should the laws provide against any one having too much power, whether derived from friends or money; if he has, he should be sent clean out of the country. And since innovations creep in through the private life of individuals also, there ought to be a magistracy which will have an eye to those whose life is not in harmony with the government, whether oligarchy or democracy or any other. . . .

But above all every state should be so administered and so regulated by law that its magistrates cannot possibly make money. In oligarchies special precautions should be used against this evil. For the people do not take any great offence at being kept out of the government—indeed they are rather pleased than otherwise at having leisure for their private business—but what irritates them is to think that their rulers are stealing the public money; then they are doubly annoyed; for they lose both honour and profit.[i]

## Theory of Art

Turning next to Aristotle's theory of art, we find that, typically, Aristotle traced our enjoyment of art to certain basic characteristics of human nature:

> Imitation is natural to man from childhood, one of his advantages over the lower animals being this, that he is the most imitative creature in the world, and learns at first by imitation. And it is also natural for all to delight in works of imitation. The truth of this second point is shown by experience: though the objects themselves may be painful to see, we delight to view the most realistic representations of them in art, the forms for example of the lowest animals and of dead bodies. The explanation is to be found in a further fact: to be learning something is the greatest of pleasures not only to the philosopher but also to the rest of mankind, however small their capacity for it; the reason of the delight in seeing the picture is that one is at the same time learning—gathering the meaning of things, e.g. that the man there is so-and-so.[j]

Thus, like Plato, Aristotle thought that art is cognitive. A poem or a picture imparts information; it does this by conveying a likeness of some object. For this reason, again like Plato, Aristotle regarded "imitation" as the essential element in art.

But, though he started with a Platonic concept, Aristotle as usual reinterpreted it in terms of his own revised theory of the forms. Plato had held that all true knowledge is of separate, intelligible forms; poems and paintings, being but copies of copies, are therefore in his view very inadequate instruments for communicating about reality. Since Aristotle held that reality is the sense world, not an abstract and separated realm, he could hold that art, though imitative, is not the failure Plato had judged it to be.

Indeed, in Aristotle's opinion, art performs an extremely valuable cognitive function, as can be seen if we compare it with history.

> It is not the function of the poet to relate what has happened, but what may happen,—what is possible according to the law of probability or necessity. The poet and the historian differ not by writing in verse or in prose. The work of Herodotus might be put into verse, and it would still be a species of history, with metre no less than without it. The true difference is that one relates what has happened, the other what may happen. Poetry, therefore, is a more philosophical and a higher thing than history: for poetry tends to express the universal, history the particular. By the universal I mean

how a person of a certain type will on occasion speak or act, according to the law of probability or necessity; and it is this universality at which poetry aims in the names she attaches to the personages. The particular is—for example—what Alcibiades did or suffered.[k]

History and poetic drama are both concerned with the lives and fortunes of individuals, but they treat this subject matter quite differently. Let us take as an example the actual career of Alcibiades, in which the necessary relation between excess and disaster was obscured by a hundred inconsequential details —details relevant to Alcibiades the man but irrelevant to this relationship. Whereas the historian-biographer must attempt to report all these details, the tragic poet operates under no such restraints. He is free to emphasize, omit, and modify—to "distort," if you will—in order to bring the significant relationships into sharp focus. The form-matter relation that, according to Aristotle, is the basic metaphysical structure of the universe is thus repeated in the relation between poetry and history. The historian's biography of Alcibiades' career, is but the matter that a poet can transform into a tragedy of ambition.

This is exactly what Euripides did, for instance, in *Medea*.[16] The raw material of this play was "history," an ancient myth, which Euripides modified to satisfy his poetic intention. Because he was under no compulsion to be faithful to the facts, he could construct a plot—a sequence of events in which the relation between excessive ambition and ruin is *dramatically* revealed, with clarity and precision and, above all, with a sense of its necessity.

Thus, though the historical Alcibiades may seem a victim of his circumstances and environment, we are convinced that Jason's tragic end was the inevitable consequence of his character. Poetry is therefore more scientific than history, for it displays relationships as necessary instead of accidental. In its own way it achieves the necessity that is the ideal of the sciences.

But, of course, the axioms of science are generalized and abstract statements of necessary connection, whereas the relations revealed in art are displayed only in the concrete individuality of a particular life in a particular environment. Poetry gives us a universal (as science does), but one that is also particular; it gives us a particular (as history does), but one that is also universal. Thus poetry is a "mean" between science and history.

Art, however, is not merely a mode of cognition. It also has an emotive aspect. Here again Aristotle began with a Platonic thesis. Plato had held not only that artists are deceitful but also that they are dangerous. Because their verses arouse violent emotions, he would have allowed them to produce only under the strictest censorship. But Aristotle viewed art as a quieter of passion, not a stimulus. Therefore, though he agreed with Plato in evaluating art on what are from one point of view extra-esthetic grounds (cognitive and moral), unlike Plato he held that art has a socially valuable function.

16 See pp. 61–62.

Specifically, according to Aristotle, tragic drama operates psychologically to relieve us of the oppressive emotions of pity and fear, just as a cathartic purges the body of some excessive "humor." It is the role of the tragic hero to work upon our emotions in this way.

> A perfect tragedy should . . . imitate actions which excite pity and fear. . . . It follows . . . that the change of fortune presented must not be the spectacle of a virtuous man brought from prosperity to adversity: for this moves neither pity nor fear; it merely shocks us. Nor, again, that of a bad man passing from adversity to prosperity. . . . Nor, again, should the downfall of the utter villain be exhibited. A plot of this kind would, doubtless, satisfy the moral sense, but it would inspire neither pity nor fear; for pity is aroused by unmerited misfortune, fear by the misfortune of a man like ourselves. . . . There remains, then, the character between these two extremes,—that of a man who is not eminently good and just, yet whose misfortune is brought about not by vice or depravity, but by some error or frailty. . . .
>
> The plot ought to be so constructed that . . . he who hears the tale told will thrill with horror and melt to pity at what takes place. . . .
>
> Tragedy, then, is an imitation of an action . . . ; through pity and fear effecting the proper purgation of these emotions.[1]

Thus, after watching the unfolding of a tragic drama, we leave the theater "calm of mind, all passion spent,"[17] and so in a state of better balance than before we saw the play.

So far we have been considering art in what Aristotle took to be its most mature form, poetic tragedy. But Aristotle thought it helpful to show that art has its origin in more elementary experiences. This genetic approach is, of course, characteristic of his whole method. In the *Politics*, for instance, he shows how the city arises from lesser communities, the family and the village;[18] and in his psychology he shows how sensation arises from nutrition, and thought from sensation.[19] His partiality for this type of approach was a reflection of his metaphysical principle of a hierarchy of structures, each of which is form to a lower, and matter to a higher, structure.

Accordingly, as we have seen, Aristotle traced the pleasure we all take in imitation to man's desire for knowledge. Imitation at any level—whether it is "the imitation of an action that is serious, complete, and of a certain magnitude" or merely a child's putting on the airs of a grownup—is always pleasurable, because its end is knowledge. To imitate anything is to identify it, to recognize it. And recognition is always a "good" because it is a kind of knowledge.

---

17 These are the words with which Milton concluded his *Samson Agonistes*. And in the preface to this dramatic poem, Milton referred to Aristotle's doctrine of catharsis.

18 See p. 288.

19 See pp. 238–43.

So much for the basis of our pleasure in imitation. The moral aspect of art can be traced to similarly elementary roots. Quite apart from the content that is being imitated and recognized, we take a natural pleasure in rhythms. Why? Because the harmonies thus experienced are communicated to our souls and induce in them a corresponding order and harmony. Thus the function of rhythm and meter, even at their most elementary level, is to produce a kind of "calm of mind." The tragic drama is nothing but the full and articulate realization of a potentiality present in the beat of feet dancing on the floor or the clap of hands together: "Imitation, then, is one instinct of our nature. Next, there is the instinct for 'harmony' and rhythm, metres being manifestly sections of rhythm. Persons, therefore, starting with this natural gift developed by degrees their special aptitudes, till their rude improvisations gave birth to Poetry."[m]

Aristotle's theory of art is in every respect a considerable advance over Plato's moralistic conception. But unfortunately, instead of making a survey of all the arts, as he made a study of constitutions of the various Greek states in preparation for his *Politics*, Aristotle virtually limited himself to one art form—dramatic poetry. Here almost for the first time, he failed to follow his own empirical program. As a result, his generalizations rest on too narrow a base to be applied without distortion to the other arts—to painting and sculpture, for instance.

## Evaluation of Aristotle's Philosophy

In looking back over this survey of Aristotle's philosophy, what is most impressive is the power of system, the way in which he used his concepts of matter and form to organize and explain every aspect of human experience. The physical world, the social world, and man's inner moral and esthetic life are all brought together in a unified world view.

Though this was certainly a massive achievement, the conceptual scheme itself is not without flaws. For one thing, matter and form were introduced as correlative concepts: Form is the "what" and matter the "this" of things. Form makes each thing a thing of some kind; matter makes each thing this particular thing of this kind. It seems odd, therefore—possibly even contradictory—to talk about unformed matter and immaterial form. Yet Aristotle insisted that there is a hierarchy of substances with an unformed matter at the bottom and an immaterial form at the top. It is easy to see why he introduced these entities. Disliking infinite series, demanding completeness, he wanted to anchor each end of the hierarchy of substances in something that would close the series definitely. Further, an unformed, or prime, matter was useful in another way: It accounted for the element of factuality, of arbitrariness, in an otherwise beautifully rational universe.

But it is one thing to see why Aristotle introduced prime matter into his system and another to give a clear account of this concept. What exactly is it? Nothing? Not quite. It must be *something*, although, being unformed, it cannot be *some* thing (that is, it cannot be anything in particular). It is, Aristotle said, the "bare possibility of being something," but this definition is hardly illuminating. Aristotle would doubtless have replied, with some justice, that our question is absurd. To demand a clear account, that is, a rational analysis, of what is precisely the irrational factor in the universe is to ask for the impossible. As regards pure form, however, Aristotle could not have resorted to this line of defense, for this ought to be the clearest of all concepts. Yet what is pure form? It is the unmoved mover, according to Aristotle. But here again his usual firm grasp of concrete reality seems to disappear in vagueness.

Another difficulty with Aristotle's basic scheme is the doubt (which has already been mentioned) about the ultimate metaphysical status of the scheme itself. Is it *merely* a conceptual scheme, merely a way in which minds like ours interpret the real? Or are the formed matters, the individual substances, objectively real and independently existing entities? This uncertainty is enough to indicate that Aristotle did not entirely resolve the Platonic puzzle about the nature of the forms and their relation to particulars.

Apart from such ambiguities as these, there are two important areas of experience in which (for quite different reasons) the conceptual scheme breaks down.

One is physics. But here we must make a distinction. Aristotle's scheme was adequate for the level of scientific knowledge and the type of scientific method available in his own day and for a long time afterwards. Indeed, as we have seen, within the limitations of this method, he made positive contributions in his own right, especially in biology. But Aristotle's method was empirical, whereas the method of modern science has been increasingly mathematical, and his philosophy of science was teleological, whereas the philosophy of modern science has been predominantly mechanistic. This does not mean that modern science is wholly right and that Aristotle was wholly mistaken, for contemporary philosophy has not yet succeeded in reconciling the empirical and the mathematical, the teleological and the mechanistic, approaches. But it does mean that Aristotle's physics was seriously one-sided.

Of course, to blame Aristotle for this deficiency would amount to criticizing him for having allowed himself to be born before the seventeenth century, something about which he hardly had a choice. So obvious is this that one would not even mention it were it not for the fact that people sometimes confuse Aristotle with Aristotelianism. It is true that his views became frozen in a monumental orthodoxy that had to be slowly and painfully overcome, but such rigidity and conservatism were totally opposed to the open-minded, intellectually curious, and empirical spirit of the man himself.

The second area in which Aristotle's philosophy is hardly adequate is religious experience. Here, however, the trouble is not so much a failure of the matter-form scheme (for later thinkers like St. Thomas were able to apply it with considerable success) as it is a possible deficiency in Aristotle's own religious appreciation. What many people have held to be the higher reaches of religious experience—the kind of mystical relationship Plato sought to express in his myths—seems to have been lacking in Aristotle.

Here as elsewhere Plato's and Aristotle's philosophies reflect the temperamental differences that have been discussed. Where Plato is whimsical and ironic, and proceeds by suggestion and indirection, Aristotle is matter-of-fact, almost pedestrian. Where Plato's writing is filled with his sense of a better and more beautiful world behind, above, beyond the world of ordinary experience, illumining that experience but transcending it, Aristotle keeps his feet firm on the ground of ordinary experience. This is his reality, and the business of philosophy in his view is to make sense of the here and now.

Yet these two world views complement, rather than contradict, each other. Aristotle certainly caught glimpses of Plato's transcendent world, as in his account of contemplation; Plato certainly held it the function of the sun to illumine the cave. Taken together, their two theories were a connected effort to solve the central problems of Greek culture. Since these have remained problems for Western societies down to our own day, the subsequent history of philosophy is in large measure the history of the enduring influence of these views.

# CHAPTER 8

# The Late Classical Period

## Political and Cultural Changes

Classical philosophy reached its constructive zenith with Plato and Aristotle, yet more than six centuries elapsed between the death of Aristotle and the emergence of Christianity as a cultural force sufficiently strong to give a radically new direction to thought. This long period was chiefly marked by the modification of classical theories in accordance with the profound social and political changes that were occurring.

The Peloponnesian War had demonstrated, for those who could see beyond the immediacy of events, both the need for a larger unity than the city-state and the inability of the Greek cities to find it for themselves. Alexander's empire marked the first attempt to form a stronger union than a mere confederation of independent cities. Alexander believed that racial homogeneity is a necessary condition of that cultural homogeneity that, in its turn, is the basis of lasting political union. He therefore attempted to overcome the old Greek prejudice (which was still strong in Plato and Aristotle) against foreigners and encouraged his soldiers to marry women from the newly conquered Asiatic provinces. He also saw that a great state requires some visible symbol of its unity. Since this could not (at least not immediately) be ties of blood brotherhood like those that had bound the members of a Greek city, he caused himself, or at least allowed himself, to be worshiped as a god by the subject peoples.

Had Alexander lived, his empire might have endured. As it was, he died at the age of thirty-three, and the state he had fashioned collapsed almost overnight.

### THE RISE OF ROME

Meanwhile, in the central Mediterranean, the successor of Alexander's universal state had already begun to rise. Rome began, as Athens and Sparta had begun, as a small, independent city-state. But, unlike the Greek cities, it managed to find a solution for the political problems that expansion and far-flung imperium entailed. Or rather, it managed to find a succession of solutions to meet the changing conditions that developed as its hegemony spread over the whole of the Mediterranean and beyond.

An example is the Romans' gradual expansion of the meaning of citizenship. Eventually, instead of being the tight little closed corporation that Athenian citizenship had been, Roman citizenship became open to all free inhabitants of the empire.[1]

While the Romans were gradually expanding their imperium through Italy and the Mediterranean world, a long-drawn-out social struggle was going on in the city itself—a struggle that was broken off only when the homeland was imperiled by external foes, and resumed as soon as the outside danger was removed. In its earliest days Rome had been a monarchy, with a council of elders and patricians, called the Senate, and a virtually powerless assembly of free citizens. When the monarchy was overthrown political power passed to the patricians, who ruled by controlling the election of the two "consuls," as the supreme officers of the new republic were called. The common people soon began to press for relief, and shortly after the beginning of the fifth century B.C. (at about the time the Greeks were fighting off the Persian invasion), they secured the right of electing special officers—"tribunes of the people"—whose

---

1 Since this did not occur until 212 A.D., the Romans cannot be said to have learned this lesson easily. At the beginning of the first century B.C., for instance, when the inhabitants of Italy were still largely unenfranchised, a rebellion against Roman authority occurred, growing out of dissatisfaction over lack of privileges. Only when the Romans failed to put it down by force of arms did they decide to extend the franchise to the dissident groups and so bring the revolt to an end.

primary duty was to protect individual citizens from arrest without due process of law.

The demand of the people for written laws was, naturally, long resisted, but finally in 452 B.C. a delegation was sent to Athens to study Solon's laws. On its return the next year, the existing unwritten law in Rome was set down on Twelve Tables. Six years later mixed marriages between nobles and plebeians were authorized. In 367 B.C. the plebeians first succeeded in electing one of their own number consul. Step by step the political differences between patrician and plebeian were removed, the final stage in this process occurring about one hundred and seventy-five years after the tribunate was established.

Meanwhile the conquest of the Italian peninsula had been completed. This brought the Romans into conflict with Carthage, then the dominant power in the western Mediterranean. After a series of wars lasting more than one hundred years (from 264 B.C. to 146 B.C.) Rome destroyed Carthage and acquired its empire. But even before this process was completed, the advance eastward began. In 196 B.C. Greece was "liberated" from the Macedonian hegemony, and by 189 B.C. the power of the other states in the eastern Mediterranean had been broken. For a time the Romans followed a policy of benevolent neutrality in Greece itself, but, as conflicts between the city-states there continued, a settlement became necessary, and in 146 B.C.—the year that Carthage was razed—Greece became in effect another Roman province.

It should be a matter of no surprise that this extraordinary territorial expansion, which continued into the next century, caused considerable political and economic dislocation in Rome itself. In the early days of the Republic, differences in rank and social status had been offset, it appears, by the frugality and simplicity of the nobles' manner of life. Cincinnatus, for instance, one of the early saviors of the Republic, was a farmer, twice called from the plow to serve his country as supreme commander.

Conquest and expanding dominion changed all this. Whereas constitutional reform tended to produce political leveling, wealth produced a new, more radical kind of distinction. The conquered territories overseas were first plundered and then taxed to support the homeland, which gradually became tax free. But this did not create economic prosperity. On the contrary, the importation into Italy of large numbers of slaves gradually ruined the old class of free farmers and small landholders. A large and virtually disenfranchised (whatever its legal and constitutional rights) urban proletariat arose, taking the place of the vigorous, independent, and largely rural population of earlier times.

As the poor became poorer, the rich were becoming richer. Proconsuls returned from foreign duty with immense fortunes, built huge palaces, and lived lives of oriental splendor surrounded by hordes of slaves and fawning clients. To advance their political fortunes, these men were able and willing to bribe the populace with bread and circuses, and the populace—already debased by their economic circumstances—were only too willing to connive at their further degradation.

## THE BIRTH OF THE EMPIRE

These economic problems and the social degeneration that ensued naturally exacerbated a political problem that was already sufficiently critical. How was the government of a small city-state to transform itself into a political system suitable to rule an empire? It took some one hundred and fifty years of bloody struggle, and the genius of Julius and Octavius Caesar, to solve this problem. With a marvelous tact, they retained all the old, well-loved Republican forms but gathered all the powers in the state, once divided among many individuals, into the hands of one man. Since no clear line was drawn between the emperor's personal affairs and the affairs of state, the emperor's personal servants—his social secretary, his bookkeeper, and such other assistants that any man of wealth might have—became Secretaries of State. Gradually a civil service adequate to administer so vast a dominion was built up. The various provinces, which in Republican days had been political plums for Senatorial politicians and had been administered by them as virtually private possessions, came under a single administration, governed by officials appointed by the emperor and acting in his name.

Doubtless this political solution was not perfect; but people often write as if, because the Empire eventually declined and fell, it was a dismal failure. This conclusion results from a comparison à la Plato of the Empire, not with other actual political systems, but with an ideal. Compared with utopia, the Empire was doubtless a failure—it did not last forever. But it endured for several centuries, and when it finally collapsed, it was still vigorous enough to transfer to Christendom much of its form and organization and to determine in large measure, therefore, the course of development in the future, down to our own day. And Rome passed on to the future more than its own political and judicial structures. Because Rome itself had been Hellenized, the attitudes and concepts of Greece became a part of the heritage of Western man.

But, of course, these insights were inevitably transformed as they were transmitted. If the large-scale organization of the Empire permitted the dissemination of Greek culture to Gauls and Spaniards whom the Greeks themselves would have scorned, its very scale colored the ideas being disseminated. Similarly, the chaotic conditions that prevailed for so long in Greece before the long arm of Rome took over were reflected in the increased value set on security, which came gradually to seem more important than independence.

The city-state milieu was on a sufficiently small scale for men to believe they could achieve security and well-being through their own efforts and through cooperation with their fellows. They had a sense, that is, of being able to control their destiny and to solve their problems. Perhaps this was an illusion; but, as long as the feeling existed, it gave men confidence and a sense of independence. They felt it was worthwhile to aim at self-improvement because the conditions of their life made them believe they had a fair chance of attaining it. All this, of course, was reflected in the ethical and political theories of Plato and Aristotle.

In the new conditions that have been described, men's values underwent an inevitable change. In a large-scale organization like the Empire it was obvious that one did not control one's own destiny. It was necessary therefore either to abandon or to alter radically the old ideal of self-improvement. One could teach oneself to accept passively whatever life brought, instead of seeking actively to alter the course of events in one's own favor. Or one could give up the attempt to achieve an harmonious, all-round development and concentrate on the inner life and one's private sensibilities. As men became convinced of the impotence of the natural man, they came gradually to rest their hopes on the supernatural. The whole value system was thus shifting away from a secular, this-worldly frame of reference.

These changes occurred, of course, only slowly. What is remarkable, really, is the persistence of Greek ways of thought beyond what might be called their normal life expectancy. It was a long time before the sense of frustration, impotence, and insecurity became too great to be contained in the rational framework of Platonism and Aristotelianism. When that time finally came the classical world was at an end. But before we reach it we must consider the ways in which Greek theories were accommodated to the political and social institutions of the Roman world.

### PHILOSOPHICAL SCHOOLS IN THE EMPIRE

In the second century B.C., when the Romans first began to interest themselves in philosophical speculation, there were five main "schools" (to use the technical term) of Greek thought. But this term is misleading insofar as it suggests an educational institution—or at least a group holding more or less identical views. It would be better, though more cumbersome, to talk about "five discernibly different types of philosophical development," for each of the so-called schools consisted of a large number of individual thinkers, living over a long period of time, who differed among themselves in many respects but who held a number of positions in common. The five schools we have to examine—schools identified as such even in classical times—are the Academics, the Peripatetics, the Epicureans, the Stoics, and the Sceptics.

The first two need not detain us long. The Academics were centered in the Academy that Plato had founded. For years after the founder's death—such was the impress of his personality—his views were handed down dogmatically by a succession of hero worshipers.[2] Like the Academics, the Peripatetics (as the members of Aristotle's rival Lyceum came to be known, because of their master's practice of walking about while lecturing) showed little originality. For the most part they were content to expound the encyclopedic learning of Aristotle.

The other Greek schools were more original. The considerable success that

---

2 Later on, by a swing of the pendulum, scepticism succeeded dogmatism at the Academy. See pp. 351–52.

they, especially Stoicism, achieved is evidence that they met some need in the culture. Each reflects one aspect of the character and temper of the post-Alexandrian world. For this reason, and because, as we shall see, they represent recurring philosophic attitudes, they will be examined in some detail.

## Epicureanism

Epicurus, the founder of this school, was born about 341 B.C. on the island of Samos in the Aegean. He visited Athens as a young man (about the time of Aristotle's death), taught in several cities where he attracted enthusiastic audiences, and then settled in Athens in 306 B.C. There he set up his school in a garden and was worshiped almost as a god by admiring pupils. He was not spoiled by this adulation but remained modest and friendly to all, freemen and slaves, men and women, adults and children. He lived simply, ate only the plainest food ("Send me a cheese," he wrote to a friend, "that I may fare sumptuously"), and found his greatest satisfaction in conversation with his friends. He died in 270 B.C.

### EGOCENTRIC HEDONISM

Epicurus' physics and his theory of knowledge have been discussed in connection with Atomism, and we have seen that in the main he followed Democritus.[3] In ethics, however, he differed radically from Democritus. The end of life, Epicurus held, is simply to maximize pleasure. Though this may sound indistinguishable from the assertions of the more extreme Sophists, Epicurus' manner of life shows that we should not identify him with advocates of living from moment to moment in the pursuit of as many and as violent pleasures as possible. Epicurus agreed that the satisfaction of any desire is per se pleasant, but he thought that the enlightened pleasure-seeker will avoid violent and extreme pleasures because of their adverse aftereffects. In general, he held, it is "better" (that is, more pleasant in the long run) to lead a simple and frugal life of self-denial. Bread and milk may not be as exciting as caviar and champagne, but they are less likely to be followed by indigestion and hangover.

> We consider that of desires some are natural, others vain, and of the natural some are necessary and others merely natural; and of the necessary some are necessary for happiness, others for the repose of the body, and others for very life. The right understanding of these facts enables us to refer all choice and avoidance to the health of the body and [the soul's] freedom from disturbance, since this is the aim of the life of blessedness. For it is

3 See pp. 79–91.

to obtain this end that we always act, namely, to avoid pain and fear. . . . And for this cause we call pleasure the beginning and end of the blessed life. For we recognize pleasure as the first good innate in us, and from pleasure we begin every act of choice and avoidance, and to pleasure we return again, using the feeling as the standard by which we judge every good.

And since pleasure is the first good and natural to us, for this very reason we do not choose every pleasure, but sometimes we pass over many pleasures, when greater discomfort accrues to us as the result of them: and similarly we think many pains better than pleasures, since a greater pleasure comes to us when we have endured pains for a long time. Every pleasure then because of its natural kinship to us is good, yet not every pleasure is to be chosen: even as every pain also is an evil, yet not all are always of a nature to be avoided. Yet by a scale of comparison and by the consideration of advantages and disadvantages we must form our judgement on all these matters. . . .

And again independence of desire we think a great good—not that we may at all times enjoy but a few things, but that, if we do not possess many, we may enjoy the few. . . . To grow accustomed therefore to simple and not luxurious diet gives us health to the full, and makes a man alert for the needful employments of life, and when after long intervals we approach luxuries disposes us better towards them, and fits us to be fearless of fortune.

When, therefore, we maintain that pleasure is the end, we do not mean the pleasures of profligates and those that consist in sensuality, as is supposed by some who are either ignorant or disagree with us or do not understand, but freedom from pain in the body and from trouble in the mind. For it is not continuous drinkings and revellings, nor the satisfaction of lusts, nor the enjoyment of fish and other luxuries of the wealthy table, which produce a pleasant life, but sober reasoning, searching out the motives for all choice and avoidance, and banishing mere opinions, to which are due the greatest disturbance of the spirit.

Of all this the beginning and the greatest good is prudence. Wherefore prudence is a more precious thing even than philosophy. . . .[a]

The desire for food (but just enough to satisfy hunger) and the desire for sleep are examples of natural and necessary desires. In contrast, the desire for sexual pleasure is natural but unnecessary, and desires for exotic foods and expensive, showy clothes are unnatural, that is, "vain and idle."

These distinctions were purportedly based on psychological fact, and they were important to Epicurus because he wanted to use them to justify his ethical theory. Necessary desires, he held, must be satisfied. Fortunately, their satisfaction is easy and (because these desires are natural and necessary) has no adverse consequences. Thus the simplest and most easily procurable food will satisfy our hunger.

On the other hand, the unnatural desires, precisely because they are unnatural, do not have to be satisfied. Though we have to eat, we do not have to eat caviar. Hence we do not suffer if these desires are not satisfied. Further, whereas the natural desires are easily satisfied, the unnatural desires are difficult to satisfy. There are two reasons why this is true. In the first place, the objects of the unnatural desires, being more exotic, are harder to come by. (Compare, for instance, the cost of bread with the cost of caviar.) In the second place, whereas there is a natural termination to the natural desires (the desire for food, for instance, is satisfied by a well-filled belly), the unnatural desires have no such limits. The more champagne we drink, the more we want. The unnatural desires are a bottomless pit that the wise man will not attempt to fill.

### DIFFICULTIES WITH EGOCENTRIC HEDONISM

But are the distinctions between necessary, unnecessary, and vain desires well founded in human psychology? Though Epicurus believed his ethics to be based on the psychology of desire, we may suspect that these alleged psychological distinctions were in fact derived from his ethics. It might be argued, for instance, that sexual release is as necessary for mental health (for some people at least) as food is necessary for physical health. Does not this make it a necessary desire for those people? And what about food, for that matter? How much food and what kind is necessary, as distinct from vain? The answer surely is that this varies from person to person. One can indeed say that a certain daily minimum intake of food (including proteins and vitamins) is necessary for health. But it is not at all clear what this necessary minimum intake has to do with ethics.

If you are an ethical hedonist and happen to like bread and milk, as Epicurus did, you will doubtless choose to confine yourself to this diet—as Epicurus did. But if you like caviar and champagne more than you dislike indigestion and hangovers, you will extend your diet to include these items, undeterred by the fact that somebody else thinks they are "vanities." Logic, it would seem, should have led Epicurus to accept this as a corollary of the pleasure doctrine. But Epicurus wanted to maintain that caviar and champagne really are vanities, that the man who enjoys them "ought" not to do so. He wanted, that is, to maintain that a man who likes caviar and champagne should nevertheless confine himself to bread and milk. But this would follow only if there were some good other (and better) than pleasure, and if bread and milk (but *not* caviar and champagne) were good in this second sense. And, of course, to argue in this way would be to abandon the Epicurean doctrine that pleasure is the sole good.

This difficulty also shows up in the Epicurean account of virtue. It follows logically from the pleasure doctrine that what people call "virtues," say, truth-telling and promise-keeping, are valuable only if they produce more pleasure than their corresponding "vices," in this case, lying and promise-breaking. For if pleasure is the sole good, the only sensible reason for telling the truth is that one will obtain pleasure thereby. Some of the time, at least, the Epicureans did argue in just this way. For instance, "I spit upon the honourable and upon those who admire it, when it does not produce any pleasure."[b] And Epicurus himself said, quite explicitly, "Beauty and virtue and the like are to be honoured, if they give pleasure; but if they do not give pleasure, we must bid them farewell."[c]

In contrast, many people hold that certain acts are "noble" and ought to be done regardless of whether they are painful and that others are "shameful" and ought to be avoided even though they might be very pleasant. As Homer reported in the *Iliad*, Achilles knew that his stubbornness had been directly responsible for the death of Patroclus. Hence he felt obliged to avenge his friend's memory by killing Hector, the Trojan champion who had slain Patroclus. Although Achilles' goddess mother warned him that if he killed Hector he would be the next to die, Achilles preferred death to dishonor. "Let me die forthwith," he replied to his mother's warning, "and be avenged on my enemy, rather than survive a laughing-stock and a burden on the earth."

Socrates, in his speech to the jury, quoted this story to illustrate his own attitude: He would rather die than weasel his way out of his predicament. While modern men, with their Judeo-Christian background, may not feel disgraced if they fail to revenge a friend's death, they may agree that there are occasions on which a too meticulous regard for one's own skin is shameful.

But, according to the pleasure doctrine, Achilles was a fool to let an illusory duty weigh against the real pains likely to be suffered in combat. It would appear that Epicurus did not like this sort of conclusion. Just as he wanted to hold that simple foods are somehow intrinsically better than rich foods, so he wanted to hold that virtue is intrinsically better than vice. According to his basic doctrine, it would be true that virtue is always better than vice if it were true that virtue is always more productive of pleasure than is vice. But, even if this could be established, it would not follow that virtue is intrinsically better. It would not be good in itself, but would be only (in the language of the *Republic*) a second-best thing, pursued because it happens to produce pleasure. It must be allowed that Epicurus' argument here is rather muddled. For instance, he maintained that "the just man is most free from trouble, the unjust most full of trouble."[d] This sounds as if he meant to maintain that just acts are necessarily a means to pleasure, but this seems clearly untrue unless the term "pleasure" is used in a restricted sense to designate a special qualitative satisfaction of some kind. It seems obvious that if pleasure means simply a titillation of the senses, unjust acts often produce pleasure.

Again, Epicurus argued: "It is not possible to live pleasantly without living prudently and honourably and justly, [nor again to live a life of prudence, honour, and justice] without living pleasantly. And the man who does not possess the pleasant life, is not living prudently and honourably and justly, [and the man who does not possess the virtuous life], cannot possibly live pleasantly."[e]

This comes close to identifying "pleasure" with the particular kind of satisfaction that accompanies "virtuous" conduct. Though Epicurus did not say exactly what he took the connection between virtue and pleasure to be, the view suggested here is quite different from what would ordinarily be understood by the proposition that "pleasure is the sole good."

It is hard not to believe that some of the popularity of Epicurus' theory stemmed from this ambiguity. The view that pleasure is the sole good attracts not only because of its simplicity, but because it appeals to the very real feeling of most people that pleasure is *a* good. On the other hand, fudging the distinction between means and end allowed Epicurus to soften the selfishness of the pleasure doctrine and to disguise the fact that it conflicts with the belief of many people that some acts are right even though they cannot be said to produce pleasure.

### REPOSE

So far only two of Epicurus' "natural" desires have been mentioned—those for food and for sleep. More interesting, and more revealing of the basic motivation of Epicurus' ethics, is the prominence he assigned to the desire for repose, which he understood both in a physical sense, as rest and relaxation from the hurly-burly of ordinary living, and in a psychical sense, as freedom from worry. If men can learn to eliminate all idle and unnecessary desires for fine living and at the same time find mental repose, they will achieve, Epicurus thought, a state of blessedness.

This suggests that, despite what Epicurus said, the supreme good in his system was not pleasure as such, but repose. And this in turn explains why he so much preferred simple, "quiet" pleasures: not because they are pleasures, but because they are quiet. It also suggests another reason for the popularity of Epicureanism in the post-Alexandrian world. An ethics that emphasized quiet and repose appealed to men who had abandoned the ideal of all-round personal development because they had found the society they lived in too complex for them to hope to control. Epicureanism provided good (that is, philosophically respectable) reasons for doing what such men already wanted to do on other grounds: to give up, to withdraw from the competition.

Now repose is certainly destroyed by competition. But it is also destroyed by worry. And the two chief worries that disrupt repose, according to Epicurus, are fear of death and fear of divine intervention in the natural processes of the world. If we can rid ourselves of these worries, it will be relatively easy to achieve that mental repose that is blessedness. Fortunately they are both groundless superstitions, and the chief value of Atomistic physics, Epicurus held, was that it served to eradicate both of them.

Fear of death is bred by our ignorance of our nature. It is obvious, assuming the Atomistic philosophy, that personal identity does not survive the death of our bodies. There is nothing about us that is not material. When, because of some particularly heavy "blow from without," or for any other reason, the atoms forming this body are scattered, this personality is at an end.

It follows that

> . . . death is nothing to us. For all good and evil consists in sensation, but death is deprivation of sensation. And therefore a right understanding that death is nothing to us makes the mortality of life enjoyable, not because it adds to it an infinite span of time, but because it takes away the craving for immortality. For there is nothing terrible in life for the man who has truly comprehended that there is nothing terrible in not living. [Death] does not then concern either the living or the dead, since for the former it is not, and the latter are no more.[f]

This is why the Epicureans interested themselves in science—not because, as Plato and Aristotle had held, knowledge is a positive good in itself, but because knowledge brings repose, the repose of a mind freed from worry. "If we were not troubled by our suspicions of the phenomena of the sky and about death, fearing that it concerns us, and also by our failure to grasp the limits of pains and desires, we should have no need of natural science."[g]

### EPICUREANISM IN ROME: LUCRETIUS

All these themes were very powerfully stated by Lucretius, the chief Roman Epicurean.[4] He lived during the time of troubles when the old Republican institutions were proving inadequate to handle the new situation created by world power and territorial expansion, and before the new imperium had been evolved, and his views reveal not only his own highly sensitive personality but also some of the tensions and strains of the age.

Like Epicurus, Lucretius was convinced that fear of death haunts men. They make the mistake of imagining themselves somehow existing in another sphere, distressed by watching the destruction of their bodies and missing themselves when they have disappeared from the world.

> Death . . . is naught to us, nor does it concern us a whit, inasmuch as the nature of the mind is but a mortal possession. . . . When we shall be no more, when there shall have come the parting of body and soul, by whose union we are made one, you may know that nothing at all will be able to happen to us, who then will be no more, or stir our feeling. . . .
> When in life each man pictures himself that it will come to pass that

---

4 Very little is known about Lucretius. He was probably born about 94 B.C., and he died in 55 B.C. According to St. Jerome, who is an unreliable witness because he lived four centuries later and because, in any case, he liked to believe the worst of wicked pagans, Lucretius was driven mad by a love philter, wrote some poems in his lucid intervals, and finally committed suicide. Virgil, who ought to have been better informed, thought him happy because he knew "the causes of things."

birds and wild beasts will mangle his body in death, he pities himself; for neither does he separate himself from the corpse, nor withdraw himself enough from the outcast body, but thinks that it is he, and, as he stands watching, taints it with his own feeling. Hence he chafes that he was born mortal, and sees not that in real death there will be no second self, to live and mourn to himself his own loss, or to stand there and be pained that he lies mangled or burning.[h]

This is the reason for Lucretius' repeated attacks on religion. It plays on these superstitious fears and exacerbates them. Crushed by the weight of religion, men grovel upon the earth. Religion, far from being holy itself, "has given birth to deeds most sinful and unholy"—deeds such as Agamemnon's sacrifice of the innocent Iphigenia at Aulis, in the mistaken belief, fostered by the priests, that her death would please the gods and permit the Greek fleet to sail against Troy. "Such evil deeds could religion prompt."[i]

Even those who claim to be enlightened, who deny that they believe in an afterlife or in hell as a place of punishment, secretly continue to do so. Indeed, fear of hell

> . . . utterly confounds the life of men from the very root, clouding all things with the blackness of death, and suffering no pleasure to be pure and unalloyed. For, although men often declare that disease and a life of disgrace are more to be feared than the lower realm of death, and that they know that the soul's nature is of blood, or else of wind, . . . these same men, exiled from their country and banished far from the sight of men, stained with some foul crime, beset with every kind of care, live on all the same, and, spite of all, to whatever place they come in their misery, they make sacrifice to the dead, and slaughter black cattle and despatch offerings to the gods of the dead, and in their bitter plight far more keenly turn their hearts to religion. . . . the mask is torn off, and the truth remains behind.[j]

Lucretius wrote so feelingly about the fear of death that we may suspect that he was himself strongly affected by the thoughts he described and that his verses were addressed more to himself, in an effort to allay his own distress, than to the public at large. However this may be, he gave a very acute psychological analysis of the way an unconscious fear of death affects everything that men do, making them restless, vacillating, and profoundly discontent.

> If only men, even as they clearly feel a weight in their mind, which wears them out with its heaviness, could learn too from what causes that comes to be, and whence so great a mass, as it were, of ill lies upon their breast, they would not pass their lives, as now for the most part we see them; knowing not each one of them what he wants, and longing ever for change of place, as though he could thus lay aside the burden. The man who is tired of staying at home, often goes out abroad from his great mansion, and

of a sudden returns again, for indeed abroad he feels no better. He races to his country home, furiously driving his ponies, as though he were hurrying to bring help to a burning house; he yawns at once, when he has set foot on the threshold of the villa, or sinks into a heavy sleep and seeks forgetfulness, or even in hot haste makes for town, eager to be back. In this way each man struggles to escape himself: yet, despite his will he clings to the self, which we may be sure, in fact he cannot shun, and hates himself, because in his sickness he knows not the cause of his malady; but if he saw it clearly, every man would leave all else, and study first to learn the nature of things, since it is his state for all eternity, and not for a single hour, that is in question, the state in which mortals must expect all their being, that is to come after their death.

Again, what evil craving for life is this which constrains us with such force to live so restlessly in doubt and danger? . . . Nor in truth by prolonging life do we take away a jot from the time of death, nor can we subtract anything whereby we may be perchance less long dead. Therefore you may live on to close as many generations as you will: yet no whit the less that everlasting death will await you, nor will he for a less long time be no more, who has made an end of life with to-day's light, than he who perished many months of years ago.[k]

In terms that anticipated some of Freud's insights, Lucretius suggested that fear of death may be the underlying, though unconscious, motive for many of the crimes men commit and the vices to which they are committed:

Avarice and the blind craving for honours, which constrain wretched men to overleap the boundaries of right, and sometimes as comrades or accomplices in crime to struggle night and day with surpassing toil to rise up to the height of power—these sores in life are fostered in no small degree by the fear of death. For most often scorned disgrace and biting poverty are seen to be far removed from pleasant settled life, and are, as it were, a present dallying before the gates of death; and while men, spurred by a false fear, desire to flee far from them, and to drive them far away, they amass substance by civil bloodshed and greedily multiply their riches, heaping slaughter on slaughter. Hardening their heart they revel in a brother's bitter death, and hate and fear their kinsmen's board. . . . Some of them come to ruin to win statues and a name; and often through fear of death so deeply does the hatred of life and the sight of the light possess men, that with sorrowing heart they compass their own death, forgetting that it is this fear which is the source of their woes. . . . Often ere now men have betrayed country and beloved parents, seeking to shun the realms of Acheron. For even as children tremble and fear everything in blinding darkness, so we sometimes dread in the light things that are no whit more to be feared than what children shudder at in the dark, and imagine will come to pass. This terror then, this darkness of the mind, must needs be scattered, not by the rays of the sun and the gleaming shafts of day, but by the outer view and the inner law of nature.[l]

Lucretius shared Epicurus' hatred of religious superstition as being disruptive of repose and seconded Epicurus' praise of frugality and the simple life:

> For the body's nature but few things at all are needful, even such as can take away pain. Yea, though pleasantly enough from time to time they can prepare for us in many ways a lap of luxury, yet nature herself feels no loss, if there are not golden images of youths about the halls, grasping fiery torches in their right hands, that light may be supplied to banquets at night, if the house does not glow with silver or gleam with gold, nor do fretted and gilded ceilings re-echo to the lute. And yet, for all this, men lie in friendly groups on the soft grass near some stream of water under the branches of a tall tree, and at no great cost delightfully refresh their bodies, above all when the weather smiles on them, and the season of the year bestrews the green grass with flowers. Nor do fiery fevers more quickly quit the body, if you toss on broidered pictures and blushing purple, than if you must lie on the poor man's plaid. Wherefore . . . in our body riches are of no profit, nor high birth nor the glories of kingship. . . .[m]

### THE APPEAL OF EPICUREANISM

There is no doubt that Epicureanism answered a real need of a deeply troubled world. In fact, the very points at which it differed most from Platonism and Aristotelianism reflect the changed conditions that have been described. Whereas Plato and Aristotle had insisted on participation in affairs, the Epicureans never tired of describing the attractions of a wise passivity.

> We must release ourselves from the prison of affairs and politics.
> Every desire must be confronted with this question: what will happen to me, if the object of my desire is accomplished and what if it is not?
> Nothing is sufficient for him to whom what is sufficient seems little.
> The greatest fruit of self-sufficiency is freedom.[n]

The doctrine that repose is blessedness and that one achieves it by reducing one's desires to the bare minimum could have appealed only at a time when city-state culture, on the basis of which Plato and Aristotle had fashioned their theories, was at an end.

The Epicureans might well have claimed to be more realistic than Plato and Aristotle had been, for the old classical world was dying and could not be revived. On the other hand, the Roman Empire, which none of these thinkers could have dreamed of, came into being and created a new order in which many of the classical ideals experienced a long Indian summer. Stoicism, to which we now turn, certainly shared some of the tendencies toward otherworldliness and internality that we have found in Epicureanism. Yet it nonetheless managed to express the continuing values of an active social and political life.

## Stoicism

The founder of this school was Zeno.[5] He was born in Cyprus, went to Athens as a young man, about 320 or 315 B.C.—just after Aristotle's death—and, after studying under the leading philosophers of the day, founded his own school about 300 B.C. The school took its name from the place where Zeno taught—a porch (in Greek, *stoa*, hence the name Stoic), or open colonnade, famous among the Athenians for its frescoes. Zeno died about 264 B.C., respected by his adopted fellow-townsmen for the simplicity and modesty of his life. He had come to Athens in the first place because of the deep impression the views of Socrates had made on him in his island home. And it was the simple ethical opinions of Socrates rather than the elaborate metaphysical theories of Plato and Aristotle that were the primary inspiration of Zeno's own views.

Already, before Zeno's appearance, a group of Socratic disciples had banded together to put into practice what they took to be the teachings of their master. These men, who were called "Cynics"[6] because of their scorn for the ordinary amenities of life, took quite a different tack from that of Plato, who also claimed to be a disciple of Socrates. Whereas Plato was interested in Socrates' method of inquiry and in the high value he assigned to the pursuit of truth, what struck the Cynics as important in Socrates' teaching was his independence of character and his indifference to circumstance. They completely ignored Socrates' dictum, "Virtue is knowledge," but clung to his belief that no harm can come to a good man.

Since poverty, pain, suffering, and death obviously can and do come to good men, the Cynics reasoned that none of these is really bad. The truly virtuous man will be indifferent to everything that happens to him. By extension, and pressing this side of Socrates' teaching to an extreme, the Cynics held that manners, customs, all the small decencies and proprieties of social intercourse, as well as the larger matters of political relationship, are without value and should therefore be ignored. Their conclusion was thus thoroughly revolutionary and completely opposed to the view of the Platonic Socrates, whose respect for law was so great that he refused to cooperate in an illegal act that would have saved his life.

In his search for the true Socratic fount, Zeno at first apparently came under the influence of the Cynics; but their anarchistic position did not long content him. The real problem for him was to reconcile the independence of the Cynic sage with the realities of political and social life of which Plato and Aristotle

---

5 Not to be confused with Zeno the pupil of Parmenides. See pp. 22–24.
6 They were called Cynics, not because of their "cynical" attitude toward human motives, but because *cynos* is the Greek word for dog, and they were thought to be doglike in their churlishness and captiousness and in their indifference to the niceties of life.

had been so fully aware. This problem Zeno and the other early Stoics left as an inheritance to the Roman Stoics.

Before examining the Romans' solution to this particular problem, let us briefly consider the other departments of Stoic thought. Zeno and the other Stoics, following the Peripatetics, made a tripartite division of philosophy into (1) logic (theory of knowledge), (2) physics (including, as with Aristotle, the natural sciences and psychology), and (3) ethics.

## THEORY OF KNOWLEDGE

The Stoics based their theory of knowledge on an extreme sensationalism. Where do our concepts come from? From perceptions, the Stoics answered. And what is perception? According to the Stoics, the mind at birth is a blank page. Objects (for example, horses) stamp impressions of themselves on the mind just as a seal stamps an impression on wax. Remembered impressions of actual horses, compared and contrasted, give rise to the general idea "horse." The form "horse" is neither an independently existing entity (as Plato held) nor a real component in a spatiotemporal substance (as Aristotle held). It is only a mental construction, a concept, which has no reality outside the mind. Though conceptualism, as this type of view is called, is not without difficulties, it has had many adherents in the history of philosophy. Hence we can hardly criticize the Stoics for having been conceptualists, but it is fair to criticize them for having been rather naïve conceptualists (unless, of course, they stated their theory more sophisticatedly in writings that have not survived). For instance, there are both true and false perceptions. That is, there are perceptions of real objects out there, and there are also hallucinations and illusions (a mirage, the bent oar in water). How are these to be distinguished? By the vividness and strength with which they are impressed upon us, the Stoics said. But this is obviously inadequate; impressions so vivid that we cannot fail to assent to them (for example, the hallucinations of a dipsomaniac) may nevertheless be false, that is, fail to represent a real object.

Aristotle's way of dealing with this problem had been to argue that real objects possess a form, whereas hallucinations and illusions do not. Veridical perception involves the transference of the object's sensible form to the percipient. This, indeed, is what makes the perception veridical. In hallucinatory and illusory experiences there is no sensible form to be transferred; this is precisely why these experiences are not veridical, even though they may be vivid and intense. Thus Aristotle had a criterion for distinguishing true perceptions from false perceptions. Unfortunately, it seems that there is no way of applying this criterion in specific cases. Hence the notion of a sensible form is not satisfactory. But at least it was an attempt to meet a genuine difficulty. The Stoics seem to have abandoned Aristotle's sensible form without even seeing the problem it was designed to solve.

## PHYSICS

In their physics the Stoics held, as would be expected from their theory of knowledge, that only matter is real. Starting from Aristotle's position that individual things are a complex of matter and forms, and rejecting, as we have just seen, his view that form is real, they obviously had to conclude that nothing exists except body. This thesis they maintained with exemplary, if misguided, logic, forcing themselves into the paradoxical position that not only god and the soul but also such properties as good and bad are corporeal. What these latter assertions meant to them it is impossible to say.[7]

However this may be, they certainly identified matter with a particular kind of body—fire. They also said that it is "god." Here, of course, we see the influence of Heraclitus. And here, as with their theory of knowledge, they seem to have overlooked difficulties that had long been recognized by other philosophers. In reverting to a Heraclitean type of view they silently passed over all the difficulties in that earlier version of materialism that the whole development of Atomism had uncovered and attempted to meet.

On the other hand, as regards the details of their physical theory, the Stoics were content to follow Aristotle's lead. Having asserted their independence of the master with regards to the first principles of physics, they were not prepared to do independent research on their own account. According to Cicero (who was certainly no unfriendly critic), although Zeno "changed a name" here and there, this "did not alter the fact that he had sprung from [the Peripatetics]."[o]

## ETHICS

In ethics, however, the Stoics made an original contribution, though even here their central concept, the notion of nature, was derived from Aristotle. The highest good for any creature, they thought, consists in acting in accordance with its nature. Happiness, they said, following a familiar line of thought, is the name for this kind of activity. But whereas Aristotle had maintained that contemplation is the supreme good, the stricter Stoics held that knowledge has only instrumental value. Like the Epicureans—and for that matter, like many modern men—they valued science only for its use. But, whereas today we are likely to value it chiefly for its technology, and whereas the Epicureans valued it chiefly because it disabuses us of superstitious fears, the Stoics valued it chiefly because it helps us discover our nature and so enables us to fit ourselves into the universe of which we are a tiny part.

What then is man's nature? In what kind of activity does natural science reveal his happiness and virtue to lie? To begin with, although the Stoics held the world to be a deterministic system, they did not believe that it is a blind mechanism like

---

[7] Modern critics have displayed much ingenuity in suggesting meanings for these propositions. See, for instance, Zeller, *Stoics, Epicureans and Sceptics*, p. 131.

that envisaged by the Atomists. Somehow or other it involves divine providence. (We have just seen that, though the Stoics held matter to be "fire," they also held it to be "god.") Moreover, the universe behaves in accordance with laws the human mind can fathom. It is therefore fair, the Stoics thought, to describe it as "rational." The universe and man, they reasoned, stand to each other as macrocosm and microcosm. Just as man's life, because he is a rational animal, involves order, law, and reason, so we can infer, because the universe displays a similar (or even more thoroughgoing) orderliness, that there is a world reason. This they variously called "Zeus," "nature," "providence," and "logos," each of these terms bringing out one facet of a complex and not always entirely self-consistent notion.

Perhaps the element in this notion that is most important historically is expressed by the term "nature," which had a long history before the Stoics employed it. It will be recalled that the conflict between the Sophists and their opponents in the fifth century B.C. had been stated in terms of a contrast between nature and convention. Is law merely a convention entered into by men for their mutual advantage, or is it somehow a part of the nature of things? Plato and Aristotle had argued, in opposition to the subjectivism of the Sophists, that there is a nature— that is, a public world. Morality, they had maintained, consists in living in conformity with that world. Though much human behavior is obviously conventional (wearing a black tie with a dinner jacket, genuflecting before an altar), much, Plato and Aristotle held, does not depend on decisions taken, or on habits formed, by men. As Aristotle wrote,

> Of political justice part is natural, part legal,[8]—natural, that which everywhere has the same force and does not exist by people's thinking this or that; legal, that which is originally indifferent, but when it has been laid down is not indifferent, e.g. that a prisoner's ransom shall be a mina, or that a goat and not two sheep shall be sacrificed. . . . Now some think that all justice is of this sort, because that which is by nature is unchangeable and has everywhere the same force (as fire burns both here and in Persia), while they see change in the things recognized as just. This, however, is not true in this unqualified way, . . . there is something that is just even by nature, yet all of it is changeable; but still some is by nature, some not by nature. It is evident which sort of thing, among things capable of being otherwise, is by nature; and which is not but is legal and conventional, assuming that both are equally changeable. And in all other things the same distinction will apply; by nature the right hand is stronger, yet it is possible that all men should come to be ambidextrous. The things which are just by virtue of convention and expediency are like measures; for wine and corn measures are not everywhere equal, but larger in wholesale and smaller in retail markets. Similarly, the things which are just not by nature but by human enactment are not everywhere the same, since constitutions also are

8 [The term translated here as "legal" also means "convention"—AUTHOR.]

not the same, though there is but one which is everywhere by nature the best.[p]

The natural, in other words, is the norm, the type, the form. Though every oak tree is just itself, with its own particular way of growth, and though there is no actually perfect example of an oak anywhere, we can evaluate actual oaks by the extent of their deviation from the norm for oak trees. The nature, or norm, "oak" is thus a certain pattern, or relationship among the parts. And, generally speaking, everything has a "nature," which is the norm for its relations to other things.

This conception of nature was picked up by the Stoics. When they said that happiness consists in activity in accordance with nature, they meant activity in accordance with the order that they conceived the universe to exhibit. In the same way that we can criticize oak trees for falling short of, or deviating from, *their* norm, we can criticize existing human institutions for falling short of, or deviating from, those relationships that express the norm of human conduct. We therefore have to distinguish, the Stoics held, between the actual laws that from time to time govern men's relations in states and the ideal relations that ought to obtain but only too often do not.

This notion of nature also suggested to the Stoics the universal brotherhood of man. If all actual codes of law ought to be evaluated in terms of a single universal law, all men everywhere ought, ideally, to be members of one universal community, citizens of one city.

The idea of a cosmopolis, or universal city, was a Stoic discovery. Though it is doubtless a logical corollary of the concept of nature that Plato and Aristotle had developed, they had been too deeply wedded to the city-state ideal to make the inference. In the new age, however, when the old *polis* had disappeared as an effective political entity, it was much easier to see that nature is not only a criterion but a universal order. Yet if it is true that men's actual experience with the Roman imperium suggested the notion of an ideal cosmopolis, it is just as true that the notion of a cosmopolis made the imperium possible. In such matters as these causality is not a one-way street. Granted that the new large-scale political unit suggested the idea to the Stoics, and granted, too, that the Empire actually had its origin in whatever sordid and realistic policies one cares to attribute to the old consuls and proconsuls, it is still true that the ideal of cosmopolis provided an ethical justification for the imperium and gave an added moral dimension to policy. Moreover, by providing Roman jurists with a useful practical distinction between the differing local laws of the various peoples of the Empire and the universal imperial law binding on all these peoples alike, it became the operating basis for assimilating these peoples and their widely differing institutions.

The influence of this Stoic concept of natural law did not stop with the Roman jurists. Absorbed into Christianity and reinterpreted as the command of the Christian God, this notion survived through the Middle Ages into the modern period. When our founding fathers drew up the Declaration and the Constitution and the Bill of Rights, they believed themselves to be putting in writing the dictates of natural law.

The ideal of cosmopolis was not the only implication the Stoics drew from the concept of nature. Another was the notion of duty. This again, of course, was not a novel idea. Hesiod and the other poets, for instance, had written about man's duty. But they had tended to associate it with the threat of divine punishment or the fear of some other evil consequence. Even with Plato and Aristotle the primary sanction for right conduct had been the individual's own happiness. Plato, for instance, had not disputed Thrasymachus' contention that a sensible man aims at his own advantage; he had merely argued that Thrasymachus was mistaken about what a man's advantage is and about how to attain it.[9]

The Stoics, on the contrary, gave duty a primacy it had never before had in Greek thought. They conceived it as wholly distinct from advantage, however long-range. Though they continued to talk of man's end as being "happiness," they thought of this state more negatively than positively. Stoic happiness did not consist (as Plato and Aristotle had held) in the all-round development of the complex human personality; still less did it consist in pleasure, that titillation of the senses that the Sophists had taken to be the good. Happiness for the Stoics was apathy, the peace of mind that comes through acceptance of the universe as it is, and a corresponding indifference to the course of events.

It follows that the Stoics believed that only our motives have moral significance. Aristotle had certainly emphasized the moral significance of the motives from which men act. This appeared, for instance, in the distinctions he drew between death by misadventure, manslaughter, and deliberate homicide.[10] The Stoics, however, went far beyond Aristotle. What is accomplished by an act, they held, matters naught; what is intended is everything. This is in part nothing but the logical result of their concentration on acceptance as the sole good. What matters morally is not the state of affairs produced by our act, but the state of mind that has led us to act. And the only moral state of mind from the Stoic point of view is acceptance—acceptance of the universe and of our place in it.

This exclusive concentration on a single motive appears also in the Stoics' utter rejection of the emotions. The earlier and more representative Greek position had been that the goodness or badness of an emotion depends on how it operates. The traditional emphasis on temperance was a reflection of this attitude. The moral aim was not to expunge the emotional side of life but to regulate it in the interests of the whole man. Though Plato showed a certain ambivalence with regard to the emotions, even he had tended toward this point of view. For instance, he had held that anger, far from being bad in itself, can and should be a useful ally of reason. And Aristotle carried this thesis even further, maintaining in effect that the essence of morality consists in taking into account the time, the place, and the

9 See pp. 170–72.
10 See pp. 279–80.

circumstances, and all the other variable factors in a situation. For him, an emotion had moral significance only within such a context. This was the meaning of moderation. The Stoics' view, by contrast, was sharply ascetic. Moderation, they held, is as bad as excess, since the supreme good is apathy.

Because Stoic virtue is unitary, it is either wholly present or wholly absent. The attainment of virtue entails a long and arduous period of preparation and training; during his novitiate the would-be sage is as wholly lacking in virtue as are those who do not even seek the true good. When virtue finally comes (if indeed it ever comes), it is attained all at once in a moment of conversion when worldly things are put away and the true perspective on the universe is achieved. In its rejection of culture, friendship, and other things generally held valuable, and in its insistence on lumping together in one indifferent mass of folly and sin all those who do not achieve the perfect serenity of the sage, this early version of Stoic ethics betrays Zeno's association with the Cynics.

Apart from its narrowness and extreme asceticism, the theory involves a number of internal inconsistencies. For instance, since the Stoic theory of knowledge had explicitly rejected the theory of forms, it is rather surprising to have forms turning up again as the norms, or natural laws, to which we ought to make our conduct conform. And again, if the universe is a deterministic system, as the Stoics also held, can men choose whether to conform or not? These questions the Stoics nowhere answered.

On the other hand, some of the Stoic insights are persuasive. Their ideal of a single society, where men act not for personal advantage but out of respect for the universal law, still has power to move us. Here, for the first time, in place of the old closed societies of earlier peoples, we have the vision of an open society in which all men, just because they are men, are equal under the law. Here is a view with obvious appeal for the Roman statesmen and jurists who were gradually forging a new kind of imperium—a universal state with a universal citizenship.

## THE APPEAL OF STOICISM TO ROMANS

Instead of rejecting Stoicism, Roman thinkers therefore attempted to purge it of its exaggerations. It was necessary, if Stoicism was to function usefully as a social philosophy in the Roman Empire, to soft-pedal "apathy." It was admirable for politicians to learn indifference to their private good, but indifference to the well-being of the community was quite another matter. The apathy of the sage, as the stricter Stoics described him, was incompatible with any activity at all, political or otherwise.

That is to say, the Stoics' original insistence on the unity of virtue had to be abandoned. Therefore, instead of emphasizing the single duty of acceptance, the Roman Stoics gave elaborate descriptions of the various duties of mankind. But in this expanded concept the original Stoic affirmation of obligation, rather than interest, was retained, so that an ascetic and altruistic tone continued to dominate Roman Stoic thought. Hence there is a marked ambivalence about much of Stoic writing. These divergent strains that merge but do not completely fuse appear, for instance, in the Stoics' attitudes toward courage. At times true courage is described as nonparticipation, as self-sufficiency, as indifference to one's fate. Suicide ("the free departure") is the sign of the really courageous man. On the other hand, courage is elsewhere described as steadfastness in the face of odds. The courageous man is one who takes his political duties seriously and unflinchingly.

Stoicism, then, never quite succeeded in developing a consistent moral philosophy, but this deficiency did not matter much to the Stoics themselves, who were less interested in philosophy as a rational account of the universe than as a rationale by which they could live in a troubled world. Stoicism, in fact, was more a religion (doubtless a rather secular religion) than a philosophical theory. This is apparent from the Stoics' tendency to use words with an emotive rather than a precisely cognitive meaning. We have already seen an example of this tendency in the great variety of terms they employed to characterize the universe itself.[11] Another is their use of the term "reason." Whereas Aristotle had made a careful and systematic analysis of reason as a mode of cognition, the Stoics used this word loosely to refer to any state of affairs of which they approved. Nevertheless, as compared with most of the views that were spreading over the Mediterranean world at about the same time—including the early versions of Christianity and the other mystery religions—Stoicism was still rational and still Greek.

With this much as an introduction, let us examine the views of several representative Roman thinkers.

## Cicero

Marcus Tullius Cicero, who was born in 106 B.C., was a brilliant lawyer. His talents in this field brought him to the consulship in 63 B.C., but election to this office was the climax of his career, for he lacked the judgment and political acumen necessary to deal effectively with the complex problems that then confronted Rome. The Republic was in its last period, and various contestants for supreme power fought a succession of bloody civil wars. In the midst of this conflict Cicero stood for the old order under which the Senate had ruled Rome, and against the new type of one-man rule. We may feel a natural sympathy with Cicero's republicanism, even while recognizing that the Senate was no longer capable of conducting affairs. The whole current of events was in fact against the policy that Cicero advocated, and he lost his life in the same struggle that destroyed the Republic itself. In 43 B.C. he was killed on the orders of Antony, one of the contenders for power after the assassination of Julius Caesar.

11 See p. 328.

In the intervals of his political career, and especially toward the end, when its failure was increasingly evident, Cicero turned to philosophy. He drew on many sources—Peripatetic, Academic, and old Roman, as well as Stoic. This is probably what most Romans did. Hence, though Cicero was not even remotely an original philosopher, he provides us with a very good example of Roman thought.

In the *De Finibus* (*Concerning the Ends of Life*) he discussed the ethical views of the rival schools. Against the Epicurean view that each individual's own pleasure is his sole good, Cicero affirmed the Stoic notion that "the Chief Good consists in applying to the conduct of life a knowledge of the working of natural causes, choosing what is in accordance with nature and rejecting what is contrary to it; in other words, the Chief Good is to live in agreement and in harmony with nature."q

### WHAT IS NATURE?

Having decided that the good is life in accordance with nature, Cicero inevitably asked the familiar question, "What is nature?" His answer reveals both his basic Stoic orientation and his typically Roman antagonism to the more extreme Stoic contention that everything short of complete virtue is equally bad. Cicero described the view of these stricter Stoics in terms that show how impractical he held it to be. They maintained, he said, "that all men's folly, injustice and other vices are alike and all sins are equal; and that those who by nature and training have made considerable progress toward virtue, unless they have actually attained to it, are utterly miserable, and there is nothing whatever to choose between their existence and that of the wickedest of mankind, so that the great and famous Plato, supposing he was not a Wise Man, lived a no better and no happier life than any unprincipled scoundrel."r

Cicero did not merely hold this position to be impractical. He also showed, very effectively, that the Stoic defense of it was an elaborate piece of verbal legerdemain. Zeno's arguments, he pointed out,

> . . . could not possibly be produced in civic life, in the law-courts, in the senate! . . . Could an advocate wind up his defense of a client by declaring that exile and confiscation of property are not evils? that they are "to be rejected," but not "to be shunned"? that it is not a judge's duty to show mercy? Or supposing him to be addressing a meeting of the people; Hannibal is at the gates and has flung a javelin over the city walls; could he say that captivity, enslavement, death, loss of country are no evils? . . . What sort of a philosophy then is this, which speaks the ordinary language in public, but in its treatises employs an idiom of its own? . . . Why, what difference does it make whether you call wealth, power, health "goods," or "things preferred," when he who calls them goods assigns no more value to them than you who style exactly the same things "preferred"? . . .
>
> Zeno's answer . . . is that while between the moral and the base a vast,

enormous gulf is fixed, between all other things there is no difference whatever. . . . These intermediate things, says Zeno, which have no difference between them, are still of such a nature that some of them are to be selected and
others rejected, while others again are to be entirely ignored; that is, they are
such that some you wish to have, others you wish not to have, and about others
you do not care.—"But you told us just now that there was no difference
among them."—"And I say the same now," he will reply, "but I mean no
difference in respect of virtue and vice. . . . The things you mentioned," he
continues, "health, affluence, freedom from pain, I do not call goods, but I will
call them in Greek *proēgmena*, that is in your language 'brought forward'
(though I will rather use 'preferred' or 'pre-eminent,' as these sound smoother
and more acceptable) and on the other hand disease, poverty and pain I do not
style evils, but, if you please, 'things rejected.' Accordingly I do not speak of
'desiring' but 'selecting' these things, not of 'wishing' but 'adopting' them, and
not of 'avoiding' their opposites but so to speak 'discarding' them." What say
Aristotle and the other pupils of Plato? That they call all things in accordance
with nature good and all things contrary to nature bad. Do you see therefore
that . . . between him and Aristotle and the rest there is a real agreement and
a verbal disagreement? Why, then, as we are agreed as to the fact, do we not
prefer to employ the usual terminology? Or else let him prove that I shall be
readier to despise money if I believe it to be a "thing preferred" than if I
believe it to be a good, and braver to endure pain if I say it is irksome and hard
to bear and contrary to nature, than if I call it an evil. Our friend Marcus Piso
was often witty, but never more so than when he ridiculed the Stoics on this
score. "What?" he said, "You tell us wealth is not good but you say it is 'preferred'; how does that help matters? do you diminish avarice? In what way?
If it is a question of words, 'preferred' is a longer word than 'good.'"[s]

## CICERO'S MODIFIED STOICISM

Though Cicero ridiculed the extreme Stoic position, he was far from rejecting
the Stoic conception of virtue. Rather, he wanted to bring this noble and altruistic
ideal into relation with the realities of daily life. It was arbitrary and perverse, he
thought, to insist that there is only one kind of act that is in accord with
nature and so appropriate for men to do. On the contrary, "No phase of life,
whether public or private, whether in business or in the home, whether one is
working on what concerns oneself alone or dealing with another, can be without
its moral duty; on the discharge of such duties depends all that is morally right,
and on their neglect all that is morally wrong in life."[t]

In his treatise, *Concerning Duties*, Cicero discussed social duties in almost
exhaustive detail. His purpose, characteristically, was hortatory, not analytical.
Hence, though the treatise might possibly make a man better, the treatise
in itself has little philosophical interest. What is significant is the fact that Cicero
was led to distinguish between (1) laws that are merely the "product of government" (that is, the enactment of some individual or group with the power to
enforce their decisions) and (2) laws that are based on the nature of things.

> True law is right reason in agreement with nature; it is of universal appli-
> cation, unchanging and everlasting; it summons to duty by its commands, and
> averts from wrongdoing by its prohibitions. . . . We cannot be freed from its
> obligations by senate or people, and we need not look outside ourselves for an
> expounder or interpreter of it. And there will not be different laws at Rome
> and at Athens, or different laws now and in the future, but one eternal and
> unchangeable law will be valid for all nations and all times, and there will be
> one master and ruler, that is, God, over us all, for he is the author of this law,
> its promulgator, and its enforcing judge. Whoever is disobedient is fleeing from
> himself and denying his human nature, and by reason of this very fact he will
> suffer the worst penalties, even if he escapes what is commonly considered
> punishment. . . .[u]

Though, as has been pointed out, both Plato and Aristotle drew a distinction
between nature and convention, Cicero formulated this distinction quite differently. In some respects his formulation resembled Hesiod's—he distinguished
sharply, as Hesiod did, between the law for man and the law for beasts. But if we
had asked Hesiod why men should obey the higher law, his answer would have
been that "Zeus the son of Cronos has ordained it." If we had asked Cicero, his
answer would have been that "reason" requires it:

> By moral worth, then, we understand that which is of such a nature that,
> though devoid of all utility, it can justly be commended in and for itself, apart
> from any profit or reward. . . . Good men do a great many things from which
> they anticipate no advantage, solely from the motive of propriety, morality
> and right. For among the many points of difference between man and the
> lower animals, the greatest difference is that Nature has bestowed on man the
> gift of Reason. . . . Reason . . . has produced conformity of character, of lan-
> guage and of habit; she has prompted the individual, starting from friendship
> and from family affection, to expand his interests, forming social ties first with
> his fellow-citizens and later with all mankind. She reminds him that . . . man
> was not born for self alone, but for country and for kindred, claims that leave
> but a small part of him for himself. Nature has also engendered in mankind the
> desire of contemplating truth. . . . This primary instinct leads us on to love all
> truth as such, that is, all that is trustworthy, simple and consistent, and to hate
> things insincere, false and deceptive, such as cheating, perjury, malice and
> injustice.[v]

Thus, according to Cicero, "reason," not Hesiod's divine will or Plato's enlightened self-interest, is the ultimate sanction for doing one's duty. This formulation was to have momentous consequences in the history of thought. First, it
provided a universal criterion by which states and their laws can be evaluated. In
fact, Cicero distinguished between a mere "assemblage of people" and a state on
the ground that an assemblage is a state only when the laws in force in it are
modeled on the eternal law of nature.

> A commonwealth is the property of a people. But a people is not any col-
> lection of human beings brought together in any sort of way, but an assem-
> blage of people in large numbers associated in an agreement with respect to
> justice and a partnership for the common good. The first cause of such an
> association is not so much the weakness of the individual as a certain social
> spirit which nature has implanted in man. For man is not a solitary or unsocial
> creature. . . .ʷ

And, second, since the law of nature is applicable to all men equally, provided
only that they possess reason, this doctrine led directly to the idea of cosmopolis:

> That animal which we call man, . . . has been given a certain distinguished
> status by the supreme God who created him; for he is the only one among so
> many different kinds and varieties of living beings who has a share in reason
> and thought, while all the rest are deprived of it. . . . Since there is nothing
> better than reason, and since it exists both in man and God, the first common
> possession of man and God is reason. But those who have reason in common
> must also have right reason in common. And since right reason is Law, we must
> believe that men have Law also in common with the gods. Further, those who
> share Law must also share Justice; and those who share these are to be re-
> garded as members of the same commonwealth. . . . Hence we must now con-
> ceive of this whole universe as one commonwealth of which both gods and men
> are members. . . .
> The universe is governed by divine will; it is a city or state of which both
> men and gods are members, and each one of us is a part of this universe; from
> which it is a natural consequence that we should prefer the common advan-
> tage to our own.ˣ

Thus all men, as citizens of one state, are fellows; and all, as subject to one law,
are equal.

> There is no difference in kind between man and man; for . . . reason, which
> alone raises us above the level of the beasts and enables us to draw inferences,
> to prove and disprove, to discuss and solve problems, and to come to conclu-
> sions, is certainly common to us all, and, though varying in what it learns, at
> least in the capacity to learn it is invariable. . . . In fact, there is no human
> being of any race who, if he finds a guide, cannot attain to virtue.ʸ

## Epictetus

Little is known about Epictetus' life. He was born about the middle of the first
century A.D. in Phrygia, in Asia Minor. It is thought, on rather scanty evidence,
that there was a Christian community in his birthplace, and it has been assumed
that Chirstianity exercised an influence on his thought. But the similarity between

some of Epictetus' teachings and those of the Christians may merely reflect the contemporary climate of opinion, to which all thinking men, Christians and non-Christians alike, contributed, and from which, in turn, they drew.

The only definite fact known about Epictetus' early life is that he was a slave in Rome during the reign of Nero. Since it was not unusual in those days for wealthy Romans to have their bright young slaves well educated, Epictetus may have owed his philosophical training to this custom. Later he acquired his freedom (how is not known) and taught in Rome until 98 A.D., when Domitian expelled all philosophers from the city. Thereafter, until his death, he taught at Nicopolis in Epirus, where a circle of pupils gathered about him. Like Socrates, Epictetus wrote nothing, but his disciples put down his "discourses." Of these a considerable number have survived.

### RELIGIOUS TEMPERAMENT

In Epictetus, the religious tendency of Stoicism is strikingly evident. Though he was acquainted with Stoic epistemology and physics, "he had no other purpose," Arrian, his friend and first editor declared, "than to move the minds of his hearers to the best things."[z] Epictetus believed that men would be better if they grasped the fact that a divine providence rules the world. This was his interpretation of that "nature" that, as we have seen, was the heart of Stoic doctrine.

> Has [the world] no governor? And how is it possible that a city or a family cannot continue to exist, not even the shortest time without an administrator and guardian, and that so great and beautiful a system should be administered with such order and yet without a purpose and by chance? . . .
>
> There is a God and . . . he provides for all things; also . . . it is not possible to conceal from him our acts, or even our intentions and thoughts. . . .
>
> God had need of irrational animals to make use of appearances, but of us to understand the use of appearances. It is therefore enough for them to eat and drink, and to sleep and to copulate, and to do all the other things which they severally do. But for us, to whom He has given also the intellectual faculty, these things are not sufficient; for unless we act in a proper and orderly manner, and conformably to the nature and constitution of each thing, we shall never attain our true end. For where the constitutions of living beings are different, there also the acts and the ends are different. . . . It is shameful for man to begin and to end where irrational animals do; but rather he ought to begin where they begin, and to end where nature ends in us; and nature ends in contemplation and understanding, and in a way of life conformable to nature.[a]

Moreover, god has made men akin to him: "But what says Zeus? Epictetus, . . . I have given you a small portion of us, this faculty of pursuing an object and avoiding it, and the faculty of desire and aversion, and, in a word, the faculty of using the appearances of things. . . ."[b] Thus man is a "fragment torn from God."

Every man has in him a "portion of God." From this belief in the kinship of god and man follow all Epictetus' specific teachings—for instance, that man has a duty to live up to this high origin, to live as befits one who knows that god is his maker.

> If you were a statue of Phidias, . . . you would think both of yourself and of the artist, and if you had any understanding (power of perception) you would try to do nothing unworthy of him who made you or of yourself. . . . But now because Zeus has made you, for this reason do you care not how you shall appear? . . . Being the work of such an artist do you dishonour him? And what shall I say, not only that he made you, but also entrusted you to yourself and made you a deposit to yourself? Will you not think of this too, but do you also dishonour your guardianship? But if God had entrusted an orphan to you, would you thus neglect him? He has delivered yourself to your own care, and says, I had no one fitter to entrust him to than yourself: keep him for me such as he is by nature, modest, faithful, erect, unterrified, free from passion and perturbation.[c]

Further, it follows that we should accept whatever god gives us, that is, whatever life brings us.

> And dost thou that hast received all from another's hands, repine and blame the Giver, if He takes anything from thee? . . . How brought He thee into the world? Was it not as one born to die; as one bound to live out his earthly life in some small tabernacle of flesh; to behold His administration, and for a little while to share with Him in the mighty march of this great Festival Procession? Now therefore that thou hast beheld, while it was permitted thee, the Solemn Feast and Assembly, wilt thou not cheerfully depart, when He summons thee forth, with adoration and thanksgiving for what thou hast seen and heard? —"Nay, but I would fain have stayed longer at the Festival."—Ah, . . . so perchance would the crowd at the Great Games fain behold more wrestlers still. But the Solemn Assembly is over! Come forth, depart with thanksgiving and modesty—give place to others that must come into being even as thyself. . . .
>
> Remember that thou art an actor in a play, and of such sort as the Author chooses, whether long or short. If it be his good pleasure to assign thee the part of a beggar, a cripple, a ruler, or a simple citizen, thine it is to play it fitly. For thy business is to act the part assigned thee, well: to choose it, is another's.[d]

Again, since all men are equally god's creatures, they are all equally members of one community. In this community the individual loses his self-identity. As a member of a greater communion, he sacrifices himself willingly, if need be, for the sake of that larger whole of which he is a part.

> A foot, for instance, I will allow it is natural should be clean. But if you take it as a foot, and as a thing which does not stand by itself, it will beseem it (if need be) to walk in the mud, to tread on thorns, and sometimes even to be cut

off, for the benefit of the whole body; else it is no longer a foot. In some such way we should conceive of ourselves also. What art thou?—A man.—Looked at as standing by thyself and separate, it is natural for thee in health and wealth long to live. But looked at as a *Man,* and only as a part of a Whole, it is for that Whole's sake that thou shouldst at one time fall sick, at another brave the perils of the sea, again, know the meaning of want and perhaps die an early death. Why then repine? Knowest thou not that as the foot is no more a foot if detached from the body, so thou in like case art no longer a Man? For what is a Man? A part of a City:—first of the City of Gods and Men; next, of that which ranks nearest it, a miniature of the universal City. . . .[e]

Although this line of thought could (and did) lead others to stress the importance of more positive social duties, Epictetus' temperament caused him to emphasize the other, asocial tendency in Stoicism—withdrawal from the world.

Ask you if a man shall come forward in the Athenian assembly and talk about revenue and supplies, when his business is to converse with all men, Athenians, Corinthians, and Romans alike, not about supplies, not about revenue, nor yet peace and war, but about Happiness and Misery, Prosperity and Adversity, Slavery and Freedom?

Ask you whether a man shall engage in the administration of the State who has engaged in such an Administration as this? Ask me too if he shall govern; and again I will answer, Fool, what greater government shall he hold than that he holds already? . . .

There is a great difference between other men's occupations and ours. . . . A glance at theirs will make it clear to you. All day long they do nothing but calculate, contrive, consult how to wring their profit out of food-stuffs, farm-plots and the like. . . . Whereas, I entreat you to learn what the administration of the World is, and what place a Being endowed with reason holds therein: to consider what you are yourself, and wherein your Good and Evil consists.[f]

Epictetus' quietism and religious piety were typical of what was coming to be the mood of the age. The whole of his teaching could be summed up, he said, in two words: "bear" and "forbear." "If a man will only have these two words at heart, and heed them carefully by ruling and watching over himself, he will for the most part fall into no sin, and his life will be tranquil and serene."[g]

## Marcus Aurelius

Marcus Aurelius (121–180 A.D.) was a member of a distinguished Roman family. As a boy he attracted the favorable notice of the childless emperor Hadrian, who arranged that his own adopted heir, Antoninus Pius, would in turn adopt Aurelius, thus assuring the succession to the Principate. Aurelius succeeded Antoninus Pius to the throne in 161, and though he was a peace-loving man, he was obliged to spend much of his time either at the frontier driving back invading barbarians or in distant parts of the Empire quelling revolts. In spite of these distractions he managed to institute a number of political and social reforms; his reign and that of Antoninus Pius were, according to Gibbon, "possibly the only period of history in which the happiness of a great people was the sole object of government."

Unfortunately, this short interval of serenity and prosperity closed with the death of Aurelius and the accession to the throne of his son Commodus, whose incompetence and violence may be taken as marking the beginning of the Empire's decline. Thus it is fair to say that with Aurelius we reach the end of an epoch. He was not only the last Stoic; he was also in a way the last great product of classical culture.

His *Meditations*, unlike the *Discourses* of Epictetus, were not intended for the instruction of others. They were random memoranda meant for himself alone, jotted down while he was on military expeditions, and reflecting his doubts and indecisions as well as his faith and his philosophy. We cannot, therefore, expect a formal philosophical theory from Aurelius. But just because he was not a technically trained scholar, his *Meditations* are valuable as an index of the degree to which Stoicism had permeated the culture of the Empire.

### CONCEPTION OF NATURE

Nature was the central concept around which Aurelius oriented his thought. But, like all the Stoics, he gave it an individual interpretation. For him nature was a cosmos in which everything is in a Heraclitean flux. Though everything sooner or later disappears by passing into something else, change is orderly and regular. As Heraclitus would have said, nothing "oversteps its measure." This orderliness is evidence, Aurelius thought, that the universe is rational and intelligent.

> Some things are hastening to be, others to be no more, while of those that haste into being some part is already extinct. Fluxes and changes perpetually renew the world, just as the unbroken march of time makes ever new the infinity of ages. In this river of change, which of the things which swirl past him, whereon no firm foothold is possible, should a man prize so highly? As well fall in love with a sparrow that flits past and in a moment is gone from our eyes. In fact a man's life itself is but as an exhalation from blood and an inhalation from the air. For just as it is to draw in the air once into our lungs and give it back again, as we do every moment, so is it to give back thither, whence thou didst draw it first, thy faculty of breathing which thou didst receive at thy birth yesterday or the day before. . . .
>
> All things are mutually intertwined, . . . and together help to order one ordered Universe. For there is both one Universe, made up of all things, and one God immanent in all things, and one Substance, and one Law, one Reason common to all intelligent creatures, and one Truth, if indeed there is also one

perfecting of living creatures that have the same origin and share the same reason.[h]

The universe, in fact, is "one living Being, possessed of a single . . . Soul; . . . it does all things by a single impulse . . . and . . . all existing things are joint causes of all things that come into existence; . . . how intertwined in the fabric is the thread and how closely woven the web." As a part of this universe, man shares in its life and in its divinity. In particular, his reason, which enables him to understand the world and his place in it, is a "morsel of the Divine."[i]

### EMPHASIS ON SOCIAL DUTIES

This sounds like Epictetus, but it led Aurelius—given his more outgoing temperament and the circumstances that had made him an emperor instead of a slave—to different conclusions. Instead of deciding that we should withdraw from affairs, he thought we should remember that "all that is rational is akin and that it is in man's nature to call for all men. . . ."[j]

From the basic obligation to "treat all men as fellow creatures," Aurelius derived a whole list of social and political duties:

> What then is it that calls for our devotion? This one thing: justice in thought, in act unselfishness and a tongue that cannot lie and a disposition ready to welcome all that befalls as unavoidable, as familiar, as issuing from a like origin and fountain-head. . . .
>
> Every hour make up thy mind sturdily as a Roman and a man to do what thou hast in hand with scrupulous and unaffected dignity and love of thy kind and independence and justice; and to give thyself rest from all other impressions. . . .
>
> The true life [does not lie] in the subtleties of logic, or in wealth or fame or enjoyment, or *anywhere*. Where then is it to be found? In doing that which is the quest of man's nature. How then shall a man do this? By having axioms as the source of his impulses and actions. What axioms? On the nature of Good and Evil, shewing that nothing is for a man's good save what makes him just, temperate, manly, free. . . .[k]

Aurelius' insistence that man is both "rational and civic" harks back, of course, to the views of Plato and Aristotle—but we heard little from them about an *obligation* to behave altruistically. For them, the primary justification for socially oriented conduct was still self-interest. But Aurelius' emphasis was on duty: "Have I done some social act? Well, I am amply rewarded. Keep this truth ever ready to turn to, and in no wise slacken thine efforts. What is thy vocation? *To be a good man*. But how be successful in this save by assured conceptions on the one hand of the Universal Nature and on the other of the special constitution of man?"[l]

This shift from interest to duty reflects a profound change in the culture, a change that is also revealed in the attention Aurelius gave to the duty of apathy, or indifference to this-worldly things: "As long then as I remember that I am a part of such a whole, I shall be well pleased with all that happens. . . . To grumble at anything that happens is a rebellion against Nature, in some part of which are bound up the natures of all other things."[m]

We have the impression that the culture was tired and discouraged. No longer was there any real hope; no longer was an appeal to progress or to self-improvement plausible. The appeal was simply to stiffen the back and endure until the end.

> Despise not death, but welcome it, for Nature wills it like all else. For dissolution is but one of the processes of Nature, associated with thy life's various seasons, such as to be young, to be old, to wax to our prime and to reach it, to grow teeth and beard and gray hairs, to beget, conceive and bring forth. A man then that has reasoned the matter out should not take up towards death the attitude of indifference, reluctance, or scorn, but await it as one of the processes of Nature. . . .
> . . . . . . . . . . . . . . . . . . . . . . . . . . . . . . . . . . . . . . . . . . . .
> Man, thou hast been a citizen in this World-City, what matters it to thee if for five years or a hundred? For under its laws equal treatment is meted out to all. What hardship then is there in being banished from the city, not by a tyrant or an unjust judge but by Nature who settled thee in it? So might a praetor who commissions a comic actor, dismiss him from the stage. *But I have not played my five acts, but only three.* Very possibly, but in life three acts count as a full play. For he, that is responsible for thy composition originally and thy dissolution now, decides when it is complete. But thou art responsible for neither. Depart then with a good grace, for he that dismisses thee is gracious.[n]

But the fact that we ought to accept death willingly when it comes does not mean, Aurelius thought, that it is right to hasten its coming. Aurelius allowed suicide only when the conditions of life make virtue impossible. "Thou canst live on earth as thou dost purpose to live when departed. But if men will not have it so, then it is time for thee even to go out of life, yet not as one who is treated ill. *'Tis smoky and I go away.* Why think it a great matter? But while no such cause drives me forth, I remain a free man, and none shall prevent me from doing what I will. . . ."[o]

Though in this passage Aurelius quoted Epictetus with approval, their views of suicide were different and reflect the ambivalence that, as we have seen, ran through Stoic doctrine. When Epictetus said that the door stands always open for us to leave the room of life whenever we choose, he represented very fairly that otherworldly attitude that, as we now know, was the wave of the future.

Aurelius, on the other hand, in limiting the conditions under which the "free departure" is permitted, in reaffirming social duties, and in trying to show that the indifference of the sage nevertheless entails certain obligations toward his fellow men, looked back to the classical community based on "the long still grasp of law."

This sense of law and order, of balance and moderation was, as has been said all along, one of the principal marks of the classical spirit. Every Stoic, from Zeno down to Marcus Aurelius, in his own way sounded this note. Even in Epictetus otherworldliness did not wholly subdue *sophrosyne*. But Marcus Aurelius was the last for many centuries to affirm the old ideal of moderation. Since he was also the last emperor of the great period of the Principate, before civilization began its long decline, he is a fitting symbol of the close of the classical world.

## Stoicism as an Operative Ideal in Roman Life

Before we leave this dying world let us briefly consider how the ideals described by Cicero, Epictetus, Aurelius, and the other Roman Stoics operated at the level of political life—how, in particular, the old Greek conception of "the long still grasp of law" was implemented in terms of jurisprudence and juridical practice.

### LAW

According to early Roman notions, a father exercised complete control over his family—over his wife, who could own no property in her own right, not even her dowry; over his children, whose lives, even when they were adults, he was at liberty to take if he chose; and over his slaves, who had no rights at all. Gradually this stern code was relaxed. At first, an exception was made for men on active duty with the armed forces. A son might, it was conceded, dispose of what he earned while under arms. Later, under Hadrian (117–137 A.D.), this right was extended to permit persons honorably discharged from the army to dispose of all their property as they chose. Limitations on the rights of a father over his children were gradually effected in other fields. The right to put one's children to death was abrogated, and permission to inflict severe punishment had to be secured from a magistrate. Similarly, a form of marriage developed in which wives did not become members of their husbands' families and in which they retained a separate estate.

As for slaves, their condition, too, steadily improved. Under the Antonines, in particular, humane legislation was introduced. Moreover, large numbers of slaves were freed by generous and grateful owners, and even larger numbers were able to purchase their freedom. In this way there arose a large population that was free but without citizenship, and a whole body of law came into existence to regulate and define the freedmen's rights. These men were often persons of ability and energy who accumulated large fortunes. The lower ranks of the civil service were almost entirely filled by freedmen, and some rose to the highest posts in the Empire. If there was not exactly a completely open course for talent, there was a gradual and continual relaxing of the restrictions that limited opportunity.

### CHARITY

Not only in the field of legislation did humanizing influences appear. The early Empire was remarkable for the interest shown in charitable enterprises. Two of many possible instances may be mentioned. Herodes Atticus, the tutor of Marcus Aurelius, gave aqueducts, race courses, theaters, and baths to many Greek cities, and on his death he left an annual money gift to every Athenian citizen. Less spectacular were the benefactions of the younger Pliny (62–110 A.D.), but they were the more remarkable since Pliny was not a wealthy man. He built a library for Como, his native town, and endowed it with a substantial annual income. He also provided a large sum for the support of the children of the poor of Como, and, because the young men of that town were having to go to Milan to complete their education, he helped to establish a local school there. In this connection he offered to pay only one-third of the cost, because, as he explained, he believed that the city would better realize the advantage of education if the parents of the boys had to contribute.

It would be ridiculous, of course, to attribute this interest in the amelioration of the condition of human life exclusively to the influence of the Stoic doctrine of the brotherhood of man. When a man of wealth allowed his slaves a share in the profits from his estates, it was often less in recognition of the slaves' humanity than in the shrewd hope that slaves who shared in the profits would work harder than those without such an interest. Similarly, the motives leading to generosity were, of course, mixed (as they are today). But the fact that a rich man could win reputation by charitable bequests, not just by magnificent display, is an indication of the humane spirit of the age.

### JUS NATURALE

Perhaps the most clear-cut evidence of the influence of Stoicism was the introduction into Roman jurisprudence of the notion of natural law. Originally the Romans, like other peoples, had recognized only one law, that for citizens. Slaves, strangers, and foreigners, not being citizens—that is, not being members of the blood brotherhood that was the basis of the primitive community—were without law. Gradually, like all peoples who engage in commerce and so perforce have extensive dealings with foreigners, the Romans had to create a law to regulate the relations between strangers living in Rome and between Romans and foreigners. This difference the Romans recognized by distinguishing between what they called the *jus civile* ("law for citizens") and the *jus gentium* ("law in use among nations," that is, laws for foreigners, for men of all nationalities). This distinction appears sooner or later in the law of all peoples, there being no great difference between Roman practice and that of, say, the Athenians, except that as the Romans acquired empire, the importance of the *jus gentium* vastly increased. This law became, in effect, international, applicable to all men as citizens of some state or other.

But now, as a result of Stoic thought, Roman jurists introduced the concept of a third kind of law, *jus naturale* ("natural law"). Natural law they conceived to be valid for all men, not merely as citizens of some state or other but as rational beings sharing in the divine reason that rules the universe. Again, whereas both the *jus civile* and the *jus gentium* were explicitly formulated codes entailing specific punishments for failure to conform, the *jus naturale* was an ideal. Failure to obey it carried not a civil but a moral sanction. Though it never appeared formally on the statute books, it affected in important ways what did appear on the statute books. Thus it caused a shift of emphasis from form, or verbal expression, to intent. Originally the law of contracts took account only of a certain sacred formula. If the proper words had been used by the parties to the agreement, there was a binding contract; if some word had been omitted or another word added, there was no contract. Gradually, however, judges began to be more interested in evidence of the intent of the parties, without regard to the particular form of words employed. The *jus naturale* also caused an ever widening expansion of the rights and privileges of citizenship, until finally all free inhabitants of the Empire became citizens. When that day came *jus civile* and *jus gentium* were finally one. But the *jus naturale* remained an ideal—an ideal for reformers and morally sensitive men to aim at. And so it remains.

The influence of the concept of natural law is only one example of the way in which Stoicism became an operative ideal[12] for the rulers and administrators of the Roman Empire. And if it was the early Greek Stoics who worked out the "ideal," it was Roman thinkers like Cicero who made it "operative." It has been suggested that the function of the Roman version of Stoicism was to temper the exaggerations of the more extreme Stoic position and make it a working philosophy. But how to do this was not learned all at once. In the early days of the Empire, Stoicism was a hot-bed of republicanism and often outspoken anti-imperial sentiment. Because social and economic conditions were in conflict with the natural equality of men, the Stoics wanted to change them forthwith. Later on, however, they came to terms with the Empire and found in its universal sovereignty a way of implementing their ideals. It became apparent that the attempt to apply these ideals all at once would destroy the state. Marcus Aurelius put this very well: "Dream not of Utopias but be content if the least thing go forward, and count the outcome of the matter in hand as a small thing. For who can alter another's conviction? Failing a change of conviction, we merely get men pretending to be persuaded and chafing like slaves under coercion."[P]

For the most part, then, Stoicism operated, not with crusading zeal, but

12  For the use of this term see A. D. Lindsay, *The Modern Democratic State* (Oxford, New York, 1947).

quietly and soberly to give meaning and significance to the lives of the politicians and civil servants who for centuries held together the Roman Empire, and with it the cultural tradition of the West. For those unnumbered and long since anonymous men who managed the affairs of empire it provided a rationale that enabled them to go about the affairs of daily life—to meet crises, to plan for the future, to work and to die—with a feeling of purpose and dignity.

## Scepticism

Finally we come to the fifth of the so-called Greek schools—Scepticism. But Scepticism was even less a formal school than the other post-Alexandrian philosophical groups. What the Sceptics had in common was a critical attitude toward what they called the dogmatism of the other schools—that is, toward what they regarded as the unjustified claims put forward, especially by the Stoics and the Epicureans, to knowledge in physics. But the Sceptics differed among themselves in respect to the degree and the extent of their scepticism. Whereas some, for instance, claimed to know that knowledge in physics is impossible, others were sceptical even of this claim. They did not maintain, they said, that knowledge is impossible; they merely noted that, as of now, they had no knowledge.

### SEXTUS EMPIRICUS

Many of the Sceptics wrote nothing; the books of those who did commit their views to writing have disappeared. For information about them we have to rely principally on Sextus Empiricus, who collected all the main Sceptic arguments in a series of treatises. But Sextus lived about 200 A.D., and the earliest recognizable member of the school was Pyrrho, who died in 275 B.C. It is important, then, as we read Sextus' arguments, to remember that he was summarizing a long and varied development.

> Our task at present is to describe in outline the Sceptic doctrine, first premising that of none of our future statements do we positively affirm that the fact is exactly as we state it, but we simply record each fact, like a chronicler, as it appears to us at the moment. . . .
> Scepticism is an ability, or mental attitude, which opposes appearances to judgements in any way whatsoever, with the result that, owing to the equipollence of the objects and reasons thus opposed, we are brought firstly to a state of mental suspense and next to a state of "unperturbedness" or quietude. Now we call it an "ability" not in any subtle sense, but simply in respect of its "being able." By "appearances" we now mean the objects of sense-perception, when we contrast them with the objects of thought or "judgements." The phrase "in any way whatsoever" can be connected either

with the word "ability," to make us take the word "ability," as we said, in its simple sense, or with the phrase "opposing appearances to judgements"; for inasmuch as we oppose these in a variety of ways—appearances to appearances, or judgements to judgements, or *alternando* appearances to judgements,—in order to ensure the inclusion of all these antitheses we employ the phrase "in any way whatsoever" . . . . "Equipollence" we use of equality in respect of probability and improbability, to indicate that no one of the conflicting judgements takes precedence of any other as being more probable. "Suspense" is a state of mental rest owing to which we neither deny nor affirm anything. "Quietude" is an untroubled and tranquil condition of soul.q

It will be seen that Sextus himself inclined toward the version of Scepticism that refused to maintain that knowledge is impossible: He did not assert that "the truth cannot be apprehended"; rather, he described himself as "persisting in the search," while marshaling a formidable array of arguments to demonstrate that truth had not yet been apprehended. When he wrote of "opposing appearances to appearances," what he had in mind was conflicting sense experiences of the same object. For instance, if someone ventures to assert that a tower looks "round from a distance," the Sceptic at once points out that it looks "square from close at hand." Of course, when Sextus attacked the validity of sense perception, he did not mean to deny that we experience what we experience; what he was denying was that we have any basis for a valid inference from what we experience to what the object is in itself.

Those who say that "the Sceptics abolish appearances," or phenomena, seem to me to be unacquainted with the statements of our School. For . . . we do not overthrow the affective sense impressions which induce our assent involuntarily; and these impressions are "the appearances." And when we question whether the underlying object is such as it appears, we grant the fact that it appears, and our doubt does not concern the appearance itself but the account given of that appearance,—and that is a different thing from questioning the appearance itself. For example, honey appears to us to be sweet (and this we grant, for we perceive sweetness through the senses), but whether it is also sweet in its essence is for us a matter of doubt, since this is not an appearance but a judgement regarding the appearance.r

As an instance of the Sceptic method of opposing judgment to judgment, Sextus cited the following: "In answer to him who argues the existence of Providence from the order of the heavenly bodies we oppose the fact that often the good fare ill and the bad fare well, and draw from this the inference that Providence does not exist."s

Thus the basic strategy by which equipollence, or suspended judgment, is to be attained consists in opposing any affirmation whatever with a contradictory affirmation. Since the latter is as plausible as the former (the arguments, or evidence, for it seem equally good), we have no way of deciding between them. So far the strategy is largely rhetorical—that is, it matters less, according to Sextus, that the arguments for the contradictory affirmations be equally strong than that they seem so, for as long as they seem equally strong, the desired suspension of judgment will be achieved.

As regards the reasoning, in distinction from the rhetoric, of Scepticism, Sextus had two main arguments. One may be called the search for a criterion; the other, the relativity-to-an-observer argument. The first consisted in pointing out that before we can assert the truth of any proposition we need a criterion by means of which we can evaluate its truth or falsity. But any proposed criterion must itself be tested—by some other criterion. This leads to an infinite regress of criteria. Meanwhile the original judgment that was to be evaluated remains in suspension.

> Of those . . . who have treated of the criterion some have declared that a criterion exists—the Stoics, for example . . . ; by some its existence is denied . . . ; while we have adopted suspension of judgement as to whether it does or does not exist. This dispute, then, they will declare to be either capable or incapable of decision; and if they shall say it is incapable of decision they will be granting on the spot the propriety of suspension of judgement, while if they say it admits of decision, let them tell us whereby it is to be decided, since we have no accepted criterion, and do not even know, but are still inquiring, whether any criterion exists. Besides, in order to decide the dispute which has arisen about the criterion, we must possess an accepted criterion by which we shall be able to judge the dispute; and in order to possess an accepted criterion, the dispute about the criterion must first be decided. And when the argument thus reduces itself to a form of circular reasoning the discovery of the criterion becomes impracticable, since we do not allow them to adopt a criterion by assumption, while if they offer to judge the criterion by a criterion we force them to a regress *ad infinitium*. And furthermore, since demonstration requires a demonstrated criterion, while the criterion requires an approved demonstration, they are forced into circular reasoning.[†]

In the relativity-to-an-observer argument Sextus pointed out, first, that what anybody perceives is relative to the state of his sense organs and, second, that the sense organs vary from species to species, from individual to individual within any species, and even from moment to moment for any individual. This general argument was developed in exhaustive, and exhausting, detail in ten "modes," or "tropes."

> The usual tradition amongst the older Sceptics is that the "modes" by which "suspension" is supposed to be brought about are ten in number. . . . They are these: the first, based on the variety in animals; the second, on the differences in human beings; the third, on the different structures of the organs of sense; the fourth, on the circumstantial conditions; the fifth, on positions and intervals and locations; the sixth, on intermixtures; the seventh, on the

quantities and formations of the underlying objects; the eighth, on the fact of relativity; the ninth, on the frequency or rarity of occurrence; the tenth, on the disciplines and customs and laws, the legendary beliefs and the dogmatic convictions.[u]

One or two examples will indicate the character of Sextus' detailed arguments. For instance, the first mode reviews the differences in the bodies of animals of different species, differences that suggest that animals of different species have quite different sense experiences.

> Sufferers from jaundice declare that objects which seem to us white are yellow, while those whose eyes are bloodshot call them blood red. Since, then, some animals also have eyes which are yellow, others bloodshot, . . . others of other colours, they probably, I suppose, have different perceptions of colour. . . . Again, when we press the eyeball at one side the forms, figures and sizes of the objects appear oblong and narrow. So it is probable that all animals which have the pupil of the eye slanting and elongated—such as goats, cats, and similar animals—have impressions of the objects which are different and unlike the notions formed of them by the animals which have round pupils. . . .
>
> If the same things appear different owing to the variety in animals, we shall, indeed, be able to state our own impressions of the real object, but as to its essential nature we shall suspend judgement. For we cannot ourselves judge between our own impressions and those of the other animals, since we ourselves are involved in the dispute and are, therefore, rather in need of a judge than competent to pass judgement ourselves.[v]

Similarly, the ninth mode (based on the frequency of occurrence) leads to suspension of judgment.

> The sun is, of course, much more amazing than a comet; yet because we see the sun constantly but the comet rarely we are so amazed by the comet that we even regard it as a divine portent, while the sun causes no amazement at all. If, however, we were to conceive of the sun as appearing but rarely and setting rarely, and illuminating everything all at once and throwing everything into shadow suddenly, then we should experience much amazement at the sight. An earthquake also does not cause the same alarm in those who experience it for the first time and those who have grown accustomed to such things. How much amazement, also, does the sea excite in the man who sees it for the first time! . . . Since then, owing to the frequency or rarity of their occurrence, the same things seem at one time to be amazing or precious and at another time nothing of the sort, we infer that though we shall be able perhaps to say what nature appears to belong to each of these things in virtue of its frequent or rare occurrence, we are not able to state what nature absolutely belongs to each of the external objects. So because of this Mode also we suspend judgement regarding them.[w]

It is important to see that the "equipollence" that these arguments of the Sceptics were designed to achieve was not a suspension of action but of judgment. The Sceptics did not want—at least most of them did not want—to destroy men's capacity to deal effectively with their physical and social environment; they wanted to destroy the pretensions of dogmatic philosophy—quite another matter. And they held that, though there is no absolute criterion by which we can conclusively distinguish between reality and appearance, between the true and the false, there are adequate criteria for making reasonable decisions in matters of day-to-day living.

## CARNEADES

This was the thesis of Carneades, one of the most distinguished of the so-called Academic sceptics.[13] Carneades, according to Sextus' account of his views, pointed out that sense impressions are not encapsulated units of experience. Each occurs within the context of others, and we evaluate the reliability of each sense experience, not by trying to compare it with the inaccessible object of which it is supposedly an "appearance," but by testing its consistency or lack of consistency within the context of other sense experiences.

> No presentation is ever simple in form but, like links in a chain, one hangs from another. . . . For example, he who receives the presentation of a man necessarily receives the presentation both of his personal qualities and of the external conditions—of his personal qualities, such as colour, size, shape, motion, speech, dress, foot-gear; and of the external conditions, such as air, light, day, heaven, earth, friends, and all the rest. So whenever none of these presentations disturbs our faith by appearing false, but all with one accord appear true our belief is the greater. . . . Just as some doctors do not deduce that it is a true case of fever from one symptom only—such as too quick a pulse or a very high temperature—but from a concurrence, such as that of a high temperature with a rapid pulse and soreness to the touch and flushing and thirst and analogous symptoms; so also the Academic forms his judgement of truth by the concurrence of presentations, and when none of the presentations in the concurrence provokes in him a suspicion of its falsity he asserts that the impression is true.[x]

Carneades realized, of course, that even complete concurrence of impressions is not an infallible guarantee: A diagnosis of fever may be mistaken even when

---

13 See pp. 316–17. At first sight it may be startling, in view of Plato's own insistence that the forms exist and are knowable, to find scepticism developing in the Academy. But there was a deep-seated strain in Plato's own thought—involving his emphasis on the transcendence of the forms—that could be pressed to the conclusion that in this spatiotemporal world absolute certainty never can be attained. After all, Plato himself had insisted that physics is at best only a "likely story." As for Carneades, he was born in Cyrene, became head of the Academy at some date earlier than 156 B.C., and died in 129 B.C.

all the symptoms are indicative of fever. But he maintained that such an occurrence is so rare that concurrence is a satisfactory criterion at the level of practice: "The rare occurrence of this kind—the kind I mean which imitates the truth—should not make us distrust the kind which 'as a general rule' reports truly; for the fact is that both our judgements and our actions are regulated by the standard of 'the general rule.'" [y]

### THE FINAL GOAL OF SCEPTICISM

Though the destruction of dogmatism, without the inhibition of action, was important to the Sceptics, it was not their final goal. The thinking of the whole school was dominated by an ethical—or, perhaps better, a religious—motive. Here the Sceptics were at one with their enemies the dogmatists. Like the Epicureans and the Stoics, the Sceptics were seeking peace of mind; they differed from their rivals merely in their conception of how peace of mind is to be attained. Whereas the Epicureans believed we reach it by coming to know that the universe is a vast mechanism in which the gods do not, and cannot, intervene, and the Stoics held we reach it by recognizing ourselves to be tiny fragments of an infinite whole, the Sceptics thought we reach it by realizing that there is no conclusive evidence one way or the other for *any* of the beliefs by which men live. As Sextus pointed out,

> We assert . . . that the Sceptic's end is quietude in respect of matters of opinion. . . . For the Sceptic, having set out to philosophize with the object of passing judgement on the sense-impressions and ascertaining which of them are true and which false, so as to attain quietude thereby, found himself involved in contradictions of equal weight, and being unable to decide between them suspended judgement; and as he was thus in suspense there followed, as it happened, the state of quietude in respect of matters of opinion. For the man who opines that anything is by nature good or bad is forever being disquieted: when he is without the things which he deems good he believes himself to be tormented by things naturally bad and he pursues after the things which are, as he thinks, good; which when he has obtained he keeps falling into still more perturbations because of his irrational and immoderate elation, and in his dread of a change of fortune he uses every endeavour to avoid losing the things which he deems good. On the other hand, the man who determines nothing as to what is naturally good or bad neither shuns nor pursues anything eagerly; and, in consequence, he is unperturbed.
>
> The Sceptic, in fact, had the same experience which is said to have befallen the painter Apelles. Once, they say, when he was painting a horse and wished to represent in the painting the horse's foam, he was so unsuccessful that he gave up the attempt and flung at the painting the sponge on which he used to wipe the paints off his brush, and the mark of the sponge produced the effect of a horse's foam. So, too, the Sceptics were in hopes of gaining quietude by means of a decision regarding the disparity of the objects of sense

and of thought, and being unable to effect this they suspended judgement; and they found that quietude, as if by chance, followed upon their suspense, even as a shadow follows its substance.[z]

Thus the underlying value system of Scepticism supports the generalizations that have already been made about late classical culture—that this was a tired and discouraged society in which peace of mind, relief from the struggle, had replaced such positive goods as social progress and self-improvement. Now, peace of mind can conceivably be won by natural means—by science or, alternatively, by suspension of judgment. But this natural peace could not hope to compete with the appeal of that deeper peace—the peace that passeth understanding—that was assured by a transcendent and otherworldly religion.

# Notes

## Chapter 1 / Pre-Socratic Philosophy

a   From the *Iliad*, translated by W. H. D. Rouse as *The Story of Achilles* (Nelson, New York, 1938), Bk. IX, pp. 171–73.

b   *Ibid.*, Bk. I, pp. 17–19.

c   *Ibid.*, Bk. XXII, pp. 425–26.

d   *Works and Days*, in *Hesiod: The Homeric Hymns and Homerica*, translated by H. G. Evelyn-White ("Loeb Classical Library" [Harvard University Press, 1926]), pp. 3, 9, 19, 21, 23, and 25.

e   *Theogony*, translated by Evelyn-White, *op. cit.*, pp. 87 and 89.

f   *Early Greek Philosophy*, translated by J. Burnet (Black, London, 1920). Compare Fragment 41, p. 136; see also Fragment 81, p. 139.

g   *Ibid.*, Fragment 47, pp. 136–37; see also Fragments 43, 44, 45, and 62, pp. 136–37.

h   *Ibid.*, Fragment 114, pp. 140–41.

i   *Ibid.*, Fragment 3, p. 133; see also Fragments 2 and 51, pp. 133 and 137.

j   *Ibid.*, Fragment 36, p. 136; see also Fragments 35, 98, 99, 119, and 126, pp. 136, 140, and 141.

k *Ibid.,* Fragment 61, p. 137.

l *Ibid.,* Fragments 23–25, p. 119; see also Fragments 11, 15, and 32, pp. 119 and 120.

m *Physics,* translated by R. P. Hardie and R. K. Gaye, in *The Works of Aristotle,* edited by J. A. Smith and W. D. Ross (Clarendon Press, Oxford, 1910–52), Vol. II (1930), 263a5 ff.

n *Early Greek Philosophy,* translated by Burnet, *op. cit.,* Fragments 5 and 6, pp. 173–74.

o *Ibid.,* Fragment 134, p. 225; see also Fragments 57 and 59, p. 214.

p *Ibid.,* Fragment 10, p. 259.

q *Ibid.,* Fragment 17, p. 261.

r *Ibid.,* Fragments 11 and 12, p. 259.

s *Ibid.,* Fragment 12, p. 260.

t *Ibid.,* Fragments 16 and 17, p. 134.

u From the *Odyssey,* translated by S. H. Butcher and A. Lang (Collier, New York, 1909), Bk. XI, p. 164.

v *Bacchae,* translated by W. Arrowsmith (University of Chicago Press, 1958), ll. 74 ff.

w *Early Greek Philosophy,* translated by Burnet, *op. cit.,* p. 103.

x Hermeias, *The Disparagement of Pagan Philosophers,* translated by A. Fairbanks, in *Selections from Early Greek Philosophy,* edited by M. C. Nahm (Crofts, New York, 1935), p. 82.

y *Early Greek Philosophy,* translated by Burnet, *op. cit.,* Fragment 29, p. 135.


## Chapter 2   /   Education Through Violence

a *The Peloponnesian War,* Bk. III, Ch. 82. This rendering is by Sir A. Zimmern, in *The Greek Commonwealth* (Clarendon Press, Oxford, 1924), p. 420.

b Quotations in this section are from Xenophon's "Constitution of the Spartans," translated by H. G. Dakyns, in *Greek Historians,* edited by F. R. B. Godolphin (Random House, New York, 1942), Vol. II, pp. 658 ff.

c *The Peloponnesian War,* translated by B. Jowett, in Godolphin, *op. cit.,* Vol. I, Bk. I, Ch. 124.

d *Ibid.,* Chs. 140–41.

e *Ibid.,* Bk. II, Ch. 65.

f *Ibid.,* Bk. V, Ch. 16.

g Quotations in this section are from "Constitution of the Athenians," translated by H. G. Dakyns, in Godolphin, *op. cit.,* Vol. II, pp. 640, 633, 640, and 634–35.

h From the anonymous translation of the *Acharnians,* in *The Complete Greek Drama,* edited by W. J. Oates and E. O'Neill, Jr. (Random House, New York, 1938), Vol. II, pp. 429–30.

i This and the following quotation are from the anonymous translation of the *Wasps,* in Oates and O'Neill, *op. cit.,* Vol. II, pp. 627 and 629.

j From the anonymous translation of the *Knights,* in Oates and O'Neill, *op. cit.,* Vol. II, p. 483.

k *Ibid.,* p. 489.

l From the anonymous translation of the *Ecclesiazusae,* in Oates and O'Neill, *op. cit.,* Vol. II, pp. 1027–30 and 1032.

m This and the following passages are from *The Peloponnesian War,* translated by B. Jowett, in Godolphin, *op. cit.,* Vol. I, Bk. V, Chs. 70, 72–77, and 81–83.

n Translated by G. Highet, in *Greek Literature in Translation,* edited by W. J. Oates and C. J. Murphy (Longmans, New York, 1944), p. 993.

o *The Peloponnesian War,* translated by B. Jowett, in Godolphin, *op. cit.,* Vol. I, Bk. V, Chs. 89–91, 97, 100–05, 111, 114, and 116.

p This and the following passages are from the *Trojan Women,* translated by G. Murray, in Oates and O'Neill, *op. cit.,* Vol. I, ll. 96 ff., 947 ff., 1207 ff., 1240 ff., 1284 ff., and 1327 ff.

q From the *Bacchae,* translated by G. Murray, in Oates and O'Neill, *op. cit.,* Vol. II, p. 282.

r From *Antigone,* translated by R. Whitelaw, in *Ten Greek Plays,* edited by L. Cooper (Oxford, New York, 1936), pp. 64–65.

s From *Medea*, translated by G. Murray, in Cooper, *op. cit.*, p. 352.

t *Ibid.*, p. 330.

u From *Medea*, translated by E. P. Coleridge, in Oates and O'Neill, *op. cit.*, Vol. I, p. 749.

v *Ibid.*, p. 726.

w *Medea*, translated by G. Murray, in Cooper, *op. cit.*, p. 333.

x *Ibid.*, p. 326.

y *The Persian Wars*, translated by G. Rawlinson, in Godolphin, *op. cit.*, Vol. I, Bk. III, Ch. 38.

z *Ibid.*, Bk. VII, Ch. 104.

a *Gorgias*, translated by B. Jowett, in *The Dialogues of Plato* (Oxford University Press, 1953), Vol. II, 576–77.

b *Ibid.*, 586.

c *Republic*, translated by F. M. Cornford (Oxford, New York, 1945), 338.

d *Ibid.*, 343–44.


## Chapter 3 / Atomism

a Fragments 6, 7, and 10, translated by C. M. Bakewell, in *Source Book in Ancient Philosophy* (Scribners, New York, 1907), p. 59.

b Fragment 11, in Bakewell, *op. cit.*, pp. 59–60.

c Diogenes Laertius, *Lives and Opinions of Eminent Philosophers*, translated by R. D. Hicks ("Loeb Classical Library" [Harvard University Press, 1925]), Vol. II, pp. 453 and 455.

d Fragment 3, translated by J. Burnet, in *Early Greek Philosophy* (Black, London, 1920), p. 258.

e *Ibid.*, Fragment 2, p. 316.

f *Ibid.*, Fragment 8, p. 323.

g *Lucretius: On the Nature of Things*, translated by C. Bailey (Clarendon Press, Oxford, 1924), pp. 31–33.

h *Ibid.*, p. 34.

i *Ibid.*, p. 38.

j *Ibid.*, pp. 38–39.

k *Ibid.*, p. 59.

l *Ibid.*, p. 47.

m *Ibid.*, pp. 40–41.

n *Ibid.*, p. 73.

o *Ibid.*, p. 68.

p *Ibid.*, pp. 90–94.

q Fragment 10, in Bakewell, *op. cit.*, p. 60.

r *Lucretius: On the Nature of Things*, in Bailey, *op. cit.*, pp. 168–71.

s *Ibid.*, pp. 73–75.

t Fragments 35, 37, 40, 41, 45, 57, 61, and 191, in Bakewell, *op. cit.*, pp. 60–61 and 63–64; *Lives and Opinions*, in Hicks, *op. cit.*, Vol. II, p. 455.


## Chapter 4 / Plato: The Theory of Forms

a *Symposium*, translated by W. R. M. Lamb ("Loeb Classical Library" [Harvard University Press, 1925]), 212, 215–17, 219–21, and 223.

b *Apology*, translated by H. N. Fowler ("Loeb Classical Library" [Harvard University Press, 1914]), 17 and 28 ff.

c *Crito*, translated by Fowler, *op. cit.*, 44 ff.

d   *Phaedo*, translated by Fowler, *op. cit.*, 116 ff.
e   Letter VII, translated by R. G. Bury ("Loeb Classical Library" [Harvard University Press, 1929]), p. 341.
f   *Republic*, translated by F. M. Cornford (Oxford, New York, 1945), 509 ff.
g   *Ibid.*, 506 ff.
h   *Ibid.*, 514 ff.
i   *Ibid.*, 533.
j   *Symposium*, translated by Lamb, *op. cit.*, 201 ff. and 206 ff.
k   *Phaedo*, translated by Fowler, *op. cit.*, 65 ff. and 74 ff.
l   *Timaeus*, translated by F. M. Cornford, in *Plato's Cosmology* (Harcourt, Brace & World, New York, 1937), 51.

## Chapter 5   /   Plato: The Special Sciences

a   *Phaedo*, translated by B. Jowett, in *The Dialogues of Plato* (Oxford University Press, Oxford, 1953), Vol. I, 453 and 456.
b   *Timaeus*, translated by F. M. Cornford, in *Plato's Cosmology* (Harcourt, Brace & World, New York, 1937), 27.
c   *Phaedo*, translated by Jowett, *op. cit.*, Vol. I, 456.
d   *Theaetetus*, translated by F. M. Cornford, in *Plato's Theory of Knowledge* (Harcourt, Brace & World, New York, 1935), 154.
e   *Timaeus*, translated by Cornford, *op. cit.*, 47–48.
f   *Ibid.*, 52.
g   *Laches*, translated by Jowett, *op. cit.*, Vol. I, 85–90.
h   *Gorgias*, translated by Jowett, *op. cit.*, Vol. II, 598.
i   *Ibid.*, 590–92.
j   *Republic*, translated by Jowett, *op. cit.*, Vol. II, 165; *Gorgias*, translated by Jowett, *op. cit.*, Vol. II, 588.
k   *Laws*, translated by Jowett, *op. cit.*, Vol. IV, 301.
l   *Republic*, translated by F. M. Cornford (Oxford, New York, 1945), 443–44.
m   *Charmides*, translated by Jowett, *op. cit.*, Vol. I, 10–11.
n   *Republic*, translated by Cornford, *op. cit.*, 434–36 and 439.
o   *Protagoras*, translated by Jowett, *op. cit.*, Vol. I, 144.
p   Passages in this section are from *Gorgias*, translated by Jowett, *op. cit.*, Vol. II, 551–53, 616–18, and 621.
q   *Republic*, translated by Cornford, *op. cit.*, 377.
r   *Ibid.*, 416–19, 451–52, 455–56, and 458–62.
s   Quotations in this section are from *Protagoras*, translated by Jowett, *op. cit.*, Vol. I, 184–85 and 186.
t   *Republic*, translated by Cornford, *op. cit.*, 545–47, 550–52, 555–58, and 562–69.
u   *Phaedrus*, translated by Jowett, *op. cit.*, Vol. III, 185–86.
v   *Republic*, translated by Jowett, *op. cit.*, Vol. II, 224.
w   *Laws*, translated by R. G. Bury ("Loeb Classical Library" [Harvard University Press, 1924]), 894–96.
x   *Timaeus*, translated by Cornford, *op. cit.*, 29–30.
y   *Ibid.*, 28.
z   *Ibid.*, 27–29.
a   *Ibid.*, 50.
b   *Parmenides*, translated by F. M. Cornford, in *Plato and Parmenides* (Kegan Paul, London, 1935), 130 ff.

c  *Sophist*, translated by F. M. Cornford, in *Plato's Theory of Knowledge* (Harcourt, Brace & World, New York, 1935), 248 ff.

d  *Timaeus*, translated by Cornford, *op. cit.*, 51.

## Chapter 6 / Aristotle: Metaphysics, Natural Science, Logic

a  *Republic*, translated by B. Jowett, in *The Dialogues of Plato* (Oxford University Press, Oxford, 1953), Vol. II, 467.

b  *Physics*, translated by R. P. Hardie and R. K. Gaye, in *The Works of Aristotle*, edited by J. A. Smith and W. D. Ross (Clarendon Press, Oxford, 1910–52), Vol. II (1930), 192b8 ff.

c  *Ibid.*, 250b10 ff.

d  *Ibid.*, 258b13 ff; *Metaphysics*, translated by W. D. Ross, in *Works*, Vol. VIII (1928), 994a1 ff.

e  *Physics*, translated by Hardie and Gaye, *op. cit.*, 260b1–5.

f  *Metaphysics*, translated by Ross, *op. cit.*, 1072a24–27.

g  *Nichomachean Ethics*, translated by W. D. Ross, in *Works*, Vol. IX (1925), 1178b7 ff.

h  *Historia Animalium*, translated by D. W. Thompson, in *Works*, Vol. IV (1910), 561a3 ff.

i  *De Anima*, translated by J. A. Smith, in *Works*, Vol. III (1931), 412a3 ff.

j  *De Anima*, II, iii, translated by P. Wheelwright, in *Aristotle* (Odyssey Press, New York, 1935), p. 78.

k  *De Anima*, translated by Smith, *op. cit.*, 424b3 ff.

l  *Ibid.*, 427a18 ff.

m  *Prior Analytics*, 24b18. This rendering is by L. S. Stebbing, in *A Modern Introduction to Logic* (Methuen, London, 1933), p. 81.

n  *Posterior Analytics*, translated by G. R. G. Mure, in *Works*, Vol. I (1928), 99b20 ff.

## Chapter 7 / Aristotle: Ethics, Politics, Art

a  *De Anima*, translated by J. A. Smith, in *The Works of Aristotle*, edited by J. A. Smith and W. D. Ross (Clarendon Press, Oxford, 1910–52), Vol. III (1931), 432a15 ff.

b  *De Motu Animalium*, translated by A. S. L. Farquharson, in *Works*, Vol. V (1912), 701a32.

c  *Ibid.*, 433b27.

d  *Nichomachean Ethics*, translated by W. D. Ross, in *Works*, Vol. IX (1925), 1094b12 ff.

e  *Ibid.*, 1094a1 ff.

f  *Ibid.*, 1102a15 ff.

g  *Ibid.*, 1115a6 ff.

h  *Ibid.*, 1123a34 ff.

i  *Ibid.*, 1109a24 and 1109b23.

j  *Ibid.*, 1103a17 ff.

k  *Ibid.*, 1109b32 ff.

l  *Ibid.*, 1135a17 ff.

m  *Ibid.*, 1145b22 and 1146b30 ff.

n  *Ibid.*, 1175a22 and 1176a4 ff.

o  *Ibid.*, 1140a24 ff.

p  *Ibid.*, 1140b31 ff.

q  *Ibid.*, 1177a11 ff.

r  *Ibid.*, 1099a31 ff.

s  *Ibid.*, 1177a34 ff.

t   *Politics*, translated by B. Jowett, in *Works*, Vol. X (1921), 1252a1 ff.
u   *Ibid.*, 1288b22 ff.
v   *Ibid.*, 1288a15–19 and 1284b28–34.
w   *Ibid.*, 1286a10 ff.
x   *Ibid.*, 1295a20–23.
y   *Ibid.*, 1292a39 ff. and 1293a11 ff.
z   *Ibid.*, 1291b30 ff.
a   *Ibid.*, 1295a25 ff.
b   *Ibid.*, 1289a38 ff.
c   *Ibid.*, 1286a7 ff., 1269a10 ff., 1287b22 ff., and 1281a43 ff.
d   *Ibid.*, 1280b31 ff.
e   *Ibid.*, 1281a4–8, 1280a32–36, and 1280a31–32.
f   *Ibid.*, 1253b15 ff.
g   *Ibid.*, 1255a5 ff.
h   *Masters of Political Thought: From Plato to Machiavelli*, M. B. Foster (Houghton Mifflin, New York, 1947), p. 262.
i   Quotations in this section are from *Politics*, translated by Jowett, *op. cit.*, 1302a17 ff., 1307b7 ff., 1305a36 ff., and 1307b25 ff.
j   *De Poetica*, translated by Ingram Bywater, in *Works*, Vol. XI (1924), 1448b5 ff.
k   *The Poetics of Aristotle*, translated by S. H. Butcher (Macmillan, New York, 1925), 1451a36 ff.
l   *Ibid.*, 1452b32 ff., 1453b4–5, and 1449b25 ff.
m   *Ibid.*, 1448b20–25.


## Chapter 8   /   The Late Classical Period

a   *Letter to Menoeceus*, translated by C. Bailey, in *Epicurus: The Extant Remains* (Clarendon Press, Oxford, 1926), 127 ff., pp. 87–91.
b   *Ibid.*, Fragment 79, p. 134.
c   *Ibid.*, Fragment 12, p. 123.
d   *Principal Doctrines*, translated by Bailey, *op. cit.*, XVII, p. 99.
e   *Ibid.*, V, p. 95.
f   *Letter to Menoeceus*, translated by Bailey, *op. cit.*, 124–25, p. 85.
g   *Principal Doctrines*, translated by Bailey, *op. cit.*, XI, p. 97.
h   *Lucretius: On the Nature of Things*, translated by C. Bailey (Clarendon Press, Oxford, 1924), pp. 133–35.
i   *Ibid.*, pp. 29–30.
j   *Ibid.*, pp. 107–08.
k   *Ibid.*, pp. 141–42.
l   *Ibid.*, pp. 108–09.
m   *Ibid.*, pp. 65–66.
n   Fragments 58, 71, 68, and 77, in *Epicurus*, translated by Bailey, *op cit.*, pp. 115–19.
o   *Cicero: De Finibus*, translated by H. Rackham ("Loeb Classical Library" [Harvard University Press, 1914]), Bk. IV, 13.
p   *Nichomachean Ethics*, translated by W. D. Ross, in *The Works of Aristotle*, edited by J. A. Smith and W. D. Ross (Clarendon Press, Oxford, 1910–52), Vol. IX (1925), 1134b18 ff.
q   *De Finibus*, translated by Rackham, *op. cit.*, Bk. III, 31.
r   *Ibid.*, Bk. IV, 21.
s   *Ibid.*, Bk. IV, 21–23 and 70–73.
t   *Cicero: De Officiis*, translated by W. Miller ("Loeb Classical Library" [Harvard University Press, 1913]), Bk. I, 4.

u   *Cicero: De Republica*, translated by C. W. Keyes ("Loeb Classical Library" [Harvard University Press, 1928]), Bk. III, xxii.

v   *De Finibus*, translated by Rackham, *op. cit.*, Bk. II, 45–46.

w   *De Republica*, translated by Keyes, *op. cit.*, Bk. I, xxv.

x   *Cicero: De Legibus*, translated by Keyes, *op. cit.*, Bk. I, vii; *De Finibus*, translated by Rackham, *op. cit.*, Bk. III, 64.

y   *De Legibus*, translated by Keyes, *op. cit.*, Bk. I, x.

z   *The Discourses of Epictetus*, translated by G. Long (U. S. Book Co., New York, n. d.), p. 2.

a   *Ibid.*, pp. 147, 144, and 20–21.

b   *Ibid.*, pp. 4–5.

c   *Ibid.*, pp. 124–25.

d   *The Golden Sayings of Epictetus*, translated by H. Crossley (Macmillan, New York, 1925), pp. 118–19 and 136.

e   *Ibid.*, pp. 44–45.

f   *Ibid.*, pp. 103 and 21.

g   *Ibid.*, p. 147.

h   *Marcus Aurelius Antoninus*, translated by C. R. Haines ("Loeb Classical Library" [Harvard University Press, 1916]), Bk. VI, 15; Bk. VII, 9.

i   *Ibid.*, Bk. IV, 40.

j   *Ibid.*, Bk. III, 4.

k   *Ibid.*, Bk. IV, 33; Bk. II, 5; Bk. VIII, 1.

l   *Ibid.*, Bk. XI, 4–5.

m   *Ibid.*, Bk. X, 6; Bk. II, 16.

n   *Ibid.*, Bk. IX, 3; Bk. XII, 36.

o   *Ibid.*, Bk. V, 29.

p   *Ibid.*, Bk. IX, 29.

q   *Sextus Empiricus*, translated by R. G. Bury, Vol. I, *Outlines of Pyrrhonism* ("Loeb Classical Library" [Harvard University Press, 1933]), Bk. I, 4 and 8–10.

r   *Ibid.*, Bk. I, 19–20.

s   *Ibid.*, Bk. I, 32.

t   *Ibid.*, Bk. II, 18–20.

u   *Ibid.*, Bk. I, 36–37.

v   *Ibid.*, Bk. I, 44–47 and 59.

w   *Ibid.*, Bk. I, 141–42 and 144.

x   *Sextus Empiricus*, translated by R. G. Bury, Vol. II, *Against the Logicians* ("Loeb Classical Library" [Harvard University Press, 1935]), Bk. I, 176–79.

y   *Ibid.*, Bk. I, 175.

z   *Outlines of Pyrrhonism*, translated by Bury, *op. cit.*, Bk. I, 25–29.

# Suggestions for Further Reading

The best course to pursue is to turn directly to the various great texts from which the selections in this volume have been drawn. Thus, instead of being content with the extracts given here, read the *Republic* in its entirety, read Aristotle's *Ethics,* and so on. Information concerning translations and editions will be found in the bibliographical notes section of this volume.

Beyond the masters themselves, here is a short list of books about them and their times that should help to make their theories more intelligible.

## PRE-SOCRATICS

J. Burnet: *Early Greek Philosophy* (London, 1920). Translations with commentaries; an indispensable work.

———— *Greek Philosophy: Thales to Plato* (London, 1914). Both readable and scholarly; includes sections on both Plato and Democritus.

E. A. Havelock: *Preface to Plato* (Cambridge, Mass., 1963). Holds that the key to understanding the history of early Greek philosophy lies in recognizing that culture in this period was just beginning to develop out of an oral stage.

W. W. Jaeger: *The Theology of the Early Greek Philosophers* (Oxford, 1947). Seeks to correct what the author feels is an exaggerated interpretation of the Pre-Socratics as scientists by emphasizing their achievements as theologians.

G. S. Kirk and J. E. Raven: *The Pre-Socratic Philosophers* (Cambridge, 1962). Detailed and careful comments on the surviving texts.

## PLATO

G. C. Field: *Plato and His Contemporaries* (London, 1930). Useful material on Plato's life and on his cultural background.

G. M. A. Grube: *Plato's Thought* (London, 1935). One of the best introductory works; the analysis is by topics instead of by dialogues.

C. Ritter: *The Essence of Plato's Philosophy* (New York, 1933). A difficult but important book by a scholar whose views have influenced other commentators.

P. Shorey: *Platonism Ancient and Modern* (Berkeley, 1938). A summary of Plato's impact on subsequent Western thought; includes a chapter indicating Plato's influence on English literature.

———— *What Plato Said* (Chicago, 1933). Useful analyses, with comment, of the individual dialogues.

A. E. Taylor: *Plato: The Man and His Work* (New York, 1927). Detailed analyses of all the dialogues, with illuminating commentary; a most useful book.

## ARISTOTLE

M. Grene: *A Portrait of Aristotle* (London, 1963). A useful and sympathetic introduction.

G. Grote: *Aristotle* (London, 1872). Still useful, especially on Aristotle's logical doctrines.

W. W. Jaeger: *Aristotle* (Oxford, 1934). A valuable study of the development of Aristotle's mind and of the chronology of his writings.

G. R. G. Mure: *Aristotle* (London, 1932). A short but very useful study of all departments of Aristotle's thought.

J. H. Randall, Jr.: *Aristotle* (New York, 1960). Argues that Aristotle's philosophy is highly relevant "for two of the most important present-day philosophical concerns, that with the analysis of language and that with the analysis of natural processes."

W. D. Ross: *Aristotle* (New York, 1924). On the whole the best single-volume treatment, by one of the editors of the English translation of Aristotle's writings.

## LATE CLASSICAL PERIOD

E. V. Arnold: *Roman Stoicism* (Cambridge, 1911). Argues that "Stoicism is the bridge between ancient and modern philosophical thought."

C. Bailey: *The Greek Atomists and Epicurus* (Oxford, 1928). An important and scholarly book by the translator of Epicurus and Lucretius.

N. W. DeWitt: *Epicurus and His Philosophy* (Minneapolis, 1954). Holds that, as a scientist, Epicurus was a continuator of the Ionian tradition and that his writings were chiefly directed against Platonism and against Scepticism.

B. Farrington: *The Faith of Epicurus* (London, 1967). Emphasizes Epicurus' role as a reformer interested in the practical problems of his day and as the opponent of Plato's ideal state.

A. J. Festugière: *Epicurus and His Gods* (Oxford, 1955). Discusses Epicureanism in the light of, and as an answer to, changes in religious belief in Hellenistic times.

R. D. Hicks: *Stoic and Epicurean* (New York, 1910). Contrasts these rival schools, which "sought by devious paths one and the same goal."

R. M. Wenley: *Stoicism and Its Influence* (Boston, 1924). Useful in tracing Stoic influence on subsequent Western thought down through the nineteenth century.

E. Zeller: *Stoics, Epicureans and Sceptics* (London, 1880). Still useful for its detailed treatment of many minor figures.

## GENERAL

A. W. H. Adkins: *Merit and Responsibility: A Study in Greek Values* (Oxford, 1960). Argues that moderation and the "quieter" virtues were less important in Greek society than has been thought.

F. Cumont: *The Oriental Religions in Roman Paganism* (Chicago, 1911). A valuable study of the mystery cults.

S. Dill: *Roman Society from Nero to Marcus Aurelius* (New York, 1905). Much interesting material on social conditions and attitudes during the Empire.

E. R. Dodds: *The Greeks and the Irrational* (Berkeley, 1956). A study of Greek religion in the light of anthropological and psychological investigations of other cultures.

M. I. Finley: *The World of Odysseus* (New York, 1954). Short and readable; excellent on mode of life, institutions, and values.

W. K. C. Guthrie: *A History of Greek Philosophy* (Cambridge, 1965). Sums up and evaluates the scholarship of many writers.

J. Harrison: *Prolegomena to the Study of Greek Religion* (Cambridge, 1922). A thorough, scholarly work including extensive materials from literary and artistic sources.

W. W. Jaeger: *Paideia* (Oxford, 1939–44). An important study of the Greek cultural ideal as formulated in literary and philosophical works.

G. Murray: *Five Stages of Greek Religion* (Oxford, 1925). An interesting interpretation by a distinguished scholar and translator.

L. Robin: *Greek Thought* (London, 1928). One of the best introductory books available on the period as a whole, from the beginnings through Plotinus.

A. E. Zimmern: *The Greek Commonwealth* (Oxford, 1931). A brilliant and readable account of social and economic conditions as a background for understanding Greek philosophy.

# Glossary

Short, dictionary-type definitions of philosophical terms are likely to be misleading, for philosophers use terms in many different ways and with little regard to common usage (on which, of course, dictionary definitions are based). Accordingly, many of the definitions given in this Glossary are accompanied by references to places in the text where the various terms in question appear in a concrete context. For terms not defined in the Glossary, consult the Index; for fuller treatment of them and of other philosophical terms, see *The Encyclopedia of Philosophy*, edited by P. Edwards (Free Press, New York, 1967). Also available are the *Dictionary of Philosophy*, edited by D. D. Runes (Philosophical Library, New York, 1942), and *Dictionary of Philosophy and Psychology*, edited by J. M. Baldwin (Macmillan, New York, 1925). The *Encyclopaedia Britannica* (eleventh edition) contains excellent articles on many philosophical terms, including some of those in this Glossary.

**Abstraction:** The power of separating, in thought, one part of a complex from the other parts and attending to it separately. Thus, to consider the color of an apple in isolation from the apple's other qualities would be to abstract this quality for attention.

**A priori:** What is known independently of sense perception and for this reason held to be indubitable. The doctrine of innate ideas (see definition) was an attempt to account for the alleged existence of a priori knowledge.

**Attribute:** See **Substance**.

**Axiom:** A proposition held to be self-evidently true and so neither requiring nor indeed capable of proof. Hence a first principle from which all proofs start. Those who deny the self-evident truth of axioms hold them to be simply postulates from which such-and-such theorems can be deduced. Thus, according to this view, the axioms of one deductive system may be deduced from another set of postulates in some other deductive system.

**Contingent:** That which may be and also may not be. Hence an event whose occurrence is not necessarily determined (see **Determinism**) by other events. Compare Epicurus' "swerve" (pp. 87–88), which is contingent because it is uncaused.

**Cosmology:** The study of the universal world process. Distinguished from ontology (see definition) chiefly by the fact that, whereas the latter asks what reality *is*, cosmology asks how reality unfolds and develops in successive stages. Thus the cosmological theory of Anaximander discussed the process by which particular things issue from and return to the "boundless" (see pp. 11–12).

**Deduction:** A type of inference (see definition) that yields necessary conclusions. In deduction, one or more propositions (called "premises") being assumed, another proposition (the conclusion) is seen to be entailed or implied. It is usually held that in deduction the movement of thought is from premises of greater generality to a conclusion of lesser generality (from the premises "All men are mortal" and "All Greeks are men," we deduce that "All Greeks are mortal"), but the chief mark of deduction is the necessity with which the conclusion follows from the premises. Syllogism is thus an example of deduction (see pp. 244–51).

**Determinism:** The theory that denies contingency (see **Contingent**) and claims that everything that happens happens necessarily and in accordance with some regular pattern or law. Thus, in Democritus' system (in distinction from Epicurus', which allowed a "swerve"), all events are determined by antecedent events in time (see pp. 84–85). Besides (1) a *scientific determinism* of this kind, it is possible to have either (2) a *logical determinism* (as with Spinoza) or (3) a *teleological determinism* (as with Augustine, who held that all events are determined in accordance with God's plan).

**Dialectic:** A term used to designate the process by which, in Plato's view, we pass from the hypothetical starting points of the various special sciences to the unconditioned first principle, or the Form of the Good (see pp. 132–35).

**Discursive:** The characteristic of the human intelligence that limits it, in the main, to a step-by-step reasoning—from premises to conclusion, from this conclusion to another, and so on. Hence to be contrasted with the all-inclusive vision of the mystic, with the possible operation of a suprahuman intellect, and with the way in which, according to Aristotle and other writers, axioms (see **Axiom**) and other self-evident principles are comprehended by the mind. Compare Aristotle's account of "intuitive knowledge" (see pp. 251–53).

**Dualism:** Any view that holds two ultimate and irreducible principles to be necessary to explain the world. The "Limit" and the "Unlimited" of the Pythagoreans (pp.

37–38) and Plato's sensible realm and realm of forms (p. 123) are examples of various types of dualism.

**Empiricism:** The view that holds sense perception to be the sole source of human knowledge.

**Epistemology:** From the Greek terms *episteme* (knowledge) and *logos* (theory, account). Hence the study of the origins, nature, and limitations of knowledge.

**Essence:** The that-about-a-thing-that-makes-it-what-it-is, in contrast to those properties that the thing may happen to possess but need not possess in order to be itself. Thus it is held (1) that we have to distinguish between those properties of Socrates that are "accidental" and so nonessential (for example, dying by hemlock) and those properties that are essential (for example, those traits of character and personality that made him the man he was). Further, it is held (2) that we have to distinguish between essence and existence (see definition): It is possible (according to this view) to define Socrates' essence exhaustively; yet when we have done so, the question still remains whether any such being exists.

**Eudaemonism:** From the Greek term *eudaimonia,* usually translated (see p. 162) as "happiness." Hence the view that the end of life consists in happiness, conceived of as an all-round, balanced, long-range type of well-being, in distinction from pleasure. Contrasted with hedonism (see definition).

**Existence:** Actuality or factuality. Contrasted with essence (see definition).

**Experiment:** A situation arranged to test an hypothesis. Contrasted with "mere" observation (see pp. 234–35).

**Free will:** The doctrine of contingency (see **Contingent**) applied specifically to human behavior; the denial that men's acts are completely determined (see **Determinism**). The question of free will is important because many philosophers hold that "ought" implies "can"—that moral judgments of approbation and disapprobation are meaningless unless the acts judged about are free, that is, under the control of the agent, who, had he so chosen, might have done otherwise. The main problems connected with free will are (1) what meaning, if any, can be attached to the notion of a free choice and (2) how the possibility of being otherwise is compatible with either (a) belief in an omnipotent and omniscient Deity or (b) the doctrine of universal causal determinism. See Index.

**Hedonism:** The view that pleasure is man's good. Contrasted with eudaemonism (see definition). *Ethical hedonism* holds either (1) that a man's own pleasure is the sole end worth aiming at (as with Epicurus, pp. 317–21) or (2) that other people's pleasure is to be taken into account. *Psychological hedonism* holds that, whatever men ought to aim at, they do in fact aim at pleasure.

**Humanism:** A variously used term. Employed (1) to describe the type of view that distinguishes man from animals on the ground that man has certain moral obligations (see, for instance, pp. 6–8). Also used (2) to contrast a secular type of ethics with a religious ethics. Thus Plato's and Aristotle's ethics could be called "humanistic," in contrast with the ethics of Augustine, on the ground that they hold man himself, rather than God, to be the supreme value. Also used (3) to designate a particular historical movement, beginning in the fourteenth century, that emphasized the study of classical literature and the revival of classical ideals.

**Idealism:** In general, any view that holds reality to be mental or "spiritual," or mind-dependent. *Subjective idealism* emphasizes the ultimate reality of the knowing subject and may either admit the existence of a plurality of such subjects or deny the existence of all save one (in which case the view is called solipsism [see definition]). *Objective idealism* denies that the distinction between subject and object, between knower and known, is ultimate and maintains that all finite knowers and their thoughts are included in an Absolute Thought.

**Induction:** A type of inference (see definition) in which (in contrast to deduction [see definition]) the movement of thought is from lesser to greater generality. Thus induction begins, not from premises, but from observed particulars (for example, the observation that A, B, and C all have the property *x*) and seeks to establish some generalization about them (for example, that all members of the class *y*, of which A, B, and C are members, have the property *x*). The main problem connected with induction is the difficulty of determining the conditions under which we are warranted in moving from an observed "Some so-and-so's have such-and-such" to the unobserved "All so-and-so's probably have such-and-such."

**Inference:** The movement of thought by which we reach a conclusion from premises. Thus we speak of inductive and of deductive inference.

**Innate ideas:** According to the doctrine of innate ideas, we must distinguish between (1) ideas that we acquire in the course of our experience and (2) ideas that we possess antecedently to all experience. Holders of this view—among them Plato (pp. 143–45)—would allow that some experience may be the occasion of our becoming consciously aware of an innate idea, but they would argue that the idea itself (for example, the idea of absolute equality) can never be found in experience.

**Intuition:** Direct and immediate knowledge. To be contrasted with discursive (see definition) knowledge.

**Judgment:** The movement of thought by which, for example, we assert (or deny) some predicate of a subject, or, more generally, by which we connect two terms by some relation. Thus, when we say "This rose is red" or "New York is east of Chicago," we judge. Following Kant, most philosophers distinguish between (1) *analytical judgments*, in which the predicate concept is contained in the subject concept, and (2) *synthetical judgments*, in which the predicate concept is not so contained; and also between (3) *a priori judgments*, which are universal and necessary, and (4) *a posteriori judgments*, which are not universal and necessary.

**Law of nature:** See **Natural law**.

**Materialism:** The doctrine that reality is matter. Whereas idealism (see definition) holds that matter is "really" the thought of some mind or other, materialism holds that minds and all other apparently nonmaterial things (for example, gods) are reducible to the complex motions of material particles. Atomism (pp. 74–107) is an example of materialism.

**Metaphysics:** The study of the ultimate nature of reality, or, as some philosophers would say, the study of "being as such." To be contrasted, therefore, with physics, which studies the "being" of physical nature; with astronomy, which studies the "being" of the solar system; with biology, which studies the "being" of animate nature; and so on. By "being as such," these philosophers mean, not the special characteristics of special kinds of things (for example, living things), but the most general and pervasive characteristics of all things.

**Monism:** The view that everything is reducible to one kind of thing, or that one principle of explanation is sufficient to explain everything. Thus the Milesians (pp. 8–14) were materialistic monists. No Christian philosopher, on the other hand, could be a monist, for the Christian must insist on an ultimate and irreducible distinction between God the Creator and the universe He created.

**Mysticism**: The view that reality is ineffable and transcendent; that it is known, therefore, by some special, nonrational means; that knowledge of it is incommunicable in any precise conceptual scheme; and that it is communicable, if at all, only in poetic imagery and metaphor.

**Naturalism**: Another variously used term. (1) In one meaning, naturalism is a view that excludes any reference to supernatural principles and holds the world to be explicable in terms of scientifically verifiable concepts. In this meaning, naturalism is about equivalent to secularism and, like humanism (see definition), can be contrasted with a religiously oriented theory like Neoplatonism. (2) In another meaning, the emphasis is on the unity of behavior; any difference in kind between men and animals is denied, and human conduct and human institutions are held to be simply more complex instances of behavior patterns occurring among lower organisms. In this sense, naturalism is to be contrasted with humanism.

**Natural law**: This term may designate (1) a pattern of regularity that holds in physical nature. Thus people talk about the "law" of gravity and hold it to be a law of nature (or a natural law) that bodies attract each other directly with their masses and inversely with the square of their distance. Those who affirm the existence of natural laws in this sense hold that these laws are necessary and universal (not merely empirical generalizations concerning observable sequences) and that they are discoverable by reason. Or the term may designate (2) a moral imperative—not a description of what actually happens in the physical world, but a description of what *ought* to happen in men's relations to one another. In this sense, too, these laws would be regarded by those who affirm their existence as being of universal application and discoverable by reason.

**Nominalism**: The view that only particulars are real and that universals (see **Universal**) are but observable likenesses among the particulars of sense experience.

**Objective**: To say that anything is "objective" is to say that it is real, that it has a public nature independent of us and of our judgments about it. Thus the question of whether or not values are objective turns on whether or not values are more than private preferences. If they are private preferences, our value judgments are subjective, and there is no more disputing about them than there is about judgments of taste: My good is what *I* prefer; yours is what *you* prefer. On the other hand, if values are objective, it follows that when we differ about them, at least one of us is mistaken. For an example of extreme objectivism concerning values, see pp. 153–74; for an example of extreme subjectivism, see pp. 68–73.

**Ontology**: From the Greek terms *ontos* (being) and *logos* (theory, account). About equivalent in meaning to metaphysics (see definition). When we inquire about the "ontological status" of something, say, perception, we ask whether the objects of perception are real or illusory, and, if real, what sort of reality they possess (for example, whether they are mind-dependent or whether they exist independently of minds), and so on.

**Pantheism**: From the Greek terms *pan* (all) and *theos* (god). Hence the view that all things share in the divine nature, or that all things are parts of god.

**Phenomenalism**: A type of view that, like idealism (see definition), holds that what we know is mind-dependent, but that, unlike idealism, generally holds that reality itself is not mind-dependent. Usually, phenomenalism does not attempt to inquire into the possible underlying causes of events, but limits itself to generalizing about empirically observable sequences.

**Primary qualities**: Those qualities thought to belong to bodies. To be distinguished from secondary qualities, which are held to be products of the interaction between our sense organs and the primary qualities of bodies.

**Rationalism:** (1) As contrasted with empiricism (see definition), rationalism means reliance on reason (that is, on deduction, on the criterion of logical consistency). Compare Zeno's attack on motion (see pp. 22–24). (2) As contrasted with authoritarianism or mysticism (see definition), rationalism means reliance on our human powers.

**Realism:** (1) As contrasted with nominalism (see definition), realism holds that universals are real, and more real than the particulars of sense experience. (In this sense, Plato was a realist.) (2) As contrasted with idealism (see definition), realism holds that the objects of our knowledge are not mind-dependent but are independently existing entities. (In this sense, too, Plato was a realist.) (3) As contrasted with idealism in still another sense, realism is the point of view that interests itself in men and institutions as they are, rather than as they ought to be. (In this sense, Plato was not a realist but an idealist.) In this sense, realism is almost equivalent to naturalism (see definition).

**Relativism:** The view that maintains our judgments to be relative to (that is, conditioned upon) certain factors such as cultural milieu or individual bias. Hence the view that we do not possess any absolute, objective (see definition) truth. The relativist need not hold that all judgments are relative; it is possible, for instance, to hold that the physical sciences yield absolute truth while maintaining that in other fields (for example, ethics and religion) there is no absolute truth.

**Scepticism:** The position that denies the possibility of knowledge. Here, as with relativism (see definition), it is possible either to have a total scepticism, like that of Gorgias (see p. 67, n. 19), or to limit one's scepticism to certain fields. Thus it is possible (as with Plato) to be sceptical of sense perception while holding that we can reach the truth by means of reason.

**Solipsism:** From the Latin terms *solus* (alone) and *ipse* (self). Hence the view that everything other than oneself is a state of oneself.

**Subjectivism:** See **Objective, Relativism,** and **Scepticism.**

**Substance:** Another variously used term. (1) In one meaning, substance is simply that which is real. Thus Aristotle called those amalgams of matter and form that he took reality to consist of "substances." (2) In another meaning, substance is about equivalent to essence (see definition). Also, (3) substance is contrasted with attribute (or property, or quality) as that which *has* the attributes. Thus substance is the underlying (and unknown) ground in which properties are thought to inhere; it is that about which we are judging when we assert properties of a subject, for example, when we say "The rose is red." Hence (4) substance is that which, unlike an attribute (or property), exists in its own right and depends on nothing else. See Index.

**Teleology:** From the Greek terms *telos* (end, goal) and *logos* (theory, account). Hence the view that affirms the reality of purpose and holds the universe either to be consciously designed (as with the Christian doctrine of a providential God) or, as with Aristotle (p. 222), to be the working out of partly conscious, partly unconscious purposes that are immanent in the developing organisms.

**Universal:** A universal is that which is predicable of many. Thus "man" is a universal because it is predicable of Washington, Jefferson, Hamilton, and all other individual men. The main problem about universals concerns their ontological status (see **Ontology**). Are they (1) separate entities distinct from the individuals of which they are predicable, (2) real but not separable, or (3) not real at all, but merely the names of likenesses shared by certain particulars? See **Nominalism, Realism,** and Index.

# Index

This is primarily an index of proper names. Thus titles and principal topics of discussion are indexed under the authors. Topics that recur in the work of several philosophers are also indexed as main entries. Page numbers in *italics* refer to quotations; those in **bold-face** refer to major discussions.